iPad® at Work®

FOR DUMMIES®

A Wiley Brand

by Galen Gruman

FOR DUMMIES®

A Wiley Brand

iPad® at Work For Dummies®

Published by: **John Wiley & Sons, Inc.,** 111 River Street, Hoboken, NJ 07030-5774, www.wiley.com

Copyright © 2015 by John Wiley & Sons, Inc., Hoboken, New Jersey

Media and software compilation copyright © 2015 by John Wiley & Sons, Inc. All rights reserved.

Published simultaneously in Canada

For general information on our other products and services, please contact our Customer Care Department within the U.S. at 877-762-2974, outside the U.S. at 317-572-3993, or fax 317-572-4002. For technical support, please visit www.wiley.com/techsupport.

Wiley publishes in a variety of print and electronic formats and by print-on-demand. Some material included with standard print versions of this book may not be included in e-books or in print-on-demand. If this book refers to media such as a CD or DVD that is not included in the version you purchased, you may download this material at http://booksupport.wiley.com. For more information about Wiley products, visit www.wiley.com.

Library of Congress Control Number: 2014950602

ISBN: 978-1-118-94928-3; ISBN 978-1-118-94929-0 (ebk); ISBN ePDF 978-1-118-94566-6 (ebk)

Manufactured in the United States of America

10 9 8 7 6 5 4 3 2 1

Contents at a Glance

Table of Contents

Introduction

If you bought this book (or are even thinking about buying it), you've probably already made the decision to use an iPad in your work. That's great, because the iPad makes a great tool for people in all sorts of businesses. Maybe your iPad is an adjunct to your computer, or maybe it's your primary computer. Either way, this book has you covered.

About This Book

Who you may be, dear reader, varies widely. Maybe you've been using an iPad for entertainment and other personal activities, or maybe you're completely new to the iPad. Maybe you're self-employed, or part of a small business that has little or no tech support. Maybe you work for a big company that has an IT department to both help you and impose rules on how you can use your iPad at work. The type of business the readers of this book do also varies widely.

That's why I cover a wide range of activities that you may do with your iPad for the purpose of work. I also cover multiple tools that you might use for each kind of task, because the right tool for you might not be the right tool for someone else.

This book helps you select and use the right tools for your work needs, as well as use the iPad effectively and safely in your work environment by addressing issues such as keeping work and personal information separate.

Here's one thing this book won't do: Teach you the basics of the iPad. Many good books are available to show you how to use the iPad itself, and several of those books come from the publisher of this book, John Wiley & Sons, Inc. Start with one of them if you are new to the iPad, and then use this book to learn how to make the iPad work at work.

If you're completely new to the iPad, I recommend that you get Wiley's *iPad For Seniors For Dummies,* by Nancy Muir. Don't let the "Seniors" in the name dissuade you: It's a great primer for anyone.

Foolish Assumptions

This book is organized by sets of functions that people do at or for work. Although I do walk you through the steps to accomplish specific tasks in apps where those tasks are complex, this book is not a recipe book for using apps. Instead it's a guide to picking the right tools and understanding how to make the iPad fit into common business workflows and practices.

I presume that you know how to do your job, so my tone is direct and uncomplicated, with no idle chitchat. I give you straightforward advice and recommendations for the right tools to do that job. Some of the issues I raise are technical or complicated because, well, that's just how work is sometimes — but I do my best to make those issues clear.

Each chapter covers a range of tools for the work you may do. I show what these tools do well and how they work at a basic level. I also let you know their limitations and requirements so that you can assess their fitness for your work.

Conventions and Icons Used in This Book

This book uses several iPad-specific terms, including:

- **Tap:** Press your finger on the screen and release it quickly.
- **Swipe:** Drag a finger across a substantial portion of the screen, often to scroll the screen's contents. Some apps use the word *slide* to describe this action.
- **Flick:** Quickly drag a finger over a short area and then release it from the screen, usually to reveal a menu button like Delete.
- **Press:** Push down on a physical button with your finger and then release it. The iPad does have a few physical buttons and switches, including Home, Volume Up, Volume Down, Sleep/Wake, and the so-called Side switch that can be set to lock the screen rotation or mute the iPad. (The iPad Air 2 does not have the Side switch, so use the corresponding controls in the Control Center instead; you access the Control Center by swiping up from the bottom of the screen.)
- **Pop-over:** A container for features and commands similar to a dialog, palette, or sheet in a computer application. You can dismiss a pop-over by tapping elsewhere on the screen.
- **Form:** A container for features and commands that you can dismiss only by tapping a button such as Done, Cancel, or OK. It's like the settings sheet in the Mac's OS X user interface.

- ✔ **Status bar:** The menu bar at the very top of the iPad screen that stays visible most of the time, displaying the time, network connection status, battery charge, and so on.

- ✔ **Home screen:** The screens that display app and folder icons. Your iPad can have as many as 15 Home screens, which you navigate by swiping sideways among them.

- ✔ **Home button:** The physical button at the bottom side of the iPad (when held vertically). Press the Home button to switch from an app to the last Home screen opened, and press it again to go to the first Home button. Double-press the Home button to enter multitasking view, which shows all running apps. Tap an app's preview screen to switch to it.

Three icons are used in this book to alert you to special content:

Tip icons point out insights or helpful suggestions related to tasks in the step lists.

Remember icons point out context or background information that will help you avoid mistakes or confusion later on.

Warning icons point out things that don't work as you'd expect or don't work correctly. I provide suggestions for how to deal with such warnings.

Beyond the Book

I have written a lot of extra content that you won't find in this book. Go online to find the following:

- ✔ **Online articles covering additional topics at**

  www.dummies.com/extras/ipadatwork

  Here you'll find out how to avoid ever losing the contents of your iPad; use the new Handoff feature to pick up from where you left off while working on another device; make your iPad act like a phone if your iPhone is close by; turn your iPad into a Wi-Fi hotspot; record your iPad's screen by using your computer and an app; and print from your iPad. Here you'll also find ten preferences in the Settings app that every business user should know.

✔ **The Cheat Sheet for this book is at**

> `www.dummies.com/cheatsheet/ipadatwork`

Here you'll find a primer on using the iPad's gestures and buttons, common Siri controls, and the apps supported by the various accounts the iPad can access.

✔ **Updates to this book, if I have any, are at**

> `www.dummies.com/extras/ipadatwork`

Where to Go from Here

The book's chapters are organized into parts so that related business issues are kept together. But you can read the chapters in any order — let your needs and questions determine what you read, and when.

But I do recommend that you start with Chapters 1 through 3, because they cover issues that many users simply don't think about when using an iPad for work, such as what iPad model to buy and how to manage business accounts and data separately from personal accounts and data. Getting these issues right will make the rest of your iPad experience a lot more pleasant, and effective.

This book assumes that your iPad is running iOS 8, the operating system released in fall 2014. Apple updates iOS roughly once each year, so you may be running an earlier or later version. (Your iPad or iTunes on your computer will alert you to both those major updates and to smaller updates that occur in between.)

Those changes may affect what you see on the screen, but you'll find the app advice and basic operational instructions to be the same whether you are using iOS 7, iOS 8, or something newer. When a change is very substantial, I may add an update or bonus information that you can download at this book's companion website, `www.dummies.com/extras/ipadatwork`.

Part I
Getting Started with iPad at Work

In this part . . .

- ✔ Finding out where the iPad can replace a computer and where it can supplement it.

- ✔ Learning about all the extra hardware you can add to your iPad so that it does more and better.

- ✔ Making sense of that iCloud thing: What it does and why you need it.

- ✔ It's all in the setup: backup, mail, contacts, calendars, and Wi-Fi — oh, my!

- ✔ Keeping your iPad — and your data — safe.

- ✔ Discovering how to be a road warrior: The right apps for that.

Chapter 1

The iPad Is Your New Computer — Much of the Time

*T*he iPad debuted in 2010, and early analysts dubbed it a "media tablet," tarring the iPad as "merely" an entertainment device for watching movies, reading books, playing games, and surfing the web. Yet from the get-go, Apple delivered world-class productivity applications in the form of its iWork suite, and since then, many developers have created thousands of apps that make the iPad a serious computer for industries of all types.

Still, many people continue to think of the iPad as an entertainment device, not as the new type of computer it truly is. If you're reading this book, you're not one of those people. You know that the iPad is a serious business tool — even though, like a PC, it's great for entertainment, too.

You can do a lot of work on an iPad — with the right apps and accessories. You may use the iPad exclusively as your only computer. More likely, you'll use it as a supplement to your computer, broadening where and how you can work.

In this chapter, I explain the iPad's role in everyday business, and why it's a great replacement or supplement for a laptop. Then I explain how to choose the right iPad model for your needs and suggest some key peripherals to complete your iPad "toolkit."

Envisioning the iPad in Your Work Day

When I go on the road for work, I no longer bring my laptop with me, and I haven't done so since 2011. I can do most of my work on my iPad, so why lug around the laptop? Plus, my iPad is one of the cellular versions, so I can access the Internet from almost anywhere. That means no hunting for the nearest Wi-Fi cafe.

If I do need to do work that my iPad has no apps for, then I can still bring the laptop with me, leaving the computer at the remote office or hotel room to do that special work when I need to. Meanwhile, my iPad is with me all the time, ready to use when needed for the many things it can do.

But you don't have to be a road warrior or work in the field to benefit from an iPad at work. I find that it's really handy in the office, too: I bring it to conference rooms to take notes that are instantly available on my computer when I get back to my desk. I look up information during the meeting to make sure decisions aren't based on bad assumptions. I show people that presentation or those budget numbers or that how-to video.

There are also times I use both my computer and iPad at the same time for work *at my desk*. In that case, the iPad becomes a second screen, letting me check some stats for a report or monitor my email while Word and Excel fill my computer's big screen. Or I can monitor a conference on my iPad while working away at my computer.

Where the iPad Can't Do the Job

As convenient as the iPad is — you can bring and use it almost anywhere — its limits are real:

- ✔ The small screen means you can't scan and work across multiple open windows as you would on a PC's larger monitor. In the iPad world, you'll find yourself focusing on one app at a time.
- ✔ The iPad doesn't support a mouse, which allows for much finer control for delicate and precision activities like drawing plans.
- ✔ A PC's physical keyboard is much faster to type on, and more accurate, too. Don't get me wrong: After you adjust to it, the iPad's onscreen keyboard is quite usable, but it ain't a computer keyboard. And you can buy an external Bluetooth keyboard for your iPad if you prefer to type on physical keys.

> ✔ Some applications don't run on the iPad at all. Some — like Microsoft Office, AutoDesk AutoCAD, and Adobe Photoshop — have iPad versions that drop some desktop features that your work may require you to use.

So, for most of us, an iPad doesn't replace our computer. But it does let us do more than a computer alone can do.

Equipping Your iPad

Before you can use an iPad at work, you need to get an iPad. Whether you buy it yourself or requisition it from your employer, you'll want to review the choices you need to make both for the iPad itself and essential peripherals for it.

Choosing the right iPad model

At any particular time, chances are that Apple has four versions of the iPad available for purchase. There's usually the current full-size model (historically with a 9.7-inch screen, diagonally measured), such as the iPad Air series, and the current smaller model, a.k.a. the iPad Mini series (historically with a 7.9-inch screen). Figure 1-1 shows the iPad Air and iPad Mini. Then there's usually the previous model of each kept on sale for those on limited budgets.

The iPad Mini is very portable, fitting into lab coat pockets and suit jacket pockets. But the screen can be hard on older eyes — you'll want reading glasses — and touch-typing is harder on its smaller onscreen keyboard. It's a great choice for folks who are rarely at a desk, which is why it's a favorite of physicians in hospitals, field technicians, construction foremen, and insurance adjusters.

The full-size iPad, the iPad Air, is also quite portable, but you can't stick it in a pocket when you need both hands to do other stuff. If you carry a briefcase or backpack, or tend to move from desk to desk or desk to conference room where you can set it down safely and easily, the iPad Air is a great choice. Its larger screen is easier to read for older eyes, and touch-typing is easier on its onscreen keyboard.

Both iPad models come in versions that support cellular networks in addition to Wi-Fi networks, and both are available in a range of internal storage capacities from 16GB to 128GB. (Note that the older models Apple sells are typically available only in the 16GB, Wi-Fi-only versions.)

Figure 1-1:
The iPad Air (left) and iPad Mini (right) represent the two basic size options available from Apple for its tablets.

The cellular option costs $130 more than the Wi-Fi–only version, but it's very handy because it lets you work almost anywhere there's a 3G or 4G (LTE) signal. Even better, cellular access is cheaper than Wi-Fi in many cases: You can pay $20 to $30 for 30 days' service of 1GB to 3GB of cellular data usage (depending on your carrier), versus $15 to $25 *per night* for Wi-Fi at a hotel, plus potentially additional Wi-Fi fees at conference centers and so on. Note that you don't need a contract for an iPad's cellular data service, though some carriers will try to sell you one. You're best off sticking with its default pay-as-you-go approach.

In the U.S., your iPad is tied to the specific carrier (AT&T, Sprint, T-Mobile, or Verizon) that you choose when you buy it, but you can use it abroad on any GSM network by buying a local SIM and getting pay-as-you-go service for it in that country.

If you're a frequent traveler who will use it to watch movies on your flights, buy as much internal storage as you can afford when you get your iPad, because you can't add more later. 16GB is fine if you're really going to use it just for work apps, e-book reading, and web use, but if you want to store your music library on it as well as a healthy collection of videos, aim for 64GB. If you're a salesperson or product manager who makes lots of presentations, aim for at least 32GB — and more if you also want to carry your entertainment with you.

Protecting your iPad with a cover or shell

You'll want a cover at least for your iPad to protect its screen, and likely a skin or case to protect the iPad's aluminum body. These add weight and bulk but will help your iPad last for years.

Apple's $39 Smart Cover is great because it magnetically attaches and detaches, so you can get it out of the way easily. By contrast, cases don't detach, so the cover is always there, folded behind the iPad when you're using the tablet. By the way, other companies make magnetically attached covers, not just Apple.

I recommend pairing a Smart Cover or similar third-party cover with a cover for the back of the iPad (these back-only covers are often called *shells*), so that you can detach the magnetic front cover when it's in the way but keep the iPad's body protected. There are many great options available from a variety of vendors, with prices ranging from $10 for a no-name version to $40 for a more durable, name-brand item.

Keeping your iPad powered

Your iPad comes with a USB cable and power block that you can connect to a wall adapter to recharge it. You may want to buy extra cables and an extra power block to keep in your travel kit so that you don't have to remember to pack it.

I also recommend you get a USB car charger if your car doesn't have a USB power outlet, as well as an extra iPad cable for the car. If you rent cars for travel a lot, get an extra to keep in your travel bag, too.

And for those who travel abroad, Apple makes a set of foreign plug adapters called the World Travel Adapter ($39) that's quite handy: You can swap out the standard Pad charger block's plug tip with the one for the country you're in, so you don't need separate charger blocks for each country. If you use a MacBook, get Twelve South's PlugBug World Charger and Power Adapter ($45; see Figure 1-2), a set of plug adapters that include a USB charging port; this combination lets you use the MacBook's power block to power both the laptop and charge your iPad (or iPhone) at the same time.

Figure 1-2:
The
PlugBug
lets you
power your
devices
almost
anywhere in
the world.

Connecting to video displays

Many business iPad owners use their tablets to make presentations, whether in conference audiences or in conference rooms. (Chapter 19 explains how to create and give presentations on your iPad.)

I recommend that you equip your conference rooms with Apple's $99 Apple TV, which lets you stream presentations and more from your iPad over Wi-Fi to the Apple TV, to which your TV or projector is connected by an HDMI cable. If your display uses the older VGA standard, you can obtain an adapter from Kanex, which sells the $60 ATV Pro HDMI-to-VGA adapter.

But not every place you'll present at has an Apple TV, so you'll need a cable adapter to connect your iPad directly to a TV or projector. Apple's $49 Lightning Digital AV adapter connects to HDMI ports, the standard on newer displays. Apple also sells the $49 Lightning-to-VGA adapter for the older VGA standard. And for those with an older iPad that uses the Dock connector instead of Lightning, Apple sells the $39 30-pin-to-VGA adapter and the $29 30-pin-to-VGA-adapter.

All these cables, adapters, plugs, and power blocks can be hard to keep track of. If your backpack or briefcase has a zippered pouch, consider keeping them in there. If not, you'd do well to store them in a zip-up mesh pouch, such as the Pack-It System models from Eagle Creek, which come in various sizes.

Adding a physical keyboard

You might want to get a Bluetooth keyboard if you anticipate doing a lot of text entry, such as to document meetings. But such a keyboard is nearly as big and heavy as an iPad, so you need a way to lug it around with you (such as in a briefcase or backpack). I own one, but I haven't used it in a couple years because I've gotten good enough with the onscreen keyboard. But I know plenty of people who find a physical keyboard really useful. My advice: Don't buy one until you know you regret not having it.

If you do want a physical keyboard, you can use any Bluetooth keyboard with the iPad. If you need a keyboard only occasionally with your iPad, you could "borrow" a Bluetooth keyboard that you already have for your computer — as long as you're not also trying to use it at the same time with that computer, of course!

But for more than occasional use, get an iPad-specific Bluetooth keyboard, which will have iPad-specific keys such as for the Home button. Logitech and Zagg both make excellent iPad keyboards, including models that can be used as a cover or case for your iPad as well. For example, Logitech offers the nicely designed Ultrathin magnetic keyboard cover, shown in Figure 1-3. Prices range from $80 to $120.

Figure 1-3:
Logitech's
Ultrathin
keyboard
cover.

Chapter 2

Setting Up Your Own iPad for Work

In This Chapter

▶ Creating your sign-in and account credentials

▶ Figuring out where to back up your iPad's contents

▶ Configuring your iPad for business email, contacts, and calendars

▶ Connecting to the Internet via Wi-Fi

A new iPad comes with Apple's software already installed or available for download from the App Store. Plus you can get additional apps from the App Store from other providers. But having apps on your iPad doesn't mean that it's ready to use for business yet — you need to set up both the iPad and some apps to work where you do.

For example, you need to set up the Wi-Fi connections so that your iPad is connected to your home and work networks, as well as to networks you might use elsewhere, such as at your favorite cafe. You also need to set up your email accounts so that you can access your email from your iPad. Ditto with contacts, calendars, and more.

This chapter explains the setup steps you need to take to get your iPad ready for business. You discover why you might want to have separate Apple and iCloud IDs rather than use the same ID for both, and how to set up those IDs in the iPad to connect to Apple's various services. You also learn about the two backup methods that Apple provides for the iPad's contents. Finally, you find out how to set up the accounts you use to access email, calendars, and contacts, as well as how to connect to Wi-Fi networks so that your iPad is connected to the world you work in.

Setting Up Apple ID and iCloud

For an iPad to access Apple's services — iTunes, the App Store, iMessage, and FaceTime — you need an Apple ID. Chances are that you already have one: If you have an account at the iTunes Store, that's your Apple ID. If you don't have one, you'll get the option of signing up for one when you first turn on your iPad and go through its Welcome screens. You can also sign up for an Apple ID via iTunes on your computer, by choosing Store⇨Create Apple ID and then following the prompts to create an Apple ID. (If you don't see this option, choose Store⇨Sign Out first.) Or you can go to `https://appleid.apple.com` from any browser to set up your Apple ID.

Most people use their Apple ID to access both Apple's online stores and Apple's iCloud sync-and-storage service, given how convenient using one ID is. And you may not want to. If someone discovers your Apple ID, he or she can then use that ID to buy media from the iTunes Store, App Store, and so on, plus access any iCloud documents, email, browser bookmarks, and even passwords. That person could also sign in to iCloud.com and have your email redirected, so you wouldn't get the notifications of his or her activities.

But don't panic: Apple has several methods to reduce the risks of such account hijackings, as Chapter 3 describes. Still, using separate Apple IDs for your iTunes and iCloud accounts can be an easy way to add an extra margin of safety to your iPad's services.

To use a different sign-in for iCloud than for iTunes, you need to create two Apple IDs (do so at `https://appleid.apple.com`) and then sign in to the iTunes Store and App Store via one ID and iCloud via another.

When you first set up a new iPad, you're asked to sign in to the iTunes Store and into iCloud, so you can enter the two IDs and passwords then. Or you can skip those steps during setup and enter them in the Settings app later, as follows and as Figure 2-1 shows:

- ✔ In Settings, tap iCloud, enter your ID and password, and tap Sign In. You can also create a new Apple ID here.
- ✔ In Settings, tap iTunes & App Store, enter your ID and password, and tap Sign In. You can also create a new Apple ID here.

If you are using a single Apple ID for both iTunes and iCloud and decide to create a separate ID for iCloud, you'll have to sign out of your iCloud account on all devices that use it, and then sign in with the new ID. The documents and settings that had been stored in your old iCloud account will not transfer to the new one. For Safari bookmarks and passwords, that's okay, because Safari will take whatever settings are stored locally on your various devices and send them to the new iCloud account. But your iCloud documents won't do that, so be sure to first copy them to your computer or local storage on your iPad and then move them back to iCloud after you've switched accounts.

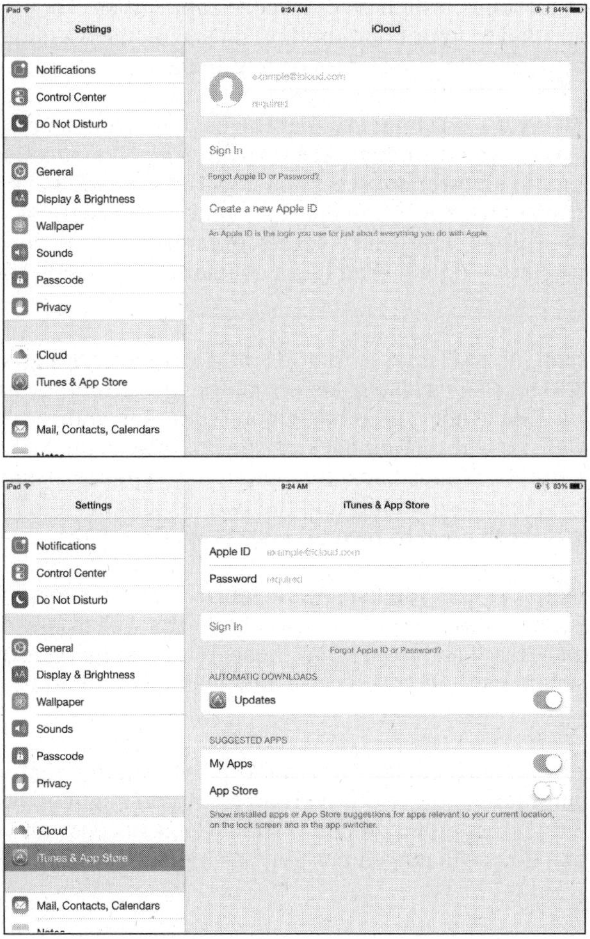

Figure 2-1: The iPad's sign-in screens for iCloud (top) and iTunes (bottom).

Choosing between iTunes Backup and iCloud Backup

Everyone should back up his or her iPad, but if you use an iPad for work, you have an extra measure of responsibility to ensure that your settings and other data are backed up so that you can retrieve them if your iPad is wiped, damaged, lost, or stolen, minimizing the downtime for you and your business.

The pros and cons of each backup option

Apple has designed the iPad so that it can work without ever connecting to a computer, using iCloud to back up key information. An iPad can also connect to a computer via iTunes, which gives it more capabilities. And even if you do connect your iPad to your computer's iTunes, you have a choice of where you back up the iPad's data: to iTunes or to iCloud.

The pros of backing up to iCloud are that the backup occurs anywhere you are, as long as you have Internet access through a Wi-Fi connection and your iPad is connected to a power source. Each day, the iPad will back up photos and videos in the Photos app's Camera Roll, your device settings, your apps' data (but not their files), your Home screen organization, all your text messages (iMessage, and — if your iPad has a cellular radio — SMS and MMS), and ringtones.

The pro of backing up to iTunes is that in addition to everything that is backed up to iCloud, iTunes also transfers all the files stored by apps on your iPad. Plus, if you enable encrypted backup in iTunes, all your passwords are backed up as well. As with iCloud backup, the iPad backs up automatically once each day. But for iTunes backup to work, both your iPad and iTunes on your computer have to be running, and the two devices need to be connected via a USB cable or both need to be on the same Wi-Fi network.

Whichever backup method you use, Apple stores for you, on its own servers, any iTunes, App Store, and iBooks purchases, as well as any documents stored in iCloud Drive. That means that these items can be restored no matter what backup method you choose and even if your iPad hasn't been backed up.

As you can see, an iTunes backup stores more but requires that you use iTunes on a computer. If you're on the road a lot, you might go weeks without a backup. Or your company might disable iTunes access on your iPad as part of its mobile device management policies (see Chapter 3), so you can't use iTunes.

Setting your backup choice

Apple doesn't let the iPad back up to both iTunes and iCloud, so you have to make a choice, unfortunately. Only you can decide the best backup location. Here's where you apply the decision you make:

✔ In iTunes on your computer, select your USB– or Wi-Fi–connected iPad from the Devices list, go to the Summary pane, and select either iCloud or This Computer (for iTunes). To enable Wi-Fi backup for iTunes, also select the Sync with This iPad over Wi-Fi option. Likewise, to enable encrypted iTunes backup, also select the Encrypt iPad Backup option.

✔ On your iPad, go to the Settings app, tap iCloud, tap Backup, and then set the iCloud Backup switch to On to enable iCloud backup and Off to enable iTunes backup.

You can change this backup choice at any time. What you can't do is have both types of backup enabled at the same time.

Manually back up your iPad

Even though your iPad will back up daily if it has a connection to the Internet or to iTunes, you can back up the iPad at any time.

For iTunes backup, select your iPad from the Devices pop-over in iTunes and click Sync to manually back up your iPad. On the iPad, go to the Settings app, tap General, tap iTunes Wi-Fi Sync, and then tap Sync Now. (If Sync Now is grayed out, make sure that iTunes is running on

your computer and is connected to the same Wi-Fi network as your iPad. The button should become active when those conditions are met.)

For iCloud backup, go to the Settings app, tap iCloud, tap Backup, and then tap Back Up Now. To see and control what is backed up to iCloud, go to the Settings app, tap General, tap Usage, tap Manage Usage in the iCloud section, and tap your iPad's name to get the screen shown below.

Setting Up Business Mail, Contacts, and Calendars

An iPad lets you set up multiple accounts, so you can work with both business and personal email from the Mail app. Ditto for your calendars and contacts. Even though you have multiple accounts active, with a unified Inbox view in Mail, their data is not commingled — your business messages are kept separate from your personal messages, so replies are from the account that received them. You can even have separate email signatures for each account, so work emails get your business info while your personal emails don't.

You manage your email, contacts, and calendar accounts in the Settings app's Mail, Contacts, Calendars pane.

To add an account, tap Add an Account and then tap the account type for the service you are adding. Your options are iCloud, Exchange, Google, Yahoo!, AOL, Outlook.com, and Other, which lets you add email services using the widely used IMAP and POP protocols.

Most businesses use Exchange (which includes Microsoft's new Office 365 service), which you set up by tapping Exchang. Some businesses use email servers running the IMAP protocol, which you set up by tapping the Other option. And some businesses use Google accounts, which you set up by tapping Google.

You can have multiple accounts for any of the supported account types, such as a personal Google Gmail account and a business one. Just create each account in turn.

Enter the settings requested for the account type you selected. (You may need to get the details from your IT department, or see what they are in your email client, such as Outlook or Apple Mail, on your computer.)

After you enter the correct settings, you choose which services to use for that account, as Figure 2-2 shows. The business services available vary based on the account type, but the possibilities are Mail, Contacts, Calendars, Reminders, and Notes. Use their corresponding switches to turn a service on or off. You can enable any combination of services per account. For example, you may want to enable your personal Gmail but not your Google contacts on an iPad primarily used for work.

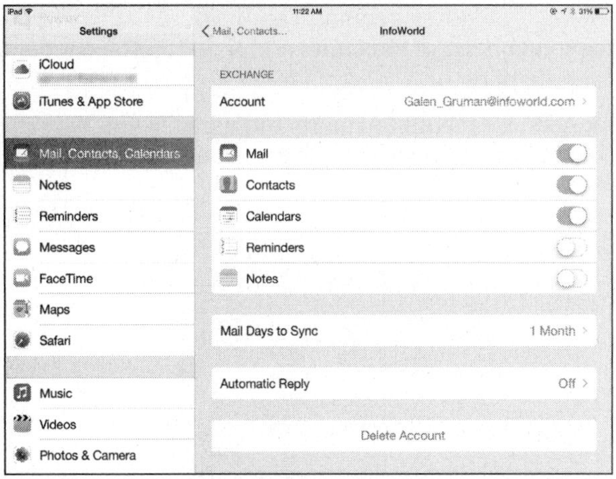

Figure 2-2:
Each mail
account
can have
several
business
services
available for
use on the
iPad.

If you use multiple devices, such as a smartphones, tablets, and computers, you can set up different service combinations for each, customizing what each device accesses based on what you use it for. After all, why wade through emails, contacts, and appointments on every device you use if you don't have to?

The corresponding iPad apps will then access your accounts' enabled business services. Here's how to move about those accounts in the iPad apps:

✓ **Mail:** In the Mailboxes list (tap Back in the upper left of the app window if you don't see it), tap the account you want to see the email for. If you tap All Inboxes, you see all emails from all accounts, as long as those emails weren't moved to folders. (You have to go to a specific account to see its folders.) You can change the order of accounts, as well as enable or disable special views such as Unread, by tapping Edit. Figure 2-3 shows the Mailboxes list being edited.

✓ **Contacts:** By default, all contacts display. Tap Groups at the upper left of the app window to get a list of accounts. If an account has a check mark next to it, it's visible. Tap Done when done.

✓ **Calendar:** In the Calendar app, tap Calendars and then tap each account you want to be visible or invisible in your calendar view. If an account has a check mark next to it, it's visible. Note that many accounts support multiple calendars each, and you can show or hide each individual calendar as desired here. Tap Done when done.

✔ **Notes:** By default, all notes display. Tap Accounts at the upper left of the app window to get a list of accounts and then tap the account you want to restrict the display to.

✔ **Reminders:** A list of accounts and its individual reminders lists appears in the left pane. Tap the account list you want to work with.

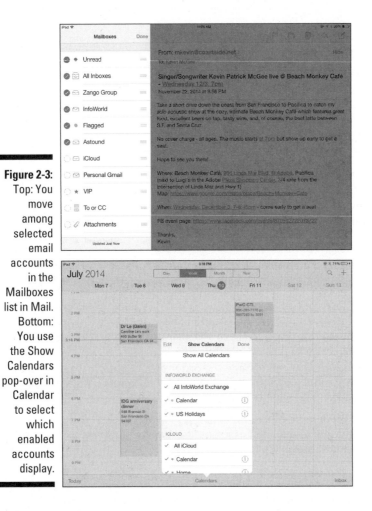

Figure 2-3:
Top: You move among selected email accounts in the Mailboxes list in Mail. Bottom: You use the Show Calendars pop-over in Calendar to select which enabled accounts display.

Connecting to Wi-Fi

Wi-Fi is how any iPad can connect to the world, or at least to a router that serves as the bridge to the Internet.

In terms of using Wi-Fi, the iPad works like any computer: You scan for available networks or enter a Wi-Fi network's name (called an SSID) and then its password. You do this by using the following steps:

1. **In Settings, tap Wi-Fi.**

   Wait a few seconds for the available networks to appear.

2. **Tap the Wi-Fi network you want to connect to, as shown in Figure 2-4.**

   If Wi-Fi is disabled, turn it on by sliding the Wi-Fi switch there.

3. **Enter the password and tap Join.** After you've joined a Wi-Fi network, the iPad will automatically rejoin it when it detects that network in the future.

In corporate environments, you may also be asked to accept a digital certificate. Doing so saves a file on your iPad that is like a second password that fills itself in for you, giving your network administrator extra assurance that your device is authorized when it later reconnects, as well as a way to keep track of the different devices that have connected.

In some corporate environments, Wi-Fi routers will also ask for additional credentials, usually the username and password you use at the office to access email and so forth (often called ActiveSync or Exchange credentials). Fill in what's required to get that access.

In hotels, airports, and cafes, connecting to Wi-Fi is just the first step to gaining access to the Internet. Usually, after a few seconds, a Safari browser window opens, requiring you to sign up for (usually paid) access or enter your account credentials for that network's provider. Sometimes all you have to do is accept some terms and conditions and look at an ad to get Internet access.

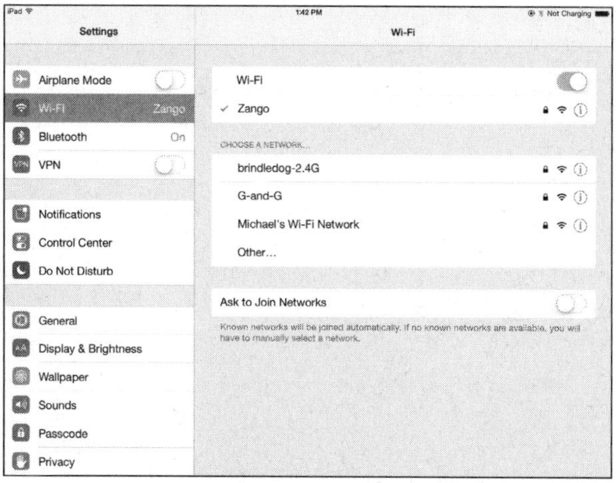

Figure 2-4:
Each mail account can have several business services available for use on the iPad.

If you don't seem to get Internet access after connecting to a Wi-Fi network in a commercial establishment, try opening Safari to see whether that forces the sign-up/sign-in pages to load. These pages don't always load automatically from the Settings app.

After you've connected to a Wi-Fi network, the iPad automatically reconnects in the future when you get in range. But you still may need to go through a web sign-up form at a commercial establishment.

If you have a cellular iPad model, you don't need to use Wi-Fi to connect to the Internet, though Wi-Fi is typically faster. My advice: Skip the high hotel, cafe, and airport Wi-Fi costs by using your cellular services in such locations, but definitely use Wi-Fi at work and home so that you don't use up your cellular data allotment where you don't have to. Hotels and airports often charge $10 to $30 a day for Wi-Fi access, which can add up to $100 or more per trip. By contrast, a 1GB or 2GB cellular plan — which provides plenty of data for email and other work uses — will cost just $20 to $30 for a month, and can be used in any location that has a cellular signal. Of course, if you do things like stream movies, you'll eat up that cellular bandwidth fast — watching a single movie can take an entire gigabyte. So be sure to price the various scenarios to get the best option for your usage.

Chapter 3

Ensuring Your iPad's Security

In This Chapter

▶ Separating personal and business info stored on the same iPad

▶ Managing device permissions for everyone in your business

▶ Securing your iPad's connections with virtual private networks

▶ Applying best practices to your iPad security

Chances are that if you use an iPad for work, it's one you bought and control, even if the company reimbursed you. Even if the company bought it, the iPad you use will all but certainly wind up containing personal information of yours in addition to business information.

That's why you need to understand how that mix of personal and business use affects the information you work with, and how to protect both yourself and your business.

This chapter shows you how to keep your personal and business data separate on your iPad, how to manage your iPad's security through a variety of methods, and how to secure your Internet connections using a virtual private network (VPN). Finally, it surveys the best security practices that I recommend you adopt in using your iPad for work. Remember: When you use your iPad for work, you have more to protect than just your personal emails and photos.

Keeping Work and Personal Data Separate

Few employees worry about the commingling of their personal and work data, but IT departments do. That's because many businesses need to monitor where company information goes, as well as what information flows through their networks, to comply with legal auditing requirements, investigate potential security breaches, and investigate other legal issues such as sexual harassment.

Anything that flows through your company's network is visible to your IT department. Any data stored on equipment, whether the company owns it or not, that connects to your company's information systems could be required in a legal case, which means that your personal equipment and accounts could be subject to access, review, and even requisition.

But don't be scared: These are worst-case scenarios that explain why your company likely has policies governing how you can access information from the company on your equipment and what personal activities you can do at the office. They also explain why your company may require you to use mobile device management software (described later in this chapter) or at least enable remote wipe on your iPad if you use it for work.

Separating work and personal isn't so easy

The best strategy for addressing these concerns is to keep information you want private off any system that accesses corporate systems. Or vice versa. In extreme cases, you'll have separate phones, iPads, and computers for work and personal use — that's the norm in the defense industry, for example.

Outside of such highly regulated industries, the formal norm has been to use company email systems only for company information, and to save your personal affairs for your home computer.

But most of us long ago crossed the work-personal divide in our computing, such as by bringing work home to work on our home PCs, accessing email from our smartphones and home PCs, and increasingly using our own iPads at the office. After all, many professionals are expected to get the job done no matter how long it takes or where they are, and to be available as needed.

The usually unspoken rule is that employers let you handle personal issues at the office or work at home sometimes to handle personal issues such as watching the kids on school holidays — you work from home, and you can do personal stuff on "work time" and even on work equipment. The expectation is that you will use personal email for personal correspondence and use the web to do personal business rather than install personal software on your work devices.

Legally, that strategy still exposes your personal devices and accounts to investigations and monitoring, but the cleaner your separation, the less likely that any investigation will need to go through your personal information.

If IT disables access to your work accounts, such as when you leave the company, your iPad may retain some of that data in its local storage. (You set how long such data is kept in the Settings app's Mail, Contacts, Calendars screen for each account.) I suggest that you delete that account from your iPad and then back up your device to iTunes or iCloud (see Chapter 2) — doing so will remove the remaining company info from your iPad and its latest backup.

Drawing a line between personal life and work on your iPad

So, what does this mean for the iPad? This section covers some strategies to use to minimize the mixing of personal and business on your tablet.

Email, calendars, notes, tasks, and contacts should be stored on separate servers

As Chapter 2 explains, the iPad supports multiple accounts for the servers that handle this information, and I recommend that you use them.

When composing emails in the Mail app, be sure the From address is from the correct account; if not, tap the current account name in your email message and choose the correct one. If you go to the Mailboxes view in the Mail app on your iPad, shown in Figure 3-1, you can tap the desired account from the Accounts list to work only in that account. This is a great way to avoid mistaken use of the wrong email account. (Tap the upper-left button on the Mail screen until you see the Mailboxes screen.)

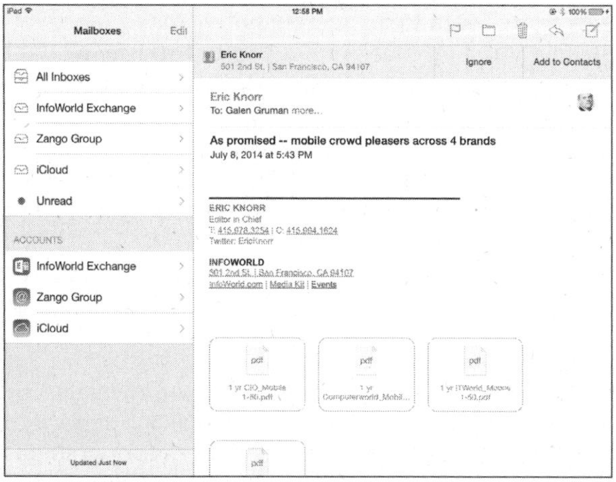

Figure 3-1: The Mailbox screen in the Mail app.

The Calendar app lets you restrict what calendars you can see by tapping Calendars and choosing the desired calendars in the pop-over that appears. But when you create an event, you can select the calendar it goes in, and because they are color coded, it's pretty easy to make sure that the right calendar is set for each event — and it's easy to edit an appointment to change the calendar it's stored in.

The Reminders app for tasks works similarly; choose the desired account from the list at the left, as Figure 3-2 shows.

Figure 3-2:
The Reminders app shows accounts at the left.

Keeping accounts straight in the Notes app is not so easy. You can't change which account a note is assigned to, for example, nor can you choose the account for a new note. So, to take meeting notes, make sure that you're using your work account, not your personal one. Tap the Accounts button at the upper left of the Notes screen to get a list of accounts, then tap the one you want to work in.

You can set the default Notes accounts on the Settings app's Mail, Contacts, Calendars screen. But it's easy to forget what your default is and inadvertently enter a note in the wrong account.

If you want to be extra safe, use different apps for personal and business data. For example:

✔ You might use Microsoft's free OWA app for work emails, contacts, and appointments (if your company uses the Office 365 service) and Apple's Mail, Calendar, Contacts, Notes, and Reminders for personal information. Figure 3-3 shows the OWA app. (OWA stands for Outlook Web Access, Microsoft's name for its Webmail website that the OWA app is based on.)

✔ You might use NitroDesk's TouchDown app ($19.99, or free if your business has an enterprise account) for work emails, contacts, and appointments, notes, and tasks (if your company uses Microsoft's Exchange server), and use Apple's apps for personal information. iKonic Apps' Mail+ is another option for Exchange users, but it supports just email, calendars, and contacts.

✔ Your company might supply a separate suite of apps for accessing corporate email, calendars, and so on. Mobile device management suites typically offer such separate app sets, as described later in this chapter.

✔ You might use Apple's apps for work functions and, say, Google's Gmail app for personal emails.

Figure 3-3:
The
Microsoft
OWA
screen
supports
email, cal-
endars, and
contacts for
Office 365
users.

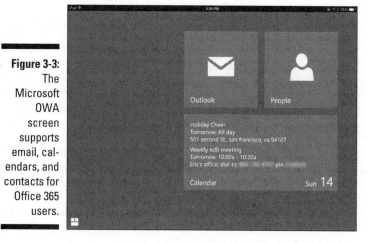

However, that "separate apps" strategy isn't as easy to do on the iPad as on a computer. The reason: There aren't alternatives to Apple's apps that work on all the popular services and cover the same range of functions.

For example, Microsoft's OWA app doesn't handle notes or tasks, and it works only if you use the Office 365 service. TouchDown covers the same bases as Apple's apps but works only with Exchange servers (which covers most larger companies). And Google has a native iPad app only for Gmail, not for Google Contacts or Google Calendar, and it has no tasks or notes tools.

About the only way to get a comprehensive alternative to Apple's apps is for your company to invest in a mobile device management service, described later in this chapter.

So, chances are that you'll use Apple's apps and will need to keep account separation clearly in mind as you use them.

Documents should be stored separately, too

A big concern among IT managers is company data being copied to devices that they can't monitor, potentially providing an escape hatch for sensitive data that they can't trace to the leaker. That concern has been around as long as the home PC, of course, but it's still real.

To work on a document, chances are that you have to make a local copy for your iPad, using the Open In service described in Chapter 17. After that's done, the document — or that copy, anyhow — is no longer under IT's control or within its ability to monitor.

But you can minimize the commingling of work and personal documents by using separate apps and storage services wherever possible.

For example, you might use Apple's excellent iWork suite consisting of the Pages, Numbers, and Keynote apps (see Chapter 5) for personal documents; and use Microsoft's also excellent Office suite of the Word, Excel, and PowerPoint apps (see Chapter 6) for business documents — assuming that your company uses the Office 365 service, which Office for iPad requires.

The Microsoft Office apps don't let you share documents with other iPad apps, other than send them as file attachments in Mail. And they restrict you to saving files only to Microsoft's OneDrive and SharePoint services, to the Dropbox cloud storage service, or to the Office apps' internal storage on the iPad, as Figure 3-4 shows, though you can copy files from other apps, including Mail, into the Office apps. Thus, Microsoft Office for iPad makes it a bit harder to share its data with the rest of your iPad.

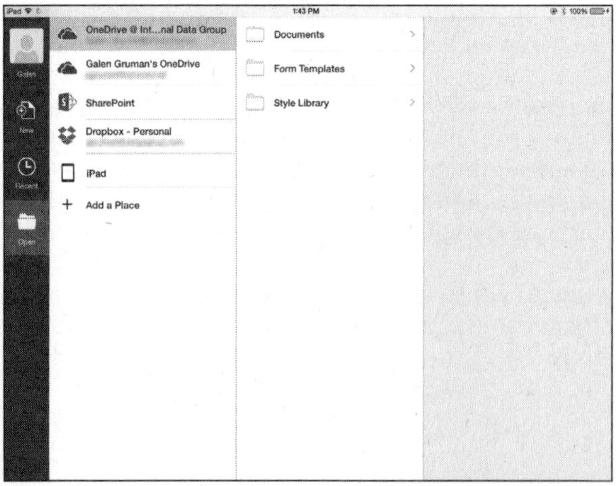

Figure 3-4: The Microsoft Office apps (Word is shown here) restrict document storage to just a few locations.

Of course, that separation is not complete. You can set up a personal OneDrive or Dropbox account and move files to it from the Office for iPad apps, and then share the files with other apps and services from the OneDrive or Dropbox app on your iPad or the OneDrive or Dropbox service from your computer. But doing all that takes a plan and some effort, so Microsoft Office is still a good option to prevent inadvertent commingling of business and personal files.

A similar strategy is to use different cloud storage services for work and business documents, such as Dropbox or iCloud Documents for personal files and Box or OneDrive for work documents. In some cases, as Chapter 16 explains, apps can directly read and write files stored on these services. Office for iPad can do so for OneDrive and Dropbox, and Apple iWork can do so for iCloud Documents and Box, for example.

Consider separating your web activities

One of the most convenient features of Apple's Safari browser is that it syncs bookmarks, passwords, and credit card information across its iPad, iPhone, Mac, and Windows versions — if you've signed into the same iCloud account on those devices, of course. But that feature also means that your personal and work web information are synced within the same account as well.

Therefore, you might consider using two browsers — one for personal and one for business. That second browser should be the free Google Chrome, which also syncs bookmarks and passwords across all devices signed into your Google account, as Figure 3-5 shows.

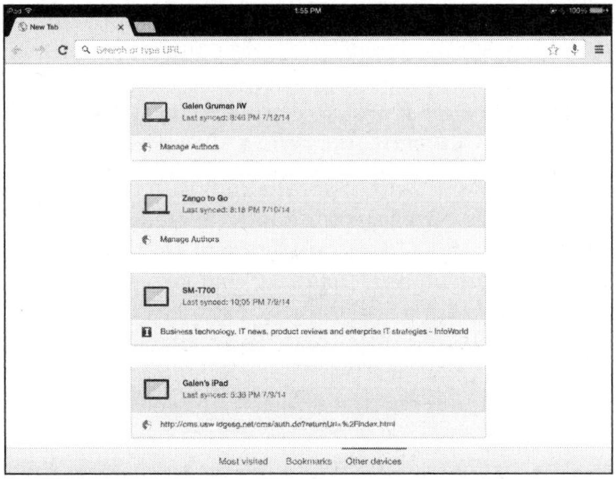

Figure 3-5: As does Apple's Safari, Google's Chrome browser syncs bookmarks and passwords across multiple devices.

You might use Chrome for work and Safari for personal business, or vice versa. Because both iCloud and Google are considered personal services by IT departments, they'd probably prefer that you use neither for work, but you don't really have a choice: Microsoft's Internet Explorer is available only for Windows, and Mozilla's Firefox is not available for iOS.

Working with Mobile Device Management

As mentioned in the preceding section, one method for separating business and professional information is to use a mobile device management server, a.k.a. MDM and EMM (for *enterprise mobility management*). These are systems that your IT department has to deploy and manage, usually for a monthly per-user fee, so they tend to be something that only larger companies use.

But even a small company can use some of these services, thanks to cloud-based small-business versions.

Popular providers include BlackBerry, CA Technologies, Citrix Systems, Good Technology, IBM, MobileIron, SAP, and Soti, though dozens of providers are out there.

An MDM server does at least two things:

- Manages user devices like iPads, such as by imposing restrictions on what networks you can access, determining what apps you can install, blocking access to iTunes and iCloud, and controlling whether you can open mail attachments in other apps. They can also remotely lock or wipe your device, disable access to corporate systems, and configure the use of virtual private networks (VPNs, described in the next section).

- Provide safe "containers" for corporate apps and data. Typically, these services provide their own apps for handling email, contacts, and calendars, and perhaps other functions. They're kept in a separate part of the iPad's memory known as a *container* that serves as a partition from the rest of your iPad's apps and data. These apps can access corporate servers for documents and other data, but they can't share that information with other apps on your iPad. These apps may also include a storage container for documents that you can browse, open from, and save to as well.

As a user, you're restricted to what your IT department has decided it will permit via MDM. If those restrictions are too onerous, all I can recommend is that you don't use a personal iPad for work but instead require your company to provide you with an alternative tool for business needs, such as a separate iPad or a laptop.

Enforcing basic security without the cost or effort of an MDM server

The iPad natively supports the Exchange ActiveSync (EAS) management policies provided by Microsoft's popular Exchange server (including the Office 365 service). It's sort of a budget MDM for small businesses, letting the company require your iPad be protected with a password (including its complexity and how often it must be changed), wipe or lock your device remotely, and remotely configure some security settings such as for Wi-Fi access points and VPNs.

The Exchange or Office 365 administrator for your company sets up which policies apply to which user groups in the management console for Exchange or Office 365.

I encourage any company of any size to at least use these policies to set basic security parameters for users' iPads. You may not need a full-blown MDM tool, but everyone should set up basics such as password requirements.

Apple has another MDM option on the cheap — two, actually. But they're Mac-only products. One is the free Apple Configurator (available at the Mac App Store), which lets you set policies similar to what EAS offers as well as impose additional restrictions and apply additional configurations. You create profiles in the application and configure the settings, called payloads, that you want included. Figure 3-6 shows the payload for passwords.

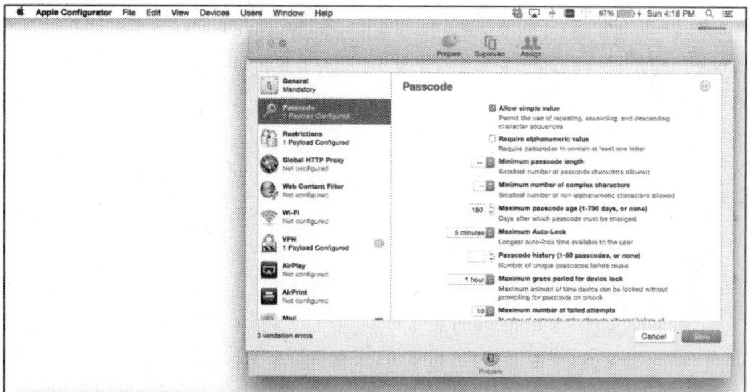

Figure 3-6:
Setting up
a configu-
ration file
in Apple
Configurator
on the Mac.

You then connect devices to the Mac running Apple Configurator and click Install Profiles in the Prepare pane to select the attached devices to install the profiles to.

Supervised mode resets the iPad and then applies all the settings to it, so it should be used only for new iPads that IT will continue to manage. Be sure to back up the iPad to iTunes, as described in Chapter 2, before resetting the iPad this way. Furthermore, only the Mac that was initially used to supervise the iPad can apply changes to the configuration changes in the future.

Then there's the $20 OS X Server application (available from the Mac App Store), which lets you remotely apply the same policies and configurations as the Apple Configuration Utility to Macs and iOS devices does. It works like the Apple Configurator, except that it ties into your company's user directory, which requires some IT administrator expertise to use.

Both the OS X Server and an MDM tool can create configuration files that set up various security and management settings so that users don't have to do the manual work — and so that IT can ensure that everyone has the correct settings. If you access those configuration files via links on web pages, through OS X Server's remote delivery feature, or as email attachments, you'll have to confirm the installation of the configuration file on your iPad, as Figure 3-7 shows.

To accept a configuration profile, you may need to disable Find My iPad temporarily. Do so in the iCloud screen of the Settings app. (I explain Find My iPad later in this chapter.)

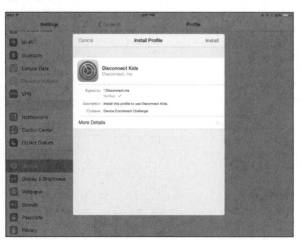

Figure 3-7:
A configuration file has to be accepted by the user to be installed.

Configuration files can be managed in the Settings app. Go to the bottom of the General pane and tap Profile to see a list of installed configurations. Tap a profile to get more details on it, as well as to get to the Delete Profile button. (But note that configuration files can be made undeletable by the user, so not all profiles will offer the Delete Profile button.)

Exploring VPN Connections

You've no doubt read the stories about hackers lurking in cafes and lounges that have public Wi-Fi access, using sniffer tools to intercept the communication between computing devices and the Wi-Fi hotspot so that they can pull out usernames and passwords that they can then sell to criminals.

The Wi-Fi snooping risk is real, though greatly exaggerated. A better target, after all, is your home network, where an attacker can camp out nearby and know it's your information he's getting. This is something that a high-level exec or rich family might be targeted for. (That's why you should always use secured networks at home, as described later in this chapter.)

So, many companies insist that you use a virtual private network (VPN) to access at least some of their systems when connecting via the Internet. A VPN provides a secure connection between your device and the corporate server, even if you connect via a network that your IT departments doesn't manage — including public hotspots, your home network, and hotel networks.

The iPad has built-in support for VPNs, including the popular Cisco IPSec variant. You set up VPN access by going to the Settings app and then following these steps:

1. **Go to the General screen.**

2. **Scroll down until you see VPN; then tap it.**

3. **In the screen that opens, tap Add VPN Configuration.**

4. **Select the type of VPN from the tabs at the top; then fill in the required information (your IT department will need to provide it).**

   Figure 3-8 shows such a setup screen.

5. **Tap Save.**

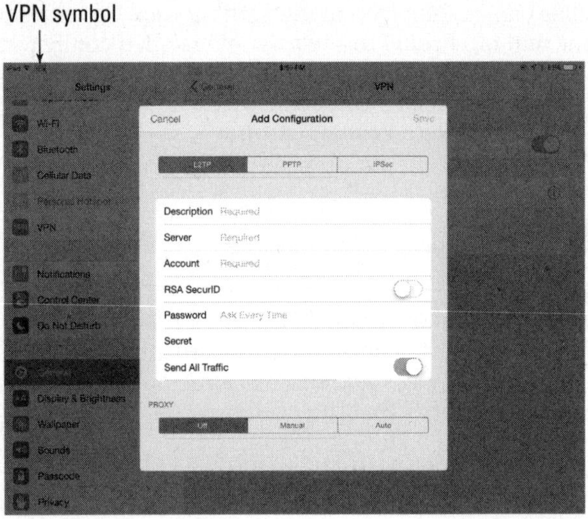

VPN symbol

Figure 3-8:
Configuring
a VPN.

To enable the VPN, set the switch at the top of the VPN screen to On. After that, you'll see the VPN option at the top-left portion of the Settings app, so you can easily turn it on or off. When you turn the VPN on, you may be required to enter a password, based on the VPN's settings.

Your iPad will work normally when an VPN is active. All that's different is that you can use some corporate resources unavailable when the VPN is not on. However, the use of a VPN can slow down your Internet activities because all communications is going through your company network first. That's a good reason to turn the VPN on only when you need to use it.

When the VPN is active, you see the VPN symbol at the left side of the iPad's status bar (refer to Figure 3-8).

You can have more than one VPN installed, as Figure 3-9 shows. But only one can be active at any one time. In the VPN screen, the one that has a check mark is the one that is turned off and on via the switch at the top of the VPN screen. To change the active VPN, turn off the VPN, select a different one from the list, and turn the VPN back on.

The VPN may automatically disconnect after your iPad goes to sleep, and it will definitely disconnect when you lose Internet access or turn the iPad off.

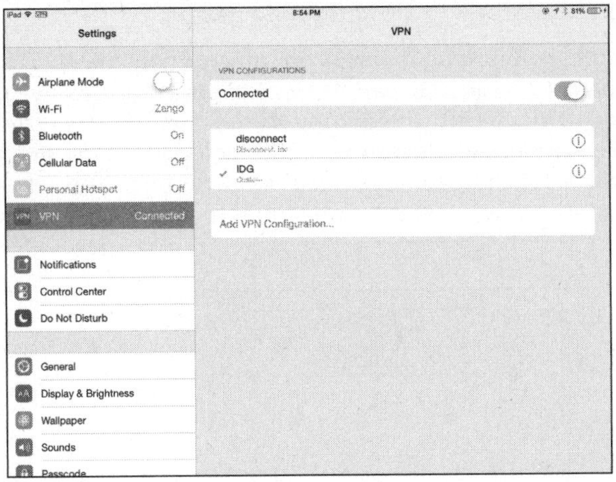

Figure 3-9:
The
checked
VPN is the
one that
is enabled
when you
turn the VPN
feature on.

Adopting Best Security Practices

You should take several steps to keep your iPad secure. After all, it's got a treasure trove of information on it that you don't want to lose or have fall into the wrong hands.

So be sure to adopt the security best practices recommended in this section in addition to the work/business separation practices earlier in this chapter, the use of VPNs also described earlier, and the backup process described in Chapter 2. And, of course, know where your iPad is!

Require a password

Every iPad should have a password enabled so that a stranger can't just wake your iPad and get access to your documents, apps, bookmarks, and so on. If your iPad doesn't have a password already set up, go to the Settings app to do so:

1. **Tap Passcode to open the Passcode Lock screen, shown in Figure 3-10.**

2. **Tap Turn Passcode On.**

3. **Enter the desired passcode.**

   It's best to use something that combines letters and numbers and isn't the same as other passwords you use so that a thief who knows one password can't access everything with it.

4. Set Require Passcode to a comfortable period.

For example, if your iPad is rarely out of your control, set it to 5 Minutes, which means that the iPad can be unused for as long as five minutes after going to sleep before requiring the password be entered to use it. (The Require Passcode options can't be longer than the Auto-Lock period you set in the General screen of the Settings app.) If your iPad contains state secrets, set it to Immediately.

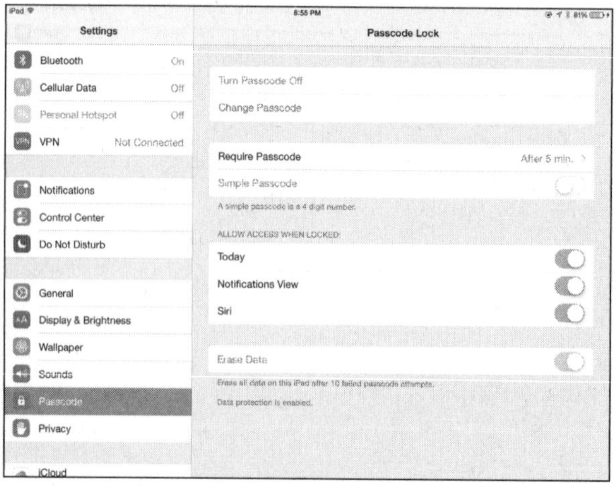

Figure 3-10: Set a password in the Passcode Lock screen in the Settings app.

Limit information to data when locked

The iPad provides a lot of access to data even when it is locked. That's really handy because you can glance at your iPad to see recent alerts and missed messages, check your calendar, turn on and off features like Wi-Fi and Bluetooth, and even issue voice commands through Siri.

In iOS 8, you can activate Siri (if your iPad is connected to power) by simply saying "Hey, Siri," so someone can get Siri to respond without even having to touch the iPad.

But maybe you shouldn't do this. On an iPhone, which you nearly always have in a pocket or your hand, these easy-access features are hard for others to use. But most people leave their iPad unattended for long periods of time, as they do their computers, so someone can easily see what information is available on your Lock screen. So maybe you shouldn't show so much there.

I recommend that you go through the following settings (in the Settings app) and ask yourself what you really want accessible on the Lock screen:

- ✔ In the Passcode Lock screen, disable any service you don't want people to use when the iPad is locked by turning off their switches. The options are Today (which shows your calendar for today), Notifications view (which shows and alerts you've missed), and Siri. (Refer to Figure 3-10 to see these options.)

- ✔ In the Notifications screen, go through the various services, including your email accounts and Messages, and decide what you're okay with being visible on the Lock screen to strangers. That way, you can leave Notifications view on in the Passcode Lock screen, knowing you've filtered the information it displays.

- ✔ In the Control Center screen, think about turning the Access on Lock Screen switch to Off so that someone can't enable or disable Wi-Fi, Bluetooth, AirDrop, or other such settings behind your back.

- ✔ In the General screen, tap Siri and consider setting the Allow "Hey Siri" switch to Off so that saying "Hey, Siri" doesn't activate Siri. (The "Hey, Siri" method works only when your iPad is connected to a power outlet.)

Limit what's monitored on your iPad

Apps can take advantage of a lot of data on your iPad to better serve you. They can access your contacts to see what your friends are sharing if they use the same social network you do. They can check your location to deliver localized restaurant recommendations, weather, and driving conditions. They can monitor your motion to track how many steps you walk each day, or to let you play games in which your movements simulate that of an onscreen character (such as snowboarding).

But many apps monitor more than they need to. You can manage what they monitor in the Settings app. On the Privacy screen, shown in Figure 3-11, go through the various services periodically to see whether you're comfortable with the access that various apps have to them. For example, why does that calculator app need to know your location? It probably doesn't, and you can block it here.

Another place where your activities are monitored is the web browser. The iPad's Safari browser tracks the websites you visit, as do third-party browsers like Google Chrome. But these browsers also have a way to disable such tracking, called private browsing.

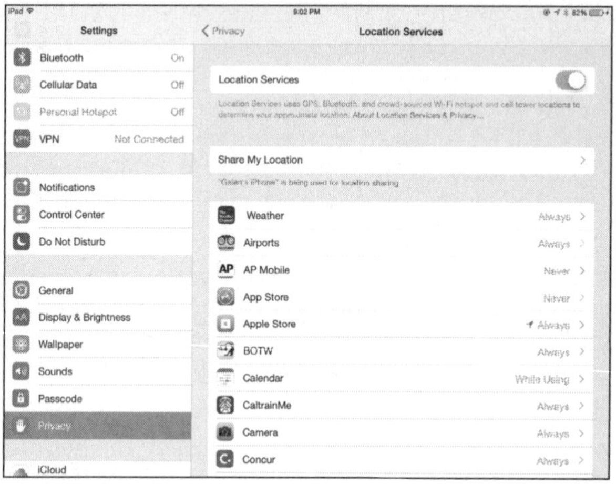

Figure 3-11:
The Privacy
screen
in the
Settings app.

If you use Safari, tap the New Tab icon at the upper right. Then tap the Private button at the upper right, as shown in Figure 3-12. Anything you visit while Private is enabled is not tracked in the browser's history. While you're in Private mode, the menu bar is dark gray, not light gray.

If you use Chrome, tap the Menu button at the upper right and choose New Incognito Tab to begin a private browsing session. You'll see the icon of a spy at the upper left of the screen as long as you're browsing privately.

Figure 3-12:
Safari's
Private
button lets
you stop
tracking the
websites
you've
visited.

Use Find My iPad

Apple has a really useful service called Find My iPad, which you should be sure is turned on. You'll find the control in the Settings app's iCloud screen.

This service lets you find your iPad from Apple's iCloud.com website on any computer, as well as from the Find My iPhone/iPad/iPod app on another iOS device — so be sure to install this free app from the App Store on all your devices.

But Find My iPad does more than help you find your iPad. It can lock or wipe the iPad remotely, if it has an Internet connection, as well as send a message to the screen (such as "Did you find my iPad? Call me at this number, please"). You can also send a noise to it, which is quite handy when your iPad is hiding under a couch, car seat, or pillow.

It also enables activation lock, so someone can't wipe your iPad and set it up with a new iTunes account (or, if you have a cellular iPad, set up a new data plan) — the person would need to know your Apple ID and password to do so.

With Find My iPad, you may not get your stolen iPad back, but at least you know the thief can't use it, either.

Chapter 4

Outfitting Your iPad for Travel

In This Chapter

▶ Using Apple Maps and Google Maps to explore locations

▶ Booking hotel rooms and flights

▶ Managing your itineraries

▶ Finding a nice restaurant

▶ Dealing with foreign languages

*Y*our smartphone is your prime travel tool when on the go because it's in your pocket, ready to help at an instant's notice. But your iPad is a great device for more involved activities, like travel planning, whether you're at home or your hotel. (Be sure to check out my recommendations in Chapter 1 for hardware equipment for travelers.)

The iPad is also a wonderful entertainment companion during your flights. You can read books and watch movies on it. In addition to buying books from the Apple iBookstore for the iBooks app and Amazon.com for the Kindle app, and buying or renting movies from the iTunes Store for the Videos app, you can also transfer your own content to the iPad via iTunes on your computer. Drag rights-free ePub and PDF files into iTunes to make them available for syncing with iBooks, and import DVD movies you own using the free Handbrake app for OS X and Windows. You can add cover art, chapter information, and so on to these ripped movies with MetaZ for the Mac or MetaX for Windows and then import them in iTunes to make them available for syncing with your iPad's Videos app.

This chapter shows you how to use maps apps to plan your travels and navigate to your destinations, how to book and manage your flights and lodging on the popular booking apps, how to work with airline apps for monitoring and checking into your flights, and how to find a nice meal when on the road. It also shows you how to use translator apps, which are handy when you travel abroad but can also be handy when working with foreigners in your office.

Getting Around: Apple Maps and Google Maps

Most people use their iPhone or other smartphone for navigating on the go, following the onscreen and spoken turn-by-turn directions from Apple Maps, Google Maps, Waze, or any of the traditional navigation apps like Navigon and TomTom.

But if you have a cellular iPad, these apps give you all the same benefits as their iPhone versions but on a larger screen that's easier for you (if you're walking) or your copilot (if you're driving) to follow.

If you're driving alone, please don't handle your iPad or iPhone to monitor driving directions. Mount the iPhone in a cradle that's visible while paying attention to the road. Or rely on its or your iPad's spoken instructions, rather than get distracted by looking at its screen on a car seat or other out-of-the-way location.

The free Apple Maps, Google Maps, and Waze require live Internet connections to display their maps, so you need a cellular device and local coverage to use them. Navigon and TomTom store maps on your smartphone or iPad, so they can navigate for you when you have no connection, such as when you are overseas or in a rural area. That's why they cost money.

But the bigger value on the iPad for these apps is to use Apple Maps and Google Maps for planning your trip. Navigation apps like Navigon, TomTom, and Waze are all about leading you in the right direction while you're on the move. They're not really designed to help you plot your course before you leave and explore the area once you're there. But Apple Maps and Google Maps can help you both navigate and explore where you are.

Getting around Apple Maps

Apple Maps is free and is preloaded on your iPad. When you open it, it figures out where you are and centers the map accordingly, as Figure 4-1 shows. But you can have it look up any location by following these steps:

1. **Enter the location in the Search field at the top of the screen.**

   Enter an address or a landmark's name (like "Statue of Liberty").

2. **Tap Search in the onscreen keyboard.**

   There you are! The map shows the area around what you were searching for, with the searched location indicated by a red pin.

Alternatively, tap the Locate button (the pointer icon) at the lower left of the Maps screen to have the iPad zoom in to your current location, as shown in Figure 4-1. *Note:* You need to be connected to the Internet via a Wi-Fi or cellular network for the iPad to discover where you are.

Tap Directions to have Maps present the directions from your current location to the location you searched, or between any locations you enter in the Start and End fields in the pop-over that appears. If you tap Start, the iPad will guide you en route, as long as it has an Internet connection. Siri will even announce the directions for you as you travel.

If you have a printer that your iPad can see over the network, you can print the map and directions. Tap Share to get the Print button.

Changing map views

You can zoom in and out using the standard iOS pinch and expand gestures: Draw your thumb and a finger close together to zoom out, and push them apart to zoom in. Rotate two fingers to rotate the screen. (And tap the compass icon at the upper right when you rotate so that you return the view's orientation to true north).

As Figure 4-2 shows, tap the Information button (the *i* icon) at the lower right of the screen to get a pop-over with more options, including a choice of views (Standard, Hybrid, and Satellite), 3D display, and traffic conditions (no color means traffic is flowing well, thin red dashed lines mean moderate slowdowns, and thick red dashed lines mean severe slowdowns).

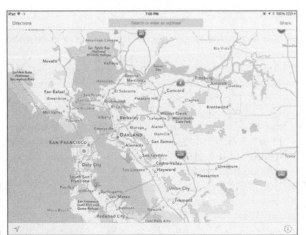

Figure 4-1:
Apple Maps.

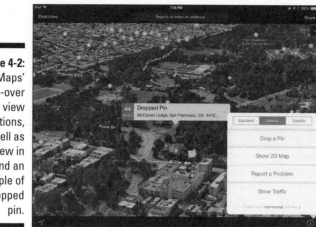

Figure 4-2:
Apple Maps'
pop-over
for view
options,
as well as
the view in
3D and an
example of
a dropped
pin.

The 3D view is most useful and impressive when you are in Hybrid or Satellite views, because you can see the elevations of hills and buildings that you just can't see in the standard map view. To change the perspective of the 3D view, touch two fingers to the screen for a second and then drag them straight up or down. Dragging them up moves you closer to viewing the horizon, whereas dragging them down brings you to a straight-down view from above.

Flagging locations

The Drop a Pin option in the Information pop-over lets you tap on the map to add a purple pin at any location. But you don't have to use the pop-over to drop a pin: Just tap and hold on the map briefly.

Tap that pin to get a banner with details on the location, including travel time and address. Tap the banner to get a pop-over from which you can get directions to or from the location, add the address to an existing contact, or create a new contact that has the address prefilled. You can also remove a pin from this pop-over.

Pins are a great way to explore a potential itinerary. When you tap the Search field, the Recents pop-over displays all dropped pins, as well as recent locations that you've obtained directions for and any locations you've book-marked. So you can use Recents to log points of interest and then select them later to provide directions if desired.

There are more pins than the purple ones you drop. Red pins indicate addresses that you searched for. And three kinds of pins are added automatically: Blue pins are gas stations and parking lots; yellow pins are commercial locations that Apple Maps knows about, such as grocery stores and museums in its database; green pins are parks.

But how do you get locations bookmarked so that they're kept for the long term? From a pin's pop-over, tap the Share icon, then tap Add to Favorites. But you don't need to have a pin to mark a location as a favorite: Simply navigate Maps to whatever location you want to bookmark — you can even just swipe through the map — and tap Share at the upper right of the screen. Then tap Add to Favorites, as Figure 4-3 shows.

Those bookmarked locations are available in the Recents pop-over: Just tap the Favorites option at the top to get a list.

At the bottom of the Favorites list is the Contacts button. Tap it to see your contacts. Grayed-out names have no address information, but names in black do. Tap a person's name to get his or her address shown onscreen; if a person has multiple addresses in your contacts card, you'll get a list of those addresses to choose from.

Syncing map locations

Apple's iCloud service keeps your various devices' Maps apps synced so that your lists of recent locations, favorites, recent directions, and dropped pins are kept the same on your iPhone, iPad, and Mac.

If you use a Mac, you can use its Maps application to create driving directions and then send them to your iPad or Phone so that they're ready for use on those devices when you are. After you create the directions on the Mac's Maps app, click the Share icon and then choose Send to name, picking the name of the iOS device to send the directions to. The directions are available in the Directions pop-over on the iPhone or iPad. What a great way to preload your devices with your itineraries!

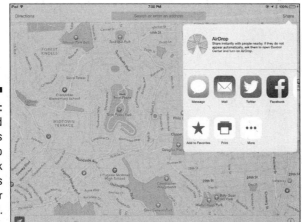

Figure 4-3: Use the Add to Favorites option to bookmark locations for later retrieval.

You can also share Apple Maps locations and directions with other people via AirDrop, which is available in the Share pop-over in Maps. What a great way to share your itineraries with fellow travelers!

The iPhone 5 and later iPhones, third-generation and newer iPads, all iPad Minis, and Macs since 2012 support AirDrop exchange with iOS devices. Chapter 17 explains how to set up AirDrop.

Going with Google Maps

Google Maps is the granddaddy of mobile maps apps, and for years it was Apple's standard Maps app. But these days, it's something you have to download yourself from the App Store, though it remains free. Figure 4-4 shows Google Maps and its menu.

Google Maps doesn't do as much as Apple Maps in some respects, but it does more in other respects. So it's good to have both apps on your iPad.

Here's what it doesn't do:

✔ Let you print maps.

✔ Provide pins for commercial locations. (It does show labels onscreen for such locations, but not pins you can tap for more details.)

✔ Share directly with other people through AirDrop or receive directions from your Mac.

✔ Provide a 3D view, though it can open your current location in Google Earth, which does.

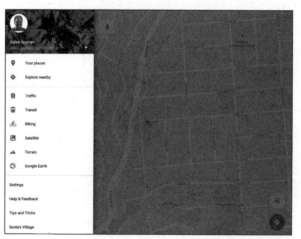

Figure 4-4: Google Maps with its menu visible.

Here's what Google Maps does that Apple Maps doesn't:

✔ Lets you save maps on your iPad. When you drop a pin or find a location:

   1. **Tap the banner for the location to open the pane shown in Figure 4-5. Or tap the Search menu and scroll down.**

   2. **Tap the More button (the . . . icon) to open the menu.**

   3. **Tap Save Offline Map in the menu.**

   4. **Tap Save at the bottom right of the screen that appears, give the saved map a name, and tap Save again.**

✔ To see that map, tap the Details button (the stack of three lines):

   1. **Tap the Your Places option in the menu to open your personal card.**

   2. **Tap the desired saved map in the Saved Places section.**

✔ Provides cycling and transit directions, as well as displays transit stops.

✔ Provides customized suggestions for nearby shopping, based on what you do on the web in the Chrome browser if you enable the Web History feature.

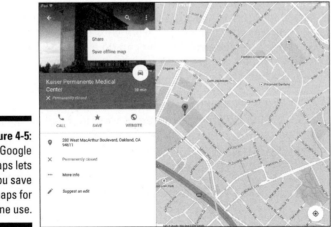

Figure 4-5: Google Maps lets you save maps for offline use.

You can share a map location via email and the Google Hangouts messaging app, as well as copy it as a graphic to paste in other applications. Follow these steps:

1. **Tap the banner for a pin or a searched location to open the details pane.**

2. **Tap the Menu button (the . . . icon) to open its menu.**

3. **In that menu, tap the Share button.**

4. **Select the desired option in the menu that appears.**

You can also save a location as a favorite by tapping the Save button in the details screen. The saved locations are in your personal card.

And Google Maps will show recent locations in the menu that appears when you tap the Search field — if you enable both Location History and Location Reporting in the Settings screen, accessed from the details pane in Google Maps. The list below the Search field shows two recent locations; tap View More Recent History below them to see more.

Booking Travel: Kayak, Expedia, and Orbitz

The iPad is a great tool not just for figuring out how to get where but also for booking travel itself. Yes, you can do that from your computer, but doing so from the iPad is often more convenient: You can do it on the couch while watching TV or during a break at a conference or meeting, when your computer is likely nowhere nearby.

There are many services for booking travel, and your company may have its preferred service that might also provide an iPad or work in the iPad's Safari browser. But if you don't have a preferred or required service, three of the most established travel booking services are definitely worth trying: Kayak, Expedia, and Orbitz. All have websites, their iPad apps also work on the iPhone, and they have versions for other smartphones as well, such as Android, so you can make and check your reservations easily almost anywhere.

Navigating Kayak Pro

Kayak has two iPad apps: the free Kayak and the 99¢ Kayak Pro. They work identically, except that Kayak Pro doesn't annoy you with ads in its screens. That's well worth the tiny cost.

The interface for Kayak Pro is quite simple: You select the type of travel you want to book using the buttons at the top of the screen, and access other features using the buttons at bottom. Its capabilities include searching for flights, hotel rooms, and car rentals; seeking travel deals based on your starting point and desired price; flight tracking for multiple flights; a view of all your Kayak-booked trips; and settings.

Kayak Pro has a really nice search facility for airlines, hotels, and car rentals. Figure 4-6 shows the screen for searching flights, which has a great set of filters such as by duration, price, airline, and stopover cities. The hotel and car screens are similar. It's quite easy to shop for services on Kayak, and that's important when you're busy.

Settings are rarely something you focus on in an app, but Kayak Pro's settings screen (accessed via the Preferences button), shown in Figure 4-7, is worth spending a little time in. There are several really key time savers in those settings:

✔ You can sign into your Kayak account, if you have one, which makes all your booked itineraries and payment info available in the app.

✔ You can enable iCloud support so that your Kayak settings are kept in sync across your iOS devices and your Mac.

✔ You can manage confirmations and alerts, as shown in Figure 4-7.

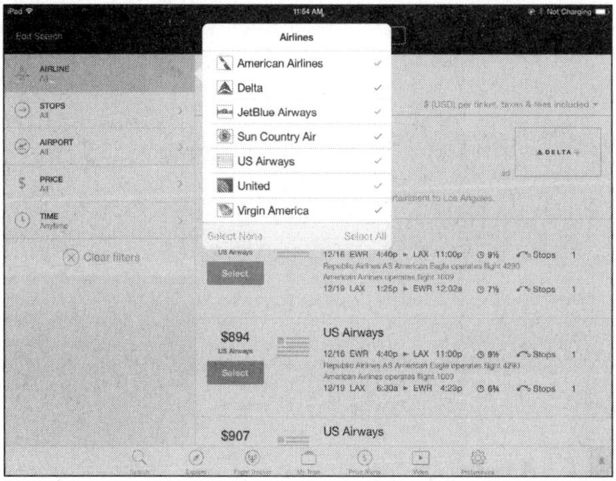

Figure 4-6: Kayak Pro's airfare search screen has lots of filters.

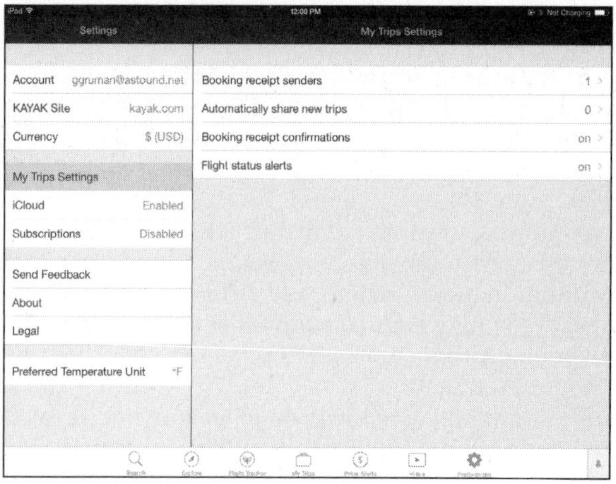

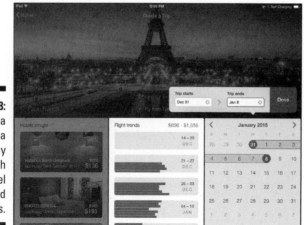

Figure 4-7:
Kayak Pro's
settings
screen has
several con-
veniences.

Engaging Expedia

The free Expedia app, shown in Figure 4-8, is much simpler than Kayak Pro, which makes it a breeze for making quick reservations when you know the area you are seeking a flight or a hotel room for. You start by entering your destination, which opens a screen showing available hotels for that night. Use the calendar at the bottom of the right of the screen to select your travel dates, and optionally use the Select Airport button at the bottom center of the screen to search for flights. Expedia shows you your options after a few moments.

Figure 4-8:
Expedia
provides a
simple way
to search
for hotel
rooms and
flights.

Expedia lets you sign into your Expedia account to track your previous and planned stays — tap the *i* button on the Home screen to sign in — but that's all you can really set. As I said, Expedia is much simpler than Kayak Pro, which means it's also not as flexible or capable.

Traveling with Orbitz

The free Orbitz app falls in between Kayak Pro and Expedia. It focuses on just making reservations for flights, hotel rooms, and car rentals. Its user interface is more spare than Kayak Pro's, though it does nearly everything Kayak Pro does in terms of making reservations. But not *everything:* Its filtering by price is less flexible, limited to sorting them, and it doesn't let you filter flights by airport stopovers.

On the other hand, Orbitz lets you build a flight by choosing the departure and return flights individually, as shown in Figure 4-9, whereas Kayak Pro shows you all combinations. The Orbitz approach is more sensible when your schedule is tight, but it takes more time to work through; the Kayak Pro approach is faster but is more sensible when you have more slack in your travel times.

For hotels and car rentals, Orbitz works similarly to how it works for flights.

The rest of the app is basic and confined to its Menu button's options: You can sign in to your Orbitz account to track your itineraries and set up payment info. You can also sign up for Orbitz rewards, a discount program that the Orbitz app keeps hounding you to join, which is quite annoying. Finally, there's a very basic flight tracker function that lets you track just one flight at a time.

Figure 4-9: Orbitz lets you select departing and return flight segments independently.

Organizing Travel: TripIt and Concur

Making reservations is only part of the travel management that you have to do. You also want to build itineraries, manage reservations, and check status. You can do some of that from the travel services' websites on your iPad, but not so much from their iPad apps. Fortunately, there are some travel management tools you can use, both from Concur Technologies.

Keeping track with Concur

One is Concur, which is a reservations and management system for companies that are clients of Concur or one of its travel-agency affiliates, such as Atlas Travel. You'll need a login name and password to use the free app (which you can get through the App Store) and your company's business arrangement with the travel agency determines what you can do with the app. For example, some companies let employees make flight reservations, whereas others don't allow this from the app (though you can still do it from the website on your iPad — go figure!).

Concur shows your itineraries, so if you book everything through your travel agent, you get the full details of the trip in one place, including confirmation numbers. Figure 4-10 shows the itinerary view. Plus, the app lets you look at alternative flight schedules and hotel rooms right from your itinerary if you need to make a change to your travel plans.

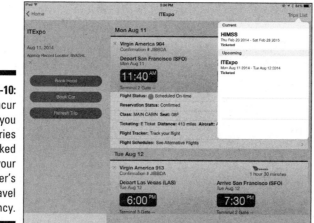

Figure 4-10:
Concur shows you itineraries booked via your employer's travel agency.

What Concur doesn't do is let you copy confirmation numbers from its itinerary view, which makes it hard to check in via an airline's mobile app because you have to remember and reenter the code. Nor does it let you add reservations to Calendar; instead, you need to use the calendar files that you get from Concur's confirmation email when you book a trip. And the flight-tracking feature in Concur requires that a $4.99 app also be installed on your iPad. Still, if your travel agency uses Concur, you should use the Concur app.

Consolidating your plans with TripIt

TripIt is *not* an app to make your travel reservations. Instead, you forward email reservation receipts to plans@tripit.com so that the app can build a unified reservation for you, as well as figure out travel directions between the various stops in your itinerary, as Figure 4-11 shows. (You have to have a TripIt account for this to work, and the emails have to come from the account you registered with.) You can add your own segments, such as a trip to an amusement park that you wouldn't reserve online.

You need to forward itineraries one at a time to plans@tripit.com; otherwise, TripIt will see only the first attachment.

TripIt is very handy because it brings all the pieces of your itinerary together. The basic TripIt app is free, but I recommend spending the 99¢ to get the ad-free version.

Figure 4-11: TripIt shows your full itinerary, even if some portions were booked separately.

But TripIt's in-app check-in features cost extra, requiring the $49 annual Pro subscription that you can buy inside the app. And you can't copy your confirmation codes from TripIt into a hotel or airline app to check in easily there. Checking flight status is also available only if you subscribe to the Pro service. Most people don't need the Pro service, but someone who's always on the road could benefit.

Jetting Off: Airline Apps and Check-In

Most airlines these days have an iPhone and Android app that you can use to check in from your phone. If you have an iPhone, most airlines also let you send your reservations to Apple's Passbook app, shown in Figure 4-12, which collects boarding passes and other tickets so that you have them all in one place. With most airports now supporting onscreen boarding passes at the security and flight check-ins, Passbook is a great convenience.

But the Passbook app works only on your iPhone, not your iPad. Still, you can check in from the Safari browser on a computer (and sometimes your iPad) from websites that enable iCloud Passbook syncing. The ticket is sent to your iPhone via iCloud in such cases, as Figure 4-13 shows. (To enable iCloud Passbook syncing on your iPhone, go to the Settings app, tap iCloud, and set the Passbook switch to On.)

Figure 4-12:
The iPhone's Passbook app collects your boarding passes.

If a site doesn't support Passbook iCloud syncing, you'll have to use the iPhone to open the airline's app to have the boarding pass sent to Passbook. That may explain why many airline apps are designed just for the iPhone, not the iPad.

Both issues — lack of support for iCloud Passbook syncing and iPhone-only apps — are annoying, but there's still reason to use such an airline's mobile app on your iPad: Running an iPhone app on your iPad lets you see everything larger and use the iPad's larger keyboard. That's handy at the end of the day when your eyes are tired but you want to check your frequent flier miles or change your seat or add a bag to your reservation.

And some airline apps, such as the free United Airlines app, have iPad versions that are better at using the screen real estate of the keyboard and typically offer more options than the iPhone or Android versions, and the iPad versions can be easier to use than the airline's website.

Some airline websites don't work on mobile devices, such as JetBlue's, because they use the Flash technology, which is supported only on Windows PCs and Macs. You'll have to use the iPad app or even iPhone app in such cases, unless you're also traveling with a laptop.

Figure 4-13:
Sites savvy to Passbook iCloud syncing can send your iPhone a Passbook ticket from your computer (and sometimes your iPad) from the Safari browser.

Dining Out: OpenTable and Yelp

When you're traveling for business, you often have your meals lined up: Your client takes you out, you eat in the hotel restaurant with colleagues, or you grab room service after a long day. But if you have the time, finding cool restaurants or local or unusual cuisine is one of the perks of being on the road.

Both OpenTable and Yelp have iPhone and Android versions, which you'll also want when you need to eat and your iPad is not with you but your phone is. iPhone users might also want to get the free Urbanspoon app, which makes it really easy to search for restaurants by cuisine; too bad it has no longer has an iPad version.

Reserving through OpenTable

OpenTable, shown in Figure 4-14, is very convenient for finding restaurants that take reservations and have them available for a party of your size at the desired time you want to eat. You can search by cuisine and/or locale to see what's available. If you want to take your colleagues or clients out and be sure that you won't be sitting at the bar for an hour before you're seated, OpenTable is the perfect travel aide. It even lets you set default filters for your searches by cuisine, price, travel distance, and neighborhoods.

By default, the app shows a tiny map to make room for ads for nearby restaurants. But you can hide those ads to see the full map, as shown in Figure 4-11, by tapping the Full Screen button near the upper right of the screen. Tap it again to see the ads.

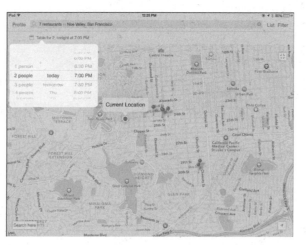

Figure 4-14: OpenTable searches available reservations at restaurants that meet your criteria.

The app is free, and you don't need to set up an account. If you do set up an account, you earn "dining points" but will get email solicitations as well.

Scouting Out Yelp

The Yelp website is widely used to find restaurants, shops, and more that people like. People vote for what they like, vote down what they don't like, and write reviews. Unfortunately, the Yelp service has been abused by businesses trying to amp up their ratings with fake reviews and by allegations that businesses that didn't advertise with Yelp saw their ratings go down.

Still, if you don't have a local guide to advise you, Yelp remains a good place to get restaurant recommendations, and you can make reservations at restaurants that accept them through the app.

Yelp's free iPad app is similar to the website, so you might think about just using the website. But the iPad app has a cleaner, easier-to-navigate design.

Translating Languages: Google Translate and iTranslate

When you're in a foreign country whose language you barely know — or simply don't know — translation services are a must. Ditto if you're researching information about a foreign company or business, whose website may have more detail in the native language than in English.

For elaborate translation you need a human translator, but it's amazing how well a translator program can do the job.

The free Google Translate is a great tool for translation because it lets you paste even large text blocks to translate, as shown in Figure 4-15, as well as translate spoken words and sentences. Pick the languages to translate between, copy or type in the text, and tap Go.

For voice translation, just tap the Microphone button and speak. The translation begins after you stop. And if you want to hear the correct foreign pronunciation of that spoken text, tap the phrase in the app and then tap the Speaker button to its right in the screen that appears.

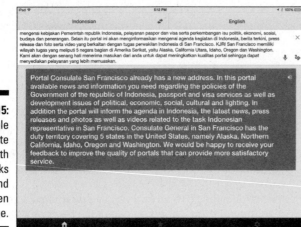

Figure 4-15:
Google
Translate
works with
both blocks
of text and
spoken
language.

Another app worth considering for translation is Sonco's iTranslate. The basic version is free, but if you want voice translation and proper pronunciation, the in-app purchase for that set of services costs $4.99. Because Google Translate offers those features at no charge, the real reason to get iTranslate is that it can convert Asian languages' characters into Roman ones (and vice versa), so you can have an easier dialog with a speaker of such languages via the iPad.

You do need an Internet connection for Google Translate and iTranslate to work (just as you do for the iPad's Siri assistant service to work). Both apps work on both iPads and iPhones, as well as Android devices, so you can have your translator on all your mobile devices.

Handling Expenses: BizXpenseTracker

One of the less pleasant chores while traveling is keeping track of your expense reports. My personal solution is inelegant but works: I keep an Excel spreadsheet on my iPad into which I log my expenses; then I print the spreadsheet when I get back to the office and file it with my paper receipts to the accounting department. Some people I know photograph their receipts using their iPad's or smartphone's camera.

There are more modern approaches, of course, in the form of expense-tracking apps and services! But I can't recommend a specific one because the right one depends on many factors outside your control. For example, if you work for a company, it likely has its own expense-management system that you'll need to use. Maybe it works on your iPad, maybe it doesn't. Some commercial expense-management systems do have iPad versions, such as those from Infor and SAP. Likewise, you might use an independent service like Expensify that charges a monthly per-user fee to your company.

If you don't have such a corporate tool provided to you and you want something more modern than an Excel or Numbers spreadsheet for tracking your expenses, get the $7.99 BizXpenseTracker app, shown in Figure 4-16.

BizXpenseTracker lets you attach files, photos, and email attachments (but not emails themselves, so you can't attach in-message receipts from emails). It can export your files to the CSV format for import into a spreadsheet as well as to PDF format, and it can send the files to your computer via Wi-Fi, a cloud storage service like Dropbox, or email.

But BizXpenseTracker can't assign accounting codes to various categories, which accounting departments often require. (Any automated reporting tool they use will do that automatically, or they'll embed those codes in the Excel expense report form that they tell you to fill out.)

BizXpenseTracker does the job well, but no app makes the process of logging expenses and gathering receipts easy — it's a drudge whether you do it on paper, on your computer in Excel, or on your iPad. What BizXpenseTracker can do is make losing those receipts during your trip less likely — if you're diligent about adding them to your reports each day, of course.

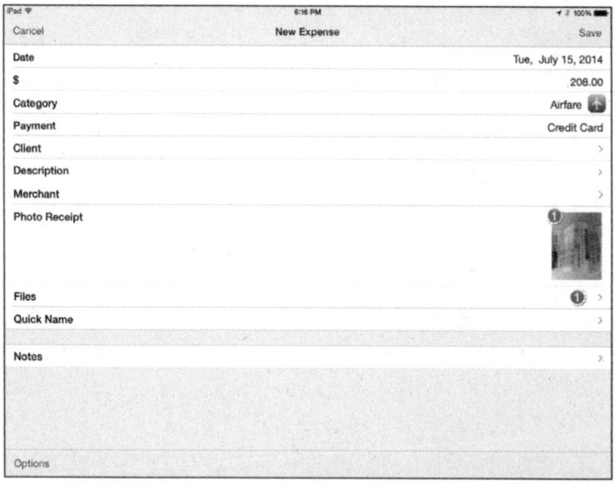

Figure 4-16: BizXpense-Tracker is a highly customizable expense-tracking tool.

Part II
Gearing Up for Productivity

In this part . . .

- All about the best iPad office productivity suite: Apple's iWork.

- Everyone uses Microsoft Office, and so can your iPad.

- Got Google? Here's how to use the Google Apps office suite.

- When a full-fledged office suite is overkill, the iPad has simpler alternatives for writing.

- Take note of that! From quick jots to sketches to voice memos, there's an app for that.

- How to be organized anywhere: Using your iPad to manage tasks and to-dos.

- Great idea! Your iPad as a brainstorming companion.

Chapter 5

Engaging Apple iWork:
Pages, Numbers, and Keynote

● ●

In This Chapter

▶ Sharing iWork documents via cloud storage services and with other apps

▶ Creating, duplicating, and deleting documents, spreadsheets, and presentations

▶ Editing, laying out, and formatting text documents in Pages

▶ Working with spreadsheets and formulas in Numbers

▶ Creating and animating presentations in Keynote

● ●

Almost everyone uses Microsoft Office, and so can the iPad (see Chapter 6). But Microsoft Office isn't the only option for editing documents, working with spreadsheets, or creating presentations on your iPad. In fact, the best office suite for your iPad is Apple's iWork, which includes Pages, Numbers, and Keynote.

In this chapter, I first explain what's in the iWork suite and how to get it, and then I describe the document management features common to all three iWork apps. Next, you see the main capabilities of the three iWork apps, with a section each on Pages, Numbers, and Keynote.

Taking a Brief Tour of iWork

The three iWork apps — the Pages word processor, Numbers spreadsheet editor, and Keynote presentation editor — are free if you bought a new iPad, iPod touch, or iPhone since September 2013, or $9.99 each if not. As with all iOS apps, you can install them at no additional charge on all your iOS devices that are signed into the same iCloud account. Apple also has Mac versions available from the Mac App Store (also free if you bought a new Mac since

October 1, 2013; $19.99 each otherwise), and both Mac and Windows users can use the free web versions in their browsers at www.icloud.com.

All three iWork apps are universal, meaning that they run on iPhones, iPads, and iPod touches. And all three open and export their corresponding Microsoft Office file formats: Word, Excel, and PowerPoint. All three support iCloud Drive, so documents created on one device are available to all your other devices that use iCloud Drive, and edits are synced across all those devices.

What you should know when using iPad productivity tools

iPads, computers, and other devices often don't have the same fonts available, even if they have the same apps. And different apps on the same device may not have the same fonts as each other. That mismatch in fonts as you move documents from one app to another and one device to another can — okay, *will* — cause text to reflow. So, that Pages document on the Mac may appear differently on Pages on the iPad, and that Pages document on iPad may appear differently in Microsoft Word on your PC. You can try to standardize on common, basic fonts like Arial, Georgia, Times New Roman, and Verdana, or you can hold off on your final formatting work until the document is on the final device and app in your workflow.

Both iWork and Google Apps can send their files to other apps via the standard iOS Share sheet, as well as receive them from other apps from those apps' Share sheet. (Microsoft Office apps cannot share their documents with other apps, but they can receive documents shared from other apps.) But remember: When you send files from one app to another, you're creating a new copy, so keeping track of which version is the "correct" one can be a challenge. All three suites really want you to keep it in the family, storing files only on their cloud storage so that only their mobile and computer apps work with them: iWork uses iCloud Drive; Office uses OneDrive and Dropbox; and Google Apps uses Google Drive. (Chapter 16 covers such cloud storage services.)

No matter what apps you use for editing, there are two keys on the iPad's onscreen keyboard that you may not know about but that are quite handy: Undo and Redo. They apply to text changes only. You get to the Undo key by tapping the .?123 key to switch to the numerals and symbols keyboard; Undo is at the lower left. You can keep undoing edits, one tap at a time. To get the Redo key, tap the #+= key to the left of the Undo key; that changes Undo to Redo and #+= to 123. To get Undo back, tap the 123 key. Tap the ABC key to get the alphabetical keyboard back.

Creating presentations and documents is often only half the battle. The other half is presenting them, whether in a conference room or through distributed documents. Chapter 18 explains how to create PDFs and ePubs from your documents, and Chapter 19 explains how to make presentations from your iPad.

Managing Documents in iWork

The three iWork apps manage documents the same way, in the Documents window that appears when you open them. Any documents you created in an iWork app — whether on your iPad, on another iOS device, on a Mac, or in iCloud.com — will appear after iCloud has had a chance to sync the files. Figure 5-1 shows the Documents window for Pages. In iCloud Drive on a Mac or PC, those documents show up in the specific apps' folders in iCloud Drive in the Mac's Finder and Windows' File Explorer, respectively.

For iCloud syncing to work, iCloud has to be turned on at each device you want synced. On your iPad, go to the Settings app and check the panes for Pages, Numbers, and Keynote to make sure that the Use iCloud switch is set to On. Also make sure that iCloud Drive is set to On in the iCloud pane in Settings. On a Mac, you manage iCloud in the System Preferences app's iCloud pane; in Windows, you manage iCloud in the Control Panel's iCloud pane, which is available if you've installed iCloud Drive. Chapter 16 covers iCloud Drive in more detail.

If you see the ↑ icon on the upper-right corner of a document's thumbnail preview, that means that changes made to it on your iPad are being sent to iCloud to update the copy on your other devices. If you see a progress bar at the bottom of a thumbnail, that means that changes made elsewhere to that document are being updated to the copy on your iPad.

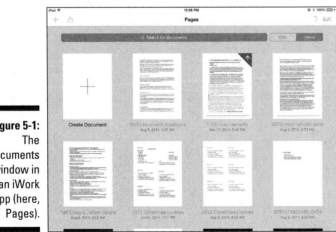

Figure 5-1: The Documents window in an iWork app (here, Pages).

At the top of the Documents window is the Search field, where you can search for documents by entering text that is in their filenames — it does not search their contents. To its right are the Date and Name buttons, which let you sort the file list by, yes, date and name.

Opening documents

The iWork apps can of course open documents stored on your iPad and synced via iCloud Drive through the app's specific iCloud Drive folder (Pages, Numbers, or Keynote). You see those documents in the Document window. Tap such a document to open it for editing. Any changes you make in that document are saved automatically as you make them.

But if your iPad is running iOS 8.1 or later, iWork can also open documents from other locations: those stored in iTunes, on a WebDAV server, in other iCloud folders, and in cloud storage services such as Box.

To access these "outside" files, tap the Add button (the + icon) at the top left of the screen and then choose the desired source:

- **Copy from iTunes:** Any files copied into iTunes for use by the app are listed. Chapter 17 explains how to put files into iTunes. The file is copied into your iPad's local storage as a separate file from the original, which remains in iTunes. *Note:* Your iPad must be visible in iTunes via a USB or Wi-Fi connection, and iCloud must *not* be enabled.

- **Copy from WebDAV:** You need to enter the WebDAV server's address and your username and password. Any compatible files you select are copied into your iPad's local storage.

- **iCloud:** Here, you can navigate to other folders in iCloud Drive. For example, if you're using Pages, the Documents window shows all documents in the Pages folder within iCloud Drive. Use this option to work with Pages documents in other folders. When you open such files, you are working on the original copy, so any changes made on your iPad are synced back to iCloud Drive.

- **More:** This option lets you add cloud storage services to the menu, based on whatever cloud storage services apps (such as Box) you have installed on your iPad. Set the switch for each desired service to On to have them appear in the Add pop-over. After you've enabled a cloud storage service, you select the desired one to get a form listing compatible files in it. (You must have a live Internet connection to do this.) When you open such files, you are working on the original copy, so any changes made on your iPad are synced back to the cloud storage service. *Note:* You'll be asked to sign into those services the first time you use them with an iWork app.

Not all cloud storage services in the More menu are actually accessible to the iWork apps, even if you set their switches to On. iOS 8.1 provides two ways for apps to directly access cloud storage services, but iWork apps support only one of those methods. Unfortunately, the list of cloud storage services shows services that support either method, so you might think you can access a storage service that you really can't. At press time, the only third-party cloud storage services to support the method used by the iWork apps were Box and OneDrive.

To quickly move among cloud storage services, tap the Locations button in the list form; a menu of other available cloud services displays.

After opening a document, to return to the Documents window in Pages, the Spreadsheets window in Numbers, or the Presentations window in Keynote, tap the Documents button at the upper left of the Pages screen, or tap the Spreadsheets button in Numbers, or the Presentations button in Keynote.

Creating, duplicating, and deleting documents

The Documents window is where you manage your documents. What does "manage" mean? It means to create new ones, copy existing ones, and delete the ones you don't want any longer. *Note:* Where I use the word "document," the term used by Pages, I also mean spreadsheets in Numbers and presentations in Keynote.

The iWork apps don't have a Save As feature after you start editing a document, so be sure to duplicate a document *before* you edit it if you want to leave the original document untouched.

To create a new document (or spreadsheet or presentation), follow these steps:

1. **Tap the Add button (the + icon) at the top left of the screen.**

   A pop-over appears.

2. **Choose Create Document (or Create Spreadsheet or Create Presentation) from the pop-over, or tap the Create Document thumbnail at the top of the Documents list.**

   A list of templates appears on which you can base the new document. Some templates are spare while others are quite sophisticated, with lots of elements' appearances predefined for you.

3. **Tap the desired template to open a new, empty document based on it.**

To copy or delete documents, there are two methods to select the ones in the Documents window that you want to act on:

✔ Tap the Edit button at the upper right of the screen.

✔ Tap and hold any document.

The toolbar at the top of the screen turns blue. Tap the documents you want to act on. You'll then see two buttons at the left of the blue toolbar: Duplicate (the icon of a page stack with a + symbol) and Delete (the trash can icon). Tap the desired button.

If you delete an iWork document on your iPad, it's deleted on all other devices as well.

Sharing and exporting documents

You might think that you can share (open in another app, send via email, make available to others in iCloud, and so on) from the same toolbar as Duplicate and Delete, but you can't. The Share button (the standard iOS Share icon) appears in the standard toolbar, next to the Add button. Tap it and then choose how you want to share:

✔ **Share Link via iCloud:** Sends a web link to the people you specify so that they can view and (optionally) edit the document from iCloud.com. (Only people with an iCloud account can edit.)

✔ **Send a Copy:** Makes a copy of the document in your choice of format for sending via Messages or Mail, or transferring to iTunes or a WeDAV server.

✔ **Open in Another App:** Makes a copy of the document in your choice of format for opening in a compatible app on your iPad. For example, you can use this to open a Word-format copy of a Pages document in Microsoft Word on your iPad.

✔ **Move To:** Moves the selected document to another folder within iCloud Drive or to another cloud storage service enabled for the iWork app, as described previously.

Most iPad apps use the Share sheet to print, but the iWork apps don't. You have to print from within a document using the Tools pop-over's Print option.

Only after choosing one of these options does the toolbar turn blue and let you select one (and only one) document to share. After you select the document, a form appears asking what format you want to share the file as — this is how you export documents. Here are the options for each of the three iWork apps:

- ✔ **Pages:** You can export a copy in the Apple Pages, Microsoft Word, PDF, or ePub formats.

- ✔ **Numbers:** You can export a copy in the Apple Numbers, Microsoft Excel, PDF, or CSV (comma-separated value) formats.

- ✔ **Keynote:** You can export a copy in the Apple Keynote, Microsoft PowerPoint, or PDF formats.

You can share a document from within a document as well, using the same Share button in its toolbar. It has the three same sharing options and export formats as you have from the Documents window.

Editing and Formatting with Pages

In an open document, tap in your text and start typing! It's that simple. Until you want to do more than type text, of course. But even then, Pages' editing and formatting tools are straightforward. In this section, I walk you through the major tool sets available in the Pages app.

Figure 5-2 shows the major editing tools:

- ✔ **Contextual menu:** Tap and hold text to select it and access any of the options, such as those shown in the center of Figure 5-2.

- ✔ **Keyboard toolbar:** When the onscreen keyboard is active, it provides text formatting controls that apply to whatever text is selected or that you are typing in.

- ✔ **Application toolbar:** The row of icons at the top of the screen has the Documents and Undo buttons at the upper left and five buttons at the right to control complex formatting, sharing, inserting objects, and more. I cover these buttons in detail in the "Using the application toolbar" section, later in this chapter.

Formatting and modifying text with the contextual menu

Tap and hold text to select it, using the drag handles to make your selection. Most of the options are the same that iOS provides any app, including Cut,

Copy, Paste, Delete, and Define (which looks up the meaning of whatever is selected). If you didn't select text, you see Select and Select All. But there are several options that only more sophisticated editing apps like Pages offer:

- ✔ **Replace:** Suggests alternative words for whatever is selected, such as when you think you misspelled something but aren't sure what the right spelling is.

- ✔ **Highlight:** Adds a colored background to the selection, similar to using a Magic Marker on paper. The button becomes Remove Highlighting if you select the highlighted text later.

- ✔ **Comment:** Inserts a sticky-note-like comment; enter the note in the pop-over that appears and tap elsewhere on the screen to save and close it. The text is highlighted with a colored background, and you'll see a note icon to the left of the line containing the commented text. Tap the icon or the commented text to open the note; tap Delete at the lower left of the note to remove it; and tap < and > at the lower right of the note to navigate through other notes in your document.

- ✔ **Style:** Displays the Copy Formatting button, which copies the formatting of the selected text so that you can then paste that formatting onto other text. To copy that formatting to other text, select that other text, tap Style in its contextual menu, and then tap Paste Style.

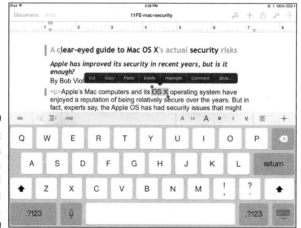

Figure 5-2:
The Pages app's main editing and formatting controls.

Adjusting text with the keyboard toolbar

The keyboard toolbar's options should look familiar because they're similar to what most computer word processors offer in their toolbars. If you tap a formatting option when text is selected, it is applied to that text; if you tap a formatting option when no text is selected, it is applied to whatever you type next at the current location.

Here are the options, from left to right:

- **Tab:** Inserts a tab character.
- **Outdent** and **Indent** (the two adjacent icons of paragraphs): The Outdent button (the icon with <) removes a level of indentation each time it is tapped, which is called *outdenting*. The Indent button (the icon with >) indents the text an additional level each time it is tapped. Both affect the entire paragraph.
- **Font:** Lets you select the font for your text.
- **Text Size:** A three-part button that lets you change the text size. Tap the small *A* to reduce the size, the large *A* to increase it, and the number between them to select a specific size.
- **Text formatting:** The three buttons here apply boldface (**B**), italics (*I*), and underline (U), respectively. If the text already has a format applied, tapping the corresponding formatting button removes it. So, for example, tapping **B** removes the bold.
- **Align (the paragraph icon):** This lets you choose the paragraph alignment: Left, Right, Centered, and Justified. The icon shows the current alignment.
- **Format Special (the + icon):** This lets you add special formatting: a comment, a hyperlink (called a *link* in this pop-over), a page break, a line break, a column break, and a footnote entry (you can then enter the footnote text in the footnote area that shows onscreen). If one or more characters are selected, you get the Link option but not the Line Break option. If no text is selected, you get the Line Break option but not the Link option.

Using the application toolbar

The most complex options reside in the application toolbar's right side: the Format button (the paintbrush icon); the Insert Object button (the + icon); and the Tools button (the wrench icon).

Adjusting document appearance with the Format pop-over

The Format button opens the Format pop-over, which has three tabs: Style, List, and Layout. Figure 5-3 shows all three tabs in a composite image.

Figure 5-3: Pages' Format pop-over's three tabs (a composite view).

In the Format pop-over's Style tab, you set local formatting using the options at the top: the text size and font, boldface, italics, underline, strikethrough, and paragraph justification. Except for strikethrough, those formatting options are also available in the keyboard toolbar.

If text is selected, what you do in the Format pop-over affects that text. If no text is selected, it affects the text you then type in.

Below those options is a list of paragraph styles. When you choose one of these, that style's formatting is applied to all the text in a paragraph. The list includes whatever was in the original Pages or Word document; for new documents, the list includes paragraph styles defined in the template used to create the document. If a paragraph has a style applied to it, you see a check mark next to the style's name in the Format pop-over's Style tab.

You cannot create new paragraph styles for your document. You cannot use any character styles the document may have (such as if it was imported from Word or Pages on a computer), nor create character styles. Fortunately, if the original document used character styles, they will be retained when you later open the document on your computer. Although you can apply local formatting to your document in Pages on the iPad, such formatting is truly local, which means that you can't assure a consistent appearance or modify all like text's appearance easily as you can with character styles — these are the reasons styles are so useful.

The List tab in the Format pop-over is simple. At the top are buttons for indenting and outdenting, duplicating what the keyboard toolbar offers. Below that is a list of bulleted and numbered list styles that you can apply to the selected text. Tap the list style you want to apply.

The Layout tab has two options:

- **Column:** Tap the – and + buttons to reduce or increase the number of columns for your document. *Tip:* What if you want multiple columns in some sections and not others? The secret is to insert page breaks using the keyboard toolbar. If you change the number of columns, the action is applied only to the current part of the document after the previous page break and until the next page break.

- **Line Spacing:** Tap the triangles to increase or decrease the space between lines in the paragraph the text cursor is active in. If you've selected text across multiple paragraphs, all those paragraphs get the new line spacing.

The Format pop-over's options change based on what is selected. The next section explains the options for the various kinds of objects you can add to Pages documents.

Creating complex documents with the Insert Objects pop-over

The Insert Objects pop-over is where you can really go to town in creating complex documents that look more like they came from a page layout tool than a text editor. The pop-over has four tabs: Table, Chart, Object, and File. Figure 5-4 shows the pop-over's Object tab, as well as an empty text box I created with it.

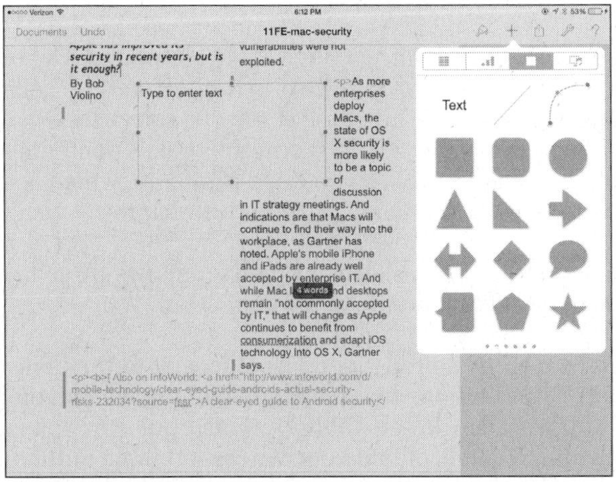

Figure 5-4: Pages' Insert Object pop-over's Object tab and the text box I created with it.

In the Object tab, swipe to the side to see the available objects in different colors. The objects are the same no matter what color you use: text, straight line, curved line (an editable Bézier curve), and various shapes from a square to a star.

Tap a shape to insert it at the current location. You can then drag the object in your document to where you want it, and resize it using the resize handles that appear at its corners when you tap it. If you tap a shape, you also get a contextual menu with the same Copy, Cut, Delete, and Highlight options as you get for text.

Tap in a shape to add text into it.

When you select a shape, the Format pop-over provides new options, as shown in Figure 5-5:

- ✔ **Style:** Lets you sets a predefined appearance for the object or create your own. To create your own, tap Style Options, which displays three tabs: Fill, Border, and Effects. Effects is the coolest, letting you add any of several drop shadow effects, changing the opacity of the object, and displaying a faded reflection of it on the page. The Border tab lets you set the color, thickness, and line type (such as dashed) for the shape's border. The Fill tab lets you select the color for the shape.

- ✔ **Text:** Provides the same options as in the previously described Style tab that's available in the Format pop-over when you're working with text.

- ✔ **Arrange:** This lets you control the shape's position relative to other objects it overlaps so that you can determine its location in a stack. You also can set how text wraps around the object, as well as the margin for the object relative to the text.

The Table tab

The Table tab provides several predefined table templates. Tap one to insert an empty table. You tap a cell to enter text in it or format the cell. To select a row or column, tap its handle at left or at top. To select the whole table, tap the circle icon at the upper left. You edit the table's contents and add rows and columns the same way as you do in Numbers, which I cover in "Crunching Numbers with Numbers," later in this chapter.

If you select the entire table, the Format pop-over shows three tabs, Table, Headers, and Arrange, which do the following:

- ✔ **Table:** Lets you apply a predefined visual format to the table. Here you can also tap Table Options to open a pop-over, in which you fine-tune the table's appearance. In the Table Options pop-over, you can set whether the table name, outside border (called table outline), and alternating row colors appear. You also can control the cell borders (called grid options) and the table text's font and size.

✔ **Headers:** Lets you set how many header rows, header columns, and footer rows the table has. These elements repeat on each page for tables that run across several pages.

✔ **Arrange:** Lets you control the stacking order and text wrap for the table.

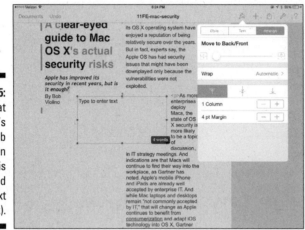

Figure 5-5:
The Format pop-over's Arrange tab for when a shape is selected (here, a text box).

If you select a cell, row, or column, the Format pop-over doesn't have the Arrange tabs, but it does have the Table and Headers tabs, plus two more:

✔ **Cell:** Shown in Figure 5-6, the Cell tab lets you set character formatting and alignment, as well as fill color, border style, and text wrap for the cell.

✔ **Format:** The Format tab lets you select the format for the cell's contents, such as Currency or Duration. It works the same as in Numbers: Tap the *i* icon to the right of a Format option to get specific formatting choices, such as the currency symbol and decimal treatment for currency.

The Chart tab

The Chart tab lets you add charts, as Figure 5-7 shows — and some really snazzy charts at that. It can do 2D, 3D, and 2D interactive. That last one, 2D interactive, lets viewers step through data on their iPads, but this works only from Pages, not if the chart is exported to ePub, Word, or PDF format.

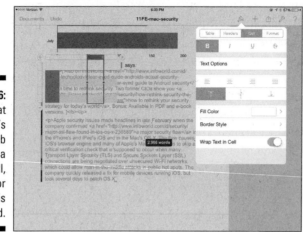

Figure 5-6:
The Format pop-over's Cell tab for when a table cell, row, or column is selected.

Scroll down horizontally through the various color options in the pop-over, and when you have the color scheme you like, scroll vertically until you find the desired chart type. Tap the one you want to insert.

Tap a chart to resize, cut, or delete it, or comment on it. You have the same options as for a shape, plus a special one: Edit Data, which lets you edit the data in the chart. Tapping Edit Data opens the form shown in Figure 5-8, where you can edit the data. Not so obvious is that if you tap and hold the handle above a column or to the left of a row, a contextual menu appears that lets you insert a column or row or delete that column or row. These chart-data handles work just like table handles do in Pages and Numbers.

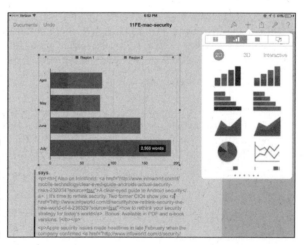

Figure 5-7:
The Insert Objects pop-over's Chart tab.

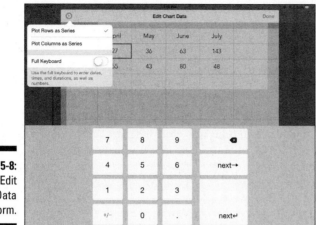

Figure 5-8:
The Edit
Chart Data
form.

The Format pop-over once again shows options specific to charts if you open it when a chart is selected. It has four tabs:

- ✔ **Chart:** Lets you change the color scheme as well as switch between 2D and 3D styles. Tap Chart Options to open the Chart Options pop-over, where you can control whether the chart title, legend, and border appear; set the font and text size; set whether value labels appear (and, if so, how they align); and change the chart type.

- ✔ **X Axis:** Lets you control how the X Axis displays, including whether its labels are visible, how numbers are formatted (such as decimal places), the scale for value display, which gridlines and tick marks appear, and how axes appear.

- ✔ **Y Axis:** Similar to X Axis, except that there are options for only the labels, gridlines, tick marks, and axes.

- ✔ **Arrange:** Has the same options for controlling the stacking order and text wrap as the Arrange tab does for tables.

The Files tab

The final tab in the Insert Objects pop-over is Files. Tap it to insert photos and videos from photo streams and albums in the Photos app. Tap the desired album or photo stream to see the photos and videos available in it, and then tap the desired item to insert it.

Tap an image or video to move it or resize it, as well as cut, copy, or delete it, or comment on it. Use the Format pop-over's three tabs to apply other formatting:

- ✔ **Style:** This lets you apply any of several preformatted drop-shadow effects, as well as add a border in the desired size, type (such as dotted), and color. When viewing the border options, scroll down to see 14 graphical frames you can apply instead of boring old border lines, such as several types of picture frames and notepapers.

- ✔ **Effects:** This gives you the same controls over drop shadows, reflection, and opacity as the Style tab's effects options for shapes.

Working with the Tools pop-over's varied options

The Tools pop-over has a grab bag of options: Find, Change Tracking, Document Setup, Settings, Set Password, and Print.

Tap Find to open the Find toolbar shown in Figure 5-9. Tap the Settings button (the gear icon) at its left to tell Find whether to match the case of what you enter, as well as to restrict matches to those that are whole words. You can also set the Find bar to only find the text or replace matches.

Use the < and > buttons to go search backward and forward in your document for the search term. Pages highlights all matches with a colored background, except that the currently found one is in white so that if you replace the text, you know which instance you are replacing.

Tap and hold the Replace button in the Find bar to get the Replace All option.

Tap anywhere outside the Find bar to close it.

You might have noticed the colored text in the screen shots in this section on Pages. Colored text indicates that revisions tracking is on in the document, so any changes made are marked as to who made them and can be approved or rejected by an editor. Pages retains the revisions tracking in Microsoft Word and Pages documents made in Pages or Word on a computer or mobile device, so the whole revisions history is maintained even as the document is moved in and out of Pages on your iPad.

To enable revisions tracking in Pages on your iPad, tap Change Tracking in the Tools pop-over and set the Tracking Switch to On. The pop-over also has the Pause switch that lets you disable revisions tracking temporarily (just remember to turn it back on!) and three view options:

- ✔ **Markup:** This shows deleted text with strikethroughs and inserted text in color (each person gets a separate color).

✔ **Markup without Deletions:** This is the default option and shows revised and new text in colors but hides deleted text.

✔ **Final:** This hides the colors of revised and added text so that you can see the document without distraction. (The revisions are still there, just not displayed.)

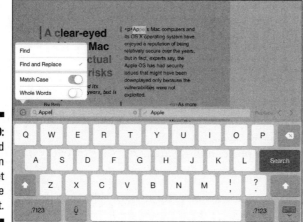

Figure 5-9:
The Find bar in Pages, set to replace text.

If you tap revised text in your document, you get a note that lets you reject or accept the revision. Doing so removes the tracking of that revision and makes the change permanent. It also shows who made the change and when, as Figure 5-10 shows. Finally, you can navigate to other revisions by using the Forward (>) and Backward (<) buttons.

The Document Setup option in the Tools pop-over opens the screen shown in Figure 5-11, where you can adjust the footer, header, and body areas of the document.

For headers and footers, tapping their area displays a contextual menu that lets you insert automatic page numbers and line breaks, as well as copy, cut, and paste text. You enter text in the headers and footers as you do in any document, and you have the same Format and Insert Objects pop-overs available for them as you do in your document.

For the body area, tapping it displays resize handles that let you resize where the main text appears in your document. You can also insert text the usual way, and insert objects via the Insert Objects pop-over. You can use the Format pop-over for any text or object in the body area.

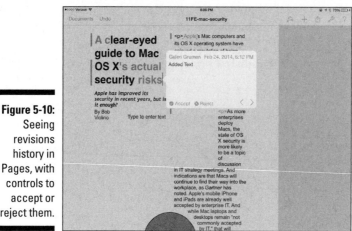

Figure 5-10:
Seeing
revisions
history in
Pages, with
controls to
accept or
reject them.

Whatever content you place in these areas displays on every page in your document.

Tap Done to save the changes and return to your document.

The Settings option in the Tools pop-over has eight switches and one field. Starting with the field Author Name, the name you enter here is the one that Change Tracking uses to know who made changes. The other options are as follows:

- ✔ **Check Spelling:** Enables spell check, highlighting any suspect words in your document with a dashed red underline. Tap a suspect word and Pages will suggest, if it can, some properly spelled alternatives.

- ✔ **Word Count:** Shows the current word count in an overlay bubble onscreen at all times.

- ✔ **Comments:** Hides comments in your document, though you can still add them via the contextual menu for text selections.

- ✔ **Ruler:** Shows the ruler at the top of the screen. The ruler does more than display your document width: You can move the margins and tab stops on it by dragging them, and insert new tab stops by tapping on the ruler — similarly to how you use the tab ruler in Microsoft Word or Pages on the computer.

- ✔ **Center Guides:** As you move or resize an object, this option displays an alignment guide at the center of an object so that you can align that object's center to a ruler position or nearby object's center.

✔ **Edge Guides:** As you move or resize an object, this option displays an alignment guide at the edges of an object so that you can align that object's edges to a ruler position or nearby object's edge.

✔ **Spacing Guides:** As you move or resize an object, this option displays an alignment guide when the current object is the same distance from a nearby object as that nearby object is to its nearby object. Using an alignment guide lets you ensure consistent space between multiple objects.

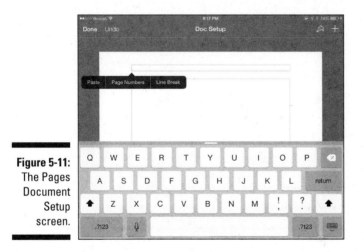

Figure 5-11: The Pages Document Setup screen.

The Tools pop-over's Set Password option lets you do what it says: set a password that is required to open the document. This is a great feature if your iPad is shared with others who should not see what you're working on. *Note:* This password applies to the current document, not to all documents and not to Pages itself.

Crunching Numbers with Numbers

When you think of spreadsheets, you probably think of someone staring at a PC's screen all day. Well, you can crunch those numbers on your iPad, too, using the Numbers app. Figure 5-12 shows a Numbers screen with a formula visible in the onscreen keyboard.

In many ways, Numbers works like Microsoft Excel, such as in how it defines formulas, how you enter data (type it in or paste it in), and how it can organize spreadsheets into multiple sheets that you navigate via tabs. So it should be an easy tool to use if you already use Excel on your computer.

How Numbers is distinct from Excel is in its contextual keyboard, which lets you format data based on the kind of data it is from the keyboard, minimizing trips to the Format pop-over. You can view the formula keyboard in Figure 5-12 as an example.

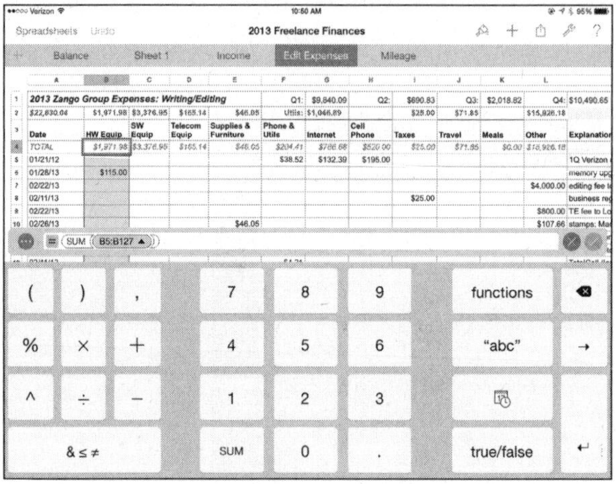

Figure 5-12: Editing a formula in Numbers.

Entering data

Tap and hold a cell to get a contextual menu with the options you'd expect: Cut, Copy, Paste, Delete, and Comment, as well as a Numbers-specific option: Fill (to set the background fill's color).

To work on a cell's contents, you double-tap the cell (which is just like double-clicking in Excel on your computer to edit a cell's contents). The onscreen keyboard appears. Its appearance varies based on the data you're working with, but all keyboard displays have three common buttons on the right side:

- **Delete:** Tapping this key backspaces one character at a time.
- **Next→:** Tapping this advances to the cell at right, making any changes you entered in the current cell.
- **Next↵:** Tapping this advances to the cell below, making any changes you entered in the current cell.

You can also tap Done in the upper right of the keyboard to accept your changes and close the keyboard.

If the cell is empty, Numbers assumes that you want to enter numbers, so it displays the Numeric keyboard, shown in Figure 5-13. The 42 icon is highlighted when the Numeric keyboard is active.

In addition to entering numbers, you can also specify how the values are displayed using the currency, percentage, ratings, and check mark buttons at left. Enter a numeric value and then tap the desired display, such as currency or stars. *Note:* For the check box display, a value of 0 has the box display as unselected, whereas any other value shows it as selected. If you tap the check box in your spreadsheet, you deselect a selected box or select an unselected box.

Three other keyboards are available:

- ✔ **Date & Time (clock icon):** Lets you enter dates. Use different buttons, such as Month, Day, and Hour, to have the keyboard change its options for that specific type of data. You can also enter durations, not just dates, by tapping the Duration button in the Date & Time keyboard; tap Date & Time button to go back to dates. Figure 5-13 shows the Date & Time keyboard.

- ✔ **Text (T icon):** Displays the standard text keyboard you see in most apps.

- ✔ **Formula (= icon):** Lets you enter formulas using the keyboard shown in Figure 5-12. (I explain how to use it shortly.)

To enter formulas, double-tap a cell, switch to the Formulas keyboard, and enter your formula. You can enter simple formulas directly from the keyboard by using the numbers and symbols on the right side.

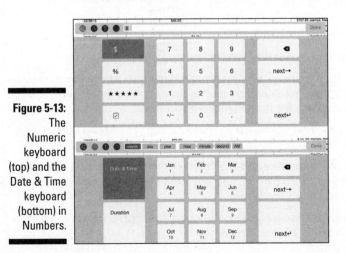

Figure 5-13: The Numeric keyboard (top) and the Date & Time keyboard (bottom) in Numbers.

Get more symbols by tapping the &≤≠ button below the symbols. Return to the first set of symbols by tapping the ()+÷ button that replaces it.

To include a cell in the formula, just tap it. (If the cell is on another sheet, no problem. Tap that sheet's name and then the cell in it.) Or drag a range to include that range (such as when summing).

If your formula has no other entries in it and you drag-select a range, Numbers assumes that you want to sum them, so you don't need to enter the Sum formula label first.

By default, when you enter a cell in a formula, the cell address is kept relative, meaning that if the cell's location changes because you added or deleted rows and columns, Numbers keeps track of the cell's new location and automatically keeps the link active to that new location. You can, however, have Numbers ignore such changes and always point to that specific row or column. Doing so is the equivalent of preceding the cell's row and/or column address with $ in Excel, such as E22, so that both column E and row 22 have fixed addresses. To accomplish this in Numbers, tap the triangle icon to the right of the cell name or range in your formula and enable the Preserve Row and/or Preserve Column switches for those whose addresses you want to be fixed. In other words, setting the switch to On acts like typing $ in front of the column or row label in Excel. (You can also just type $ directly in the formula yourself, as in Excel.)

You can much get more complex in your formulas with the buttons at the right side of the keyboard, as follows:

- **Functions:** Tap this to get the Formulas pop-over, which has these two tabs:

    - *Recent:* Shows formulas you've used recently, for easy access

    - *Categories:* Lets you find any formula

    You tap a formula to insert it in your overall formula in the Formula keyboard. When you do so, Numbers shows the required data fields. Tap a field to enter the data for it, as Figure 5-14 shows.

- **"abc":** Opens the Text keyboard so that you can type literal text in your formula. Tap Done to return to your formula.

- **Date & Time (the calendar-and-clock icon):** Opens the Date & Time keyboard so that you can type date and duration entries in your formula. Tap Done to return to your formula.

- **True/False:** This inserts a False condition in your formula; tap it again to convert that False to True.

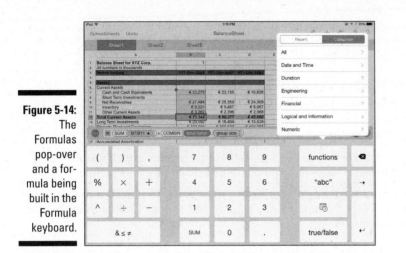

Figure 5-14:
The
Formulas
pop-over
and a for-
mula being
built in the
Formula
keyboard.

When you're done entering a formula, tap the green ✔ icon at the upper right of the Formula keyboard. Tap the red X icon to delete the formula (such as to start over).

Formatting cells, rows, columns, and tables

Spreadsheet users often spend as much time making their spreadsheets look good as they do perfecting their formulas.

Working with cells, columns, and rows

Tap a cell to select it for formatting. To select a row, tap the handle to its far left; to select a column, tap the handle above it — just as you would do in Excel with the mouse. Drag over a range of cells to select that range. And tap the circle icon at the upper left of the sheet to select the entire sheet.

If your sheet has several tables on it (which Numbers lets you create from its Insert Objects pop-over; tap the + icon at the upper right), they each have their own circle icon and their own column and row handles.

When you tap a row or column handle, its contextual menu (see Figure 5-15) provides several options that any spreadsheet user would expect Numbers to offer:

✔ **Insert:** Inserts a row or column before the selected one.

✔ **Sort:** Sorts the spreadsheet's or table's contents based on the content of the selected row or column, with options to sort in ascending or descending order.

✔ **Fit:** Resizes the row or column so that its contents are all visible. (This option does not appear if the contents are already fully visible.)

✔ **Hide:** This hides the column or row from view. To unhide a row or column, select the next row or column and choose Unhide from the contextual menu.

When selecting cells, rows, and columns, there are two other options to look for (also shown in Figure 5-15):

✔ **Resize:** Look for a resize icon (⋮⋮ for columns, = for rows) in the handle and drag it to resize the row or column.

✔ **Change Selection:** Look for small circles in the center of the selection boundaries for rows and columns, or in the corners for a range of selected cells. You can drag these to increase or decrease the selection's range, such as to increase the number of cells included. Again, this is similar to Excel's selection handles on a computer.

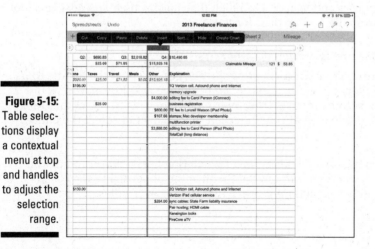

Figure 5-15: Table selections display a contextual menu at top and handles to adjust the selection range.

Adjusting the appearance of text and cells with the Format pop-over

The Format pop-over in the upper right of the screen (the button is a paint-brush icon) is where you apply formatting to your table and cells, such as alignment, background colors, borders, and text wrap.

The first three tabs in the Format pop-over — Table, Headers, and Cell — work the same as they do in the Pages Format pop-over (see the section "The Table tab," earlier in this chapter).

The Format tab, though, is special to Numbers. This tab lets you apply the display formatting to the data in cells. For example, you choose Currency and then tap its *i* icon to see the available currency options, such as symbol and decimal places. The composite view in Figure 5-16 shows both the overall Format tab and the specific Currency options. (In the Numbers app, you see only one at a time.)

Unusual options in the Format tab are Slider, Stepper (which uses + and – buttons to let users increment or decrement values), Pop-Up Menu, and Checkbox. These are all features you'd expect to find in an app's user interface, not in a spreadsheet. They let users change data in the spreadsheet using app-like controls rather than enter numeric data, making it easier for employees to update common spreadsheet forms.

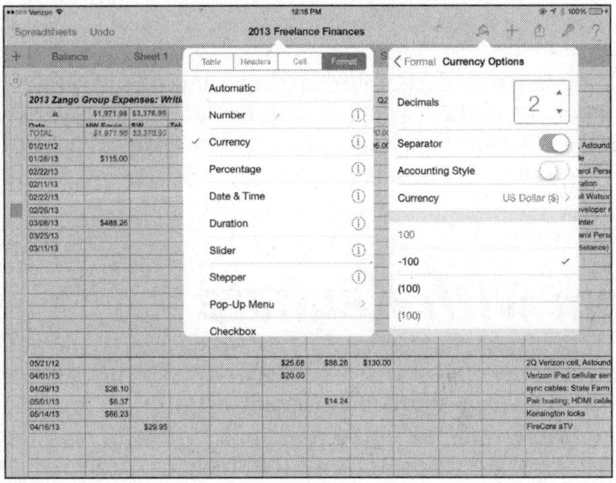

Figure 5-16: The Format pop-over's Format tab in Numbers, with the Currency options also shown.

Creating, naming, duplicating, and moving sheets

I mention earlier in the chapter that a spreadsheet can have multiple sheets. They're very easy to work with, and the following actions should be familiar to Excel users:

- ✔ To create a sheet, tap the Add button (the + icon) at the left side of the list of sheets, below the toolbar.
- ✔ To edit a sheet's name, double-tap its name — just as you would a cell — and enter its new name.
- ✔ To move a sheet, just drag it within the sheets' tabs.
- ✔ To duplicate or delete a sheet, tap its tab once and then tap it again to display its contextual menu, which will have two options: Duplicate and Delete.

Working with the Insert Objects and Tools pop-overs

The Insert Objects pop-over (the button is a + icon) lets you insert tables, charts, shapes, and files into your spreadsheet. It works just like the Insert Objects pop-over in Pages, which I cover in the "Adjusting document appearance with the Format pop-over" section, earlier in this chapter's section on Pages.

Likewise, the Tools pop-over (the button is a wrench icon) works like that in Pages, which I cover in the "Working with the Tools pop-over's varied options" section, earlier in this chapter's section on Pages. It just has fewer options in Numbers than in Pages: Find, Settings, Set Password, and Print.

Dazzling Them with Keynote

As good as Pages and Numbers are, my favorite iWork app is Keynote, which lets you create really dazzling presentations. Keynote was created for Apple cofounder Steve Jobs so that he could use Apple software, not Microsoft's, to make his world-famous product introduction slides. And that pedigree shows.

A Keynote presentation is made from slides. If you use Microsoft PowerPoint, it's the same structure you already know: You have master slides that are the templates for the slides you add. Slides are composed of images and text, each in its own box. Slides can have transitions between them, and objects on slides can have effects display on them as they appear (called *builds* or *animations*). Figure 5-17 shows a Keynote presentation with a text box selected, and its contextual menu.

Whereas this chapter covers how to create your Keynote presentation, Chapter 19 provides guidance and tips on giving the presentation you create.

Figure 5-17: A Keynote presentation, with a text box's contextual menu displayed.

Creating a presentation

When you create a presentation in the Documents window (see the section "Managing Documents in iWork" at the beginning of this chapter), Keynote asks you to choose a template. That template contains the master slides for your presentation.

You cannot create or modify these templates in Keynote for the iPad. You have to create or modify templates in Keynote on the Mac by editing the master slides in a document and then opening a copy of that document in Keynote on the iPad to use as if it were a template (if you've chosen not to use one of Keynote's predefined templates). *Note:* Windows PC users can't create or modify master slides, either, even via Keynote in iCloud. Only Mac users can.

After choosing a template, your new presentation opens with the slide pane at the left and a single slide in it. Follow these steps to start working on the elements of your presentation:

1. **Tap the Add Slide button (the + icon) at the bottom of the pane to open a pop-over of master slides.**

2. **In the pop-over, tap the master slide that you want to base your new slide on.**

   Note that when you have multiple slides, the new slide is added after whatever slide is currently selected in the pane.

   Figure 5-18 shows a new slide, as well as the Add Slide pop-over.

   If you have an existing slide that you want to use as the basis for a new slide, just tap and hold it for a second to open its contextual menu, and then choose Copy. Move to the location where you want to insert the copy, tap and hold that slide, and choose Paste from its contextual menu. (The contextual menu also lets you cut or delete the slide.)

3. **Double-tap the text boxes to enter or paste text.**

4. **Tap the Add button (the + icon) on a graphics box to open a pop-over that lets you import photos or other images from the iPad's Photos app.**

   You can also insert tables, charts, shapes, and image and video files onto a slide in a new box using the Insert Objects pop-over (its button in the toolbar has a + icon); it works just like the Pages Insert Object pop-over, which I cover in the "Working with the Insert Objects pop-over" section, earlier in this chapter in the section on Pages.

Figure 5-18:
A new Keynote slide, as well as the Add Slide pop-over where you choose the master slide to use for the new slide.

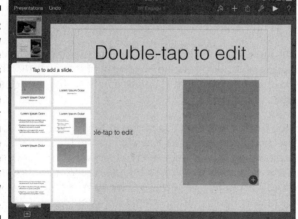

You can copy, duplicate, paste, cut, and delete objects such as text boxes and graphics boxes by tapping them and choosing the desired option from the contextual menu that appears after a moment. Figure 5-15, shown earlier in this chapter, shows such a contextual menu.

To select multiple slides, tap and hold on one, then tap on each additional slide you want to select. It works like Ctrl+clicking in Windows or ⌘+clicking on the Mac.

You can also drag objects within a slide, and use the resize handles in the center of each border segment to reshape it — as you would do on a computer when using Keynote or PowerPoint.

Finally, you can rearrange slides by dragging them within the slides pane to a new location. To drag a slide, tap and hold it until it "pops up" to let you know it's selected. Don't release your finger from the screen, but drag it to a new location, releasing your finger when it's where you want it.

Applying formatting, transitions, and animations

When your slides' content is in reasonable shape, you can focus on the fine-tuning. Of course, you could fine-tune each slide as you create it. I prefer to get my basics in place before fine-tuning, but if doing each slide in full glory one at a time is your preference, you can easily work with Keynote that way.

To select multiple objects, such as to move or delete them en masse, tap and hold one and then tap the others. Release your finger from the first object when done, and apply whatever option you want from the contextual menu, or drag them together within the slide.

Formatting slide objects

You can apply various formatting to slide objects, such as text boxes and graphics boxes. You do so via the Format pop-over, which you open by tapping the Format button (the paintbrush icon). Some of the options in the Format pop-over are the same as the options for Pages:

- ✔ **For text boxes,** the Style tab and Text tab work as they do on Pages, as I explain in the "Adjusting document appearance with the Format pop-over" section, in the Pages section earlier this chapter.

- ✔ **For graphics boxes,** the Style tab works as it does in Pages, as I explain in the "The Files tab" section, in the Pages section earlier this chapter.

That still leaves some tabs in the Format pop-over that work differently in Keynote than in Pages:

- **For text boxes,** the Arrange tab lets you control the relative placement in the stack of overlapping elements, as the Pages version does. But it also has options to align the text within the box (top, middle, or bottom), to specify the number of columns for the text in the text box, to specify the margin between the box's edge and the text within it, and to lock the box to its current location so that it can't be accidentally moved.

- **For graphics boxes,** the Arrange tab has the same stack control as for text boxes and to lock the object's placement on the slide. But it also has buttons to flip the object horizontally and/or vertically.

- **For graphics boxes,** the Image tab has

  - *The Edit Mask button:* Lets you change the crop of the image via a slider that appears, essentially changing the box shape to show more or less of the image in it.

  - *The Reset Mask button:* Removes the crop entirely, showing the entire image. The Instant Alpha button temporarily shows the whole image so that you can drag across it to make the colors you drag over invisible, as Figure 5-19 shows. (For example, if you drag your finger over a dark-blue region, all similar dark blues are made invisible by Instant Alpha.) In the floating bar that appears at the bottom of the screen, tap Reset to return to the previous settings, or Done to apply them.

  - *The Replace button:* Lets you replace the image with another from the Photos app.

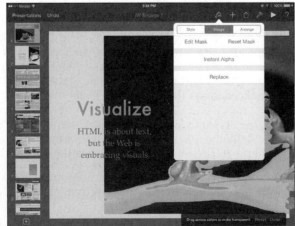

Figure 5-19: Using the Instant Alpha tool to remove colors.

Applying transitions to slides

Having cool effects between slides is a time-honored part of making presentations. Your slides can spin into oblivion, replaced by the next slide; they can rotate to display the next slide; they can sparkle as the new slide emerges in a transporter-like effect from *Star Trek*. But they won't do any of these things unless you apply the animations in the first place.

For the first animation in your presentation, tap a slide to select it and then tap Animation in the contextual menu that appears a moment later. The Keynote toolbar turns blue and the Transitions pop-over appears, as shown in Figure 5-19.

Tap an effect to select it for that slide (tap None to remove the transition effect), and tap the Options tab at the bottom of the pop-over to get any specific controls for that effect, such as duration and angle, as Figure 5-19 also shows in its composite of the pop-over's two tabs. Tap the Play button at the upper right of the pop-over to see how your transition looks.

You can go straight to the animation view by choosing Transitions and Builds in the Tools pop-over (tap the wrench icon).

After you've entered this animation view (the blue toolbar), tap each slide in turn. A pop-over appears with the name of any currently applied transition (or None, if it has no transition) and a + icon that if tapped opens the Transitions pop-over shown in Figure 5-20 to let you select and manage the transition for that slide.

You cannot apply an animation to multiple slides, so you may want to apply it to the first slide in your presentation as you create it, and then duplicate that slide for each new slide. This way, the animation is copied to each copied slide as well.

To see how the transitions look, you can tap the Play button (the right-facing triangle icon) in the toolbar. Tap the screen to advance to the next slide or build. Use the pinch gesture to end the playback.

When you're done with your animations, tap the Done button in the toolbar to return to the standard editing view.

Applying builds to slide objects

Animations can be applied to objects on a slide, not just to entire slides. Keynote call those *builds*.

You add animations to an object very much as you do to slides: Tap an object to display its contextual menu. Tap the Animate option to enter the animation view (blue toolbar) that you get when adding transitions to slides. You now see a pop-over with two labels: Build In and Build Out. Build In is what happens as the object appears; Build Out is what happens as you display the next object (or slide).

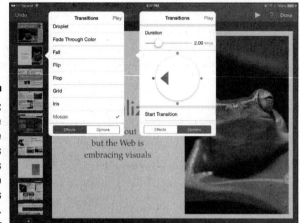

Figure 5-20:
A composite image of the Transitions pop-over's Effects tab and Options tab.

If you have lots of builds on a slide, and they each have both build-ins and build-outs, your presentation is going to be distractively gimmicky. When it comes to special effects, restraint is the wiser course.

Tap the + icon next to the build you want to apply. Select the build in the Effects tab of the pop-over that appears. Then go through the other tabs to fine-tune the presentation of that build (Figure 5-21 shows them all in a composite view):

- ✔ **Options:** Set duration and build-specific options such as angle of entry or exit for an effect.

- ✔ **Delivery:** Available for text boxes, this tab lets you control how the build is applied to your text. The default is All At Once, which makes the build run just once for the text box. But you can choose to have it run for each paragraph.

- ✔ **Order:** All builds for the current slide appear here, and you can rearrange their order by dragging each to a new location. Note the number that appears on the slide for each object with a build effect; that number is the object's order of presentation within the slide.

Figure 5-21:
Applying
a build:
Choose the
effect in the
pop-over's
Effects tab
and cus-
tomize its
display in
the other
tabs.

You can play a build within the pop-over, or you can play back the entire presentation using the Play button in the toolbar — both work just as they do for slide transitions.

Using the Tools pop-over

The final part of Keynote is the Tools pop-over, which you open by tapping the wrench icon in the toolbar. It has the same Find and Set Password options as Pages, which I cover in the "Working with the Tools pop-over's varied options" section in this chapter's earlier section on Pages.

Using Settings options

The Settings options are almost the same as in Pages, with the addition of the Slide Number switch. If set to On, this shows the slide numbers on the slides themselves (that is, on what the audience sees).

Adding presenter notes

One tool you'll likely use a lot is Presenter Notes. This tool lets you add notes to each slide that only you will see during your presentation, and that you can also include in your printouts — just like how PowerPoint works.

When you open this tool, the toolbar turns blue and a blank screen appears. Note which slide is selected in the pane at the left: The text you type becomes the notes for that slide. (You can edit the content as you would edit text in any app.) Tap another slide to select it and enter its notes.

When you're done, tap the Done button at the upper right of the screen.

Using presentation tools

The presentation tools option opens a pop-over with several options:

✔ **Interactive links:** Tap this option and then tap the object or text selection you want to apply a link to. A pop-over appears that lets you link to another slide in your presentation, to a web page (a URL), or to an email address. Tap Done when done. Now, depending on what you chose, tapping that object in your presentation will go to another slide or the web page in Safari, or it will create a new Mail message to the email address you linked to (which is handy for presentations that you distribute to others to view on their own and in which you provide contact information).

✔ **Soundtrack:** Tap this option to add one or more songs from your Music app to the slideshow. You can set songs to play once or to loop. Note that these songs aren't associated with a particular slide, so they begin playing when you begin your presentation. (To delete a song, swipe to the left over its name and then tap the Delete button that appears.)

✔ **Presentation Type:** Tap this option to have the presentation play continuously (the Loop Presentation switch), to restart if it's been idle a while (such as for kiosks where someone walked away mid-presentation), and to control playback:

• *Normal:* The slideshow plays back in slide order and can be remotely controlled (see Chapter 19).

• *Links Only:* Meant for kiosk-style presentations, only items that have links within the presentation will display. Essentially, you're using Keynote to build a self-contained virtual website that plays through Keynote and requires the user to tap each item to go to its link. Such presentations cannot be remotely controlled.

• *Self-Playing:* Also meant for kiosk-style presentations, the presentation plays itself once started — just once unless the Loop Presentation switch is set to On.

Chapter 6

Opting for Microsoft Office 365: Word, Excel, and PowerPoint

Almost everyone uses Microsoft Office on his or her computer, but until spring 2014, it wasn't available for the iPad, forcing most people to use Apple's iWork (see Chapter 5) on their mobile devices instead. That works fine, but Windows users especially wanted a native Microsoft office suite for their iPad to get a more similar working experience on their PC and iPad. Office for iPad delivers on that desire.

Office is, of course, the corporate standard for editing text documents, spreadsheets, and slide show presentations. Having Office on the iPad makes the Apple tablet able to do much of the "real work" that we all do on our computers — and using Office provides a familiar tool for doing that work. This chapter explains how to use Office on your iPad.

Understanding Office Subscriptions

The three Office apps — the Word word processor, Excel spreadsheet editor, and PowerPoint presentation editor — are free to download. Individual users can use many of the editing capabilities at no charge if you have a Microsoft account, but you need an Office 365 subscription to use all the capabilities. Subscriptions start at $70 per year for an individual, $100 for a family, and $99 per employee for a business. Large businesses can negotiate pricing for custom versions of the Office 365 suite, such as to add other Microsoft tools like Exchange email, SharePoint document management, and Lync conferencing.

Subscription-only features include 1TB of storage per person in the Microsoft OneDrive cloud storage service; ability to work with files stored in the Dropbox cloud storage service; full revisions tracking; and full access to Office's paragraph styles and to the chart, image-formatting, and table tools.

This chapter assumes that you have an Office 365 subscription.

Business users must have an Office 365 business subscription to do any editing. In addition to the full Office suite, a business subscription includes access to corporate file shares via OneDrive for Business and, optionally, to SharePoint. You can access these features only by signing in via a corporate email address that your IT staff has preregistered with Microsoft. So, if you try to avoid paying for a business subscription by using a personal Microsoft account instead, you won't be able to work on documents stored in those corporate file shares.

If you have an Office 365 subscription (personal or business), you have rights under most plans to use Office on one computer (Mac or Windows PC) and two mobile devices (any combination of iPad, iPhone, and Android device) for a single-user subscription or as many as five computers and five mobile devices for a family subscription. Business users are typically able to use up to five devices per employee; for a business license, "devices" include iPads, iPhones, Android devices, Macs, and Windows PCs.

After you sign in to an Office 365 app to "activate" that access on your iPad, it signs you into all Office apps on your iPad.

Be sure to read the sidebar about using iPad productivity tools in Chapter 5 to avoid common frustrations, such as font changes when exchanging files with Office apps on your computer.

Managing Documents in Microsoft Office

The three Office apps manage documents the same way in the Documents window that appears when you open them.

At the left of the Documents window is a pane with as many as five buttons, as shown in Figure 6-1 and described here:

- ✔ **User (a silhouette or your photo):** Tap this to sign in or out of your Microsoft account, as well as to sign in or out of the OneDrive, OneDrive for Business, Dropbox, and/or SharePoint cloud storage services. *Note:* You can have more than one account of each type active for storing documents in.

- ✔ **New (the document icon):** Tap this to open a pane of templates that you then select as the basis for your new document.

- ✔ **Recent (the clock icon):** Tap this to display a pane of the documents you've opened recently, starting with the most recent one. You can also pin documents to the top of the pane, even if it wasn't recently opened, for quick access to it later. Tap the Pin button (the pushpin icon) to the right of a document's name to add it to the Pinned list at the top of the pane.

- ✔ **Open (the folder icon):** Tap this to open a pane with two columns: The first column shows you the various storage locations available (see Figure 6-1), including on the iPad itself (a local file) and any documents in it. If a storage location has folders, you see those folders and can tap them to open a third column to show its contents. Keep tapping folders to move through your folder hierarchy.

- ✔ **Activate (the shopping-cart icon):** If visible, tap this button to verify that you still have an active Office 365 account. You'll be asked to do this periodically to be able to continue to use the full Office capabilities.

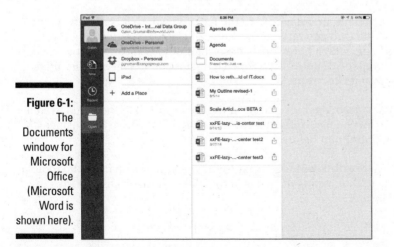

Figure 6-1: The Documents window for Microsoft Office (Microsoft Word is shown here).

Gotchas in how Office 365 stores documents

Any documents you create in an Office app on your iPad, iPhone, Android device, or Windows 8 PC (or on a Windows 10 PC, tablet, or smartphone when that operating system becomes available in late 2015) are by default stored in Microsoft's OneDrive cloud storage, though you can force the apps to store the documents locally instead. That means you need an active Internet connection to open them and should save them quickly to make a temporary working copy on your iPad. If you lose your connection, Office will save the files on your iPad until your connection resumes, at which point it will sync any changes made on your iPad with the original version. New documents are likewise synced with OneDrive if created when you had no Internet connection.

Corporate users may discover that their IT departments have configured Office 365 to store their files in OneDrive for Business and/or SharePoint instead. And you might have access to OneDrive, OneDrive for Business, and SharePoint from Office — the first for personal documents if you have a personal Microsoft account (such as on your home PC) and the others provided by your business through the corporate Office 365 account it provides you.

Mac users and Windows 7, Vista, and XP users have to jump through some hoops to work with SharePoint, OneDrive, or OneDrive for Business (not available for the Mac when this book went to press but expected in late 2015). Ask your tech support staff for help navigating how Microsoft's pieces fit together, because when this book went to press, each platform's version of Office worked differently in terms of managing files.

Opening and creating Office documents

To open a document, first navigate to the location where it is stored via the Open pane in the Documents window. You can also open a document from the Recents pane, which I previously described. And you can use the iPad's Open In feature (see Chapter 17) to open a document in Mail or other iPad app in the desired Office app.

Tap a document to open it for editing. If the file is stored in the cloud, wait a few moments for the file to transfer from OneDrive, OneDrive for Business, Dropbox, or SharePoint before it opens.

If you see "[Compatibility Mode]" next to the document's name in the toolbar after opening it, that means the file is in the older .doc format, not the current .docx format.

To create a document, tap New in the Documents window. This opens a pane of document templates. Tap the one you want to base the document on, and your document opens. I recommend that you save the document immediately, which you do by following these steps:

1. **Tap the File button (the document icon at upper left).**

2. **In the form that appears, tap Name to open the Save As form, where you enter a name in the Name field and select the storage location for that new document.**

3. **Tap Save.**

    By default, Office apps automatically save changes to documents. To disable that feature, set the AutoSave switch to Off.

If a document is open, you can return to the Documents window by tapping the Documents button (the ← icon) at the upper left of the screen.

Renaming and storing Office documents

One of the more mystifying aspects of the Microsoft Office apps is the ability to name and move documents. Document management is, frankly, haphazard and incomplete.

For example, the Office apps on the iPad cannot rename documents, nor can they move documents from one folder to another or one cloud storage service to another, or from the cloud to permanent storage on your iPad.

But the Office apps *do* let you move documents that are stored locally on the iPad to OneDrive cloud storage by following these steps:

1. **Tap the iPad location in the Open pane in the Documents window and then tap the Share button.**

    The Share button is the icon showing an up arrow (↑) in a box, located to the right of a document name you want to move off your iPad.

2. **In the pop-over that appears, choose Move to Cloud.**

3. **In the form that appears, choose the cloud storage service to move it to.**

    You can also navigate the cloud storage service's folders to move the file to a specific folder. In addition, you can give the moved file a new name or keep the existing name.

4. **Tap Save in the upper right.**

You also can delete documents from the Documents window no matter where they are stored: In the Documents window's Open or Recents pane, tap the Share button to the right of a document and choose Delete in the pop-over that appears.

You can duplicate documents in Office apps — just not from the Documents window. From *within* a document, tap the File button and then use the Duplicate button in the File pop-over to rename and copy a document.

The File pop-over is also where you print documents, from its Print menu option, and where you can revert to the last saved version, using the Restore option.

You can also rename, duplicate, and delete documents, as well as create folders, from the Dropbox, OneDrive, and OneDrive for Business apps on your iPad — for any documents stored there, that is — as well as from your computer's Dropbox, OneDrive, OneDrive for Business, and SharePoint virtual disks or from those services via a computer's web browser.

Sharing Office documents

Office can't share files to other iPad apps, though it can receive them. So you have to email yourself the apps to open them from Mail in another app, or go to the separate OneDrive or OneDrive for Business cloud storage app where Office stores its files and then use the iOS Share to send them to your other iPad apps.

The Share sheet is the standard method in iOS for sharing files with other apps, as well as for sending files via email and text messages and for printing. (See Chapter 17 for more about the Share sheet.)

To share a file from an Office app, you have two methods:

✔ From the Documents window's Open or Recents pane, tap the Share button (the icon showing ↑ in a box) to the right of the document name and choose the desired sharing option.

✔ From within an open document, tap the Share button (the person icon) and choose the desired sharing option:

• *Email as a Link:* Sends a web link to the document in OneDrive

• *Email as Attachment:* Sends the document itself within an email

• *Copy Link:* Creates a web link to the document in OneDrive that you can then message or otherwise send to someone else

If you share a file as an email attachment from within the document, you can choose to send it in its native Office format or as a PDF file. You don't get the PDF option if you share the document from the Documents window.

Editing and Formatting with Word

In the Word app, open a document, tap in your text, and start typing. Of course, you'll want to do more than that. As with the other Office apps, Word has a very straightforward, clean interface for editing and formatting. The tools for naming and moving your document are a bit confusing, but not so the editing and formatting tools.

Using the contextual menu

When you select text (by double-tapping a word), a contextual menu appears near the text and provides the standard iOS contextual menu's editing options: Cut, Copy, Paste, and Delete, as well as Speak (to have the iPad say aloud the selected text) and Define (to look up the term in the iPad's internal dictionary or on the web). No formatting commands are available from the contextual menu.

When you insert the cursor between letters in text (by tapping and holding where you want to insert it), such as to type new text at that location, a contextual menu appears. It provides the standard iOS options for text insertion: Select, Select All, and Paste. It also has Office's own Insert option, which lets you then insert your choice of a tab or line break.

Touring the Word toolbars

Word has five working views that determine what controls are available to you via their toolbars. While working in your document, you switch among them as needed to do the following:

- **Home:** Apply basic formatting such as font, text size, paragraph alignment, and bulleted and numbered lists
- **Insert:** Insert layout objects such as headers and footers, tables, graphics, and text boxes, as well as special kinds of text attributes such as hyperlinks, page numbers, and footnotes

✔ **Layout:** Manage page orientation and margins, columns, breaks, and sections.

✔ **Review:** Check spelling, manage comments, get word counts, enable revisions tracking, and manage how revisions are displayed and which are accepted and rejected

✔ **View:** Enable document rulers and set page views

Figure 6-2 shows a composite image of all five working views' toolbars, with the active tab indicating which toolbar you're viewing.

The toolbar in Word — as well as in Excel and PowerPoint — also holds the Undo and Redo buttons no matter what working view is active.

Formatting text in Home view

When you're editing or writing text, you use the Home view to format that text, either by paragraph (such as a bulleted list) or character (such as the font).

If a formatting button affects entire paragraphs, using that button affects any paragraphs that you have selected text in; if no text is selected, that button affects the paragraph the text cursor is active in.

If a formatting button affects just characters, using that button affects any text you have selected. If no text is selected, the formatting button affects any text that you then type.

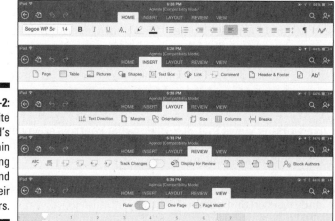

Figure 6-2: A composite of Word's five main working views and their toolbars.

Here are the paragraph-oriented buttons (the first is at the far left of the toolbar; the others follow the highlighting tool):

- ✔ **Styles:** Shown in Figure 6-3, this button lets you apply a predefined paragraph style, such as from the document template or a document created in Word on a computer. *Note:* Word for iPad cannot modify or create paragraph styles. Also, it does not support character styles, which applies formatting to strings of text rather than entire paragraphs, such as when you have the first few words after each bullet in a different font than the rest of the paragraph.

- ✔ **Align Left, Align Center, Align Right, and Justify:** These buttons control how text aligns to the left and right margins.

- ✔ **Line Spacing:** This button opens a pop-over in which you choose the desired line spacing.

- ✔ **Bullets:** The Bullets button opens a pop-over that lets you choose the bullet style for the paragraph, which is formatted as a list item. Bullet choices include the ✓ character. Use the None option to revert a paragraph to a nonlist style.

- ✔ **Numbering:** This button opens a pop-over in which you choose the numbering style for the paragraph, which is formatted as a list item. Use the None option to revert a paragraph to a nonlist style.

- ✔ **Outdent and Indent:** This moves the paragraph's block indent to the left (outdent) or right (indent). The first increment is the same as for a list; the subsequent increments move to the next half-inch mark on the ruler.

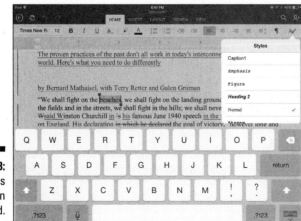

Figure 6-3:
The Styles pop-over in Word.

Following are the character-oriented buttons on the Home toolbar, starting from the far left:

- ✔ **Font:** This lets you select one of the iPad's available fonts.

- ✔ **Text Size:** This lets you select the text size, or use the + and – buttons to increase the size one point at a time.

- ✔ **Boldface, Italics, and Underline:** These apply (or remove) the indicated formatting to or from text. For example, if the selected text has, say, boldface already applied and you tap the B button, you remove the boldface from that text.

- ✔ **Formatting:** This button pens a pop-over in which you can select strikethrough, subscript, and superscript formats, as well as Text Effects, which provides several outline and drop-shadow effects. Here you also find the Clear Formatting option, which removes all formatting (except styles) applied to the currently selected text.

- ✔ **Highlight Color:** This button opens a pop-over in which you choose a color to apply behind the text, as if you had drawn over it with a felt-tip marker.

- ✔ **Font Color:** This button's pop-over lets you choose a color to apply to your selected text. Tap the Custom Color button at the bottom of the pop-over to create your own text color.

The Show/Hide Invisibles button (the ¶ icon) at the far right of the Home toolbar toggles the Invisibles view, which shows marks for spaces, paragraph returns, and so on when highlighted and hiding them when not highlighted.

Adding and formatting page objects in Insert view

The Insert working view mixes several types of elements, some that you apply to text and some that are part of your document layout.

Several of the Insert toolbar's buttons — Table, Pictures, Shapes, and Text Box — open a new toolbar with options specific to the object you are inserting. I cover those tools in the next several sections.

The Insert toolbar also has one layout-oriented button: Page, which inserts a page break at the current cursor location and positions the cursor at the top of the new page.

The Insert toolbar's other controls are text-oriented controls and are as follows:

- ✔ **Link:** Lets you insert a hyperlink to a web page through the selected text.

- ✔ **Header & Footer:** This pop-over lets you add, edit, and remove headers and footers. The header and footer appear on the page and fit within the document's margins. You can edit their contents as you can any other text. Tap Close to return to your document. You can have just headers, just footers, both, or neither.

- ✔ **Page Numbers:** Lets you control how page numbers appear in your document. The options are

  - *Show # on First Page:* Set this switch to On if you want the page number to appear on the first page of the section or document.

  - *Position:* Choose to display the page number in the header or footer.

  - *Alignment:* Choose to show the page number in the left, center, or right side of the header or footer, or in the inside margin or in the outside margin (to the side of the header or footer).

  - *Format:* Choose the numbering style, such as Arabic (1, 2, 3, . . .), Roman (i, ii, iii, . . .), or letter (A, B, C, . . .). The Roman and letter numbering styles are available in both uppercase and lowercase variants.

If you're working on a document whose page numbering was defined in Word on your computer, the numbering isn't editable unless you set the Numbering switch to Off and then back to On in the Page Numbers pop-over. Also, you can't restart page numbering within sections in Word for the iPad, though such numbering set in Word on your computer is preserved.

- ✔ **Footnote:** Adds a footnote at the current cursor location and creates a footnote text box at the bottom of the page for you to enter the footnote text in. Word renumbers the footnotes as you add new ones so that they display in the order they appear in your document, not the order in which you created them.

Creating and formatting tables in Table view

When you insert a table — or select an existing one — the Table working view appears in the toolbar, with controls for tables, as Figure 6-4 shows.

Word's tables are simple and so are the controls you use to work with them. You have all the formatting available for cells' contents that you have for any text in your document, but there are no table-specific controls such as deci-mal align or currency selection.

You can apply formatting such as background colors to cells. Double-tap a cell to select it and then drag its handles to extend the selection to other cells. To select an entire table, tap anywhere in it, and then tap the table selector handle at its upper-left corner, as Figure 6-4 also shows. You cannot select entire rows or columns, except by dragging the selection handles over them.

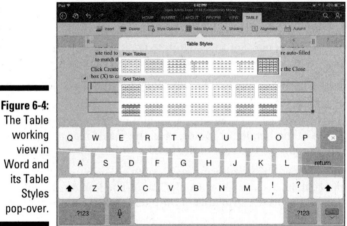

Figure 6-4:
The Table working view in Word and its Table Styles pop-over.

With cells or the entire table selected, you can use the following buttons to apply formatting to them:

✔ **Insert:** This pop-over lets you insert a row above or below the current cell's row, or a column to the left or to the right of the current cell's column.

✔ **Delete:** This pop-over lets you delete the current cell's row or column, or the entire table.

✔ **Style Options:** This pop-over's options are meant to be applied to spe-cific rows and columns, not the entire table or individual cells. You can specify the row type — header, total, or banded — for the selected row to override the formatting specified for that row by the table style applied. Likewise, you can specify the column type (first or last) to over-ride the formatting for that column specified by the table style. Finally, the Repeat Headers option — available only if the first row in a table is selected — repeats that row as the header on each page if the table runs across multiple pages.

✔ **Table Styles:** This pop-over's options apply the selected table style to the entire table (even if only one cell is selected). Table styles can include color borders, row color and shading (bands), and special formatting for the first and last columns, the header row, and the total row (where you total your numbers, such as in a budget).

✔ **Shading:** This pop-over lets you apply shades and colors to the selected cells.

✔ **Alignment:** This pop-over lets you specify the text alignment within a cell: Left, Center, or Right for horizontal alignment and Top, Middle, or Bottom for vertical alignment.

✔ **AutoFit:** This pop-over lets you have Word figure out how to size the table based on your selected option:

  • *AutoFit Contents:* Adjusts rows and cells to best fit the contents.

  • *AutoFit Page:* Makes the table fill the page width and adjusts the columns accordingly.

  • *Fixed Column Width:* Honestly, this doesn't do anything.

You can resize a table by dragging the handle at its lower-right corner, but you cannot resize individual columns or rows manually.

Formatting and manipulating images in Pictures view

If you insert a picture or select one in the document, the Picture working view appears, as shown in Figure 6-5.

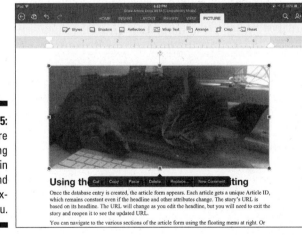

Figure 6-5:
The Picture working view in Word and its contextual menu.

Tap and hold a picture to get the contextual menu, which lets you delete the picture as well as cut, copy, and paste it. You can drag a picture within your document to a different location, and you can use the resize handles on a selected image to resize it — just as you would do with a mouse on computer.

Here are the Picture working view's buttons:

- ✔ **Styles:** Lets you apply any of a couple dozen fancy framing effects.

- ✔ **Shadow:** Lets you apply any of a couple dozen shadow effects.

- ✔ **Reflection:** Lets you apply any of nine reflection effects below your picture.

- ✔ **Wrap Text:** Lets you control how text interacts with the picture. By default, text flows so that the text above the picture continues below it. But you can change that configuration to make the text flow around its sides, to make text flow behind or in front of the image, or to anchor the image to a specific spot in text so that it flows with that text.

- ✔ **Arrange:** Lets you control how the picture appears when it overlaps other objects. You can move the image up or down through the stack of overlapped images; those objects behind it in that stack are obscured by the part of picture that overlaps them, and the objects in front of it obscure any part of the picture they overlap.

- ✔ **Crop:** Lets you crop out unwanted parts of an image, such as to show just part of it. After you select a picture and tap this button, the sizing handles become cropping handles, and you crop the image by moving the handles — similar to using the cropping tools on your computer. But you also get a contextual menu with several predefined crops: Original (the original image is shown in its entirety); 1:1 (a square portion); and 3:2, 4:3, and 16:9. Tap Reset to undo your crop.

- ✔ **Reset:** This pop-over has two options:

  - *Reset Picture:* Undoes all your picture formatting

  - *Reset Size:* Leaves your formatting but returns the image to its original size

Adding boxes, ovals, lines, and other shapes in Shape view

The Shapes pop-over contains more than 40 options for shapes that you can insert. When you insert a shape or select an existing one, the Shape working view appears in the toolbar.

Tap the shape to open its contextual menu, which has the usual Cut, Copy, Paste, and Delete options, plus one specific to shapes: Add Text. If you choose Add Text, you convert the shape into a text box with that shape. (To edit its text later, choose Edit Text from the contextual menu.)

The Shape toolbar's buttons are as follows:

- ✔ **Insert:** Inserts a shape into the document.
- ✔ **Shape Styles:** Opens a pop-over with several predefined styles for your shape, including various combinations of color backgrounds, outlines, and drop shadows; some also have text formatting predefined.
- ✔ **Fill:** This pop-over shows background colors predefined by the document's template. Use the Custom Color button at the bottom of the pop-over to create your own color.
- ✔ **Outline:** Works like the Fill pop-over except that it applies to the shape's border (called *outline* in Word).
- ✔ **WordArt Styles:** Opens a pop-over with the same fancy text formats as the Text Effects options in the Home working view's Formatting pop-over, described in the "Formatting text in Home view" section, earlier in this chapter.
- ✔ **Wrap Text:** Works like the Wrap Text pop-over for pictures, covered in the "Formatting and manipulating images in Pictures view" section earlier in this chapter.
- ✔ **Arrange:** Works like the Reorder pop-over for pictures, also covered in the "Formatting and manipulating images in Pictures view" section, earlier in this chapter.

Creating and formatting text boxes in Shape view

When you insert a text box — or select an existing one — the Shape working view appears in the toolbar. No, that's not a mistake: It does open the Shape working view, and there is no Text Box working view.

A text box is basically a plain, square shape — no background, no outline, no drop shadow — that you type text into. You can then reshape it using the control handles, and you can move it by dragging it. You also can format the box's appearance using the Shape working view's toolbar.

Just as you use the Edit Text option in a shape's contextual menu to edit its text, so you use the same option to edit a text box's contents. And to format the text in a text box, go into the editing mode via Edit Text and then switch to the Home working view to get Word's text-formatting controls.

Specifying page attributes in Layout view

The Layout working view's buttons (see Figure 6-6) let you format the pages themselves, as opposed to their text or objects. Here are the buttons in this view:

- **Text Direction:** Rotates all text in the document to 90 degrees, 270 degrees, or Horizontal, which means no rotation (the default setting).

- **Margins:** Lets you choose the outside margins for your document. You can't specify the margin's size, such as in inches. Instead, you choose from predefined margins such as Narrow and Wide. The Mirrored option is meant for double-sided printed documents, and gives more space to the inside margins so that when the paper pages are bound together the text doesn't "fall" into the inside area where the binding is.

- **Orientation:** This pop-over has two options: Portrait and Landscape, to determine whether the page is taller than wide (Portrait) or wider than tall (Landscape).

- **Size:** Lets you choose the paper size from the common U.S. and European paper sizes.

- **Columns:** Lets you apply columns for the current section (covered in the next bullet) or, if the document has no sections, the entire document. *Note:* You cannot apply columns to a text box.

- **Breaks:** Opens a pop-over with several options. Two are page-oriented:

  - *Page:* Forces a new page at the current location, and places your text cursor at the top of the page following the new one.

  - *Column:* Forces a new column at the current location. If your document is a single-column document, this acts like a page break.

  - *Section:* A section break adds a new section to your document at the current cursor location and determines how page flow is affected by that new section. You can choose Next Page, Continuous, Next Page, Even Page, and Odd Page. The Continuous option has no effect on the document's pagination, but the other section options create a page break as their names indicate. Odd Page, for example, ensures that the new section begins on the next available odd-numbered page, inserting a blank page at the end of the previous section if necessary to accomplish that.

  If you have a section that begins on a new page, any header or footer added to it applies to just that section, replacing any header or footer defined for the previous section. (I explain how to add headers and footers in the "Adding and formatting page objects in Insert view" section, earlier in this chapter.)

Figure 6-6:
Editing a
header in
Word.

Tracking changes, commenting, and proofing in Review view

The Review working view in Word is where you enable and manage tracked changes — the additions and deletions that show up onscreen in your document as you edit it.

The Review view has controls that affect how tracking displays and works, and it has controls to move through and approve or reject specific revisions.

The first controls described here are the universal controls. To enable revisions tracking, set the Track Changes switch to On, as shown in Figure 6-7; if the document had revisions tracking enabled on your computer, it will remain enabled on the iPad. Use the Display for Review pop-over to determine how revisions display onscreen. Your options are

- ✔ **All Markup:** Shows all markup onscreen.

- ✔ **No Markup:** Hides all revisions so that you see only how the final document will appear if all the changes are accepted. (Changes are still tracked, just silently.)

- ✔ **Original with Markup:** Show the original document with the later revisions indicated as deletions, not as additions. This view assumes that the author will reject most of the changes to the original and so presents them as deletions to confirm or reject, whereas the All Markup view (called Final Showing Markup in Word for Windows and Mac) assumes that the author will accept most changes, so it presents them as additions to confirm or reject.

- ✔ **Original:** Hides all the revisions to show the original version. (Changes are still tracked, just silently.)

✔ **Show Markup:** Opens a pop-over that lets you control what revisions are visible: comments, insertions and deletions, and formatting. It also lets you show all revisions in balloons to the side of the document or just comments and formatting revisions in balloons to the side (text revisions are shown in the document itself through strikethrough for deletions and underlining for additions).

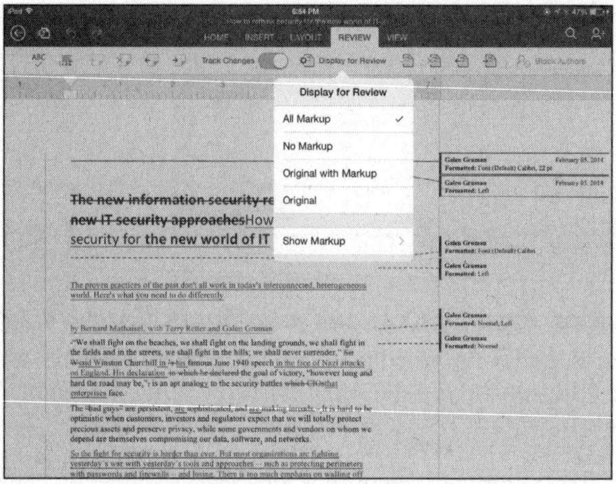

Figure 6-7:
Revisions
tracking
enabled in
Word, with
the Display
for Review
pop-over
visible.

There are three other universal controls available, but they're unrelated to revisions tracking:

✔ **Block Authors:** A feature available only to Word documents saved in the .docx format and stored on OneDrive or SharePoint, it lets you prevent others from editing the document. Tap the Block Authors button at the far right of the toolbar, and then choose Block Authors from the Block Authors pop-over. You release the blocks by choosing Unblock All My Blocked Areas in that pop-over.

✔ **Spelling:** Tap this button (at the far left of the toolbar) to open a pop-over in which you enable spell-checking and grammar-checking. You also specify the language for Word's spell-checking and grammar-checking. *Note:* Word indicates questionable spelling with red squiggly underlines and questionable grammar with green squiggly underlines.

✔ **Word Count:** Tap this button to open a pop-over that shows the number of words and characters for your document. By default, this feature ignores text in text boxes and footnotes, but you can include that text in the count by setting the Include Additional Text switch to On in the pop-over.

The other buttons in the Review view's toolbar let you manage the individual revisions in the document. The four buttons at the left work with comments and are, from left to right, as follows:

- ✔ **Add Comment:** Inserts a comment at the current cursor location, displaying a comment bubble in the right margin for you to enter your comment text in.

- ✔ **Delete Comment:** Deletes the current comment.

- ✔ **Previous Comment:** Moves to the previous comment in the document, meaning the first one before the current cursor location.

- ✔ **Next Comment:** Moves to the next comment in the document, meaning the first one after the current cursor location.

The four similar buttons to the right of the Display for Review button manage revisions:

- ✔ **Accept Revision:** Makes the current revision a permanent part of the document, treating it as if it were part of the original text and removing the information as to what was changed, who changed it, and when.

- ✔ **Reject Revision:** Removes the revision, reverting the text to the original.

- ✔ **Previous Revision:** Moves to the previous revision in the document, meaning the first one before the current cursor location.

- ✔ **Next Revision:** Moves to the next revision in the document, meaning the first one after the current cursor location.

Enabling rulers and setting page view in View view

The View working view has just a few controls:

- ✔ **Ruler:** Set this switch to On to display the document ruler, which shows margins and tab stops. You can move those items by dragging them, just as you do via a mouse in Word on your computer. You can also add a tab stop by tapping the ruler at the desired location.

- ✔ **One Page** and **Page Width:** These buttons, respectively, show the document so that an entire page fits onscreen (One Page) and so that the text fits within the width of the screen (Page Width). You might use One Page to see how an entire page looks with all its elements, rather than print it to paper just to get that complete view.

Crunching Numbers with Excel

Excel was the first visual spreadsheet editor, back in 1985 on the Mac and later in Windows. It has since become the standard tool for spreadsheet work, so having Excel on the iPad is a big deal. And it's an easy tool to use if you're already familiar with its use on your computer.

Like Word, Excel relies on working views to group its various features:

- **Home:** Edit cell contents and apply formatting.
- **Insert:** Insert tables, charts, pictures, shapes, and text boxes.
- **Formulas:** Find the formula you want so that Excel inserts it for you. You can create and edit formulas in any view, but the Formulas view provides easier access to different formula categories.
- **Review:** Add and manage comments.
- **View:** Control the display of various items in your spreadsheet.

Figure 6-8 shows these working views' toolbars.

Figure 6-8:
Excel's five main working views and their toolbars.

Entering data into cells

In any working view, you tap a cell to work on its contents. The onscreen keyboard appears, as does the Formula Bar at top, as Figure 6-9 shows.

The onscreen keyboard is pretty much the standard iOS keyboard, with two exceptions:

✔ Above the keyboard to the left appears the list of current sheets in the Excel workbook. When the keyboard is not open, the list of sheets appears at the bottom of the screen.

✔ Above the keyboard to the right appear two buttons: Abc and 123. The Abc button shows the standard keyboard, and the 123 button shows Excel's numeric keyboard, shown in Figure 6-10. You get a numeric keypad, cursor keys to move among cells, various special symbols, and the Sum button (the Σ icon) to add the Sum formula in the current cell.

If a button has a green upper-right corner, tap and hold that button to get alternative symbols, such as ¢, £, €, or ¥ from the $ key.

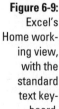

In the numeric keyboard, you can also tap Return (the icon shown here in the margin) in the far right of the keyboard to accept your changes and move the cursor to the next cell below. Tap and hold Return to get the ↓ key instead, which inserts a hard return in the current cell.

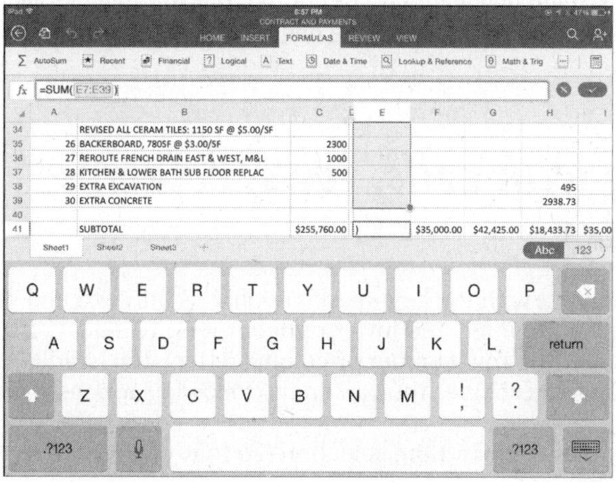

Figure 6-9: Excel's Home working view, with the standard text keyboard.

In the Formula Bar, enter your formula as you do in Excel on your computer. Tap a cell to include it in the formula, and tap the *fx* button to open a list of available formulas to insert one into the Formula Bar for the current cell. Tap the Clear button (the X icon) to erase the formula, and tap the Accept button (the ✓ icon) to accept the formula (or tap the Enter key on the keyboard).

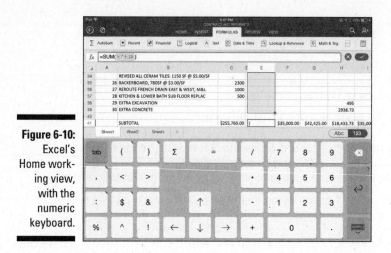

Figure 6-10:
Excel's
Home work-
ing view,
with the
numeric
keyboard.

TIP

To make a cell reference absolute, add $ in front of the row and/or column values you want to make sure don't change as you copy or move the referenced cells. For example, the cell address $E15 will keep the column set to E even if the referenced cell is moved or copied, but the row will be updated if the cell's location changes. Making the cell address E15 ensures that neither will change.

Working with cells, rows, columns, and tables

To select a cell, tap it with the keyboard hidden; it is outlined and shows selection handles at its upper-left and lower-right corners. To select rows or columns, tap its label (the row number or column letter); the handles appear in the center of the longest side. You can do the following actions with selections:

- ✔ Drag a handle to expand the selection (so that you can apply formatting, for example).

- ✔ For cells only, tap and hold a cell until its border animates and its content "bounces" slightly onscreen; then drag it to move it and its contents to another location, overriding whatever was in the cell you moved it to.

- ✔ For rows and columns only, drag the resize handle (the = icon for rows and the ‖ icon for columns) on their labels to resize their depth or width, respectively. (The onscreen keyboard has to be hidden for the resize handle to display.)

- ✔ Tap a cell, row, or column and then quickly tap it again to display the contextual menu.

For cells, the contextual menu's options are Cut, Copy, Paste, Paste Format, Clear, Fill, and Wrap. The Cut, Copy, Paste, and Clear options do what they do in any app: cut, copy, paste, and delete the contents. Here's what the other three options do:

- ✔ **Fill:** Fills the selected cells with the formula (or value, if it has no formula) in the first cell in the selection, essentially copying its formula (or value) to all the selected cells.

- ✔ **Wrap:** Enables text wrap for the selected cells, making the cell deeper if needed to display all the text.

- ✔ **Paste Format:** Pastes the formatting (but not the contents) of the cell you last copied.

For rows and columns, you don't get the Paste Format, Fill, or Wrap options, but you get the following additional options in the contextual menu:

- ✔ **Insert Above (for rows) or Insert Left (for columns):** Inserts a new row or column next to the current location.

- ✔ **Delete:** Deletes the current row or column.

- ✔ **Hide:** Hides the current row or column. To unhide a hidden row or column, select the rows or columns on either side of the hidden one; then choose Unhide in the contextual menu.

- ✔ **AutoFit:** Makes the row or column resize to fit the text within it.

To select an entire sheet, tap the triangle icon at the upper-left corner of the sheet. You get the same contextual menu options as for cells, except there's no Paste Format option.

When you select cells, columns, rows, or tables, you can use the formatting features in the Home working view on the selection, as covered later in this chapter.

Finally, you'll see a list of sheets in your workbook at the bottom of the screen if the keyboard is hidden, or above the keyboard if it is visible. Tap a sheet's name to move to it, or tap the plus sign (+) at the right of the tabs to add a new sheet. Double-tap a sheet's tab to edit its name. Tap and drag a sheet's tab to reorder it. Tap the active sheet's tab to get its contextual menu, which has options to delete, duplicate, and hide the sheet. (To unhide sheets, tap the active sheet's tab and choose Unhide from its contextual menu.)

Formatting cells in Home view

The Home working view (refer to Figures 6-9 and 6-10) is where you apply formatting to cells and their contents. Several of the buttons on the Home toolbar work just like their Word counterparts, so refer to the "Formatting text in Home view" subsection in the Word section, earlier in this chapter, for details on Font, Text Size, Boldface, Italics, Underline, Fill Color, and Font Color. The Alignment button also works as it does in Word's Table view, also covered earlier the "Creating and formatting tables in Table view" subsection in the Word section.

The other buttons in the Excel Home view are specific to Excel:

- ✔ **Cell Borders:** Lets you apply borders to the selected cells, just as the same button in Excel on your computer does. But you find fewer options on the iPad than on a computer; for example, there is no double-line border option for the iPad.

- ✔ **Merge Cells:** If at least two adjacent cells are selected, this button merges them into one cell.

- ✔ **Number Formatting:** Opens a pop-over in which you select the display formatting for the cell's numeric content, such as Currency or Date. These work as they do in Excel on your computer, providing options such as currency symbol, number of decimal places, and so on as appropriate for the specific display format.

- ✔ **Cell Styles:** Opens a pop-over with several predefined cell formats that you can apply to selected cells. These predefined formats typically combine background fills, text colors, and borders to give you single-tap selection of complex formats. You can, of course, create your own the old-fashioned way by using the Fill Color, Font Color, and Cell Borders buttons in combination.

- ✔ **Insert & Delete Cells:** Lets you insert cells, columns, and rows at, as well as delete them from, the selected cell's location. As in Excel on a computer, you can choose whether the insertion or deletion affects the entire row or column or just the selected cells.

- ✔ **Sort and Filter:** If at least two adjacent cells are selected, this pop-over lets you sort their contents in ascending or descending order within their column(s). If you've set the Filter switch to On, a downward-pointing triangle icon appears in the first cell; tap it to open the Sort and Filter pop-over, which contains options to filter out specific data (such as blank values) from what displays onscreen in the sort.

Adding objects such as charts via Insert view

The Insert view lets you insert various objects in your document. The Table, Pictures, Shapes, and Text Box objects work just as they do in Word, so refer to the details on them in the earlier part of this chapter that covers Word. (See the "Creating and formatting tables in Table view," "Formatting and manipulating images in Pictures view," "Adding boxes, ovals, lines, and other shapes in Shape view," and "Creating and formatting text boxes in Shape view" subsections, respectively.)

The one Excel-specific object is the chart. You can have Excel recommend appropriate charts based on the selected data by using the Recommended button, or you can choose specific types by using the Charts button. Both open pop-overs with the available options. (You can also change an existing chart by selecting it and then choosing a new option in the Recommended or Charts pop-overs.)

Figure 6-11 shows the Recommended pop-over and a chart it built, as well as the Chart working view that appears when you insert or select a chart.

After you insert a chart, select it to move it elsewhere in your sheet. You can also resize it using the resize handles that appear. Its contextual menu has the Cut, Copy, and Delete options.

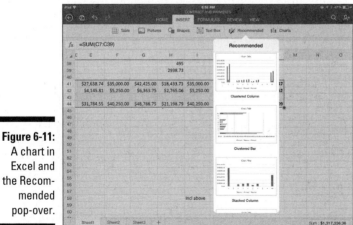

Figure 6-11: A chart in Excel and the Recommended pop-over.

Excel does a good job of building charts from your data, but you'll likely want to refine them further. You do that with the tools in the Chart working view, as follows:

- ✔ **Recommended:** Opens the Recommended pop-over so that you can apply a different recommended chart type to the current chart.
- ✔ **Types:** Opens the Chart Types pop-over so that you can apply a different chart type to the current chart.
- ✔ **Layouts:** Opens a pop-over with choices of layouts for the current chart type, meaning where labels, keys, and gridlines appear.
- ✔ **Elements:** Opens a pop-over in which you specify the formatting for chart elements such as its title, data labels, legends, lines, and trendlines.
- ✔ **Colors:** Opens a pop-over with sets of colors that you can apply to the chart to set the palette of colors used.
- ✔ **Styles:** Opens a pop-over with predefined styles for the current chart type, including colors and fonts.
- ✔ **Switch:** Swaps the X and Y axes in your chart.
- ✔ **Arrange:** Available only if the chart overlaps another object. You can move the chart up or down through the stack of overlapped objects; those objects behind it in that stack are obscured by the part of the chart that overlaps them, and the objects in front of it obscure any part of the chart they overlap.

When the chart's appearance is to your preference, you can edit the various titles it may have, such as chart title, axis titles, and key titles. Tap and hold the title to make the title editable; then change the text to whatever you want.

Getting to formulas in Formulas view

The Formulas working view in Excel is, frankly, not terribly useful. All it really does is divide the various categories of formulas into their own buttons, as well as provide the Recent button for quick access to frequently used formulas. But you can access all the same formulas in any working view from the Formula Bar using its *fx* button.

The Formulas view also has the Calculate button (the calculator icon), which forces the spreadsheet to update all calculations. Because Excel updates calculations as you edit them or change values, it's also not that useful.

Working with comments in Review view

The Review working view in Excel is similar to that in Word but has options only for viewing comments, navigating from one to the next, and deleting them. You can't add comments in Excel on the iPad.

Managing spreadsheet display in View view

You use the View working view in Excel to control whether several items display onscreen: the Formula Bar (it always displays if you edit a cell, so hiding it here means that it's hidden only when a cell is not being edited), the list of sheet tabs, the label headings for rows and columns, and cell gridlines.

The reason to turn off the display of the Formula Bar, gridlines, sheet tabs' list, and label headings is to make more of your spreadsheet visible on the iPad's screen, such as if you find yourself constantly scrolling to see rows and columns that otherwise would fit onscreen.

The View working view also has the Freeze Panes button, which opens a pop-over with three options: Freeze Panes (anything above and anything to the left of the current cell's location), Freeze Top Row, and Freeze First Columns. Freezing the panes means that the frozen parts always display onscreen, and any scrolling occurs only in the unfrozen parts. This is handy to keep rows and columns in view that label what data they contain so that you know what the numbers are that you're looking at — otherwise, those labels would scroll offscreen.

Dazzling Them with PowerPoint

Although I prefer Apple's Keynote (see Chapter 5) for presentation work, Microsoft's PowerPoint is also a good tool for creating and editing slide shows. It provides master slides that serve as the templates for the slides you add. Slides are composed of images and text, each in its own box. Slides can have transition effects as you move among them.

Chapter 19 explains how to give presentations from PowerPoint, such as when you're on stage and you want to control when the audience sees each slide, have your speaker notes visible only to you, and be able to "draw" on your slides as you speak to highlight certain content live.

As with the other Office apps on the iPad, PowerPoint uses working views to group its features:

- ✔ **Home:** Format text as well as insert new slides, text boxes, and shapes.

- ✔ **Insert:** Insert new slides, tables, pictures, videos, shapes, and text boxes — yes, there is some duplication with the Home view.

- ✔ **Design:** Format the slide show's basic elements: its themes, slide size, and background image.

- ✔ **Transitions:** Apply transitions — special effects that appear as you move from slide to slide.

- ✔ **Animations:** Similar to transitions, these special effects are applied to elements on the same slide, appearing as you reveal each element (called *builds*) in turn.

- ✔ **Slide Show:** Preview your slide show and work in Presenter view. (Chapter 19 covers these features.)

- ✔ **Review:** Show comments and move among them.

Figure 6-12 shows the toolbars for PowerPoint's main working views.

Figure 6-12:
Power-
Point's
seven main
working
views and
their
toolbars.

Creating a presentation

When you create a presentation in the Documents window (see the section "Managing Documents in Microsoft Office," early in this chapter), PowerPoint asks you to choose a template. That template contains the master slides for your presentation.

You cannot create or modify these templates in PowerPoint for the iPad. You have to create or modify templates in PowerPoint on your computer by editing the master slides in a document and then opening a copy of that document in PowerPoint on the iPad to use it as a de facto template (rather than choosing a predefined template).

When your new presentation opens, you see the slide pane at the left, with a single slide in it for you to start working on. At the bottom of the pane is the Add Slide button (the + icon). In the left side of the Home working view's toolbar and in the left side of the Insert working view's toolbar, you have the New Slide button to insert a new slide. A pop-over appears with various master-slide formats to choose from. *Note:* If you have multiple slides, the new slide is added after whatever slide is currently selected in the pane.

Figure 6-13 shows a new slide as well as the New Slide pop-over.

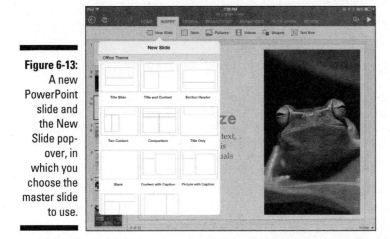

Figure 6-13:
A new PowerPoint slide and the New Slide pop-over, in which you choose the master slide to use.

If you have an existing slide that you want to use as the basis for a new slide, just tap and hold it for a second to open its contextual menu; then choose Copy. Move to the location where you want to insert the copy, tap and hold that slide, and choose Paste from its contextual menu. (The contextual menu also lets you cut and delete the slide.) Or choose Duplicate to make a copy right after the current slide.

Double-tap the text boxes to enter or paste text. To add other objects, go to the Insert working view and tap the button for the desired object type: Table, Pictures, Videos, Shapes, and Text Box. The Table, Pictures, Shapes, and Text Box pop-overs work just as they do in Word, so refer to the "Adding and formatting page objects in Insert view" section in the earlier coverage of Word in this chapter to understand how to use these pop-overs and the objects they insert.

The Videos pop-over is a PowerPoint-only feature, but it inserts videos from the Photos app the same way as the Pictures pop-over inserts photos from the Photos app. However, you won't find a Videos working view for inserted videos as you do a Pictures view for inserted pictures. All you can do with an inserted video in PowerPoint is select it to move, resize, copy, cut, paste, or delete it.

You can also drag objects within a slide and use the resize handles in the center of each border segment to reshape an object — the same as you do on a computer when using PowerPoint.

Finally, you can rearrange slides by dragging them within the slides pane to a new location. To drag a slide, tap and hold it until it "pops up" to let you know it's selected. Don't release your finger from the screen, but drag it to a new location, releasing your finger when it's where you want it.

Applying formatting and transitions

You can fine-tune each slide as you create it, or you can get all the slides set up and then fine-tune them all in one sitting. Because PowerPoint doesn't let you select multiple objects at one time, I suggest fine-tuning each type of object first and then copying those objects as needed for use in other slides. This way, all the formatting work gets copied, too.

Formatting slide objects

You can apply various formatting to slide objects, such as text, shapes, text boxes, and pictures. You do so via the Home, Picture, Shape, Text Box, and Table working views' various formatting buttons, which work the same as in Word (covered earlier in this chapter).

Applying transitions to slides

Having cool effects between slides is a time-honored part of making presentations. Your slides can disappear behind virtual curtains, replaced by the next slide; they can fade into the next slide; they can be crumpled into a ball and displaced by the new slide. But they won't do any of these things unless you apply the animations in the first place.

You apply transitions in the Transitions view. Select the slide in the slide pane that you want to apply the transition to; then tap the Transition Effect to get a pop-over of available transitions (shown in Figure 6-14).

Figure 6-14:
The
Transition
Effect pop-
over in
PowerPoint.

Some transitions let you control some aspects of how they work, such as the direction they move in. If so, the Effect Options button is no longer grayed out; tap it to get a pop-over of available options for the current slide's transition effect.

If you want to apply a transition effect to all slides in your presentation, PowerPoint makes that easy:

1. **Select the slide whose transition you want to apply to all slides.**

2. **Tap the Apply to All Slides button in the Transitions view.**

Applying animations to slide objects

Use the Animations view's tools to apply transition-like special effects to individual objects on a slide — such as when you have several items you want to display, or "build," one by one — perhaps each bullet in a list, for example.

After you select the object to which you want to apply an animation effect, tap the button for the desired effect:

- **Entrance Effect:** Opens a pop-over (shown in Figure 6-15) with about three dozen effects that display when the object first appears, or builds, on the slide.

- **Emphasis Effect:** Opens a pop-over with a couple dozen effects that display after the object has appeared on screen. You use emphasis effects to highlight an object, such as this year's net profits, sometime during your presentation.

✔ **Exit Effect:** Opens a pop-over with the same effects available for entrance effects; the exit effect displays as you move to the next object in a build or, if there are no further builds, in the slide, when you advance to the next slide.

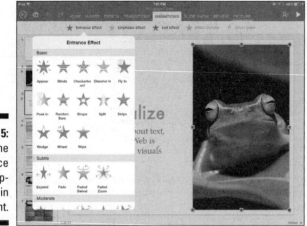

Figure 6-15: The Entrance Effect pop-over in PowerPoint.

To change the effect applied, select the object and tap the button for the type of effect you want to change; then select the new effect in the pop-over.

You can apply multiple effects to the same object: one of each type. For each effect applied, you'll see a square with a number in it. The square's outline is color coded to match the color of the effect (the color of the star to the left of each effect button) so that you know what type of effect it is.

The order in which you add emphasis effects determines the order in which they appear in your slide. (The order of entrance and exit effects depends on the order in which the objects were created.)

Tap an effect's number to display a contextual menu with the Delete option; tap Delete to remove that effect.

Previewing your presentation

To see how your presentation will look to an audience, tap the Play button (the right-facing triangle icon at the far right of the toolbar) to enter Presenter view. PowerPoint begins the slide show from whatever slide is currently active.

Swipe to the left to advance to the next build or slide. Swipe to the right to go back to the previous build or slide.

To exit the playback, tap and hold the screen until a toolbar appears at the top of the screen; then tap Exit Slide Show. Or just use the pinch gesture (pull your thumb and a finger together on the screen) to exit the playback.

Adding presenter notes

One PowerPoint tool you'll likely use a lot is Presenter View. This tool lets you add notes to each slide that only you will see during your presentation, and that you can also include in your printouts.

Chapter 19's "Presenting with PowerPoint" section explains this tool in detail, but here's the quick version of how to add notes:

1. **Tap the Presenter View button to see your slides (at the bottom); tap a slide to open it.**

2. **Double-tap in the notes area on the left side of the screen to enter or edit its text. (Tap the Notes button, the page icon, at the top if the text area is not visible.)**

3. **Repeat Steps 1 and 2 for each slide you want to add notes to or edit notes for.**

4. **Tap End Slide show at the upper left of the screen to return to the standard PowerPoint editing view.**

Chapter 7

Looking to Google Apps: Docs, Sheets, and Slides

*I*n addition to Microsoft Office and Apple's iWork, the other major office productivity suite is Google Apps: Docs, Sheets, and Slides. It's the least capable of the major iPad office sites by far, but many people do use Google Sheets and Docs on their computer browsers. So, having the corresponding apps on the iPad can be handy, even if you use iWork or Office as your main iPad office tool.

This chapter shows you what Google's apps for text, spreadsheets, and presentations can do for you.

Managing Documents in Google Apps

When you open a Google Apps app for the first time, you're asked to sign in with your Google account, such as your Google Drive or Gmail sign-in. After you're signed in, the app shows all available documents on the Google Drive cloud storage service (described in detail in Chapter 16).

When you work in Google Apps, you need a live Internet connection to work on documents stored in Google Drive, which is the default location for your documents.

By default, Google Drive displays documents as thumbnails in its Documents window, as shown in Figure 7-1. But tapping the List icon at the upper right of the toolbar changes the view to a list; then, when you're in List view, the button becomes the Thumbnails button, which you use to bring back the Thumbnails view.

When I say "documents," I mean not just the text documents in Google Docs but also the spreadsheets in Google Sheets and the presentations in Google Slides.

Tap the Menu button (the icon that shows three lines) at the upper left of the screen to choose what documents display:

- ✔ **Recent:** Shows all Google Docs and Microsoft Word files available in your Google Drive account and stored in the Google Docs app on your iPad.

- ✔ **Starred:** Shows only documents that you've marked as favorites. You mark these items within a document (not in the Documents window) by tapping its More button (the rotated . . . icon) and then tapping to select the Starred option there.

- ✔ **Incoming:** Shows documents being shared with you by others from their Google Drive accounts.

- ✔ **On Device:** Shows only documents stored on your iPad in a Google Apps app. You can move a document to your iPad by tapping the More button, either in a document itself or from a document's thumbnail or listing in the Documents window. Then you choose Keep on Device.

- ✔ **Google Drive:** Opens the Google Drive app and shows all documents stored in Google Drive.

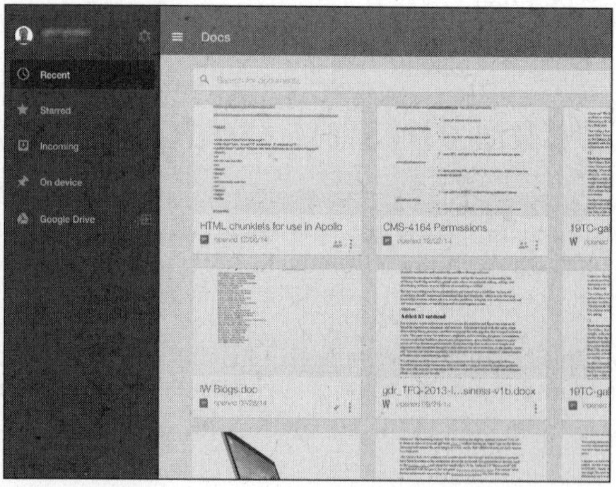

Figure 7-1:
The Documents window for Google Apps (Docs is shown here), with the Menu pane open at the left.

The Menu pane also has the Settings button (your account name). Tap it to open a form in which you can sign out of your Google account and into another, as well as require a password to open the current Google Apps app (handy for keeping work documents inaccessible to family members at home who use your iPad).

The More menu for each document in the Documents window is where you manage your documents:

- **Rename:** Lets you rename the document.
- **Share & Export:** Lets you send the file as an email attachment, print it, export to PDF or Microsoft Office format (via the Send a Copy option), save the file in the equivalent Google Apps format (if it's an Office file) or the equivalent Office format (if it's an Apps file), and share the file so that other users can edit it on Google Drive. *Note:* The Share & Export menu is also available within documents from the More menu there.
- **Keep on Device:** Stores the document on your iPad, so it's available even when you have no Internet connection.
- **Details:** Opens a pop-over that shows the format, last modification date, creation date, and storage location for the document.
- **Remove:** Deletes the file.

To create a document, tap the Add button (the big + icon) at the lower right of the Documents window. Give the document a name in the form that appears, and tap Create. None of the Google Apps apps support style sheets or templates, so you get a simple document with no such predefined formatting.

To open an existing document, tap its name. Then tap in the document to work on it. At the upper left of the screen, the Accept (the ✓ icon) button appears. Tap it to end your editing session (your changes are saved as you make them). The toolbar also has the Undo and Redo buttons that you use to roll back unwanted changes or reinstate rolled-back changes that you decide you want to make after all.

To return to the Documents window, tap the ← button that appears in the Accept button's place.

Editing with Google Docs

Google Docs has only basic editing capabilities for both Microsoft Word files and Google's own Google Docs format. When you open a document, the toolbar at the top of the screen shows those capabilities, which apply to selected text or, if no text is selected, to whatever you type next:

✔ **Boldface (B), Italics (*I*), and Underline (U):** These buttons apply the specified formatting, or remove it if that formatting is already applied.

Formatting (the A icon): This button opens a pop-over with two tabs (see Figure 7-2):

- *Text:* Lets you apply boldface, italics, underlines, strikethrough, paragraph style, font, text size, text color, and background (highlight) color. *Note:* The strikethrough and paragraph-style options are not available for Word files, just files in the Google Docs format.

- *Paragraph:* Lets you apply left, right, center, or justified alignment to paragraphs, as well as indent them, outdent them, indent or outdent their first lines, and make them into numbered or bulleted lists. There are no options for bullet or numbering styles. *Note:* The first-line indent and outdent options are available only for Microsoft Word files, not files in the Google Docs format.

The More button (the rotated . . . icon) opens the More pop-over, which has the Find & Replace option. This option opens the Find & Replace bar, shown in Figure 7-3, at the top of the screen, where you enter your search text and optional replacement text. Use the caret (^) button to search backward; the button with an upside-down caret symbol to search forward; the Replace button to replace the current found instance; and All to replace all occurrences. Tap the Close button (the X icon) to close the Find & Replace bar.

Figure 7-2:
The Formatting pop-over in Google Docs, with both tabs shown in this composite.

Figure 7-3:
The Find &
Replace bar
in Google
Docs.

The More pop-over also offers these options:

- **Page Preview:** This opens a separate window that shows how the document will look if printed. In that window, tap the More button to open the Actions pop-over, from which you can open the document in a compatible app, open it as a web page in Safari, or print it to your choice of an AirPrint– or Google Cloud Print–compatible printer. When done, tap the Close button (the X icon) to close that preview window.

- **Details:** Opens a pop-over that shows the format, last modification date, creation date, and storage location for the document.

- **Share & Export:** Lets you send the file as an email attachment, print it, export to PDF or Word (via the Send a Copy option), save the file in the Google Docs format (if it's a Word file) or the Word format (if it's a Docs file), and share the file so that other users can edit it on Google Drive.

- **Keep on Device:** Stores the document on your iPad, so it's available even when you have no Internet connection.

- **Star File:** Marks the document so that it appears in the Starred view in the Documents window, as described previously in the "Managing Documents in Google Apps" section.

If you're working with a Microsoft Word file, you get two additional options in the More pop-over:

- **Spellcheck:** If selected, this option causes Docs to highlight suspect words in your document with a red squiggly underline.

  You can tap a word to open the contextual menu and use the Replace option to see what words the iPad's internal dictionary suggests that you use instead.

- **Track Changes:** If selected, this option shows any revisions tracked previously, as well as opens a toolbar at the bottom of the screen with the Tracked Changes and New Comment buttons (see Figure 7-4):

  - *Tap Tracked Changes* so that the word On appears to its left to enable revisions tracking. A + button appears to the right of all revisions; tap it to get details as to the change, who made it, and when — plus buttons to accept or reject it.

- *Tap New Comment* to add a comment at the current location; a speech bubble icon appears to right of any comment.

- *Tap the caret (^) button and the upside-down caret button* to move back and forward, respectively, through comments and revisions.

- *Tap Hide* to hide the Track Changes toolbar — and to stop further revisions tracking until you reenable the Track Changes in the More pop-over.

The Track Changes check box in the More pop-over is obscured by the onscreen keyboard if the keyboard is visible. Hide the keyboard to see the Track Changes check box.

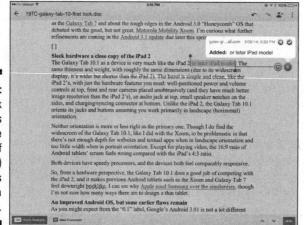

Figure 7-4: The Track Changes bar (at the bottom of the screen) and details about a revision.

Crunching Numbers with Google Sheets

Google Sheets is, like Google Docs, also basic, though it's adequate for simple uses such as expense reports and table- and list-style spreadsheets. As with all Google Apps, you create the new spreadsheet document in the Documents window, as described previously in the "Managing Documents in Google Apps" section.

Working with cell, rows, columns, and sheets

You tap a cell to select it, and can change the selection area using the resize handles at its upper-left and lower-right corners. The contextual menu options for selected cells are Cut, Copy, Clear, and (if more than one cell is selected) Merge. (If you select cells that were already merged into one, the contextual menu displays the Unmerge option.)

You tap a row or column using its label (row number or column letter), and use its selection handles (the circles in the center of the longest area) to expand or reduce the selected rows or columns. Tap a row or column header for a moment to get the contextual menu, whose options include Cut, Copy, Clear, Delete, and Merge Rows or Merge Columns.

To insert a column or row, tap the Insert button (the + icon) and choose Column Left, Column Right, Row Above, or Row Below to insert the desired item. You can also insert rows or columns from the contextual menu if rows or columns are selected: You'll see the Insert x Before and Insert x After options; x is replaced by the number of rows or columns currently selected.

You also can use the resize handle (the = icon for rows, ‖ icon for columns) on a selected row or column, to make a row or column larger or smaller.

At the bottom of the screen are tabs for each sheet in the workbook. Add a new sheet by tapping the Add button (the + icon) at the far right. Tap and drag tabs to rearrange them. Tap the menu button (the down-pointing triangle) on a tab to open the pop-over shown in Figure 7-5. Here, you can delete, duplicate, and rename the sheet, as well as freeze the panes to keep the number of rows at the top and columns at the left that you specify in place as you scroll through the rest of the document, so that any headers remain visible to help you know what you're working on as you navigate the spreadsheet.

Formatting a cell's content

Cells are where the action is in a spreadsheet, containing the data, formulas, and their visual presentation, a.k.a. formatting. The formatting-oriented options in Google Sheets's menu bar are, from left to right:

- ✔ **Color (the paint bucket icon):** This pop-over has two tabs — Text Color and Fill Color — that work the same way: Tap a color from the row at the top to display various shades of that color below. Tap the desired color to apply it.

✔ **Boldface (B), Italics (*I*), and Strikethrough (S):** These buttons apply the specified formatting, or remove it if that formatting is already applied. *Note:* The strikethrough option is not available for Microsoft Excel files, just for Google Sheets files.

✔ **Formatting (the A icon):** This pop-over, shown in Figure 7-6, has two tabs:

- *Text:* Lets you apply boldface, italics, underline, strikethrough, text size, text color, and font to text, as well as set its horizontal and vertical alignment within its cell. *Note:* The underline and strikethrough options are not available for Microsoft Excel files, just for Google Sheets files.

- *Cell:* Lets you apply fill color, borders, and number format (such as currency or date) to the cell, as well as enable text wrap. If multiple cells are selected, the Merge Cell switch converts them into a single cell, as well as lets you unmerge them later.

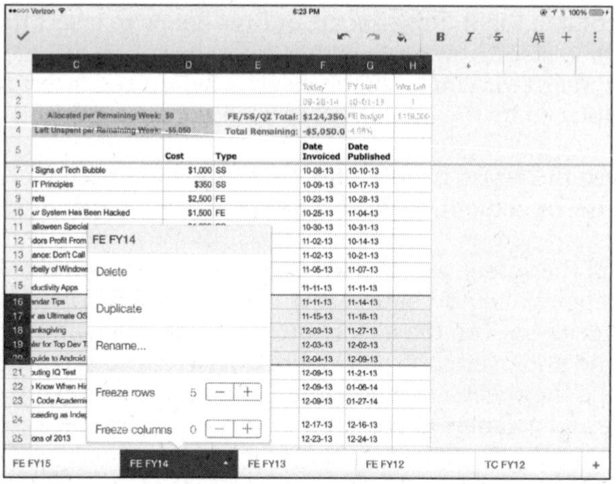

Figure 7-5:
The Track Changes bar (at the bottom of the screen) and the details of a revision shown in Google Docs.

So what about working with formulas? I hope you remember the various formulas you use in Excel or Numbers, because Google Sheets lets you enter them but offers no help with them, such as showing you the components of any formula, or even what formulas are available.

If you look closely at Figure 7-6, you can see a simple formula in the bar above the keyboard. When you tap into a cell to edit it, that bar is where you type in any formulas you want to use. You can tap a cell to enter its location in the formula, and you can use $ within cell addresses to lock the cell reference, as you can in Excel and Numbers. When you're done with your formula, tap the Accept button (the ✓ icon) to the left of the bar; the keyboard hides when you tap that button.

Figure 7-6:
The Formatting pop-over for Sheets, with its two tabs shown in a composite.

Engaging Them with Google Slides

The third component of Google Apps is the newest: Slides. It's the tool you use to create and modify slide show presentations.

Creating a presentation

After you create the new slide show in the Documents window, as described in the "Managing Documents in Google Apps" section, earlier in this chapter, you see the slide pane at the left, with a single slide in it for you to start working on. At the bottom of the pane is the Add Slide button (the slide-and-+ icon).

When you tap Add Slide, the Add Slide pop-over appears with a selection of master slides you can select, as Figure 7-7 shows. Choose a master slide to create a new slide based on it. *Note:* If you tap Add Slide and have a slide selected in the slide tray, the new slide is based on that selected slide and inserted after that selected slide.

If you have an existing slide that you want to use as the basis for a new slide, just tap and hold it for a second to open a blue toolbar at the top of the screen; then choose Copy. Move to the location where you want to insert the copy, tap and hold that slide, and choose Paste from the toolbar. (The toolbar also lets you cut and delete the slide, as well as select all slides for deletion or copying.) Tap the Accept button (the ✓ icon) at the far left of the toolbar to close the blue toolbar; then tap in a slide to resume editing.

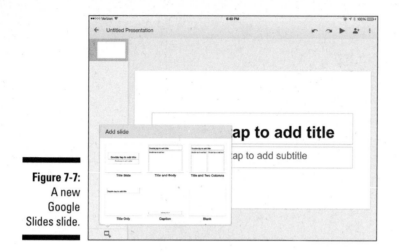

Figure 7-7:
A new
Google
Slides slide.

Double-tap the text boxes to enter or paste text.

The toolbar has the Insert button (the + icon). Tap it to open the Insert pop-over, which lets you insert a text box or insert any of more than 120 shapes.

If you are editing a PowerPoint file (rather than a Google Slides file), you can also import images from the iPad's Photos app or take a photo using the iPad's camera.

If you are editing a Google Slides file (rather than a PowerPoint file), you can also insert various types of lines and mathematical equations into your slides.

You can select and then drag objects within a slide, and use the resize handles in the center of each border segment to reshape it — as you would do on a computer when using PowerPoint or Keynote.

Tap an object and then tap it again after a moment to open the contextual menu, which has the usual options: Cut, Copy, Paste, and Delete.

Finally, you can rearrange slides by dragging them within the slides pane to a new location. To drag a slide, tap and hold it until it "pops up" to let you know it's selected. Don't release your finger from the screen, but drag it to a new location, releasing your finger when it's where you want it.

Applying formatting

You can fine-tune each slide as you create it, or you can get them all set up and then fine-tune them all in one sitting. Because Slides doesn't let you select multiple objects at one time, I suggest that you fine-tune each type of object first and then copy an object as needed for use in other slides so that all the formatting work gets copied, too.

If you select a text box, the Formatting pop-over (tap the toolbar's A icon to open it) provides the same Font and Paragraph tabs as Docs does for text files. Refer to the "Editing with Google Docs" section, earlier in this chapter, for details on the Formatting pop-over. If you select a text box, the formatting is applied to all its contents; if you select specific text within the text box, the formatting is applied only to that selection.

If you select any object, including text boxes, the Formatting pop-over has an additional tab: Shape, which is shown in Figure 7-8. It has just two options:

- ✔ **Fill Color:** Lets you set the background color for the shape.

- ✔ **Stacking Order:** Lets you control where an object appears relative to objects that overlap it. Objects in front of it obscure the object where they overlap; the object obscures other objects behind it where they overlap. Use the slider to move the object up or down the stack.

Figure 7-8:
The Shape tab in the Formatting pop-over in Google Slides.

Adding speaker notes

One tool you'd expect in a slide-show editor is Speaker Notes, which lets you add notes to your slides. Tap the More button (the rotated . . . icon) to open the More pop-over and then tap Show Speaker Notes to display the notes text at the bottom of the slides. For each slide, you can enter the notes in that box, as well as edit existing text.

In contrast to Keynote and PowerPoint, Google Slides doesn't let you view your speaker notes while presenting, so they don't do you any good while presenting. They might be useful for people you hand the presentation document to for later reference, though.

Chapter 8

Getting Productive with Alternative Writing Tools

In This Chapter

▶ Editing files from the top cloud storage services with UX Write Professional

▶ Editing and formatting documents in UX Write Pro

▶ Focusing on just the writing using Markdown formatting in Byword

Yes, Virginia, there are office productivity suites other than those from Apple, Microsoft, and Google. Chapters 5 through 7 cover those suites, but in this chapter I cover two tools that you should consider if you prefer to work with something different. Maybe those tools feel too complex for you, for example. Or you're the kind of person who wouldn't be caught in a big-box store like Walmart and doesn't want to work in the productivity app equivalent.

Staying Flexible with UX Write Professional

A big limitation in the Apple Pages, Google Docs, and Microsoft Word is that they steer you to their cloud storage services: iCloud Documents, Google Drive, and OneDrive and SharePoint, respectively. Many of us like using a service like Box or Dropbox as a network file share, where all the files we're working on are stored and accessible from any device (see Chapter 16). You can move files from these cloud storage services into Pages, Docs, or Word, but with only a few exceptions you can't open or save back to them directly, making version control tricky and cumbersome.

The $24.99 UX Write Professional doesn't have that limitation: In addition to working with files on your iPad, it can open files from and save them to the

Box, Dropbox, Google Drive, and Microsoft OneDrive services, as well as to any Internet-accessible file server that uses the WebDAV protocol. It also has some features that Pages, Docs, and Word don't.

You can get the free version of UX Write and subscribe to the Pro features for $1 per month. That's a great way to check out whether UX Write Pro is worth its full $24.99 price for your needs. Just note that the free UX Write is not very useful unless you subscribe or buy the Pro features, which you must do from within UX Write as an in-app purchase.

Accessing the cloud in UX Write Pro

UX Write Pro opens to the My iPad screen, which lists any documents stored locally on your iPad. To work with files stored elsewhere, tap the Storage Location button at the left side of the screen. In the form that appears, tap My iPad to open files and create new ones locally on the iPad; tap WebDAV or one of the four cloud storage services — Box, Dropbox, Google Drive, and Microsoft OneDrive — to move to that service's "drive." If you tap a service that you haven't signed into before, UX Write Pro will ask for your sign-in credentials for that service and then save them for future use.

You need a live Internet connection to work with cloud storage services or a WebDAV server.

When you open a storage location, you see a list of existing files and folders, as Figure 8-1 shows. Navigate to folders by tapping them; navigate back a level by tapping the < button at the upper left of the screen. Tap a filename to open it, and tap the + button at the upper right of the screen to create a new document or a new folder. (More on new documents shortly.)

A cloud icon to the right of a filename means that the file needs to be downloaded to your iPad so that you can work on it; after it's downloaded, the icon changes to one of a floppy disk (remember those?) and a cloud, so you know the file is stored on your iPad but is also synced to the cloud storage service. Figure 8-1 shows both icons.

UX Write Pro can open only two file formats: HTML and Microsoft Word. And for Word, it can open only the 2007 (or later) file format, which has the filename extension `.docx`, not the earlier Word 97 format (`.doc`).

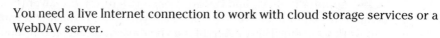

You can use more than one cloud storage service in UX Write Pro. Tap the Storage Location button at the left side of the screen to open the form displaying locations; then tap the icon for the one you want to work in now. What you can't do is work in multiple locations simultaneously; you have to move among them one at a time.

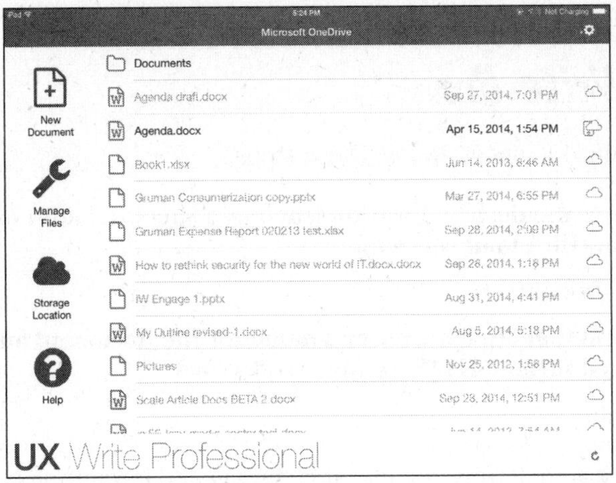

Figure 8-1:
UX Write
Professional
displays
your cloud
storage
service's
files and
folders.

To refresh the folder and file list, tap the Refresh button (the curved-arrow icon) at the lower right of the screen. Tapping that button updates the list with any changes made on the cloud storage service, such as from another device.

You can also move and delete documents, as well as create new folders, in your cloud storage account from within UX Write Pro; just follow these steps:

1. **Tap the Manage Files button at the left side of the screen.**

2. **Select the files and/or folders you want to work with by tapping the circles to the left of their names.**

   Tap Select All at the bottom right of the screen to select everything displayed.

3. **Tap the button at the bottom of the screen for the desired function: New Folder, Rename, Copy, Move, or Delete.**

   If you tap Copy or Move, a window appears showing available folders; tap the destination folder and then Move Here, or tap Cancel to cancel the operation. *Note:* If you tap New Folder, any selected files are not moved into it; you have to select them again and use Copy or Move to put files in the new folder.

4. **Tap Done when you're, um, done.**

Creating a new document in UX Write Pro

To create a new document, follow these steps:

1. **Navigate to the desired location (such as a specific folder on your iPad or at a specific cloud service).**

2. **Tap New Document.**

3. **In the form that appears, enter a name for the document and choose the desired format: HTML or Microsoft Word.**

4. **Tap Create.**

That's all there is to it! Now you can start typing and formatting to your heart's content.

Editing and formatting in UX Write Pro

You enter text the usual way, and you use the standard iPad selection tools to select, cut, copy, and paste text.

Select text and then tap the appropriate button from the menu bar at top to apply the desired formatting:

- **Formatting:** This menu usually displays Heading 1; tap it to select a different predefined paragraph style and apply that style to the current paragraph or selected text. The Formatting pop-over contains two really useful options:

  - *Direct Formatting:* Opens a new pop-over that lets you set the font, font size, text color, and text background color, paragraph justification, first-line indentation, line spacing, margins, and borders.

  - *Edit Styles:* Lets you edit the attributes of existing paragraph styles and create your own (via the green + button — something you can't do in Pages, Docs, or Word. In the screen that appears, you get the same formatting options as in the Formatting and Direct Formatting pop-overs. Figure 8-2 shows the style editor. Tap Done after creating or modifying a specific style, and tap Back to Document to return to editing mode.

- **Boldface (B), Italics (I),** and **Underline (U):** These buttons apply the specified formatting to the selected text.

✔ **Format (the A icon):** This button displays the Formatting bar, shown in Figure 8-3, below the menu bar. Not to be confused with the previously described Formatting pop-over, the Formatting bar has options for font, text size, text color, text background highlight color, line height, and paragraph alignment. *Note:* The ¶ "button" does nothing because it's really part of the four alignment buttons adjacent to it.

✔ **Lists (the bulleted-list icon):** This button displays the List bar, which has buttons for bulleted lists, numbered lists, outdenting, and indenting. There's also the No List button to remove all list formatting from the selected paragraphs.

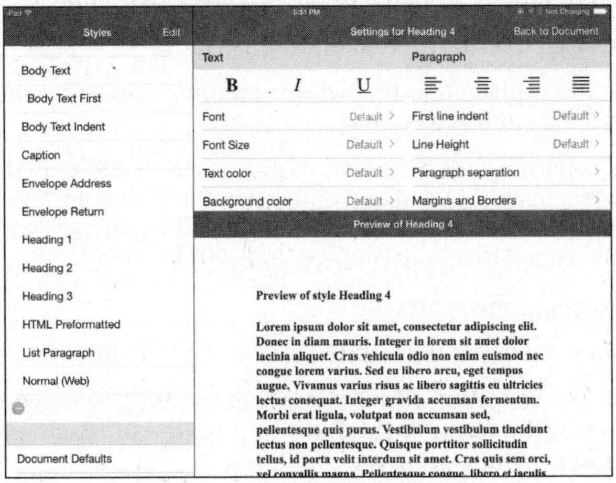

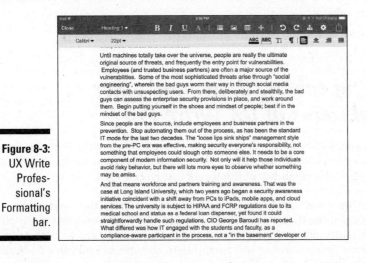

Figure 8-2:
UX Write Professional's style editor.

Figure 8-3:
UX Write Professional's Formatting bar.

The keyboard in UX Write has an extra row of keys at the top. The first two buttons on the left side are meant for text selection and highlighting, and work in concert with the arrow keys that appear on the same row when either is selected. I find the iPad's native text insertion and selection easier to deal with.

Searching for text in UX Write Pro

To search for text, follow these steps:

1. **Tap the Settings button (the gear icon) at the right side of the menu bar; then tap Find & Replace in the pop-over that appears.**

2. **Enter the search term in the Find field.**

   If you want to replace that text with something else, enter the replacement text in the Replace field.

   Optionally, set the Case Sensitive switch to On to find only text whose capitalization matches what you entered in the Find field. Likewise, set the Regular Expression switch to On if you want to search for text patterns, an advanced concept that you can learn more about at www.regexone.com.

3. **Tap OK to begin the search.**

   The first occurrence is highlighted in your document.

4. **Tap the Forward button (the right-facing triangle) to move to the next occurrence of the term, or the Back button (the left-facing triangle) to move to the previous occurrence.**

   Tap Replace to replace the found term with the replacement you specified previously.

5. **Tap Done when you're done searching.**

Inserting tables, links, and other special items in UX Write Pro

To insert a special item, such as a table or hyperlink, place the text cursor in your text where you want that item to be inserted and then tap the appropriate button from the menu bar at the top of the screen:

- **Image:** Inserts an image from the Photos app or from the current storage location (so that you can insert image files that aren't on your iPad!). You have options to change the image's width and to assign both an automatic figure number and a caption to the image. You can't do those things in Pages, Docs, or Word.

✔ **Table:** Inserts an empty table with the number of rows and columns that you specify. As with images, you can set the table's width and assign both an automatic table number and a caption to it.

✔ **Insert:** Opens a pop-over from which you can insert a web link (hyperlink), cross-reference, footnote, end note, table of contents, figures list, or tables list — these are particularly useful in academic and government documents.

Moving and deleting text with outlines in UX Write Pro

Another neat feature in UX Write Pro is the outline feature, which you access from the Outline button in the menu bar (the icon looks like an org chart). The top-level paragraphs (Heading 1) are shown; tap the disclosure triangle to see any subsections (Heading 2, Heading 3, and so on), as Figure 8-4 shows. Tap any section to jump to it.

But the real power of the outline tool is that it lets you delete or move the entire block of text in the current section, from its headline to the next one. (So be careful!)

To move a section, tap Edit and then drag a section's move handle (the icon of three lines). To delete an entire section, tap the red – icon. (To work with a subsection, tap the disclosure triangle next to a main section to see its subsections. No triangle means no subsections.) Tap Done when you're done.

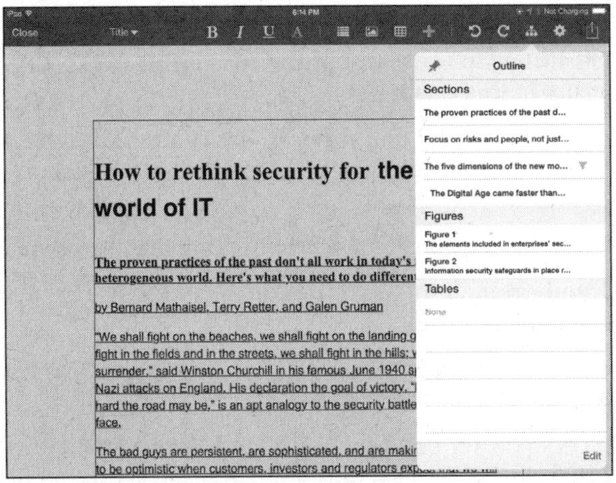

Figure 8-4: UX Write Professional's outline tool lets you move and even delete whole sections.

Sharing, printing, and other tasks in UX Write Pro's Share and Settings options

There are a few final areas of UX Write Pro you should know: the Share options and the Settings options, both of which are available in the menu bar through the standard iOS icons. The gear is for Settings and the square with the up arrow is for Share.

The Share pop-over has four basic options: Print, Create PDF, Email, and Open In. These options do the standard things that they do in any iPad app.

The Settings options are a little more interesting, as many are actually not settings but functions:

- **Manage Subscriptions:** If you are paying $1 per month for the Pro features, this is where you can see when your current subscription ends as well as renew your subscription.

- **Find & Replace:** Lets you find and optionally replace text, as described in the "Searching for text in UX Write Pro" section, earlier in this chapter.

- **Spell Check:** Launches the spell checker. After you tap it, all suspect words are highlighted in your document. You navigate them the same way you do a search, using the Back and Forward keys. Tap Replace to either change the highlighted text or, if it's correct, add the term to the dictionary so that UX Write doesn't flag it again. Tap Done in the menu bar when done.

- **Word Count:** Shows the character, word, and paragraph counts for the current document.

- **Styles:** Opens the same screen as tapping Edit Styles in the Formatting pop-over described in the "Editing and formatting in UX Write Pro" section, earlier in this chapter.

- **Page Layout:** Lets you set line spacing, how paragraphs are separated (first-line indent or space between), page size, and margins for the current document.

- **Language:** Sets the language for spell-checking for the current document.

- **Heading Numbering:** If this switch is on, headings are automatically numbered academic style.

- **Look & Feel:** Lets you set the text size, color scheme, and keyboard color for the app's user interface.

- **Language:** Lets you set the default language for UX Write Pro, for any document that doesn't have a different language set in the previous Language option.

✔ **Auto Correct:** Lets you turn on auto-correction for when you type, as well as specific automatic text substitutions as you type and customize the dictionary used for auto-correction.

✔ **Typesetting:** Affects how your document is printed and converted to PDF. WebKit is the default option, but its creators are slowly adding support for a widely used academic format called LaTeX that allows for more precise renderings. But when this book went to press, the LaTeX support was too minimal to really use.

Getting Down to Basics with Byword

UX Write Pro, described in the previous sections, is pretty sophisticated. But many people actually want a text editor that does less. For them, an editing format called Markdown is perfect: It does just the basics and nothing more, allowing writers to focus on writing, not formatting.

There are several Markdown editors for the iPad, but my favorite is the $4.99 Byword. It works with iCloud and Dropbox, so you can access your files — plain-text format (`.txt`) only — from other devices easily and keep them all synced.

And if you pay an additional $4.99 via the in-app purchase, you can publish your content to the WordPress, Tumbler, Blogger, and Scriptogram blogging platforms, as well as to the Evernote note-taking service.

The settings for Byword are minimal, and you access them via the Menu button (. . .) at the upper right of the screen. In the pop-over that appears, tap Preferences. You can configure the default font and the default text size, as well as enable or disable auto-capitalization, auto-correction, and spell checking. You can also enable Dark Theme, which displays your documents as white type on a black background — it's designed for those who write in bed and don't want to disturb their partners. (Seriously.)

That Menu pop-over is also where you print your document and export it to an HTML file, PDF file, email attachment (HTML, PDF, RTF, or plain text). You can also choose to copy the document in HTML format so that you can paste it into a website editor or other HTML editor. Finally, you can tap Share to open the iPad's standard Share pop-over, such as to send your text to a social network or open it in another app.

But as I said, Markdown editors like Byword are all about the writing. When you create or open a document in Byword, you get a spare interface — Byword has no menu bars, for example. All formatting controls are in the onscreen keyboard, as Figure 8-5 shows.

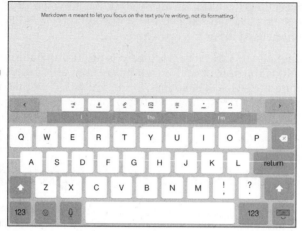

Markdown is meant to let you focus on the text you're writing, not its formatting.

Figure 8-5:
Byword
keeps
everything
simple, with
all format-
ting options
in the
keyboard.

To get the menu bar and its two options — File List and Menu — hide the keyboard using the standard iPad Hide Keyboard button in the lower right of the onscreen keyboard.

In that top row are the < and > keys to move your text cursor, just like their equivalents on a computer keyboard. (You can also just tap where you want to insert the text cursor.)

The Byword keyboard's top row is also where the formatting controls are (the white keys). From right to left, you tap the key to do the following:

- ✔ **Insert a tab character.**
- ✔ **Insert a heading character (#).** One # character means Level 1, two # characters means Level 2, three means Level 3, and so on.
- ✔ **Insert a link.** You enter the hyperlink text between the brackets ([]) and the URL itself between the parentheses.
- ✔ **Insert an image.** You enter the image caption between the brackets; the image's file path or URL goes within the parentheses — you can't actually insert an image itself here.
- ✔ **Apply a list.** Tap this key once to make the current paragraph a bulleted list, twice to make it a numbered list. A third tap removes the list attribute (but keeps the text).

✔ **Emphasize text.** Tap this to insert an emphasis indicator (*) at the beginning of the text you want to emphasize (make italic), and tap it again at the end of the text to insert a second emphasis indicator that tells a Markdown editor to revert to normal text. For example, "I *love* cheese" will present as "I *love* cheese."

✔ **Undo:** Undoes whatever you just did, whether formatting or typing.

A good guide to Markdown's formatting syntax is available from its creator, John Gruber, at `http://daringfireball.net/projects/markdown/syntax`.

Chapter 9

Taking Notes

Most of us jot stuff down on whatever we have at hand — the back of an envelope, a notepad, and a sticky note are all fair game. With an iPad, you can jot away in as many locations as you want, without needing to find pen and paper. And those notes can be shared across your devices and with other people with little to no effort. Try that with the back of an envelope.

People take notes differently, and there are as many note-taking apps as there are note-taking styles. In this chapter, I survey the field to cover the major bases.

Navigating Apple Notes

Your iPad comes with Apple's Notes app, and it's a very serviceable note-taker, if not one that is full of bells and whistles. It takes notes, lets you share them, and that's pretty much it.

Entering and formatting notes

To enter a note, tap the New Note button at the upper right of the screen, and begin typing, as Figure 9-1 shows. That's it! Your notes are saved automatically as you type them.

To delete a note, tap the trash- can icon at the upper right of the screen. It goes bye-bye!

You position and select text the usual iOS way, and use the standard menu that appears when you select text to cut or copy it, or paste in text previously cut or copied. Use the Insert Photo option to insert an image from the Photos app. (This option is not available for Exchange accounts; I explain how to use accounts later in this chapter.)

You also get several options if you have selected some text:

- **B/U:** Opens a submenu in which you choose Bold, Italics, or Underline.

- **Replace:** Shows suggested alternative words for the highlighted word; this is meant to get spelling suggestions.

- **Define:** Opens the iPad's built-in dictionary to show the word's meaning so that you know you're using it correctly. The pop-over that shows the definition has two options:

  - *Manage:* Lets you download foreign-language dictionaries to add to your Pad's linguistic knowledge

  - *Search Web:* Searches the web for that term so that you can get more information on it

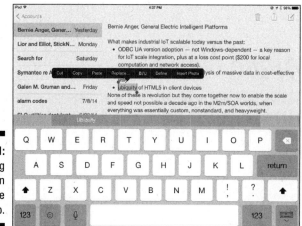

Figure 9-1:
Working with text in the Apple Notes app.

You may have noticed the bullets in the note in Figure 9-1. But you can't find a way to format bulleted lists in Notes on your iPad. So how did I get them? I cheated. I typed that note in Notes on my Mac, which does support such formatting. The iPad preserves that formatting, even if it can't create it.

On the left side of the Notes app, you see a list of your notes. Move to a note by tapping the desired note, whether to read it or edit it. Swipe up in that list to reveal the Search box, which you can use — wait for it! — to search for notes that contain the search term's text.

Sharing your notes

Say you're taking meeting notes to distribute to your team via email or have a shopping list to send your spouse via text message. From the note you want to share, tap the Share icon at the upper right of the screen and then tap the desired sharing method from the pop-over that appears: AirDrop, Message, Mail, Copy, or Print. (Copy copies the entire note into memory so that it can be pasted in another note or app.)

That's all there is to it.

Syncing your notes

Although it's not obvious, Notes does have the big advantage of syncing notes across any (or all) of several accounts you may have, including iCloud, Exchange (Server version 2007 or later), Gmail, and many IMAP email accounts. This means that notes entered in Notes are available on any device that uses the same accounts.

For example, if you create a note in your iCloud account, the Notes app on all your iPads, iPhones, and Macs have the same note available to them, and changes made on one device affect the note on all the others. Likewise, if you create a note in your Exchange account, you see that note in Microsoft Outlook as well on your PC or Mac.

The trick is that you need to use the same account for your notes on all devices for them to see that note. Most people have just one such shared account — usually their iCloud account — but you may also have another account that you use for your business, so your personal notes and business notes stay separate.

To move among accounts, tap the Accounts button at the upper left of the Notes screen. You get a list of active accounts at the left, as Figure 9-2 shows. Tap the account to see only that account's notes. New notes you create will be in that account until you switch accounts.

So what happens if you're in All Notes view, which shows all your notes from all accounts? I'm glad you asked: New notes are automatically created in the account you specify as the default for Notes in the Settings app. In the Settings app, tap Notes in the list at the left; then tap Default Account to specify that default account from the list of accounts that appears.

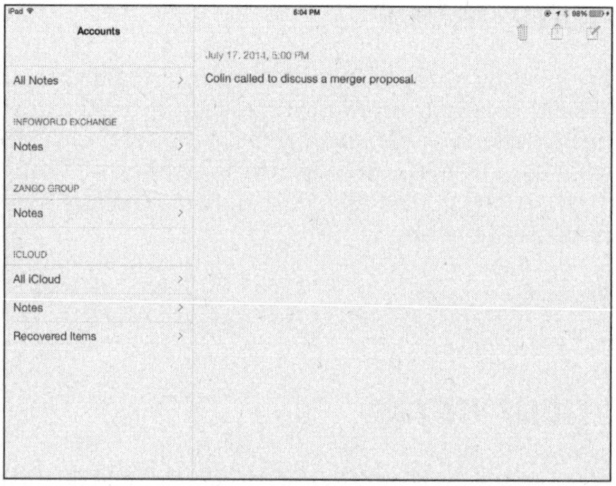

Figure 9-2:
Apple's
Notes lets
you use
multiple
accounts
for syncing
notes.

Getting to notes outside Apple's world

Most other services like Exchange and Google don't have note-taking apps that work like Notes. Instead, they typically make their notes available via email clients. But you won't see those notes in Apple Mail on an iPad, iPhone, or Mac — you must use the Notes app on those devices to see your notes.

Notes synced via an Exchange account appear in the Notes section of Microsoft's Outlook app for Windows and OS X, as well as in the Notes folder of Microsoft's Outlook Web Access webmail service. But Microsoft's OWA app (its version of Outlook for the iPad and iPhone) does *not* show these notes; you have to use Apple's Notes app instead.

Notes synced via a Google account show up in the Notes folder in the Gmail app for your Android device, iPad, or iPhone. And you see them if you read your Gmail on Google's website from your browser, as well as in the Notes folder in Outlook for Windows or the Mac.

Ditto for IMAP-synced notes: You see them in the Notes folders in Outlook, Gmail, and Android's Email app, as well as when reading email on the web at sites like Yahoo! and Outlook.com.

So how do you get Notes accounts? You also find these in the Settings app, but in the Mail, Contacts, Calendars screen. Tap an account that you want to sync notes through; then set the Notes switch to On. Do the same for any iOS device you have, as well as in OS X's Internet Accounts system preference. If an account doesn't have a Notes switch, it can't sync notes.

Exploring Evernote

Evernote is one of the most popular note takers out there. It started as a web application but now has apps for the iPad, Mac, Windows PC, and other devices. You set up an Evernote account and then sign in with it on each device you use Evernote on. That way, all your devices sync their notes, and every device has the current set of notes.

Evernote is popular because it supports both notes and reminders, and lets you send notes to your Evernote account via email, which makes the process of adding information you want to refer to later very easy.

The Evernote app is free, and the service's free version meets most people's needs. You can upgrade to the premium service for $45 per year. Its capabilities include PDF annotation, whiteboarding during meetings, and searching within documents.

Creating notes

When you first open Evernote on your iPad (after you've signed in), you get the very simple All Notes screen that displays a grid of "cards" for your existing notes. Although simple, that display isn't that easy to navigate. But you can get a more compact view in an easier-to-navigate list format by tapping the elephant icon at the top left of the screen. The resulting List view is shown in Figure 9-3.

In List view, tap the icon for the type of note you want to create:

- **Text:** Creates a simple note.
- **Camera:** Takes a photo with the iPad's camera and saves it as a note.
- **Photos:** Imports images from the Photos app and saves them as a note.

✔ **Reminder:** Sets up an alert that sends you an email at a specified date and time, as well as presents an alert message on your iPad.

✔ **List:** Creates a note with check boxes so that you can indicate items that are completed as you do them.

You can change the color scheme for the List view by tapping Settings and then tapping Customize Home Screen in the pop-over that appears.

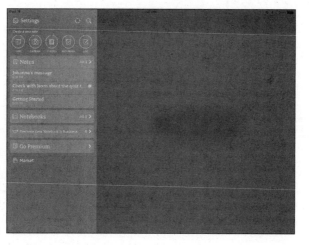

Figure 9-3:
The List
view in
Evernote.

Editing notes

As you add notes, they display in the Notes section below the welcome screen's icons. Tap a note to open its details as well as edit it.

If you select text, you can cut, copy, and paste it, apply basic character formatting, get suggestions for alternative words, and look up a word in the iPad's dictionary — the standard text options on the iPad.

Changes you make are saved as you type. Other notes appear at the left, so you can open a different one.

Figure 9-4 shows a note and the options you get at the top of the screen for it:

✔ **Add Reminder:** Converts an existing note to a reminder or lets you edit an existing reminder for that note. If your note already has a reminder, you see the date for the reminder next to the Add Reminder icon.

✔ **Attach Image or Audio:** In the menu that appears, you can have Evernote import an image from the Photos app or take one using the iPad's camera. The Audio option tells Evernote to use the iPad's microphone to record whatever it can hear.

✔ **Search:** Searches the current note for whatever text you enter.

✔ **More (the . . . icon):** Opens a menu where you can open the standard iOS Share pop-over for sharing and printing, simplify or remove the text formatting of the current note, and delete the note.

Figure 9-4:
A note in
Evernote.

You also the Info icon (the *i* in a circle) in the upper-right area of a note. Tap this icon to get the option to add tags to your notes. Tags are basically labels that you use to help identify similar notes. In List view, you find the Tags button below the list of notes; tap it to display all the tags you've used. Tap a tag to see all notes using it.

Evernote lets you create notebooks, which are essentially folders for notes. By default, your notes are added to the All Notes view. If you want to work in a specific notebook, tap the Home icon (the elephant head) and then tap Notebooks. You then get a list of existing notebooks as well as the New Notebook option to, well, create a new notebook.

To move a note into a different workbook, tap the Workbook name right above the note when viewing or editing it, as you can see in Figure 9-3, and choose a different workbook for it.

Adding notes to Evernote via email

One of the cool features in Evernote is the capability to email it a note and have it added to your workbooks, with the email's information retained. You get a special email address to send notes to, which you can find by signing into Evernote from a browser and opening your account settings. When you send email to that address, you add to the end of the subject line the codes Evernote uses to figure out what to do with the email you sent:

✔ *@notebook*: Notes goes into your default notebook unless you specify one using a code at the end of the subject line.

For example, to send a note to the Work Priorities notebook, add the code @Work Priorities to the end of the subject line.

✔ *#tag:* Add as many tags as you want at the end of the subject line, each indicated with the # symbol. Tags must be one word each.

✔ *!reminder:* Entering just an exclamation point (!) at the end of the subject line sets up a reminder without an alarm. To add an alarm to the reminder, add the word *tomorrow* (such as !tomorrow) or a date (such as !2015/08/15).

Sketching with PhatPad

A frustration that many people have with taking notes on an iPad or a computer is that you have to type them. This means that you can't make sketches. But the iPad has a touchscreen, so it does let you draw with your finger or a stylus. That's where the $7.99 PhatPad comes in: It's a note taker that lets you create drawings in your notes as well as record audio in your notes. How cool is that?

Working with the pen

Drawing is easy: Just start drawing with your finger or stylus on the blank screen that appears when you tap the + icon at the top of the file list. Just be sure that the Draw button (the pen icon at upper right) is active, which it is by default.

To delete lines and shapes that you've drawn, tap the Erase button (which looks sort of like a chalkboard eraser) and then draw through whatever you want to delete. If the eraser touches part of a line or curve, it erases the whole object.

You can change the thickness and pen color of the "pen" by tapping the palette icon at the upper right of the screen. The icon in the center of the pen wheel that appears toggles between pen thickness and color.

Navigating your notes

To navigate PhatPad, tap the Grabber tool (the hand icon); now your gestures don't draw anything, but instead do the iPad's standard scroll, rotate, expand, and pinch gestures. Swiping horizontally moves you among pages, as does tapping the < and > icons on either side of the current page number at top.

Notes are saved automatically as you work with them. To create a new note, tap the Add button (the + icon) at the upper left of the screen. To see previously saved notes, tap the Files button (the icon of two pages) next to it.

Writing by hand

What PhatPad can't do is use the iPad's onscreen keyboard to type. To write text, you turn on its handwriting recognition, shown in Figure 9-5. To do so, you tap Insert Text in the Tools pop-over, which you access via the Tools button (the wrench icon) in the upper left of the screen.

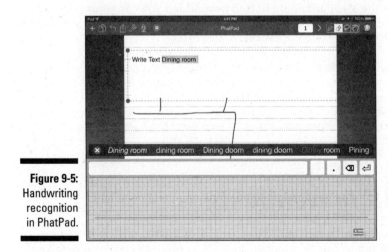

Figure 9-5:
Handwriting recognition in PhatPad.

You can convert existing handwritten text to typewritten text by selecting it with the Selection tool (the lasso icon): Draw a rectangle around the handwriting, and when you release your finger from the screen, a menu appears. Tap Convert to Text. The Selection tool also lets you change the pen ink and thickness for any selected drawings, handwriting or not, as well as delete, copy, cut, and move the contents.

Adding audio to your note

To add a sound recording to your note, tap the Record button (the microphone icon) at the upper left of the screen; then begin speaking or playing the audio you want added to the current note. You can tap Pause to pause the recording and then tap Pause again to resume.

Tap Stop when done, or Cancel (the X icon) to throw away that recording. If you do save the recording by tapping Stop, the Record button becomes the Playback button (speaker icon); tap it to play your recording.

You can have only one recording per note.

Sharing and syncing

PhatPad has the standard Share button from which you can print your note, email it, send it to Evernote, export to PDF, send to other PhatPad users over Wi-Fi, and share with social networks.

It can also sync files to the Box, Dropbox, Google Drive, and Microsoft OneDrive cloud storage services, but you have to manually initiate that syncing. To do so, go to the files list and tap the Sync button (the icon of two curved arrows); then choose the desired service to sync with. I recommend that you periodically sync your notes to your cloud storage service so that you have a backup.

Noting It All in Notability

The $4.99 Notability is similar to PhatPad in that it lets you sketch and record audio in your notes. But Notability also lets you type via your onscreen keyboard — at the expense of not having PhatPad's handwriting recognition. So, if you see yourself as a mostly typing kind of note taker, Notability is a better option than the keyboardless PhatPad.

Storing, sharing, and organizing notes

Notability can store notes to Box, Dropbox, Google Drive, and any storage server that uses the WebDAV protocol to provide file access. It also supports iCloud, so your notes are automatically available to your other iOS devices that have Notability installed. You set up your cloud storage accounts and turn on iCloud in the Settings window; in the main Notability screen (where your notes are listed), tap the gear icon.

The Share icon in that main screen, shown in Figure 9-6, lets you email, print, and otherwise share your notes to or with other apps (via Open In), devices (via iTunes), and the supported cloud storage services.

The Share icon is also available within a note to share that note.

Notability has the concepts of dividers and subjects, which are basically ways to categorize your notes. A subject holds multiple notes, and a divider holds multiple subjects. To create a divider or subject, tap the + icon at the upper left of the main screen; then tap Create Subject or Create Divider, as desired.

To create a note, tap its subject and then tap the pen icon at the upper right of the screen. To import a note from a cloud storage service, tap the Import button to the left of the pen icon.

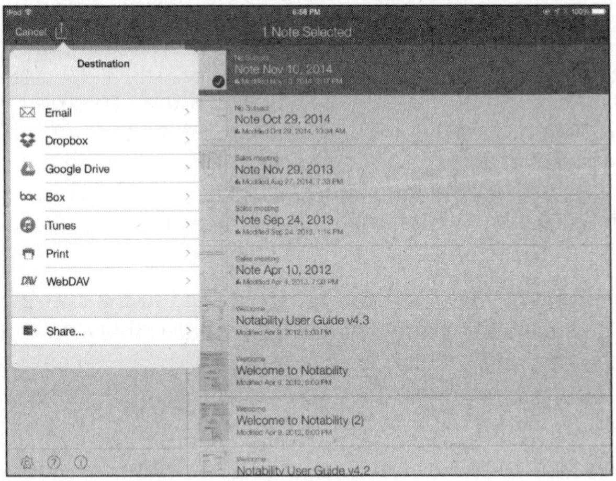

Figure 9-6: Notability's file list is where you can share notes with others.

Working on a note

When a note is open, you see a row with the following icons at the top that let you choose the type of content to add or edit, as Figure 9-7 shows:

- ✔ **T:** Activates the keyboard; tap it and then tap the screen to be able to type. The text begins at the far left of the screen and doesn't wrap around any drawings. To create a text box that you can move and resize, tap and hold until the +Text Box menu appears; then tap it to create a text box to type in.

- ✔ **Pen:** Activates the drawing mode; use your finger or a stylus to draw anywhere onscreen. Tap the icon twice to change the thickness and color of the pen's "ink."

- ✔ **Marker:** Activates the highlight drawing mode. It works just like the Pen icon, except that the "ink" is translucent, so whatever is under what you draw with it is still visible.

Unless you create a text box or use the drawing tool described later, text and drawings can't be moved after they've been inserted.

- ✔ **Eraser:** Lets you erase an object by swiping over it.

- ✔ **Scissors:** Lets you draw a marquee around objects and then tap the screen to get a menu through which you can cut, copy, or delete the selection or apply a new "ink" color and/or thickness to it.

- ✔ **Hand:** Lets you scroll through your pages. (You can stay in one of the other icon modes and scroll by using two fingers at the same time.)

- ✔ **Microphone:** Lets you record audio to add to your note. Tap it to start recording; tap it again to stop. An indicator shows the total recording time for all the recordings in the current note. Each note can have multiple recordings attached to it. After you stop recording audio, an arrow icon appears next to the microphone; tap it to get playback controls as well as the gear icon, which opens a pop-over where you can manage (read: delete) recordings.

- ✔ **+ (plus sign):** Lets you insert images from the Photos app; a photo taken by the iPad's camera; a drawing (called a figure) that you can move within the note; and a web clip (a screen shot of a web page that you can tap to open the actual web page). This icon also lets you add sticky notes.

- ✔ **Pages:** Lets you show or hide a list of pages for the current note.

To return to the main screen, tap the Back button (the < icon) at the upper left of the screen. Your notes are saved automatically as you work on them.

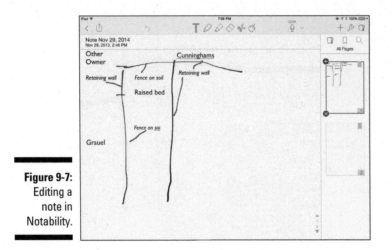

Figure 9-7:
Editing a
note in
Notability.

Annotating Notes with OneNote

Microsoft Office users likely know and use OneNote, the note-taking
companion to Word, Excel, and PowerPoint. But unlike those apps, the free
OneNote app does not require you have an Office 365 subscription to use it
for business purposes. However, you do need a free Microsoft account, such
as from a Windows 8 PC, OneDrive account, Hotmail or Outlook.com account,
or Office 365 account.

Working with notebooks

As with Office for iPad, OneNote opens and saves its notes only to and from
Microsoft's OneDrive cloud storage service and its SharePoint enterprise
storage server. Both are commonly used in business, so OneNote works well
as your business note taker, separate from your personal notes that you may
take in another note-taking app.

In OneNote's Notebook list, shown in Figure 9-8, you'll see each notebook
you've created, and you can tap Create Notebook to create more. You can
think of a notebook as a file folder for your notes. If you create a notebook,
a window opens in which you give it a name and select where the note is
stored, assuming that you have multiple OneDrive accounts (such as a personal one and a business one). Most people have just one, so the option to
select a location won't give you a choice.

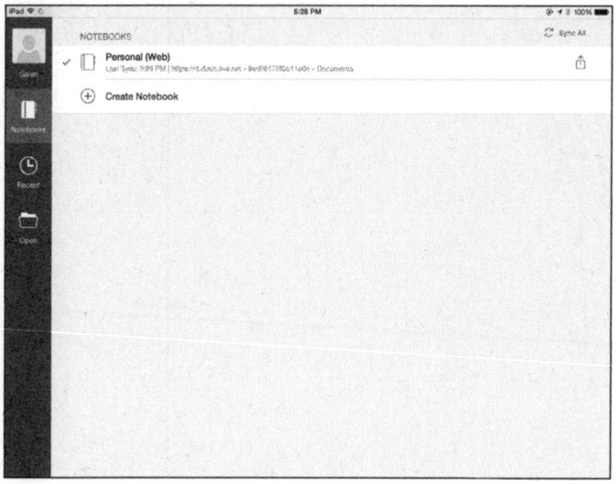

Figure 9-8:
OneNote's
Notebook
list.

Be careful how you name your notebook. You can't edit its name on the iPad after the notebook has been created. You have to rename it using the OneNote app on your PC or Mac.

To open a notebook, just tap its name in the Notebooks list. After you've opened a notebook, you can go back to the Notebooks list by tapping the Back button at the upper left of the screen (the ← icon).

If you want to open a notebook that's not already on your iPad, you need Internet access to get notebooks from OneDrive or SharePoint, which is where they're stored. Tap the Open button in the Notebooks list and navigate to the desired notebook; then tap it.

To sync the iPad and OneDrive/SharePoint versions of your notebooks when you have an Internet connection, tap the Share icon to the right of a note-book in the Notebook list and tap Sync Now in the pop-over that appears.

The equivalent Sync This Notebook button is also available after you open a notebook from the File pop-over, which you open using the File button (the icon of an arrow intruding onto the left side of a page) at the upper left of the screen.

Working with notes

When you open a notebook, you see the distinctive Microsoft toolbar at top, with tabs for Home, Insert, and View, and icon buttons for the current tab's options immediately below. Below that is a set of tabs, including Quick Notes, and Unfiled Notes. You can create more tabs by tapping the + icon. Each tab contains notes pages — which is what you'd probably just call a note. Basically, each page is a separate note, tabs can store several pages each, and notebooks can store several tabs' worth of notes.

Tap the tab you want to add a note in, or see a note in; then, on the right side of the screen, tap Add Page to create a new note in that tab or the name of the desired page below to open it. Figure 9-9 shows a note with these user interface elements visible.

Every note has a title, which you can edit, at top, followed by an automatically created date and time below it, which you cannot edit. Below that is the free space for your notes. Tap in that space and begin typing. Unlike most note-taker apps, OneNote lets you have multiple text boxes in a note, so if you tap elsewhere in that white space, you're adding a new text box there. This setup lets you organize your text visually on the page rather than in strict vertical order such as in Apple's Notes. Figure 9-9 shows a second text box being added to a note.

Figure 9-9:
Entering a second text box in a note in OneNote.

Formatting notes

If the Home tab is active, you get the text-formatting options for notes in OneNote. They should be familiar to you if you use Word. They are, from left to right, Font, Text Size, Boldface, Italics, Underline, Strikethrough, Text Color, Highlight Color, Bulleted List, Numbered List, Outdent, Indent,

Alignment, and Styles. But there are four buttons that are probably new to you unless you use OneNote on your computer:

- ✔ **To Do:** Adds a check box in front of the current paragraph so that you can check off tasks as they are completed.

- ✔ **Important:** Adds a star icon in front of the current paragraph to indicate that it's, well, important.

- ✔ **Question:** Adds a ? (question mark) icon to mark a paragraph as a question, perhaps containing items you want to review or ask about in a meeting.

- ✔ **Tag:** Lets you add a tag to the current paragraph to indicate its meaning to you. There are 27 such tags available, including Remember for Later, Definition, and Source for Article. Each tag displays as its own icon in front of the current paragraph.

Using other OneNote features

The Insert tab lets you insert tables, pictures (from the Photos app), photos (from the iPad's camera), hyperlinks, and the current date.

If you're using iOS 8.1, the File button in the Insert tab supports iCloud Documents, so you can insert documents stored in that Apple storage service, as well documents stored in other iOS-compatible cloud storage services such as Box, Dropbox, and Google Drive. (Chapter 16 explains how to use iCloud Documents.)

The View tab lets you change the page's view level, change its page color, and enable the spell-checker as you type.

The top menu has five other options worth noting:

- ✔ **Undo** (the left-facing curved arrow icon)

- ✔ **Redo** (the right-facing curved arrow icon)

- ✔ **Search** (the magnifying-glass icon)

- ✔ **Share** (the person icon), which lets you email the note as a PDF file, email the link to the note on OneDrive, or copy the link to the note on OneDrive to paste into a text message or other app's text

- ✔ **Full Screen** (the icon of two arrows), which hides and shows the toolbars

Keeping It Simple with Notes for Box

Box is a popular cloud storage service (see Chapter 16) that recently added its own note-taking feature, storing its notes with all your other documents on Box.

To use Notes for Box, you have to have a live Internet connection — the notes are created and stored on Box's servers, not on your iPad.

In the Box app, open the side menu by tapping the icon of a ← in a box at the upper right of the screen. Then tap the + icon at the top of that menu. Now tap Create New Box Note, and wait a few seconds for the tool to load.

What you get is a very simple note-taking tool, shown in Figure 9-10, that has minimal formatting features: There are buttons to create bulleted, check-marked, and numbered lists, and to indent and outdent paragraphs. That's it. You can use formatting such as boldface, italics, and underlines by selecting text and using the standard iPad text menu's **B/U** menu option. That's it!

Notes consist of a title and the note text. No more.

In the note's side menu, you have options to copy, move, rename, and delete the file. Your notes appear in the Box file list with your other documents.

You may not see Box notes in your Box Sync folder on your computer. If not, you can see (and edit) them in your browser after signing into your Box account at the Box website.

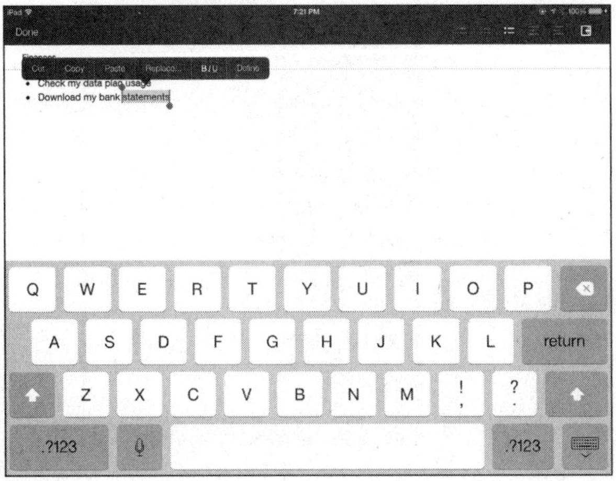

Figure 9-10:
A note in
Notes for
Box.

Recording It with WaveRecorder and TapNotes

Sometimes you don't want notes as much as a recording, whether for review later or transcription. As the commercial says, there's an app for that.

Using WaveRecorder

My favorite recording app is the $1.99 WaveRecorder. You don't record notes with it; you record conversations, meetings, lectures, and so on.

To start recording, you tap the red Record button, which creates a new "note" and begins recording. If you leave the app to do something else, the recording continues, and you see the iPad's status bar turn red to let you know that recording is still on.

In the screen that appears while you are recording (see the left side of Figure 9-11), you see fields for the note title and any notes you want to add to it, such as who attended. You can type in your own meeting notes as an adjunct to the recording if desired.

The WaveRecorder app does not display in landscape mode, so the screen is always in portrait orientation.

Figure 9-11: Recording in Wave-Recorder (left) and Wave-Recorder's list of saved recordings (right).

The text's default is quite small, but you can increase it to something readable using the Text Size slider at the bottom of the screen.

To pause a recording, tap the Record button again. To stop the recording, tap the black Stop button. When the recording stops, you get a screen that lists all the recordings, as the right side of Figure 9-11 shows. Tap a recording to see any notes in the window at right; tap the Play button to hear the recording. The scrub bar at the top lets you move within the audio file so that you can skip to other locations in the audio.

WaveRecorder saves audio files in Apple's AIFF format. If you need to convert it to the common MP3 format, you can do so in iTunes. Choose File⇨Open to import the file into iTunes. Open the iTunes Preferences dialog and click Import Options in the General tab. In the Import Using menu, choose MP3 Encoder. Click OK; then click OK again to close the Preferences dialog. In the music library, right-click the audio file and choose Create MP3 version. You can drag that MP3 file to the Mac Desktop or Windows File Explorer to create copy to share with others. (AIFF is better for importing music than MP#, so be sure to change Import Using back to AAC Encoder when done.)

At the bottom of the screen are several buttons that act on whatever recording is selected:

- **Web Access:** Makes the audio recording available to your computer's browser over Wi-Fi using a URL that displays.
- **Email:** Sends the audio file to an email address that you specify.
- **Trim:** Lets you edit out portions of the audio file.
- **Delete:** Deletes the audio file.

Using TapNotes

WaveRecorder's developer hasn't updated the app in years, which is fine except for one aspect: Its capability to connect to Dropbox no longer works. I haven't found another recording app as good as WaveRecorder, but if you want something more modern, a decent alternative is the 99¢ TapNotes, shown in Figure 9-12.

In TapNotes, you can type in notes as the app records; you can also pause and restart recordings, and keep recording when you're using other apps. You can even add time markers to your notes so that you can find specific segments more easily later.

Figure 9-12:
Recording in
TapNotes.

But TapNotes doesn't share files as easily as WaveRecorder does: You have to use Open In from the Share sheet to copy the MP4 (not MP3) audio file to a cloud storage service such as Box or Dropbox; then copy, email, or otherwise share it from there.

TapNotes also stores audio files in a calendar view, associating them to a date. It's not so easy to find recordings whose dates you don't recall, but you can open a side menu that lists all your recordings in one place.

Chapter 10

Tackling Tasks and To-Dos

*W*hen you rely on an iPad, you tend not to have paper or a place to keep those reminder lists. But several apps are available to take the notepad's place as well as sync your tasks or to-do items (they mean the same thing) to other devices. These apps can even issue you reminders automatically.

In this chapter, I cover a variety of apps that help you manage your to-do items and tasks, from simple lists to complex projects.

Running through Reminders

Your iPad comes with Apple's own to-do manager, Reminders. Like Apple Mail, Calendar, and Notes, you can set Reminders up to sync tasks with several services you may have, including your iCloud and Microsoft Exchange/Office 365 accounts. That way, your to-do lists stay synchronized across all your devices.

You set up Reminders syncing in the Settings app's Mail, Contacts, Calendars screen. Tap an account to see what services it can sync; if you see Reminders, set the switch to On to enable that service's to-do items in the Reminders app.

I have to say that beyond its support for multiple accounts, Reminders is a pretty basic to-do app. Each task consists of a single entry, so you can't put multiple items together, such as for a list of issues you want to make sure are addressed in a meeting or a list of groceries to get on the way home. Instead, each such item is a separate reminder.

Using the accounts list

Most iPad users don't realize they have accounts, but everyone has at least one: his or her iCloud account. A business user likely has additional accounts set up, at least for email — you very likely have an Exchange account set up, for example, to access your work email and calendars, as Chapter 12 explains. An account is a central repository that all your devices — computers, tablets, and smartphones — can access to get services such as email, calendars, contacts, notes, and to-do items.

By using different accounts for personal and business needs, as Chapter 3 recommends, you keep all your data available to you on the iPad, but in a way that keeps them separate from each other. Should you leave your company and your account is deactivated, your iPad no longer can get those services — but your personal data from your other accounts are unaffected.

Many of Apple's apps, including Reminders, thus are built to support multiple accounts. In Reminders, you can see the to-do items for just one account at a time, so you will likely find yourself switching among accounts. That's easy enough: Tap the accounts list on the left side of the screen — each account appears there — to see its items or add an item to it.

To add lists to an account, follow these steps:

1. **Tap the account you want to add the new list to in the accounts list at the left of the screen.**

2. **Tap Add List at the bottom left of the screen.**

3. **In the pane that appears at right (shown in Figure 10-1), give the new list a name.**

   Optionally, choose the desired color for the list's name by tapping the desired color's circle button (a row of them appears under the list's name, as Figure 10-1 shows). Color coding can help you more easily distinguish, say, work lists from personal lists.

4. **Tap Done.**

Figure 10-1:
Adding a
list to an
account in
Reminders.

You can change the color of the task later, like so:

1. **Tap the list in the accounts list.**

2. **Tap the Edit button in the tasks list in the right pane and then tap Color to select a different color.**

3. **Tap Done.**

Unfortunately, Reminders doesn't let you see all your to-do items in one list; you can see only a single list's items at any one time. Well, not quite: You *can* see all your to-do items that have a reminder alarm set, across all your lists, in the Scheduled list available toward the bottom of the left pane.

You can manage your accounts' lists by tapping the Edit button at the bottom of the accounts list. Tap the Delete button (the – icon in a red circle) to delete a list and all its to-do items. Drag a list's Reorder icon (the three bars) to move it to a new position within the accounts list.

Creating to-do items in Reminders

To create a new to-do item, tap the list it should go in and then tap in the blank area of the tasks pane on the right of the screen. Type your task details. That's it!

Well, that *can* be it if you want, but as you enter your task's description, notice the Details button (the *i* icon) that appear to its right. You can tap this icon to get more options in the Details pop-over, as Figure 10-2 shows. Within this pop-over, you can enable alarms, set an alarm date and time, and make it a repeating alarm. You can also indicate the task's priority, move it to a different list, and add notes to the description. Tap Done when, um, done.

You'll get the notifications of any alarms on your iPad and other iOS devices using the same account. You can control how those notifications appear in the iPad's Settings app. Tap Notifications and then tap Reminders to get a set of options for how the Reminder alert will appear, such as whether they display in the Lock screen, what sound (if any) they play, and how they appear onscreen (as a fleeting banner at top or in an alert box that you must manually dismiss to continue working).

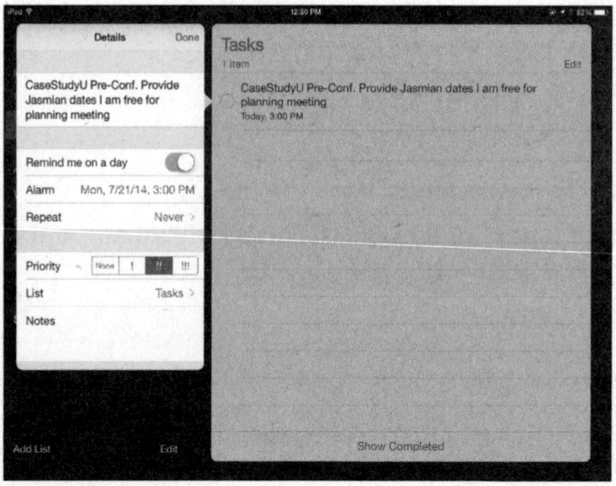

Figure 10-2:
Setting an alarm for a to-do item in Reminders.

Editing and marking to-do items

It's as easy to edit a task as it is to create it: Just tap inside the item's text to edit it as you would text in any app. Tap the Details icon to open the pop-over for Alarm and other settings to adjust those.

To mark a task as completed, tap the circle to its left. Completed tasks disappear from the standard Reminders view, but you can tap Show Completed at the bottom of a list's task pane to see those you previously marked as completed.

Sharing to-do lists

Reminders lets you share to-do lists with other people — that is, as long as they use Reminders, they have an iCloud account, and your list is in iCloud. To share a list, follow these steps:

1. **Tap a list in the iCloud account section of Reminders.**

2. **Tap the Edit button in the tasks pane at the right.**

3. **Tap Sharing to open a pop-over in which you add the name of a person (or multiple people) to share the list with.**

4. **Tap Done when you're done.**

All the people you share with will see this list in Reminders on their iPad, iPhone, or Mac, or from another device if they go to iCloud.com in a browser. They can add items, mark them off, and otherwise manage them. Sharing lists is great for a family, work group, or club to keep everyone in sync as to what needs to be done and what has been done.

Sifting Tasks with Toodledo

The $2.99 Toodledo brings you more control over your tasks than Reminders, but it can sync only to the Toodledo app on your other devices (iOS, Android, and BlackBerry) or to PCs or Macs via the Toodledo website at a browser. That is, it doesn't use accounts like iCloud or Exchange to sync its data across your devices, but instead Toodledo uses its own website as its hub.

Also, Toodledo can't share task lists. Its Share sheet, for example, can share only an individual task (as if it were a note), and only via Twitter or email. And it can't set up shared task lists as Reminders can. (Chapter 17 explains how to use iOS's standard Share sheet capability.)

The real power in Toodledo resides in its Settings screen (shown in Figure 10-3), which you get to by tapping Settings at the bottom of the screen. In the Settings screen, you decide which fields appear for your tasks:

1. **Tap Fields & Defaults in the left pane.**

   In the Fields & Defaults pane that appears on the right, there are two sections: Fields Used and Unused Fields.

2. **Drag fields between the Fields Used and Unused Fields sections using the Reorder icon (the three bars) for each field you want to move.**

   Any fields in the Fields Used section will be available for your tasks in Toodledo.

3. **Tap the Tasks button at the bottom of the screen when done to return to the tasks view.**

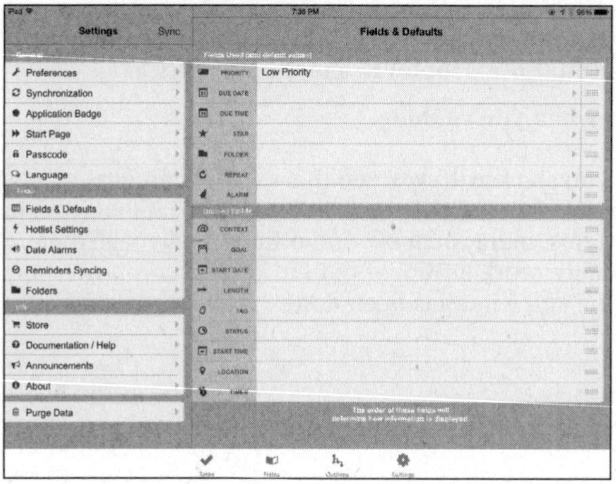

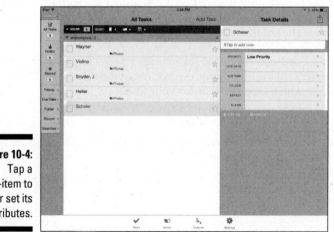

Figure 10-3:
Toodledo
lets you
customize
the fields
available for
your to-do
items.

After you set up the fields you want to display and in the order you want to display they, you can use any or all of them for your tasks, as Figure 10-4 shows. Just tap a to-do item to open it; then tap the desired field from the list that appears to its right.

Figure 10-4:
Tap a
do-item to
see or set its
attributes.

Adding and deleting tasks

Adding a task is straightforward:

1. **Tap Add Task.**

2. **Type in the task's title.**

3a. **Tap Edit to get the available fields, and fill in those that are relevant to the task.**

3b. **Or tap Add to add the task with just a title.**

   Either way, the task is added to your list. You can tap the task to show the fields available, at which point you can fill in those relevant to the task.

4. **(Optional) Enter a note for the task in the Tap to Add Note field that appears in the upper right of the screen when you select or create a task.**

You place a task into a folder by using the Folder field, which is with all the other fields, such as Priority and Due Date.

Deleting a task is even easier: Just flick to the left over a task and tap the Delete button that appears.

Marking and organizing tasks

As with most task managers, you just tap the check box to the left of a task to mark it as completed. Tap the Star to mark a task as a starred one. (You get to decide what meaning that star has, such as "important," "seriously, don't forget," or "my boss wants this.")

Where Toodledo stands out is in the two ways it lets you manage the display of your tasks.

First, you can choose which tasks to show via the All Tasks, Hotlist, and Starred buttons at the left side of the screen, or by using the five menus also available there: Priority, Due Date, Folder, Recent, and Searches.

The Searches feature lets you save complex search criteria (such as a combination priority, due date, and folder) for reuse later — a real time saver. But you have to set up saved searches at the Toodledo website, not in the app. Any searches you set up on the website display when you tap the Searches button, if your iPad has an active Internet connection; tap the saved search you want Toodledo to run.

By default, Toodledo decides on its own what tasks are marked as Hotlist ones — that is, the tasks it deems urgent or important and so wants to call out in a separate list. But you can set up your Hotlist rules in the Settings screen by tapping Hotlist Defaults in the list at the left and then Different Settings in the pane at right. You can combine priority level, due date, and star status to define what goes in the Hotlist.

The second way Toodledo helps you display your tasks is by using the filters. At the top of the tasks list are four buttons that let you control how your results display: Show, Sort, Second Sort, and Third Sort. Show lets you decide whether you show completed tasks and future tasks, and the three Sort menus let you combine up to three filters — such as Date Added, Folder, and Alphabetical — for the display order.

Drilling Down with Todoist

As is usually the case with to-do apps, Todoist is designed to work with the Todoist service, so it doesn't sync tasks over iCloud or Microsoft Exchange. The app is free, as is the basic service, though you must sign in with your Google, Facebook, or Todoist account. If you want to be able to add labels or set up reminders, you need to upgrade the $29-per-year premium service. Business accounts are also available that let work groups share task lists.

The Todoist app lets you view your tasks organized as projects or filtered by priority, assignee, or date. In the left part of the screen, tap Reports or Filters to decide how to view your tasks.

Working with projects

The concept of organizing projects is what makes Todoist stand out. You can create projects and subprojects, a structure that lets you organize your tasks in ways many to-do apps can't. You can break a project into several component groups. Likewise, you can set up subtasks for your tasks, meaning that you can show the various parts of a complex task — *subtasks* — as separate entities, yet keep them grouped with the overall task they belong to. Figure 10-5 shows an example of grouping subtasks within a task.

To create projects and subprojects, follow these steps:

   1. **Scroll to the bottom of the left side of the screen.**
   2. **Tap Add Project.**

3. **Enter a name for the project in the Name field.**

4. **Set the Sub-project field to your choice of No (not a subproject), Level 1, Level 2, or Level 3.**

5. **(Optional) Set the color for the project or subproject using the Color menu.**

6. **Tap Done.**

7. **Tap Edit at the bottom of the project list.**

8. **Drag the projects and subprojects so that the subprojects are under their parent projects, and in the order you want them.**

9. **Tap Done.**

When editing the project list, tap the Details button (the *i* icon) to edit a project's attributes. You also delete it (and any task entries) here by tapping Delete Project.

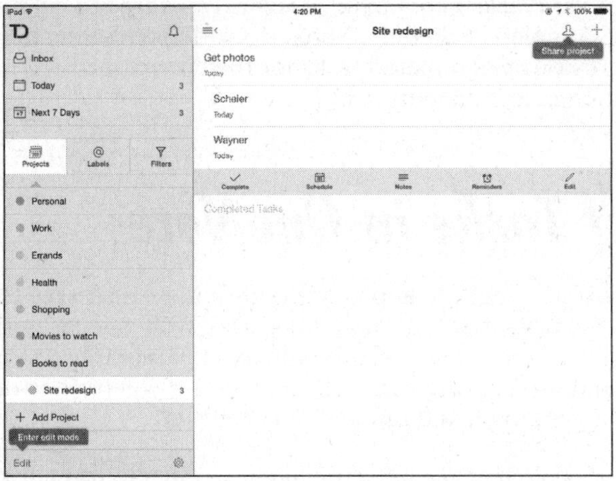

Figure 10-5:
Nesting subtasks within a task in Todoist.

Adding and editing tasks

Adding a task in Todoist is easy: Just tap the Add button (+ icon) in the upper right of the screen. When you do that, a form pops up, as shown in Figure 10-6, where you enter the salient details, including the task details and the project to store it as part of, as well as the optional aspects: due date, priority level, and subtask level. Also, if you've subscribed to the Premium service, audible alarms (a.k.a. reminders) or labels, you enter those details here. Tap Done when you're done.

Figure 10-6:
Adding
a task in
Todoist.

After you create a task, you tap its project or use the Filters view to find it. You see the relevant tasks in the pane at right. Tap a task to get buttons for its options: Complete, Schedule, Notes (to add notes), Reminders, and Edit. (To see previously completed tasks for the current project, tap the Completed option below the buttons.)

Checking Off Tasks in OneNote

Although Microsoft's OneNote app is primarily a note taker (see Chapter 9), it does have some task-oriented capabilities, too. Well, one task-oriented capability: You can add a check box to individual paragraphs in your notes using the To Do button in OneNote's Home view. All you have to do is select somewhere in a paragraph and tap the To Do button.

That check box is tappable, meaning that you can tap it to display a check mark for a completed task (tap it again to remove the check mark, such as if you selected an item by accident).

You can't manage your to-do items other than to add/remove the check boxes and select/deselect them, so OneNote is no substitute for a full-fledged task manager. But it does let you commingle to-do items in your notes.

Managing Task Details in Quip

The free Quip Docs, Chat, Spreadsheets app is part of the larger web-based Quip service meant for collaborative task management centered around documents more than list-style reminders. The Business subscription ($12 per month per user) lets work groups collaborate more directly and with more functions than the free version provides, though the free version does let you share task folders with other Quip users.

People in a Quip group can review those documents, which can include everything from draft specifications lists to check-off lists that people can use to track what's done. And Quip uses actual emails to let people know when there's a change, a new task, or other item of note.

You don't have to be a group to use Quip — it works fine for a single person as well, acting as your repository for projects' draft documents and task lists. In terms of content richness, that's more flexible than other task managers. But you don't get capabilities like scheduled alarms or syncing with servers such as Microsoft Exchange, Google, and iCloud.

Working with the Desktop, Inbox, and task folders

You create your task folders in Quip by using the New Folder icon near the upper right of the screen (it looks like a folder with a plus sign). To open a task folder, just tap it.

Both task folders and documents reside on the Desktop, as shown in Figure 10-7. It's essentially the same concept as the Desktop in Windows and the Mac.

On the left side of the screen is a list of task documents called the Inbox. (Tap the Inbox button at the bottom of the screen if this list isn't visible.) On the right side of the screen, you see the Desktop, which shows thumbnails of tasks and task folders.

In the Inbox, you may see names of tasks that aren't visible in the Desktop because they reside within folders. You need to open their folders to see them in the Desktop.

In the Inbox, you can filter your view of task documents using the Search box and the Unread, All, and Private buttons at the top of the Inbox. (A private task document is one that you haven't shared.)

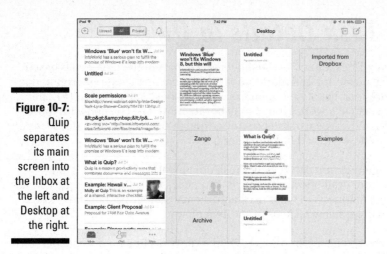

Figure 10-7:
Quip
separates
its main
screen into
the Inbox at
the left and
Desktop at
the right.

So how do you share a task folder? Tap and hold the folder in the Desktop. In the pop-over that appears, tap Sharing to invite other people via email to participate in the folder in Quip. Or tap Send Link to send a web link to the folder so that others can open it in Quip.

Creating and editing a task document

Creating a task document is really easy in Quip:

1. **Tap the New Document button (the page icon) at the upper right of the screen.**

   If a folder is open, the document is placed into that folder; otherwise, it is on the Desktop.

2. **Tap the default document title "Untitled" to highlight it. Then enter a more useful name for it.**

3. **Tap the blank area below the title to begin entering your text.**

   When you select text, the contextual menu appears. In addition to iOS's standard Cut, Copy, Paste, Replace **B**/U, and Define options, the contextual menu for text in Quip includes these options:

   - *Format as Code Block:* Highlights the text as computer code. To make it regular text again, select it and choose De-Nerdify (seriously) from the menu.

   - *Highlight:* Lets you add a comment to the selected text.

   - *Link:* Lets you add, edit, or delete a hyperlink in your text.

When you're on Quip's website (`www.quip.com`) in a computer's web browser, you can see your edits to task documents. The truth is that the Quip website is a more powerful tool than the iPad version.

But the Quip iPad app does have several useful features for your notes that you might not see at first. That's because they are accessed via a row of buttons (shown in Figure 10-8) that appears above the onscreen keyboard as you type — and you can be forgiven for not seeing them:

- ✔ **Keyboard (the ABC icon):** Switches back to the keyboard if you are using another function.

- ✔ **Paragraph (the icon of a bulleted list):** Opens a pop-over with formatting options for heading size and list type (bulleted, numbered, and checked).

  If you format a paragraph as a headline, the Paragraph button's icon changes to an H followed by an S (for small), M (for medium), or L (for large), based on the headline size applied. Likewise, if you format it as a list, the icon changes to represent the kind of list it is. You'll also see Indent and Outdent buttons if you've formatted a paragraph as a list.

- ✔ **Insert (the icon of two screens):** Opens a pop-over with seven options:

  - *Image:* Inserts an image from the Photos app or takes a picture with the iPad's camera.

  - *Spreadsheet:* Inserts a spreadsheet in which you can enter text (such as for tables) and Excel-like formulas. Tap the calculator icon that appears in the button bar to get a special keyboard designed for numeric and formula entry. Tap the Spreadsheet icon that appears in the button bar to open a pane with formatting options such as boldface and spreadsheet editing options such as for inserting a new column. Tap another cell to return to the standard keyboard.

  - *Checklist:* Inserts a checklist into your task. A checklist has check boxes to the left of each entry, so you can check off individual items as you complete them.

  - *Person:* Inserts the @ symbol, after which you type a person's name. If the person is a Quip user, you can tap that name to send a message to him or her.

  - *Document:* Asks you to begin typing a document name stored at the Quip website; as you do so, a reference to it in the form of a link (also preceded by @) is inserted. Tap that link to see the document.

  - *Link:* Lets you insert a hyperlink's URL.

  - *Code:* Inserts a blank paragraph formatted as code, meaning that the text is formatted in a typewriter font and has a gray background behind it.

✔ **Mention (the @ icon):** Lets you add a person or document reference at the current location. Yes, that's what the Person and Document options also do in the Insert pop-over.

✔ **Comments (the icon of a thought balloon):** Adds a comment to the current location. After you enter a comment, tap Send to send the comment to your document (weird, huh?). You see a comment icon in the document where you inserted it. And if you go to Quip on your computer's web browser, you can view all comments in one place there. But you can't see that consolidated set of comments on your iPad.

✔ **Done:** Tap this button to hide the keyboard so that you can see your task in the full iPad screen. (You don't have to tap Done to save your changes; they're saved automatically as you type.)

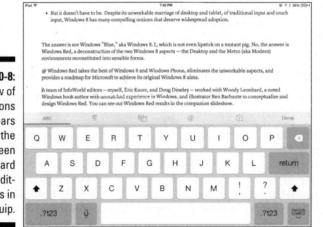

Figure 10-8:
A row of buttons appears above the onscreen keyboard when editing tasks in Quip.

There are three more buttons to note when working on a task document. These appear at the upper right above the document:

✔ **Share:** Tap this button either to send someone a link to the document so that he or she can work on it in Quip or to invite collaborators for this document. In other words, this button provides the same sharing options that you get for folders.

✔ **Pin/Unpin:** Tap the Pin button (a hollow pushpin icon) to put your document directly on the Quip Desktop; the button turns solid when you've pinned the document. You unpin it from the Desktop by tapping the solid Pin icon, which makes the icon hollow again.

✔ **Settings:** Tap the button (a gear icon) to get a grab bag of capabilities: Sharing, Copy, Link, PDF (saves the document as a PDF file), Print, Theme (which lets you apply a different visual theme to the document), Export to Microsoft Word (which then lets you use the standard iOS Share sheet to email, message, print, or open the document in another app), and Delete Document.

 When viewing task documents on the Desktop or in a folder, tap and hold on a document's preview for a second or so to get a pop-over with the following options all in one handy place: Sharing (same as the Share button's Sharing option in a document), Link Sharing (same as Share button's Link option in a document), Copy (which copies the entire document), Move (to move the document to a different task folder), Pin to Desktop/Unpin from Desktop, and Delete Document.

Importing document files

You can also import documents into Quip — but only if they are Word, RTF, or plain-text files — from Box, Dropbox, Evernote, and Google Drive, as well as from other apps and email attachments via iOS's Open In feature.

To import a document via Open In, tap the Share button in your email or other app; then tap Quip in the list of available apps. (Some apps, such as Pages, require you to choose the format for the text before choosing the app; be sure to select a supported format such as Word, RTF, or text-only.) You then see the document in your Desktop workspace in Quip.

To import from Box, Dropbox, Google Drive, or Evernote, scroll to the bottom of the task list in All view and tap Import Documents; then tap the name of the service to import from. You'll find the imported document in a folder named Imported from *service* (with *service* being whatever storage service you use); changes made to the document are synced back to the original version in the cloud service.

Chatting about projects

Another feature in Quip worth knowing about is Chats, which you get to by tapping the Chats button at the bottom of the Inbox. Here, you can chat with other Quip users, allowing you to discuss your projects in real time.

It works just the same as any other chat service: Enter a contact to chat with (from your iPad's Contacts app, Google Contacts, Yahoo!, Outlook.com, or an email invite you send) and then start messaging when the other person responds.

Managing Your Work with OmniFocus

One of the most expensive apps described in this book, Omni Group's $29.99 OmniFocus 2 for iPad, is also the only one that requires you run iOS 8 or later. And it's a long-beloved project-management tool — much more than a to-do manager — that continues to set the standard for iPad project-management tools. (There's a separate, $19.99 iPhone version and a $39.99 Mac version, but no Windows version.)

OmniFocus has two basic organizational methods: inboxes and projects. An inbox is what it sounds like: a virtual tray for whatever is due. A project is a set of related tasks (called *actions* in OmniFocus). A project shows just its tasks. An inbox shows all tasks due that are not in any project — think of it as the stuff you need to do outside your projects. You can have multiple inboxes, and you can have multiple projects. Figure 10-9 shows a project with a task being added.

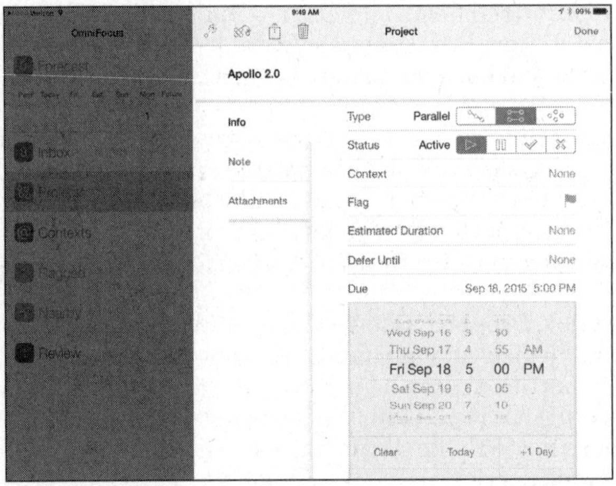

Figure 10-9: Adding a task (action) in Omni-Focus 2.

Touring OmniFocus's views

OmniFocus also has multiple views in addition to the Inbox and Projects views (tap Home in the upper left if you don't see the list of views):

  ✔ **Forecast:** Shows a timeline for the selected day, with the number of tasks indicated in the next five days. Tap Future to get a list of all tasks due after that five-day period. If you give OmniFocus permission to access your iPad's calendar, you also see that in the timeline, as

Figure 10-10 shows. *Note:* If you didn't give permission when you first launched OmniFocus, you can do so in the Settings app's OmniFocus pane, via its Privacy option.

✔ **Contexts:** Shows your inbox and project tasks organized by categories, which OmniFocus calls *contexts*. You specify the context when you create or edit an inbox, project, or task.

✔ **Flagged:** This shows any tasks you've flagged, using the Flag option when you create or edit an inbox, project, or task.

✔ **Nearby:** Shows any tasks near your current location. OmniFocus compares your current location to the address or map location that you added to a context to determine what is nearby.

✔ **Review:** Lets you review the status of a project on a scheduled basis, such as weekly, as explained later in this chapter.

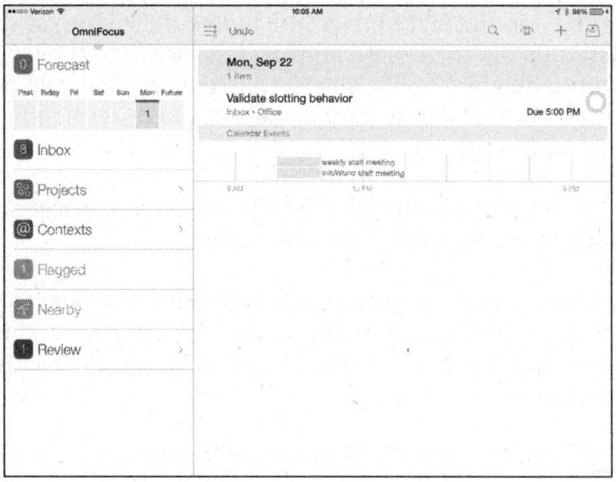

Figure 10-10: OmniFocus's Forecast view.

Creating projects, inboxes, and tasks

To create a project in OmniFocus, follow these steps:

1. **Tap Projects in the left pane.**

   Make sure that you still see the OmniFocus pane at the left, not the pane that has Home at the upper left.

2. **Tap the Add button (the + icon).**

3. In the pop-over that appears, choose New Project.

You can also choose New Folder, which creates a folder that can contain tasks or projects. You use folders to organize complex projects by providing subprojects, as I explain later in this chapter. Any folders appear in the Projects list.

To create a context, follow these steps:

1. Tap Contexts in the left pane.

You see all the current contexts.

2. Tap the Add button (the + icon) and Choose New Context to add a new context at the top level.

If you want a context to be a subcontext to another, tap that context name *before* adding the new context.

To delete a context, tap the List button (the bulleted-list icon) at the top of the Contexts list; then tap the Delete button (the – icon) to the left of any context you want to delete. You'll also see the Reorder icon (the three lines) to the right of each context name; drag a context's Reorder handle to move it to a new location within the list.

To create a task, click the Add button (the + icon) at the top right of the screen, and choose New Action or New Inbox Item.

A quick way to create a new inbox task is to tap the New Inbox Item button (the inbox icon) at the upper right of the screen. Whether you add an inbox item or a task this way, you get the form shown in Figure 10-9, with these fields in the Info pane:

- **Title:** Tap the Untitled Item field and enter the name for the task.

- **Project:** In the New Inbox Item pane, be sure that Info is active (bold-faced; tap it if not). Select an existing project by tapping the label None to the right of the Project label. That opens a pop-over listing available projects; tap the project to add the task to. Or leave Project set to None so that it's not assigned to a project (in other words, to make it an Inbox item). *Note:* You can add the task to a project later, if that project doesn't yet exist. Just tap the task in the Inbox or in the Miscellaneous project list to edit it and choose the project to assign it to then.

- **Type:** Your choices are Sequential, Parallel, and Single Actions.

- **Context:** Choose a context from the pop-over that appears when you tap this field, if desired.

- **Flag:** Tap the icon if you want the task to appear in the Flagged list. Tap it again to remove it from that list.

✔ **Estimated Duration:** Tap this field to get a control bar where you choose Minutes or Hours; then use the + and – buttons to increase or decrease the time increments. If you want to remove the duration, tap the X icon.

✔ **Defer Until:** Tap this field to get the standard OS time scroller, where you can set the date and time for this action's deferral. You can also just tap Clear, Later (which picks a random date in the future), +1 Day, +1 Week, +1 Month, and +1 Year. The +1 buttons set the time for that period from the current date, so +1 Week is a week from today, for example.

✔ **Due:** Tap this field to set the due date. It works just like the Defer Until option except that Due has the Today button instead of the Later button.

✔ **Repeat:** Tap this field to set the task as one that repeats.

The Note pane lets you add notes to the task, and the Attachments pane lets you add a photo (from your iPad's camera or your Photos app) or voice recording to the task.

Tap Save to save the task and close the form, or tap Save+ to save the task and open a blank form in which you create another new one.

Managing projects

After your projects have tasks, you can mark tasks as done, review your projects, add more tasks later on, and reorganize your projects.

Marking actions and projects as done

Marking an action as done is simple: In any of the views that show the action, tap the big circle to the right of its name to mark (with a check mark) it as complete. That's it! (Tap a item to remove the check mark if it's not completed.)

You can also mark a project as done by opening the project and tapping the Completed button (the ✓ icon) in the Status area. Other statuses you can set are On Hold (the pause icon), Dropped (the X icon), and Active (the play icon).

Reviewing projects

To review projects, first you need to make the project reviewable. To do so, tap and hold a project's name in the right pane — tapping and holding a project's name in the left pane does nothing. In the contextual menu that appears, tap Review. As Figure 10-11 shows, you then see the Reviewing bar at the bottom of the right pane for that project and can come back to that Reviews view by tapping Reviews in the left pane.

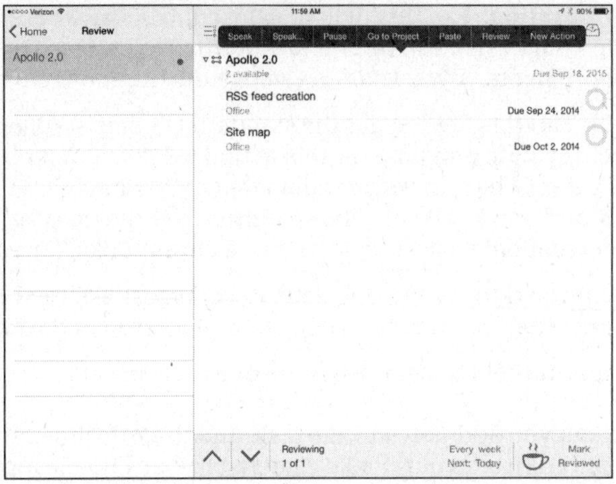

Figure 10-11:
Reviewing
projects in
OmniFocus.

Tap the "Every" or "Next" text to the left of the coffee-cup icon at the bottom of the pane to get the Project Review pop-over, where you set how often you want to review the product and when the next review date is. The text changes to that setting.

Tap Mark Reviewed at the bottom right of the screen to mark the project as reviewed until the next review date comes up.

If you have multiple projects set for review, you can navigate among them using the caret (∧) and (∨) caret buttons — or just scroll through the projects in the right pane.

Finally, you can control what you're reviewing by tapping the View button (the eye icon) and choosing First Available (only the first task in each project), Available (all tasks), Remaining (all active tasks), or All (includes completed and dropped tasks).

Reorganizing projects

When you create tasks, you typically add them to a project. But you may discover that some tasks that aren't in a project need to be added to one, or that tasks may need to move to a different project. You may have created folders to contain tasks and now want to make those tasks part of your projects.

To simply move a task from one project to another, tap the task to edit it and choose a different Project in the Project field. But you can do more by using the two buttons at the upper left of an task's form:

- ✔ **Move Inside Another Item (the icon of a circle with an arrow into another circle):** This button makes the current task a subtask of another task, as well as lets you move a subtask up to a higher-level task or into the project's main level. *Note:* The View button (the eye icon) controls which tasks are visible for moving this task into.

- ✔ **Convert (the icon with five circles and a curved arrow):** This button makes the task into its own project if you choose Convert to Top Level Project. If you have folders, you can choose to put the new project in a folder.

If you open a folder, you can move it and its contents into another folder to create a folder hierarchy. Use the Move Inside Another Item button to do that.

I explain earlier how to create folders, and I just explained how to move tasks into folders. But how do you get projects into folders? By tapping a folder in the Projects list and then tapping the Add button (the + icon) and choosing New Project in the pop-over. What you cannot do is move an existing project into a folder — only new projects and existing tasks.

Chapter 11

Outlining and Brainstorming

*W*e all organize thoughts differently, but organizing them — whether through brainstorming or outlining — is usually a critical step to developing project plans, proposals, and so forth.

The iPad makes a great tool for such organizing because it's usually at hand, so you can do your organizing almost anywhere you are when inspiration strikes or deadlines force you into action. Creativity often doesn't happen on a schedule, and with the iPad, it doesn't have to.

But creativity does come with a price: The apps for this category are costlier than for many other business app categories. You've been warned! And if you're thinking that, at least for outlining, you can just use Microsoft Word or Apple Pages to do that work, think again: The iPad versions of these apps don't have an outline view, much less outlining capabilities as their computer versions do.

This chapter covers commonly used apps that let you create textual outlines or visual outlines (a.k.a. mind-mapping), whether for fleshing out the intended contents of a document or for brainstorming.

Running the Gamut with OmniOutliner

The $29.95 OmniOutliner for iPad has a strong following among Mac users (the $49.95 Mac version has long had a dedicated following; there is no Windows version). OmniOutliner is both a very simple outlining tool that's easy to use and a complex one that lets you choose how rich you want your outlines to be.

OmniOutliner exports its outlines to a variety of formats, including the web's HTML, the industry-standard OPML format for outlines, and the Microsoft Word `.docx` format.

What OmniOutliner does not do as easily as create outlines is import ones that have been created elsewhere. Importing an outline created in Microsoft Word is especially problematic, even though you see Word listed in iOS's Open In pop-over when you try to import a `.docx` file from Mail or another app into OmniOutliner. So if you use a Windows PC, it's best to use OmniOutliner on the iPad as your sole outlining tool. If you use a Mac, it's best to use OmniOutliner for iPad with OmniOutliner for Mac so that you can exchange outlines between your tablet and computer. Either way, after you're done working on that outline, you can bring it into Word or Pages for your actual writing.

OmniOutliner also doesn't support iCloud or cloud storage services like Box or Dropbox, though you can use Open In from those apps to send an outline file to OmniOutliner, as well as use Open In (via the standard iOS Share sheet, covered in Chapter 17, when selecting outlines in OmniOutliner) to send those files to a cloud storage service. It's a bit of work, but possible.

Creating and editing outlines

When you open OmniOutliner, you should see your local documents. If you have set up an Omni Sync Server account (which you can do from the web at `https://manage.sync.omnigroup.com`), you see two large buttons when you sign in: one called Omni Sync Server and one called Local Documents. Tap the one that has your files or is the one in which you want to create new ones. You can move between them by tapping the Locations button at the upper left of the screen; that is, when you're working in one, you tap Locations to make these options appear.

Creating an outline

To create a new outline, tap the Add button (the + icon) at the upper right of the Documents screen. Then choose a template from the set that appears. Using the templates can be handy, but note that their sample text comes with them, so you need to delete that text in your new document.

As Figure 11-1 shows, the basic template is essentially empty, with an empty line (which OmniOutliner calls a *row*) ready for your input.

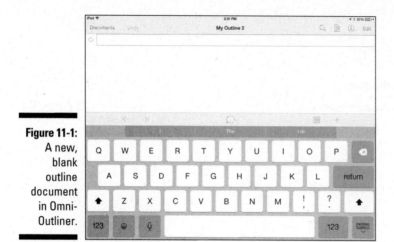

Figure 11-1:
A new, blank outline document in Omni-Outliner.

To put text in your outline, just begin typing! Tap Return or tap the + button above the onscreen keyboard to create a new line, and use the Indent button (the ← icon) and the Outdent (the → icon) button in the row that appears above the onscreen keyboard to change the level of the current line. (Tap Indent to move the line a level down, and Outdent to move the line a level up.

Moving and manipulating lines

To move a line, follow these steps:

1. **Tap the Edit button at the upper right of the screen.**

2. **Tap the lines you want to move to select them.**

3. **Tap the Move button that appears at the bottom of the screen.**

4. **Tap within your outline where you want to move the selected lines to.**

5. **In the menu that appears, choose Above, Below, or Inside to determine where the moved lines appear relative to the location your tapped.**

   Tapping Inside nests the moved lines into the tapped location, essentially inserting them there at a lower level in the outline.

You probably noticed other options at the bottom of the screen, which you can see in Figure 11-2: Cut, Copy, Delete, Group, and Move. Cut stores the deleted line in memory so that it can be pasted elsewhere, whereas Delete doesn't — the line is simply gone.

When you cut or copy lines in OmniOutliner, you don't see a Paste option at the bottom of the screen. Instead, you tap and hold at the location you want to paste the cut or copied lines and use the Paste option in the menu that appears.

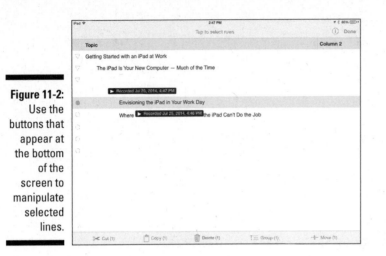

Figure 11-2:
Use the
buttons that
appear at
the bottom
of the
screen to
manipulate
selected
lines.

The Group option begins to show some of OmniOutliner's sophistication. Select multiple lines and tap Group to, well, group those lines. (You can ungroup them by tapping Ungroup.) Notice how the circle icon to their left changes to a triangle, as you can see at the top of Figure 11-2. Tap the triangle icon to hide or reveal everything below that line in that group.

Adding audio comments

OmniOutliner has a cool capability: adding audio recordings to your outlines. Tap a line or text within a line; then tap the Comment button (the speech bubble icon above the onscreen keyboard). The Comment button disappears, with a Pause/Record button, audio level indicator, time indicator, and Done button (the check mark icon), as Figure 11-3 shows.

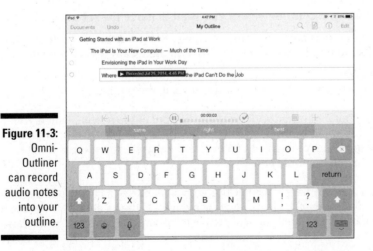

Figure 11-3:
Omni-
Outliner
can record
audio notes
into your
outline.

You can have as many recorded comments in your outline as you'd like. (They display as a black bar with a Play icon and the recording data and time.) Just tap one to play it.

Adding notes

Another button above the onscreen keyboard lets you add notes. Unsurprisingly, it's called Notes, and its icon looks a paragraph. Tap it to insert a note at the current location; tap outside that line to complete the note.

You can show or hide notes by tapping and holding the Notes button until two buttons appear onscreen: Show Notes (its icon shows a bulleted list with one line each) and Hide Notes (its icon shows a bulleted list with two lines each). They do what you'd expect!

Inserting columns

Outlines are usually composed of just lines, indented to show their internal hierarchy. But OmniOutliner also supports columns, which let you make sophisticated outlines that act more as project management documents. For example, you can add a check box column, a date column, a numeric column, a pop-up list column (a type of menu), and a duration column. By default, columns are rich text, meaning text to which you can apply formatting.

To create a column, follow these steps:

1. **Tap the Content button (the icon of a wrench in a page) at the upper right of the screen; then tap New Column at the bottom of the pop-over that appears.**

2. **Be sure the Columns pane is active; tap it if not.**

3. **Make your desired selections in the Column options that appear.**

   These options include Name (the column's name); Style (the same options as in the Text Styles pop-over); and the type of column: Rich Text, Number, Date, Duration, Pop-up List, and Checkbox, as shown in Figure 11-4. **Note:** Tap a type's *i* icon to get further options, such as to set the choices you want to appear in the pop-up list or the format for numbers (such as percentage or currency).

4. **Tap Columns when done.**

5. **Tap outside the pop-over to close it.**

To edit a column, tap any column in the Content pop-over's Columns list to edit its attributes, if desired.

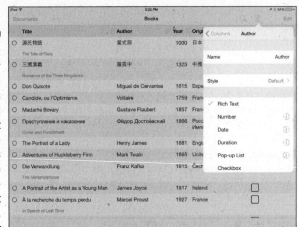

Figure 11-4:
OmniOutliner
lets you add
columns
of several
different
types, mak-
ing outlines
more like
project man-
agement
documents.

Changing the column type removes any text or other data that exists in your outline for that column. Tap Undo at the top of the screen immediately after closing the pop-over to restore any inadvertently removed text.

To move or delete a column, tap Edit in the pop-over; then use the Delete buttons (the – icon) and Reorder buttons (the two lines) to remove and rearrange columns, respectively.

Formatting outlines

For most people, an outline's formatting is simple because they do the formatting in their final document. But OmniOutliner lets you do fancier formatting because users often create documents in the app that don't get moved to Microsoft Word or Apple Pages for further development — the outlines become project documents or complex task lists.

The templates available for new documents give you a taste of that available formatting. To apply formatting to an existing outline's text, tap the Text Style button (the *i* icon) at the upper right of the screen; then apply boldface, ital-ics, or underline (which you can also do with the standard iOS text-selection contextual menu's **B/U** option); choose an existing style; or create your own by scrolling down the Text Style pop-over and tapping Customize Style.

The pop-over is called Text Style when you've selected text within a line and is called Row when the entire line is selected. The options are the same either way.

You can format an entire outline from the Contents pop-over:

✔ In the Styles pane, you can apply a template theme, as well as apply paragraph and character formatting via the Whole Document, Level 1 Rows, and Notes menus. Create a new style by tapping New Style at the bottom of the pop-over, and delete or reorder styles by tapping Edit.

✔ In the Document pane, you can set the zoom level, background color, and color for alternate rows (as you would do in a spreadsheet or table to make it easier to distinguish rows from each other).

Working with documents

Tap the Documents button at the upper left of the screen to return to your Documents view, whether that is Local Documents or Omni Sync Server. You see thumbnails for all your documents, as Figure 11-5 shows.

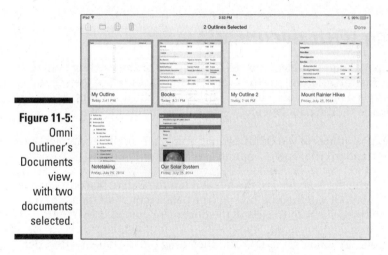

Figure 11-5:
Omni Outliner's Documents view, with two documents selected.

You tap a document to open it. But you can do more. Tap and hold a document, or tap Select and then tap one or more documents to get a row of buttons at the upper left of the screen, as follows:

✔ **Share:** Lets you email or open a document in another app (you're asked which format to export the shared document as), as well as create a template based on the selected document. *Note:* If more than one document is selected, this button doesn't respond.

✔ **Move To (the folder icon):** Lets you move the selected documents to a different folder as well as create a folder to move them into.

> ✔ **Duplicate (the icon of two pages):** Creates copies of the selected
>   documents in the current location.
>
> ✔ **Delete (the trash can icon):** Deletes the selected documents.

To get help with OmniOutliner, tap the Settings button (the gear icon) in the
Documents view and then tap OmniOutliner Help. There's also a free, excellent e-book manual for OmniOutliner available at the iBookstore; just search
for "OmniOutliner" to find it.

Going Basic with Cloud Outliner

If OmniOutliner does way more than you need, consider the $4.99 Cloud
Outliner at the other end of the spectrum. The app is very simple, with the
bonus advantage of being able to sync outlines with Evernote, a popular
note-taking tool covered in Chapter 9.

Working with documents

When you open Cloud Outliner, you see a simple list of any existing outline
documents. Tap the Add button (the + icon) at the upper left of the screen
and then enter a name for your outline. Tap > to edit the document, as
described in the "Editing documents" section, later in this chapter.

You can import outlines in the OPML format from Mail and other applications
by using the standard iOS Open In option (see Chapter 17).

To delete a document, just flick to the left and tap the Delete button — just as
you would in Mail. Or tap the Edit button (the pencil icon) and then tap the
Delete button (the – icon) to the left of the document you want to delete.

To reorder your documents, tap Edit and then drag the document's Reorder
handle (the icon of three lines) to the desired new location.

Editing documents

To edit a document, tap the > icon to the right of its name in the documents
list. You see the screen shown in Figure 11-6. Here are the actions you can
take in this screen:

> ✔ Double-tap a line to select it so that you can insert or edit its text.
>
> ✔ Tap + to add a new line.

✔ Tap the up and down triangle buttons to move a line within the outline.

✔ Tap the left and right triangle buttons to indent or outdent a line to establish the hierarchy for your lines.

✔ Drag its Reorder handle (the icon of three lines) to move a line to a different location in the outline.

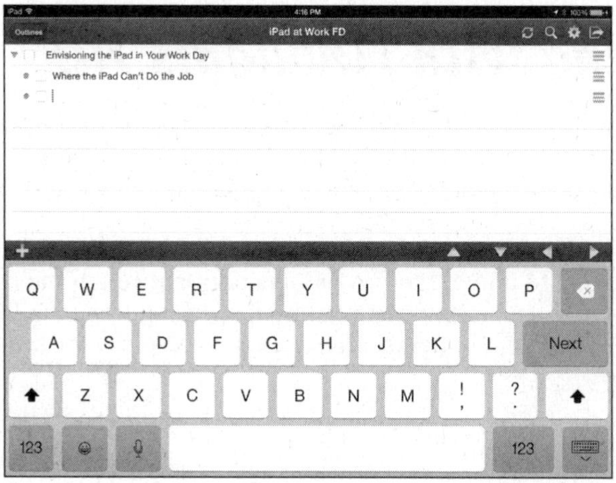

Figure 11-6:
An outline
in Cloud
Outliner.

Text formatting in Cloud Outliner is nonexistent, but you can cut, copy, and paste using the standard iOS contextual menu for selected text.

By default, your outline items show check boxes. You can disable them by tapping Cloud Outliner's Settings button (the gear icon) and setting the Show Checkboxes switch to Off. Other options here include Hide Checked Items and Hide Unchecked Items (for using Cloud Outliner as a simple task manager), Adjust Row Heights to Fit Text, and Expand All, Collapse All, and Uncheck All.

Sharing and syncing documents

Believe it or not, I'm almost done telling you about Cloud Outliner. Just two controls are left to know about in a document.

One is the Share button, which opens the Share pop-over from which you can email an outline as an OPML file, open it in another OPML-compatible app, and send it to Evernote. If you have sent an outline to Evernote, the Share pop-over shows two new options: Remove from Evernote and Log Out from Evernote. The logout option prevents Evernote and Cloud Outliner from syncing the outline, essentially making the two versions independent.

To sync an outline, tap the Sync button (the icon with two curved arrows). That's the second control available in a document. This feature syncs not just with Evernote but also, via iCloud, with Cloud Outliner on your other iOS devices and Mac (there's a $9.99 Mac version, but none for Windows). iCloud syncing is enabled by default; you manage it in the Settings app's Cloud Outliner pane.

Mind-Mapping with iThoughts HD

Outlining is not, of course, the only mechanism for collecting and organizing your thoughts. Outlines are quite useful for linear progressions of ideas, such as the organization of a history book, legal argument, movie script, and so on.

But nonlinear connections are also quite useful to understand, especially when you're trying to understand a complex notion through the relationships of its many components. That relationship-diagram approach is called *mind-mapping*, and the $9.99 iThoughts HD is a great tool to use for brainstorming in this manner.

iThoughts HD has a version available for the iPhone called just iThoughts; it's a free download if you buy the iPad version. There's also a version of iThoughts for the Mac (but not Windows): the $47.99 iThoughtsX. You can share files among all three.

The process of mind-mapping is simple operationally — you draw shapes (called *nodes*) that contain words and then connect them to figure out how they relate. But it is mentally challenging because those relationships require thought, and as you map out more relationships, you may rethink ones you made previously. If you were using paper, you'd use a pencil and do a lot of erasing as you draw and redraw those relationships. But on an iPad, you can do that tinkering without worrying about the remnants of erased lines remaining on your page.

Creating a mind map

Because mind-mapping is primarily a visual endeavor, the user interface of iThoughts HD may seem a little odd at first. For example, you start with a blank canvas, not a folder hierarchy. Tap the Maps button (it looks like an open book) and then tap the Add button (the + icon) in the lower right of the pop-over that opens. Choose Map or Folder in the menu that appears.

In the Maps pop-over, any folders that exist are shown, as are any mind maps that you didn't create in a folder. (To create a mind map in a folder, open that folder first and *then* tap Maps and choose Map.)

The Maps pop-over is where you navigate to all iThoughts mind maps stored on your iPad. The three buttons at the bottom of the pop-over control how the mind maps are displayed: Favorites, Most Recent, and Folders (the default view).

Tap and hold a mind map in the Maps pop-over and then choose Add to Favorites to mark it as a favorite. You also see the Duplicate menu option, which lets you copy an existing mind map.

When you create a mind map, you get an almost-blank canvas that has a central node in the center. This is your "root" node. A root node is one that everything else relates to, so everything ultimately leads back to it. As I explain in the next section, you don't have to have just a single root node in your mind map, but you do need to start somewhere, so iThoughts HD creates the first node for you.

Adding nodes and setting their relationships

To create a mind map's relationships, tap the node you want to add the relationship to and then use the buttons at the upper right of the screen for the following:

- ✔ **Child (the icon shows one relationship indented below the other):** Adds a node that is subordinate to the selected one, meaning that it's a child to the current node (its parent). In other words, it is a subordinate thought or a component of that other thought.

- ✔ **Sibling (the icon shows two unindented relationships):** Adds a node that is equal to the selected one, meaning that it's a sibling to the current node. In other words, it's an independent thought at the same level as the selected thought. *Note:* This button is active only after the root node has at least one child.

- ✔ **Comment (the icon of a speech bubble):** Adds a comment to the selected thought.

- ✔ **Related topic (the icon of two connected objects):** Lets you connect the selected node to another node that you then tap. These relationships are freeform, meaning whatever they mean to you.

✔ **Group (the icon of a dotted-line shape):** Lets you group items together inside a shape so that you know they have a special relationship (in your mind, anyhow). When you tap Group, the selected node and its children are grouped via a shaded outline.

As you add nodes, enter the text for them. Double-tap a node to add or edit text if the node isn't already ready for text input (the onscreen keyboard will appear).

Figure 11-7 shows a simple mind map with child, sibling, and related relationships, as well as a group and a comment.

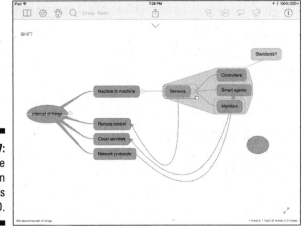

Figure 11-7:
A simple
mind map in
iThoughts
HD.

From these building blocks, you can create very complex webs of relationships for whatever you are exploring.

If your map gets overly complex, you can hide child nodes temporarily quite easily. Notice that minus sign (–) icon in a circle to the right of a node that has child nodes? Tap it to hide those child nodes. It becomes a plus sign (+) icon; tap it to unhide those nodes.

Remember when I said that you can have more than one root node? Here's how you add new nodes not connected to existing nodes: Tap and hold for a second or two on the screen where you want to add that new node. And there it is! ***Note:*** iThoughts calls these *floating nodes*.

There's something else you can add to your mind map: doodles, which are freeform drawings. The process is not so obvious, so follow along carefully:

1. **Tap any node or object in your mind map.**

   You see a square appear in the node's lower-right corner.

2. **Tap that square and then tap Doodle in the menu that appears.**

3. **Select the line thickness, line type, and color from the options at the top of the screen.**

4. **Use your finger to draw whatever you want.**

5. **Repeat Steps 3 and 4 for additional components of this doodle.**

6. **Tap Done when done.**

   The doodle appears near the object you had initially selected, but you can drag it elsewhere if desired.

Keep in mind that the mind map is a canvas, and you can scroll and zoom on it using the standard iOS gestures to drill down into your mind map, move among its sections, and zoom out to see the whole thing.

Use the Undo and Redo buttons if you inadvertently add the wrong kind of relationship, group, or other item.

Editing and formatting mind maps

If you want to get fancy, you can in iThoughts HD, such as to create stunning mind maps that you might present in a meeting. But before I get to those formatting capabilities, let me explain the basic editing you can do.

Editing and formatting text in mind maps

If you select text within a node, you get the usual iOS contextual menu options for text selections: Cut, Copy, Paste, Replace, **B**/U, and Define. Plus you get three options that are special to iThoughts HD:

- ✔ **Research:** Opens a Search page showing the results for whatever term is in that node. When in that search mode, you can change the search service using the compass icon in the upper right of the screen, such as to WolframAlpha or Google Scholar.

- ✔ **Make Topic(s):** Makes a child node for each selected word (each word becomes the label for the new corresponding node).

✔ **Add to Note:** Adds the selected text to a note attached to that node. You see a little note icon in the node indicating that you have a note there. Tap it to have the note appear above the mind map in a drawer that opens. *Note:* A note is not a comment; a comment appears on the mind map as a type of node, whereas a note is inside the node.

When you select a node that has text in it, you see some options above the onscreen keyboard. They're not really that useful because you can use standard iOS editing functions for all but one of them. But here's what they do:

✔ **Open selection menu (↑):** Opens the standard iOS contextual menu for text selections.

✔ **Move Left a Word (|Word) and Move Right a Word (Word|):** Navigates your text cursor through the currently selected text.

✔ **Move Left (the left triangle) and Move Right (the right triangle button):** Moves one character left or right, respectively.

✔ **Open Text Style Pop-over (A):** Lets you adjust the text size, font, color, formatting, and alignment of the selected nodes' text.

Formatting maps and nodes in mind maps

You can change how your mind maps are displayed using the Settings button (the gear icon). It lets you change the canvas color, font, style of the link lines, and the map layout.

For the map layout, the default style is horizontal, which adds new nodes to the left or right. But you can switch to Vertical, which adds them below and above; Top Down, which has them flow down from the top; and Fishbone, which has them flow to the right from the root node. You can also enable Rainbow Colors, which applies different colors to nodes based on their relationships. Changing these settings changes the layout of your current map.

If you tap an object, the standard iOS contextual menu appears with the Cut, Copy, Paste, and Delete buttons. Plus the Research button is also available for text selections.

To select multiple nodes, tap and hold the Shift button with one finger and then tap each node with another finger. Release both fingers when you're done selecting.

For a specific node, you have a lot of formatting options via the Format pop-over. To open it, tap the *i* icon at the upper right of the screen. It has six panes, from left to right:

TIP

✔ **Icons:** Inserts icons to the selected nodes.

Tap and hold an icon and then tap Add to Favorites to add it to the pop-over's Favorites list.

✔ **Palette:** Applies a color from the swatches that display, or you can choose a specific color by tapping More to show the color picker.

✔ **Shape:** Lets you choose the shape for the selected objects.

✔ **Text Style:** Lets you adjust the text size, font, color, formatting, and alignment of the selected nodes' text. (Yes, these are the same options available via the *A* icon when editing text.)

✔ **Project Settings:** This pane, shown in Figure 11-8, lets you set indicators such as degree of progress, start and due dates, estimated time frame for the research or delivery effort, and resources (a list you create of resources needed for the selected nodes). This pane's capabilities transform iThoughts HD from just a mind-mapping tool to a project-estimation tool.

✔ **Related Items:** Lets you associate a library image (iThoughts HD–provided artwork to help decorate nodes), a photo from the Photos app, a photo you take with the iPad's camera, a doodle, a link to another mind map, or an email address. *Note:* This pane's options are available only if a single node is selected.

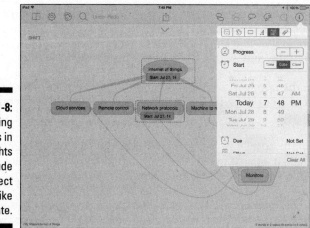

Figure 11-8:
Formatting
options in
iThoughts
HD include
project
settings like
start date.

Sharing mind maps

After you've created a mind map, you can share it with others by using the Share button at the top of the screen. The Email and Open In options work as they do in any iOS Share sheet (see Chapter 17), but three options are special to iThoughts HD:

- ✔ **Cloud:** Lets you share the mind map with others via the Dropbox cloud storage service (if you have a Dropbox account, of course).

- ✔ **Image:** Exports an image of your mind map that can then be sent to other people or apps, as well as printed, via the standard iOS Share sheet.

- ✔ **Task Reports:** Creates an email listing your choice of the tasks embedded in your mind map or the resources noted for the mind map. (You set both the tasks and resources reports in the Project Settings pane of the Format pop-over.)

Sketching with Skitch

Mind-mapping is great if you are trying to model complex relationships, but sometimes your visual brainstorming needs are much simpler. For example, maybe you really just need a way to draw annotations on an image, to make notes for, say, a design project or room layout. That is, in that old-fashioned paper-and-pencil way.

The free Skitch app is great for such annotations. As Figure 11-9 shows, Skitch lets you draw on and add text to photos. It also lets you create your own drawings as well as mark up websites (it takes a screenshot of the page you want to annotate) and, with a $1.99 in-app purchase, PDF files.

When you open the app, you see a list of albums from the Photos app. (If you have no photos on your iPad, Skitch asks you to take one. Do so if you want to annotate a photo!)

At the bottom of the screen is the menu of items you can annotate: Photos, Camera (from your iPad's camera), Map, Web, PDF, and Draw (create your own drawing). Tap the desired option to begin.

At the right side of the screen is the menu button for the kinds of annotations you can do — freeform lines, text, arrows, and so forth. At the left side is the menu button for your pen's color and thickness. Those two tools are all you need to use Skitch — well, them and the Undo, Crop, and More buttons at the top. (More lets you clear all annotations and rotate the image.)

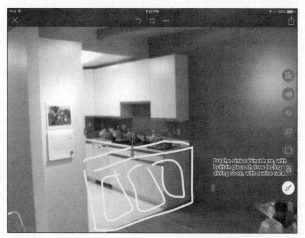

Figure 11-9:
An anno-
tated photo
in Skitch.

When you're done with your work, you tap the Close button (the X icon) at the upper left, which gives you the option to save the annotated image to the Photos app or cancel.

Skitch has one more set of options: those that display when you tap the Share button. The Share button in Skitch doesn't open the standard iOS Share sheet, but instead puts three buttons at the bottom of the screen that, when tapped, show their options in the space between the buttons and a preview version of your annotated image, as Figure 11-10 shows.

Figure 11-10:
Skitch's
nonstandard
presentation
of Share
options.

The three buttons are

- ✔ **Meeting:** Displays any meetings in the Calendar app scheduled to start no more than an hour earlier from now or an hour later from now, so you can send the meeting attendees an email with the annotated image during, right before, or right after the meeting.

- ✔ **Share:** Lets you send the annotated image via Mail, Twitter, Facebook, or Messages; send the image to Evernote (if you buy the annual $44.99 service in-app purchase); and open the image in another compatible app on your iPad.

- ✔ **Save:** Lets you save the image to Evernote on your iPad (you need to sign in from Skitch, though) or Photos, as well as copy the image to the Clipboard so that you can paste it into another app. (Yes, the Save options pretty much duplicate what you can do via the Open In choice in the Share options.)

You have one more option when you tap Share from your image: The Caption button at the upper right of the screen. Tap it to enter a caption for your image; then tap Done on the onscreen keyboard. The caption is placed at the bottom of your annotated image.

Part III
Collaborating and Communicating

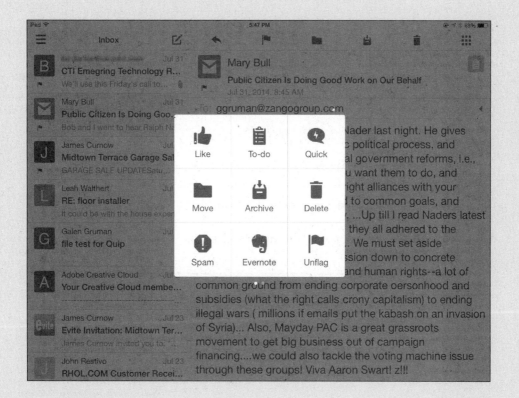

Visit www.dummies.com/extras/ipadatwork for tips on how to use the new Handoff feature to sync your work across devices.

In this part . . .

- ✔ Let's face it: We all live in email. Whether you use Apple, Microsoft, or Google, the iPad has got you covered.

- ✔ Staying in touch is easy with the iPad's contacts and calendar tools.

- ✔ Who needs a phone? Use your iPad to join the conversation.

Chapter 12

Wrangling Email, Contacts, and Calendars

*T*he iPad's built-in personal information management (PIM) client apps — Mail, Contacts, and Calendar — are really powerful and should be your portals to email, contacts, and calendars, even if that data isn't in Apple's iCloud service.

Still, there are reasons to use other PIM apps instead of or in addition to Apple's offerings, such as to manage business and personal information separately. In this chapter, I explain how the iPad works with such PIM information for the major PIM account providers, such as Google and Microsoft. Although Apple's PIM apps are highly capable, you may prefer to use other client apps, whether because your company requires you to use a specific app or because a non-Apple client has extra features that appeal to you.

Understanding How the iPad Connects to PIM Accounts

Many people struggle with the notion of *accounts,* a core foundation for how the iPad — as well as computers and smartphones — works with PIM information such as email, contacts, and calendars. This section explains the accounts concept and how the iPad works with the variety of accounts available for PIM information.

On a home PC, you may be used to having your email, appointments, and contacts stored locally on just that PC, so you have to use that PC to use that information, or be sure to enter it into your other devices. But in a business environment, much of that information is stored on servers so that it's accessible from multiple devices and to multiple people — for example, for group calendars or corporate staff directories. Using an account ensures that there is just one master copy of the information shared across all devices, with changes made at one device synced to all the others that use the same account.

You will have at least one account — iCloud, Exchange, or Google — that provides one or more of the PIM services to your devices. But most people will have multiple accounts, such as Exchange for work use and Google for personal use. The iPad can work with as many accounts as you have.

Most PIM clients can work with the popular PIM services out there, so they can be your one-stop shop for all your email accounts, all your calendar accounts, and all your contacts accounts.

For email, the commonly used PIM accounts are the following:

- ✔ **Microsoft Exchange:** This supports both the locally hosted versions used by most businesses and Microsoft's Office 365 cloud service.

- ✔ **IMAP:** Used by many smaller businesses and most companies that provide you with your own domain. Several popular services use IMAP, including Apple's iCloud, Google's Gmail, Yahoo!, AOL, and Microsoft's Outlook.com (the former Hotmail).

- ✔ **POP:** The ancient protocol that your Internet service provider (ISP) may still offer.

A *domain* is a unique web destination, such as wiley.com or zangogroup.com. You have to register a domain and then pay a web host a fee to keep it running for you. If you have a small business, pay the $100 or so annual cost to maintain your own domain — it's much more professional to have your own domain than to use something like gmail.com or outlook.com in business. I can recommend Verio.com for buying domains and Pair.com for hosting them; both are inexpensive, and they don't spam you, as GoDaddy and other heavily advertised providers do.

For calendars, the commonly used PIM accounts are Exchange, Google Calendar, and the CalDAV standard used by many services.

Exchange versus IMAP versus POP

If you work for a large business, someone else has given you your account information and already chosen whether to use Exchange, IMAP, or POP for your email. (Exchange also supports calendars, contacts, notes, and tasks, whereas IMAP also supports notes. Chapter 9 covers notes and Chapter 10 covers tasks.) The IT people at your business likely chose Exchange or IMAP — and for the same reasons you should choose them if you are a small business that has no IT department to rely on.

The POP method is the oldest and least flexible of the three, so it's also the cheapest to provide. By default, whatever device reads an email gets that email downloaded, and the original is then deleted from the server to save space. If you have multiple devices, having POP means that your emails are fragmented across all your devices.

There is a work-around, however: On each device, set the POP server to retain emails for at least a week so that each device has a chance to access the emails before they are deleted. On your iPad, go to the Settings app, tap Mail, Contacts, Calendars, tap your POP account, tap Advanced, and set the "save" period in the Delete from Server menu. Note that if you set different periods on different devices, the shortest period "wins." And note that your email provider may limit how much mail you can store before it begins automatically deleting

your email, so don't set the retention period too long.

The IMAP method is newer than POP, but it's not exactly new. It keeps messages on your server so that all devices have a shot at accessing them. Working with multiple devices is therefore easier, but your email storage can grow infinitely.

To avoid the infinite storage issue, your IMAP server is typically set with a maximum storage period. You can set the storage period for your account on your iPad. Go to the Settings app, tap Mail, Contacts, Calendars, tap your IMAP account, tap Account, tap Advanced, and set the "save" period in the Remove menu. Again, note that if you set different periods on different devices, the shortest period "wins."

The Exchange method is the newest, but again it's not new. You have no way to set the "save" period from your iPad's Settings app. The Exchange administrator sets this period from a Microsoft management application like Exchange Server or System Center on a PC or through a browser. If you use Office 365 or a hosted Exchange service, the administrator will have a web page and login to manage such settings. An Exchange administrator can also manage which devices get access to the server and set policies that the devices must honor to gain access. This latter approach is the best way to go if you can afford it.

For contacts, the commonly used PIM accounts are Exchange, Google Contacts, and the CardDAV standard or the LDAP standard used by many services.

Beyond all the items mentioned in this section, there's really nothing left to support other than IBM's Lotus Notes and Novell GroupWise, but even those servers now use an Exchange-compatible front end called Exchange ActiveSync to work with various email, calendar, and contacts apps.

When you set up your PIM accounts on the iPad, you see the following services: iCloud, Exchange, Google, Yahoo!, AOL, and Outlook.com. Tap the desired service and follow the prompts; the iPad will configure for you whatever protocols (like IMAP or CalDAV) such services may use behind the scenes. For services not listed, tap Other and then choose the specific protocol, such as IMAP, POP, CalDAV, CardDAV, or LDAP, that the service uses.

Accessing It All with Apple's Mail, Contacts, and Calendar

For email, Mail supports the following: Exchange, IMAP, and POP. It also supports several popular types of IMAP accounts, including its own iCloud, Google's Gmail, Yahoo!, AOL, and Outlook.com.

For calendars, Calendar supports Exchange, Google Calendar, and any service that uses the CalDAV standard, such as Yahoo!.

For contacts, Contacts supports Exchange, Google Contacts, and any service that uses the CardDAV standard, such as Yahoo!, or the LDAP standard.

When you set up your iPad, you all but certainly set up an iCloud account or signed in with an existing one (such as one you've set up on your iPhone or Mac, or in iTunes), as Chapter 2 explains. For most people, having an iCloud account works really nicely as your personal account because it not only provides email, calendars, contacts, notes, and reminders but also syncs settings such as Safari bookmarks and passwords across all your Apple devices. And it supports shared calendars, so you can have a shared calendar with your family and a separate one for yourself. Or you can have multiple calendars within that iCloud account, some shared (with different people per calendar, such as the soccer team's parents, or your siblings for your parents' medical appointments) and some not (such as your bookie appointments) — whatever make sense.

But if you use Google or some other service for your personal email, contacts, and calendars, that's fine — they work on the iPad, too. Likewise, you can use any service for your business email, calendar, and contacts.

In all cases, you set them up via the Settings app's Mails, Contacts, Calendars pane. Tap Add Account, choose the account type to add (tap Other for IMAP or POP mail, for CalDAV calendars, or for CardDAV or LDAP contacts), and enter in the requested information. The services you configure in the Settings app become available to Apple's PIM apps.

In most cases, the information you enter on the iPad is the same as what you would enter on a computer. The exception is for Exchange — or can be. If you use Microsoft Outlook at the office, IT may have set you up with a direct account. But those don't work in Mail, Contacts, and Calendars. Instead, you

Notes for Exchange users

Exchange is the name of Microsoft's server for email, contacts, calendars, notes, and tasks. But many people call it Outlook, because that's the name of the Microsoft application in Windows and on the Mac used to work with Exchange. Outlook can also work with other email services, such as Google's, and Apple's own Mail app can work with Exchange. So, try not to use the terms Exchange and Outlook as synonyms — they're not!

If you're the kind of person who works on a lot of devices — a home computer, a work computer, a tablet or two, and a smartphone — pay attention: Exchange limits the number of active connections an account can have, usually to ten. That sounds like a lot of headroom, but for EAS connections such as on the iPad, each service — email, contacts, calendars, reminders, and notes — counts as a connection. Ditto for using Exchange with Apple's PIM apps on the Mac and iPhone, or Google's PIM apps on

Android. Or apps on any device from a company other than Microsoft.

So obviously, if you have a tablet, smartphone, and Mac all turned on and connected to the Internet, you can easily surpass ten active EAS connections if they all tend to sync around the same time. If you do exceed the limit, you'll get delays in syncing, and even some accounts that stop syncing on some devices. So turn on only the Exchange services you really want to be active on each device. Or turn off devices that aren't really being used — for example, shut off your home computer rather than let it sit idle (and checking Exchange periodically) while you're at the office.

Note: Connections from Microsoft's own Outlook and OWA apps count as one connection per device, no matter how many services are turned on for that device. No, that's not fair!

have to use Exchange ActiveSync credentials, which means that you need to know the external server. That server is usually the same as you would use to access Outlook Web Access from your browser, such as owa.*domain*.com or webmail.*domain*.com), though it will likely be outlook.office365.com if you use Outlook 365.

If you set up an Exchange account, you also set which services are enabled for syncing, as well as how far back the account syncs email using the Mail Days to Sync option. And you can set up an out-of-office reply using the Automatic Reply option. (Just remember to turn it off when you're back!) Figure 12-1 shows the setup screen for Exchange in the Settings app.

In the Mail, Contacts, Calendars pane in the Settings app, you set most of your preferences for Apple's apps: Mail, Contacts, Calendar, Notes, and Reminders, such as default accounts (for new entries in an app), email signatures, display order for contact names, and default alert times for calendar entries.

Spend a few minutes going through these options to customize your iPad experience. Most provide a brief explanation of what they do.

As I mention in this book's intro, I assume that you have basic iPad skills, or that you have a good introductory book to help you learn them. Therefore I don't cover all the ins and outs of using Mail, Calendar, or Contacts. I do, however, show you specific techniques that a business user should know, particularly those that are not readily obvious.

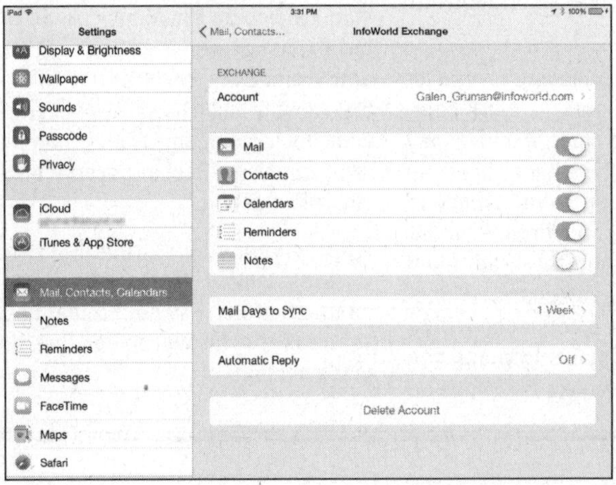

Figure 12-1:
The setup
screen for
Exchange in
the Settings
app.

Managing your accounts and Inboxes in Mail

If you're using Mail for both business and personal email, you can use a few tricks for clarifying which account you're using so that you don't mix up where messages are coming from.

Knowing what account sends your email

The first thing to do is set your default email account. That's the one new messages are sent to if you're composing an email from All Inboxes or other multiaccount Inbox in Mail. Ditto for email sent by other apps — those that use Mail to do the actual delivery, anyhow.

You set that default in the Settings app's Mail, Contacts, Calendars pane, by tapping Default Account in the Mail section and choosing the, um, default account.

If you're in an account-specific Inbox, or reading messages from a specific account, your new message is sent from that account regardless of what your default is. Mail assumes that if you're looking at messages from, say, your work account, you want new messages to come from that same work account.

Likewise, when you reply to an email, Mail sends it from the account the email was sent to so that the reply to a message sent to your business account will come from your business account.

You can always change which account an email (whether a new email or a reply) is sent from by selecting a different account in the From field when composing an email.

Setting up your signatures

The second thing to do so is make sure that you have a different email signature for each account you have, as Figure 12-2 shows. You do so in the Settings app's Mail, Contacts, Calendars pane, using the Signature option toward the bottom of the Mail section. Tap Per Account to set a separate signature that is automatically inserted at the bottom of each message you send. In the figure, you can see that I have set one personal signature (for my iCloud account) and two business ones (for my freelance business and my day job).

Tap a signature to edit it. You can't use formatting such as boldface or colors, but you can use paragraph returns to separate lines. When you're done, leave the Settings app or go elsewhere in the Settings app. Your edits are saved as you type them.

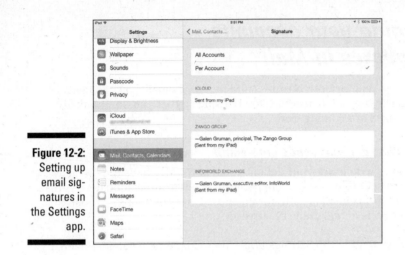

Figure 12-2:
Setting up
email sig-
natures in
the Settings
app.

Moving among email accounts

When you have multiple accounts set up in Mail, you see them listed twice in
the left pane of the main Mail screen, as Figure 12-3 shows.

At the top are your Inboxes, which by default shows All Inboxes (a unified list
of messages in all your accounts' Inboxes — meaning not in account folders),
the Inbox for each account, and Unread (which shows all unread messages
across all your account Inboxes).

You can choose what Inboxes display, and in what order, by tapping the
Edit button. Rearrange Inboxes by dragging each Inbox's Reorder handle
(the icon of two lines) to a new location in the list. Select or deselect the
Inboxes you want to display. Most are smart mailbox folders, which are
filtered lists from all your accounts, such as Flagged, Today, All Drafts, and
Attachments. At the very bottom is the Add Mailbox button; tap it to add
a specific mailbox folder to the Inbox list. Tap Done when you've arranged
your Inbox display as you prefer.

The other section of the left pane is accounts, which shows each account
activated in the Settings app. Tap an account to see any mailbox folders it
has, and tap a mailbox folder to see its contents. (Navigate back up your mailbox folder hierarchy by tapping Mailboxes at the top left of the screen.)

You can rearrange the accounts the same way you rearrange inboxes: Tap
Edit above the Inboxes section, scroll down, and use the Reorder handles to
reorder the accounts.

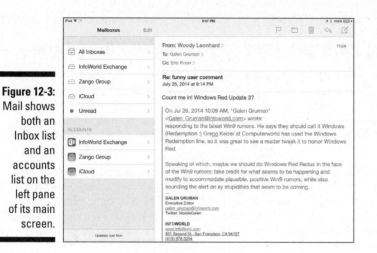

Figure 12-3:
Mail shows both an Inbox list and an accounts list on the left pane of its main screen.

You can't reorder the mailbox folders within an account, but you can create a new mailbox folder by going to the account and then tapping Edit above the mailbox folders list. Then you have these options:

✔ **Tap New Mailbox at the bottom to add a mailbox folder to the current account.** In the Name field that appears, enter a name for the new mailbox folder. In the Mailbox Location menu that appears, tap the account name to get a list of all current mailbox folders so that you can choose where to insert the new one. Tap Save when done. The new mailbox folder is synced to all your devices that use this account.

✔ **Tap a mailbox folder to edit its name change its location, or delete it.** Tap Save when done.

Tap Done when you're done editing your mailbox folders.

To move messages to a mailbox folder, tap the Folder icon at the top of a message and then tap the desired mailbox folder from the list that appears on the left pane. Or tap the Edit button above the message list in the left pane, select each message you want to move (which places a check mark next to them), tap Move at the bottom of the pane, and then select the mailbox folder to move them into.

Tracking an important conversation

When you get new emails, you'll likely see them on the your Lock screen, in the Notification Center (swipe down from the top of the screen to open this), or, for a few seconds, on the top of your Home screen or current app screen. What you see in those notifications, and when, depend on what you've set up for each Mail account in the Settings app's Notifications pane.

Navigating multiple messages at the same time

When you're replying to an email or writing a new email, you often realize that you need to look at the original email or another email to get some relevant information. But for iOS versions before iOS 8, after you had begun composing an email on the iPad in Mail, you couldn't switch to another email. All you could do was tap Cancel and then tap Save Draft to save the current message in your Drafts folder, get that other information, go to your Drafts folder, and reopen the draft message to continue working on it.

Well, that tedious process is no longer necessary as of iOS 8. You can open and even compose other emails while other email drafts are in progress. It's devilishly easy: Simply drag down the bar at the top of the message sheet to the bottom of the screen. It anchors itself there, as the left side of the following figure shows, and you can navigate Mail to read other messages, reply to other messages, and compose other messages. You can pull down any other message you're writing to the bottom of the screen as well so that you can have several in progress at the same time.

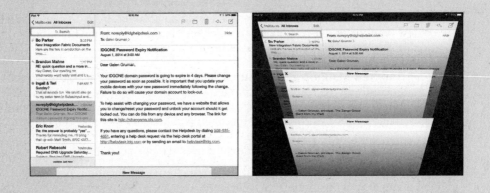

If you have only one in-progress email anchored to the bottom of the screen, tap it to reopen it. If you have several, tap the anchored-message bar to open the screen shown at the right of the figure, from which you pick the message you want to open. (If you use an iPhone, this screen should look familiar: It's the same method for navigating open tabs in Safari on the iPhone.)

If your iPad is used primarily for work purposes, in the Settings app's Notifications pane, set your work email to show up in the Lock screen and at the top of other screens in what is called a banner. But don't set up personal email accounts. If your iPad is primarily for personal use, do the opposite!

When you open Mail, you'll of course see new messages in the Inbox, as well as in the mail list for the accounts your messages are sent to. Also, iOS 8 has added another kind of notification that lets you track responses to specific conversations as Figure 12-4 shows.

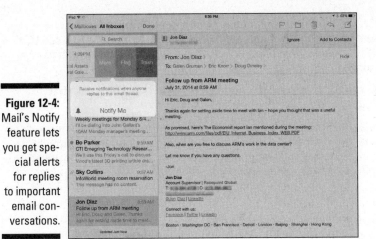

Figure 12-4:
Mail's Notify feature lets you get special alerts for replies to important email conversations.

This new notification is called Notify Me, and you can set it up for any conversation (a.k.a. a *thread*). When reading a message, tap the Flag button (the flag icon) at the top of the message, choose Notify Me in the menu that appears, and choose Notify Me again to confirm. Or in a message list, flick to the left over a message, tap More, choose Notify Me, and choose Notify Me again to confirm. To stop notifications, do the same, but choose Stop Notifying. (You don't have to confirm that.) Then, when you get a new message in this thread, a notification displays on your iPad screen, no matter what app you're currently using.

Be careful when using the flick gesture to get the More button. If you flick too far to the left, the three buttons — More, Flag, and Delete — become one button: Delete. It's really easy — too easy, in fact — to accidentally delete an email with this gesture.

So what notifications do you get from Notify Me? That's up to you. If you have Notify Me enabled for at least one conversation in Mail, you can set up what that notification is like in the Settings app. To set up what type of notification you get from Notify Me, follow these steps in the Settings app:

1. **Tap Notifications to open the Notifications pane.**

2. **Tap Mail to open the Mail pane and make sure that the Allow Notifications switch is set to On.**

   You see all your active accounts; tap any one to set or alter its notifications. Likewise, tap Show in Notifications to set how many emails (from all accounts) display in the Notification Center.

3. **Tap Thread Notifications.**

   This sets up the notifications for Notify Me. *Note:* If you don't see this option, that means there are no email conversations for which Notify Me is turned on.

4. **Set the sound, type of alert, and other options in the pane that appears.**

   I recommend setting the type of alert to a higher level than your normal alert level for Mail accounts. For example, if you usually set email notifications to display as banners, I suggest you set Notify Me notifications to display as alerts, which interrupt what you are doing when they appear.

Creating business cards from emails

iOS has long had the capability to use a tool known as a *data detector,* which recognizes information such as a phone number or address in an email and lets you tap that information to act on it. For example, you can tap a number to add it to Contacts (or call it from an iPhone), or tap an address to get a map of that location.

iOS 8 takes the concept further. It scans each email you read to see whether it has contact information in it that's not in the Contacts app. If so, it displays a bar at the top of the message (see Figure 12-5) asking you whether to add that information to Contacts. Tap Add to Contacts to add all the information it detects; a pop-over appears, letting you choose to create a new contact from the detected information or add it to an existing contact (such as to fill in missing information).

Figure 12-5:
Mail detects when an email contains contact information that's not in your address book and lets you add it with a tap.

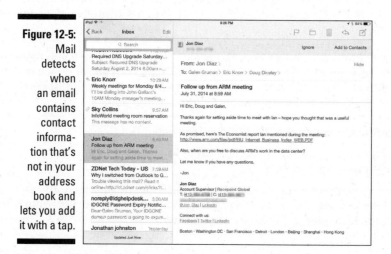

In an era when paper business cards are rarely used, this cool feature provides a great way to add to your address book, which is then kept up-to-date on all your devices through iCloud, Exchange, or Google.

Telling people you're not available

If you use Exchange (or Office 365) for your email, you know how valuable its Automatic Replies feature is (previously called Out of Office). With it, you set up automated messages as replies to anyone who emails you during a specified period so that people get a message saying you are on vacation or traveling and to contact so-and-so in your absence or just wait till you're back.

If you use Microsoft Outlook on your computer, you'll find that feature baked in for easy access. If you use Mail on the Mac, you can get to it by right-clicking the Exchange account in your mail list and choosing Out of Office. But how do you do it on the iPad? Until iOS 8, you had to go to the Outlook Web Access web page that your company set up to manage Automatic Replies — an awkward experience.

But now you can set up Automatic Replies directly on the iPad, in the Settings app's Mail, Contacts, Calendars pane. Just follow these steps:

1. **Tap your Exchange account from the accounts list.**

2. **Tap Automatic Reply.**

   Automatic Reply is the iPad's name for Out of Office.

3. **In the sheet that appears, set the Automatic Reply switch to On, enter an end date (if desired), and add or edit the Away Message field's contents.**

   A *sheet* is a settings window that appears over the current screen; you can't move or leave a sheet until you tap Cancel or Save (or Done, in some cases). It's like an unmovable dialog.

   If you don't specify an end date for Automatic Reply, remember to turn off this switch when you're back — otherwise, people will keep getting the automated reply.

On a PC or a Mac, or via Outlook Web Access, you can set two away messages: one for people at your company and one for people outside the company. But when you set up Automatic Reply on the iPad, everyone gets the same message.

I wish that iCloud, Gmail, and other IMAP accounts supported the Automatic Reply feature!

Managing your accounts and address book in Contacts

As with Mail, Contacts can work with a variety of electronic address books, including those in iCloud, Exchange, and Google, plus any server that's CardDAV- or LDAP-compatible. If you make a change to a contact, or add one there, all devices that use the same contacts account get the change. You set up your accounts in the Settings app's Mail, Contacts, Calendars pane, setting the Contacts switch to On for any account whose contacts you want available on your iPad.

Also as you can with Mail, you can access all your contacts from all your accounts, such as when composing an email or initiating a FaceTime chat.

Setting your default contacts

Just as you do with Mail, you should be sure to set your default Contacts account so that new contacts are added to the account you expect them to be in. You do so in the Settings app's Mail, Contacts, Calendars pane, by tapping Default Account in the Contacts section and choosing the, um, default account.

Adding new contacts

When you add a contact from within the Contacts app, you can force the contact to go in a specific account by hiding the others before adding a contact. To hide the other accounts and add a contact to a specific account, follow these steps:

1. Tap Groups in the upper-left corner of the screen.

2. Deselect all accounts other than the one you want to add the contact to.

3. Tap Done.

4. Tap the Add button (the + icon) at the top of the screen, enter the contact's information, and tap Done.

5. Tap Groups again.

6. Select all the accounts whose contacts you want to be visible on the iPad.

7. Tap Done.

You can't create groups on the iPad, though any groups in your contacts lists are retained on the iPad. Groups have another limitation: Although you can turn specific groups off in Contacts (follow the preceding Steps 1–3 but deselect just the specific groups you want to hide), doing so has a perverse effect: People who are members of no groups are also hidden when you hide any group. That's not right!

You can't move a contact from one account to another from your iPad; you need to do that on your Mac using its Contacts application by selecting the contacts' cards and moving them to the account you want them to be in. On a PC or Android device, you have no simple way to move contacts from one account to another, unfortunately. And you can't move contacts from an Exchange account to another account, even in Contacts on the Mac.

Linking contacts across accounts

Because Contacts can access contacts from multiple accounts, you can have several versions of a person in your contacts list. In Contacts on your Mac, you can merge and link such duplicates by selecting them and choosing Card⇨Merge Selected Cards. That command merges multiple cards into one if they are in the same account, and it links multiple cards on different accounts so that they appear to be one card, even though their information continues to be spread across the various accounts that person shows up in.

On the iPad, you can also link cards. In the Contacts app, select a person from the contacts list and tap Edit. Scroll to the bottom of the Edit pane and tap Link Contacts. Now choose the other instances of that person to link each instance together. The person will now appear just once in the contacts list of the Contacts app, yet each account's card for that person is retained as is. The unified card on the iPad shows the cards that are linked to it, as Figure 12-6 shows.

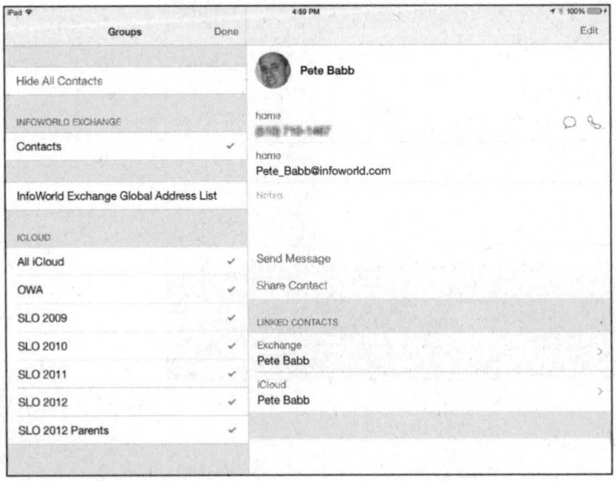

Figure 12-6: Contacts lets you link cards from multiple accounts.

Quickly contacting recent contacts

For most people, the Contacts app serves as an organizer for your address book, plus as a way for other apps to look up information about people. For example, Mail uses Contacts to find a person's email address when you tap the + icon while composing an email in Mail, and Calendar uses the Contacts app to show people's birthdays.

That information is also used by Messages, a text messaging app, and FaceTime, an audio and video chatting app, both of which come preinstalled on the iPad. (Chapter 13 covers Messages and FaceTime.) Messages can look up a person's mobile phone number to send an SMS text message, or look up the person's iCloud account to send an iMessage. FaceTime can look up the person's iCloud account to do an audio or video chat.

iOS 8 makes it a bit easier to contact people you tend to contact often or have contacted recently. When you open the app switcher by double-tapping the Home button or swiping four fingers up from the bottom of the screen, the app switcher shows not just recently used apps but also recently contacted people. Tap a person to get available options for contacting him or her; these options are Messages, FaceTime Audio, and/or FaceTime Video, as Figure 12-7 shows.

If you don't want recent contacts to show up in the app switcher, go to the Settings app's Mail, Contacts, Calendars pane, tap Show in App Switcher in the Contacts section, and set the Recents switch to Off.

Figure 12-7:
The app switcher shows recent contacts and lets you contact them via Messages and, if they have iCloud accounts, FaceTime.

Managing your accounts and appointments in Calendar

If you've read this chapter from the start, this statement will sound familiar by now: Calendar lets you connect to any of several accounts for your appointments — iCloud, Exchange, Google, and any service that uses the CalDAV standard — so that your appointments remain synced across all your devices. And you can see all your appointments in one place, even though they are actually stored on the separate servers of your various accounts.

As with Mail and Contacts, you enable calendar access for an account by setting the Calendar switch to On for that account in the Settings app's Mail, Contacts, Calendars pane. Also, you set the default calendar account in the Calendars section of the pane by tapping Default Calendar.

Handling invitations

Calendar automatically displays any meeting request that you receive via email as long as it uses the industry-standard .ics file format. Virtually every calendar program generates this .ics format. (You'll see those invites in Mail as well, in the message they came in.) Invites that come from other Exchange users to your Exchange account also show up automatically in Calendar.

You can tap Accept, Decline, or Maybe in the Mail app to respond to an invite you see there. If you tap Accept or Maybe, the event is added to your default calendar unless you specify a different calendar in the menu that appears.

You can also handle invites in Calendar. By default, invites that you haven't acted on show up on your calendar as gray events with a dashed outline. Tap the event to accept or decline it.

You don't have to hunt for such events, though: Tap the Inbox button to open the pop-over shown in Figure 12-8. It has two panes:

✔ **New:** Shows invitations you have not responded to, including updates to previously accepted invites.

✔ **Replied:** Shows the meetings you've responded to and what your response was. You'll see three buttons for each event — Accept, Maybe, and Decline — with the button for the current status highlighted.

You can change that invite's status by tapping a different button for a specific invite.

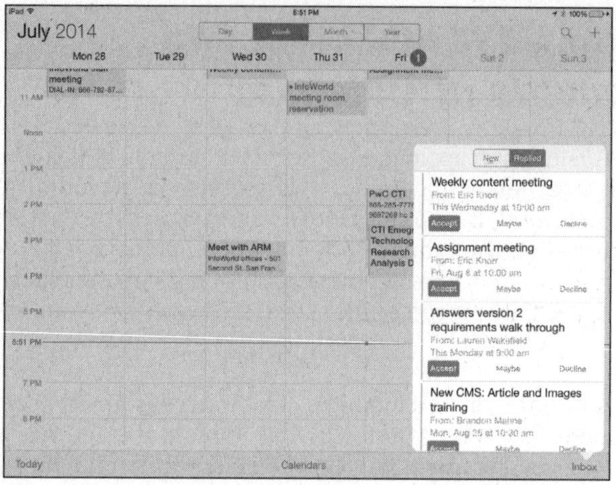

Figure 12-8:
Calendar
lets you see
the status
of meet-
ing invites
in one
location.

Calendar also has an option to add invitees to appointments you set up. To invite people to an event, follow these steps:

1. **Open or create the appointment in Calendar and tap Invitees in the pop-over that shows the event details. (The upcoming Figure 12-9 shows such a pop-over.)**

2. **In the To field in the Invitees pop-over that appears, enter the person's email address or, if that person is in your Contacts with an email address, his or her name.**

   Calendar looks up the name as you type it, displaying any matches so that you can select the one you want.

3. **Add more people, if desired, by typing a comma after an existing name.**

4. **Tap Done to send the invitation via email or Exchange, depending on the accounts you and the invitees use.**

If the event is in an Exchange calendar and the person you're inviting is also an Exchange user at your company (meaning that you're using the same Exchange server), the Invitees pop-over will show whether the person has a scheduling conflict with your event. It even suggests times when people (who are using the same Exchange server, that is) are free to meet, in case you want to reschedule at that more available time.

Managing events

Look again at Figure 12-8. If this (print) book were in color, you would see all the events showing up in different colors. Each color represents a specific account, so you know at a glance whether an appointment is for work or a personal matter. You set the colors for your accounts by tapping the Calendars button at the bottom of the screen and then tapping the *i* icon next to a calendar to get a color list.

To add an event, tap the Add button (the + icon) at the upper left of the screen. To search existing events, tap the Search button (the magnifying glass icon).

For both new and existing events, you can add and change all sorts of infor-mation in that pop-over, as Figure 12-9 shows. Options include making an event repeat, setting a reminder alert, getting drive-time estimations and location maps (if the address is in the Location field), and adding notes. (Options don't display if they're not available for a specific account or if they are for an invite someone else sent.) Just tap a field to edit it. You can also change the status of an accepted or decline event.

To change an existing appointment from one calendar to another, just tap the event, tap the calendar shown in the pop-over that appears, and select a dif-ferent calendar from the list. *Note:* If someone else created the event through an invite, you may not be able to change the calendar it's on, for technical reasons that don't matter because you have no control over them.

If you use Exchange, you'll be happy to know that iOS 8 added a useful Exchange feature to the event pop-over: the Private switch (shown in Figure 12-9, at bottom right). If you slide that switch to On, other Exchange users in your company can see that you have an appointment at that time but they can't see any of its other details.

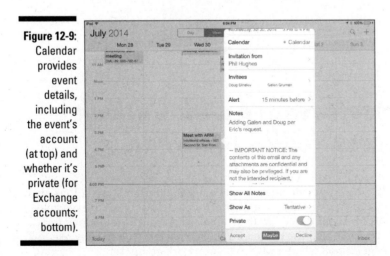

Figure 12-9:
Calendar
provides
event
details,
including
the event's
account
(at top) and
whether it's
private (for
Exchange
accounts;
bottom).

You did know that Exchange calendar events are public to other users in your company unless you mark events as private, right? Or set them all to be private? (You can do that in the preferences settings for Calendar on the Mac or for Outlook in Windows or on the Mac.)

Managing calendar display

In the Calendars pop-over, you can hide or show specific calendars by tapping a calendar's name to remove or show the check mark.

And, often important for business use, you can tell Calendar to show declined events in your calendar, as Figure 12-10 shows. (Declined events appear as a gray block, with a stripe to the left side in the color of the account.) This feature can be handy if someone complains that you skipped a meeting: You can see quickly that it was set at the same time as another meeting you just couldn't skip.

Figure 12-10:
The
Calendars
pop-over in
Calendar
lets you
control
which
calendars
display, and
what color
their events'
back-
grounds
have.

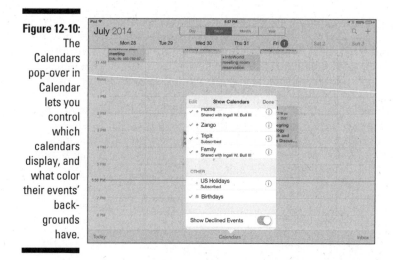

Going Microsoft-Native with Outlook for Web Access (OWA) for iPad

If you use Exchange email at work, you probably use Microsoft's Outlook application. It's the corporate standard, even though other applications such as Apple's Mail for the Mac also work with Exchange. Microsoft makes a version of Outlook for the iPad as well. It's called OWA, short for Outlook for Web Access, which is also the name for the web page that you likely use to access your office email when away from your work computer.

The OWA for iPad app is free, but you or your company must pay for an Exchange Online or Office 365 subscription to use it. If you also use an iPhone, you will use the separate OWA for iPhone app.

 You can't use OWA for iPad if your Exchange server is locally hosted, meaning running on your own company's servers. The app works only with the "hosted" Exchange or Office 365 cloud service provided by Microsoft and select providers. You'll instead have to use Apple's PIM apps or a mobile device management service's PIM clients to access a locally hosted Exchange server. (Chapter 3 explains mobile device management.)

Knowing when you can and should use OWA

OWA lets you work with your email, calendars, and contacts in Exchange, but not your notes or tasks. (You can use Apple's Notes and Reminders apps for these, as Chapters 9 and 10 explain.)

You might wonder why you'd bother with OWA, given how nicely Mail on the iPad works with Exchange. Honestly, the only good reason is because your company insists that you use OWA. Your company has a legitimate reason to insist: To keep your work and personal email completely separate.

Although Mail separates different accounts' email behind the scenes, you can easily send an email from one account to another without IT's awareness: Just forward or reply to the work email by changing the email's From field to your personal account before sending. You might think your company is paranoid, but some businesses have to comply with strict rules on tracking business communications, such as to prevent insider trading or show an accurate correspondence history in case of a lawsuit.

Signing in to OWA

When you first use OWA, you need to sign in with your Exchange Online or Office 365 credentials, which your IT department can give you. (You can probably find them in the settings for Outlook on your computer as well.)

You may also need to establish a PIN; your IT administrator may have configured Exchange Online or Office 365 to require one. If so, you need to enter that PIN each time you want to check your email, calendar, or contacts in OWA.

OWA lets you pick which Exchange service you want to use from its Go To screen, shown in Figure 12-11. Those services are

- ✔ **Outlook:** For email
- ✔ **Calendar:** For appointments
- ✔ **People:** For contacts

If you open OWA and go straight to mail, calendars, or contacts, tap the Go To button at the bottom left (it looks like two squares on top of a rectangle) to get that Go To screen to use a different Exchange service.

Figure 12-11:
OWA's Go
To screen.

Working with email

The default Outlook screen shows a list of emails at the left and the currently selected email on the right, including any related emails from a conversation (also called a *thread*). Tap an email in the message list to view it. You can narrow down the display of emails by tapping the desired filter: All, Unread, To Me (this excludes any emails where you were in the Cc or Bcc field), and Flagged.

Figure 12-12 shows the default screen with an email in a conversation. You may see just a summary for other emails in a conversation; tap them to expand that summary to display the full message instead.

Figure 12-12:
The typical OWA screen for email that's part of a conversation.

Managing and composing emails

Numerous controls are scattered about the Outlook screen, some affecting the current email and others affecting the way mail is presented. First, here are the controls that apply to the current email.

At the upper right of the screen are three buttons:

- ✔ **Expand/Collapse Thread:** Shows the full conversation or collapses the conversation to just the headers. If you see two stacked caret (^) characters, that means you can expand the conversation. If you see two stacked upside-down caret characters, that means you can collapse it. (Both of these caret characters appear here in the margin.) If your conversation has just one message, the buttons expand or collapse that one message.

- ✔ **Trash:** Deletes the entire conversation.

- ✔ **More (the . . . icon):** Displays other options, as Figure 12-11 shows: Mark as Unread, Flag, Move (to move the thread to a different folder), and Ignore (which deletes the conversation from your Inbox and deletes any more replies as they come in).

Within a message itself are two buttons to the right of the header:

- ✔ **Reply (the icon of two left-facing curved arrows):** Lets you reply, reply to all, or forward that particular email.

- ✔ **More (the . . . icon):** Displays other options: Mark as Unread, Flag, Mark as Junk, and Delete. That Delete option is what you use to delete a specific message in the conversation, rather than the whole conversation.

You may also see an Action Item bar in some messages. If OWA detects what it thinks are tasks in the email's text, it shows this bar. Tap it to create a reminder from what it thinks it has found.

To create a new email, tap the New button (the + icon) at the upper left of the screen and then compose your message in the form that appears, as Figure 12-13 shows. Use the To, Cc, and Subject fields as you would with any email app. Enter your text in the message body — and no, you can't apply formatting such as boldface, italics, or indents to your text selections in OWA.

Figure 12-13:
Composing
an email in
OWA.

Here are the buttons involved in composing emails, both new messages and replies or forwards of existing ones:

- ✔ **Send (the flying-letter icon):** Sends the message.
- ✔ **Attachments button (the paperclip icon):** Lets you add a photo from the Photos app or your iPad's camera.
- ✔ **Apps (the icon of two boxes):** Lets you work with OWA add-ons such as templates, if available.
- ✔ **Cancel (the X icon):** Closes and discards the message.
- ✔ **More (the . . . icon):** Opens a menu with the following options:
    - *Show Bcc:* Displays the Bcc field
    - *Show From:* Shows you the account the message will be sent from
    - *Check Names:* Verifies that names you enter are in the Exchange contacts list

• *Set Importance:* Marks the message priority

• *Show Message Options:* Opens a sheet in which you can request a delivery or read receipt as well as mark whether a message should be considered confidential or otherwise sensitive

Working with mail folders, views, and search

The Outlook screen has other options scattered throughout that let you work with other Exchange features.

To the left of the message list is the Expand button (the » icon). Tap it to see a list of favorite (frequently used) folders, people with whom you correspond frequently (tap a name to see just emails from that person), and (if you scroll down) a list of all folders for your email account. Figure 12-14 shows the expanded view. Tap the Collapse button (the « icon) to hide this view.

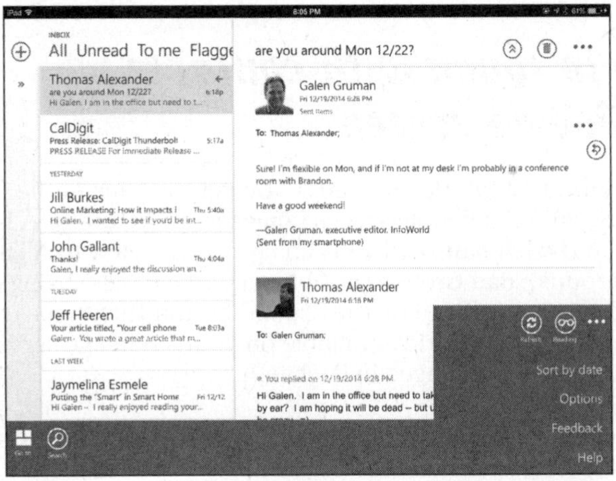

Figure 12-14: OWA's expanded Outlook view lets you see folders and frequent correspondents.

OWA auto-collapses this expanded view when you perform an action, so you'll find yourself frequently reopening it. You have no way to keep it open until you decide you're done with it.

At the bottom of the Outlook screen are your other options:

✔ **Go To (the icon of two squares on a rectangle):** Closes the Outlook screen and returns you to the Go To screen shown earlier in Figure 12-11.

✔ **Search (the magnifying-glass icon):** Lets you search your email.

✔ **Refresh (the icon of two curved arrows chasing each other):** Checks for new emails.

✔ **Reading (the eyeglasses icon):** Hides or reveals the message list. You use it to let a message take the whole screen.

✔ **More (the . . . icon):** Lets you:

- *Change how messages are sorted:* If messages are currently sorted by date, you see the Sort by Conversation option to change that setting so that all messages in a conversation appear together, as shown earlier in Figure 12-12. If messages are currently sorted by conversation, you see the Sort by Date option to change that setting so that all messages are sorted by date and not grouped into conversations.

- *Change other email settings:* Tap the Options option to see the screen shown later in Figure 12-21.

Getting in touch with contacts on the People screen

OWA uses a consistent interface, so after you get the hang of the Outlook screen, working with the People screen comes more naturally. A list of contacts appears at the left side, and you can narrow the view to All, People (meaning no groups), and Groups (meaning no individuals) using the buttons at the top of the contacts list. Use the Expand button (the » icon) to show the various contacts and directories available on your Exchange server, including conference rooms if managed in Exchange.

When you select a person from the contacts list on the People screen, you see all the information available for that person in Exchange, as Figure 12-15 shows, in what OWA calls a *card.* Tap the Edit button (the pencil icon) at the bottom of the screen to edit a person's information in the form that appears. Tap the Save button (the diskette icon) to save your changes or the Cancel button (the X icon) to ignore them.

To create a new contact, tap the New button (the + icon) at the upper left of the screen to get the same form.

If a person appears multiple times in your contacts list, you can link those separate entries into one so that the person appears just once. To do so, tap one of the entries for that person, scroll down to the bottom of the right pane, and tap Manage. Any duplicate entries are shown, which you can then link to the current card. You can also search for people to link, such as if a person uses a nickname.

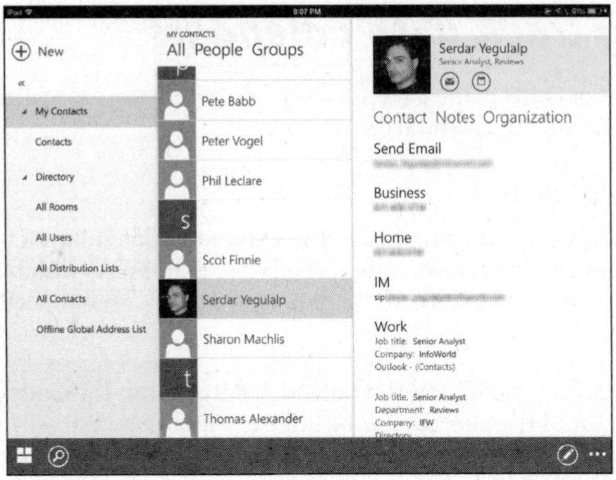

Figure 12-15:
OWA's
expanded
People view
lets you
see your
contact's
information
as well as
available
Exchange
directories.

There's not much more to the People screen than what I've described so far. But here are a couple more features: Under a person's name, you may see the Mail and/or Calendar icons; tap Mail to send that person an email, and tap Calendar to invite that person to an appointment. If you've added notes to a person's card, you can view those notes by tapping the Notes button under the person's name. Tap Contact to see that person's contact information. Tap Organization, if available, to see information about that contact's manager, reports, and division information for companies that use Exchange to track that detail.

You use the Search button (the magnifying glass icon) at the bottom left of the screen to, well, search for people.

Use the More button (the . . . icon) on the bottom right of the screen for these additional features:

- ✔ **Sort Contacts:** Lets you sort contacts by first name, last name, company, home city, work copy, or when added.

- ✔ **Display Name Order:** Lets you choose whether people's names appear in *first last* or *last first* format (no matter how they are sorted).

- ✔ **Delete:** Deletes the current card.

One person you won't easily find in the People screen is yourself. You're not listed in your contacts, for example. And probably not in All Contacts. After all, why would you need to contact yourself? But if you want to view and edit your own entry in Exchange, go to the expanded view in the People screen (tap the » icon) and tap Offline Global Address List, if available. You should find yourself there.

Keeping track with calendars

The final piece of OWA is the Calendar screen, where you can view and manage your Exchange calendar.

Using calendar views

Figure 12-16 shows the month view in the expanded Calendar view; use the Day, Work Week (which shows only weekdays), Full Week (which includes weekends), and Month buttons at the bottom of the screen to switch calendar views.

To jump to today's schedule in the Calendar screen, tap the Today button at the lower right of the screen; it looks like a paper calendar with a triangle above it. Your view won't change, but the current date will be highlighted in the week and month views.

In the expanded view (tap the Expand button, which is the » icon — not shown in Figure 12-16 because the view already expanded), you get a list of available calendars, including other people's calendars that you've been given access to, to view or manage them (something you do in Outlook on your computer, not from your iPad).

Tap a calendar's name at the bottom left of the screen to display its events (a check mark appears to the left of its name) or hide it (the check mark goes away). In Figure 12-16, you can see both my appointments (in blue) and my boss's appointments (in green).

Figure 12-16:
OWA's
expanded
Calendar
view lets
you see the
month at
a glance,
as well
as other
available
calendars.

Today button

Handling event details

To get details about an event, tap it to get a pop-over, as shown in Figure 12-17. You get basic details such as the host, the date and time of the event, and any notes for the event.

If you are in Month view, you have to close the expanded view to be able to see the event details. At the right side of the screen, you see an agenda column for the selected day; tap the event in the agenda to see its details. Tapping the event in the Month view itself simply displays that day's events in the agenda list.

If you tap the pop-over, you can get even more details:

✔ **Host info:** Tap the host's name to open his or her contact card.

✔ **Your status:** For events you were invited to, tap one of the three invitation buttons to change your participation status: Accept (the check mark icon), Maybe (the ? icon), and Decline (the X icon).

✔ **More details:** Tap anywhere else on the pop-over to open the screen shown in Figure 12-18. Here, you can change the reminder alert setting, add an email reminder for the meeting; see the full list of attendees; reply to the organizer or to all participants; delete the appointment; and view the series details for a repeating event.

Tap outside the details screen to close it and return to the calendar view.

Figure 12-17: The pop-over for event details in OWA.

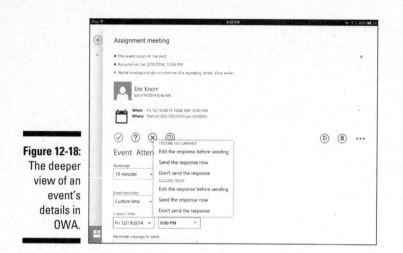

Creating and editing events

Of course, you can create new events in the Calendar view of OWA, as well as edit details of events you created.

To create an event, follow these steps:

1. **Tap the New button (the + icon) at the upper left.**

   A form for your event opens, as Figure 12-19 shows. The basic form has fields for the event name, location, date and time, and duration.

2. **Tap More Details.**

   This opens a form in which you can also invite attendees, set a reminder, mark the event as private, select the calendar in which the event appears, add notes, and set the event as a repeating one, as shown later in Figure 12-20.

3. **Tap the Schedule button (the icon of a calendar and a small clock) at the top of the screen.**

   Here, you can view the proposed event time in your calendar to see whether you have any conflicts with the new event.

4. **Tap either the OK button (the check mark icon) or the Cancel button (the X icon) in that calendar view to return to your event-creation screen.**

5. **If your company uses Microsoft's Lync meeting service, such as part of an Office 365 subscription, tap the Online Meeting Settings to set up an online Lync meeting invitation with the meeting URL created for you.**

6. **Tap the Save button at the top of the screen (the diskette icon) to create the event, or tap the Cancel button (the X icon) to cancel it.**

To edit an event, tap it to display its pop-over, as shown earlier in Figure 12-17. Tap the Edit button (the pencil icon) to edit its details, as shown in Figure 12-20. *Note:* If no Edit button appears, you can't edit the event, likely because someone else created it and either invited you or placed it on your calendar.

The forms for creating and editing events are the same as what you see in Figure 12-20, with two exceptions, both in the menu that appears when you tap the More button (the . . . icon). When editing events, that menu offers two options that aren't available when creating them:

 ✔ **Delete Event:** Does exactly what it says it does.

 ✔ **Forward:** Lets you send the event details to someone else via email.

Setting OWA options

In OWA's Outlook, People, and Calendar screens, the menu that appears when you tap the More button at the bottom right of the screen has the Options option. The Options pane that opens lets you control the default settings for all of OWA, not just for the particular service you're in.

Figure 12-19: The basic form for creating an event in OWA.

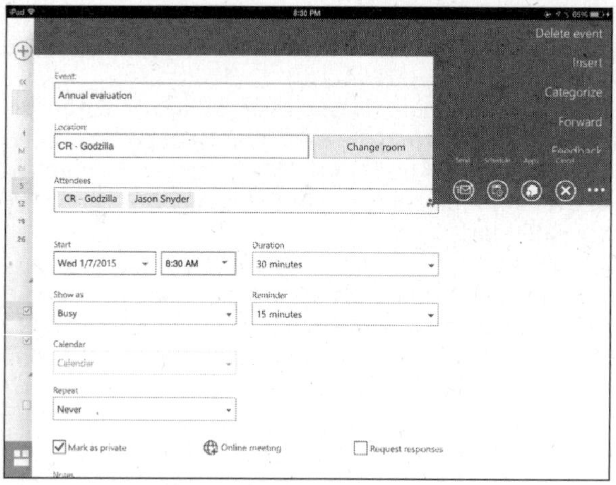

Figure 12-20:
The full
options
for editing
an event's
details in
OWA.

The options in the Options pane are as follows:

- **Automatic Replies:** Select the Automatic Replies box to enable the Exchange Out of Office feature, shown in Figure 12-21. As with Outlook or Mail on a computer, you can send separate replies to people in your organization and to people outside your organization, as well as restrict automatic replies to only people in your Exchange contacts list. What you cannot do in OWA for iPad is specify a start and stop date for the Out of Office replies, as you can on your computer or in Apple's Mail app for the iPad.

- **Time Zone:** Set your current time zone here, such as if you are traveling and want to see time stamps and calendar entries in the now-current time zone.

- **Email Signature:** Enter the text for the automatically appended signature that OWA adds to your message. Or tell OWA to use the signature you set up for Exchange in Outlook on your computer or via OWA on the web. Or tell OWA not to include an automatic signature at all.

- **Photo:** Change the photo for your account by selecting a new one from the Photos app.

- **Passcode:** Enable, disable, or change your OWA passcode here, as well as set how long OWA must be idle before it asks you for that passcode. *Note:* Your IT organization may have set policies in Exchange that force you to have a passcode and set a minimum timeout period. If so, you'll find some options unavailable for this setting.

✔ **Contact Sync:** Enable or disable access to Exchange contacts stored on your iPad. If you disable syncing, your Exchange contacts aren't available for use by other apps, such as FaceTime and Messages.

✔ **Offline Folders:** This option lets you set up as many as five folders to be synced automatically to your iPad so that their contents are available even when you don't have an Internet connection. (Your Inbox and Drafts folders are always synced, so these five are in addition to those two.) Other folders' contents are synced only when you go to those folders in OWA and have a live Internet connection.

Tap the Done button (the check mark icon) to close the Options screen.

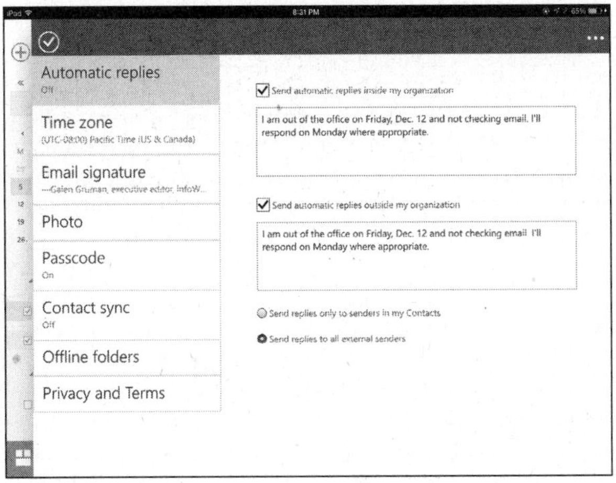

Figure 12-21: OWA's Options screen.

Going Google-Native with Gmail

If you use Google's Gmail service, you can, of course, access it from the iPad's own Mail app if you set up Gmail in the Settings app's Mail, Contacts, Calendars pane. But you may want to use the separate Gmail app, which is free, to keep your Gmail email separate from your other email. For example, maybe you use Gmail for business and iCloud for personal matters, so you'd use the Gmail app for Gmail and the Mail app for iCloud.

The Gmail app is very straightforward and is similar to other email apps: It shows a message list at the left side and the current message on the right side, as you can see in Figure 12-22.

Figure 12-22:
Gmail's
message
view.

The Gmail app can access only Gmail, not email from other services. If you use the Google Calendar or Contacts services, unfortunately you can't use Google iPad apps for them — there aren't any. You'll need to use the iPad's Calendar and Contacts apps instead.

You may need to sign in to Gmail using your standard Google account user-name and password. After you sign in, the Gmail app usually remembers your info, so you likely won't have to sign in again on your iPad. But you can switch accounts, if you have multiple Gmail accounts, by tapping the Manage Accounts button (the icon of a person and a gear) at the bottom left of the Gmail screen.

Creating new emails

To create a new email in Gmail, tap the New icon (the pencil icon) at the top of the screen. A simple form appears in which you enter the recipients in the To field (type in a name to have Gmail look it up from your contacts list, or enter the actual email address) and the email subject in the Subject field. To Cc or Bcc someone, tap the Cc/Bcc button to display those fields.

Tap the Attachments button (the paperclip icon) to insert a photo from the Photos app or a file from your Google Drive cloud storage account.

Type your message in the message body. Select text to open the standard iOS text selection menu, from which you can apply boldface, italics, or underlines via the B/U button.

When you're done, tap the Send button (the icon of a paper airplane) at the upper right of the form. Or tap Cancel (the X icon) at the upper left of the form to discard the message or save it as a draft in your Drafts folder.

Working with messages

To read a message, tap it in the messages list at left. You can use the Search field at the top of the messages list to search the current folder. (I explain in the next section how to move to other folders.)

When reading an email, you get the Reply button at the upper right; tap it to get a menu with two choices: Reply and Forward. If you're one of several recipients, a third option appears: Reply All.

Above the Reply button is the Star button; tap it to flag the message as starred. Doing so makes it available via the Starred folder described later.

At the upper right of the email pane are three other buttons:

✔ **Archive (the icon of a box with a plus symbol):** Removes the message from your Inbox but keeps a copy in the All Mail folder for later access.

✔ **Delete (the trash can icon):** Removes the message from your Inbox and moves it to the Trash folder; after 30 days the message is permanently deleted from the Gmail server and thus from your Trash folder.

✔ **Menu (the triangle icon):** Offers the following options in its pop-over:

- *Move:* Lets you move the message to a different folder.

- *Label:* Lets you assign a category for later sorting.

- *Mute:* Tells Gmail to ignore any more messages that come in reply to this one, and removes the email from the Inbox. (You can still find it in the All Mail view I explain later.)

- *Report Spam:* Tells Google that a message is spam; this helps block further emails from that person and moves the message to the Spam folder.

- *Print:* Uses Google's Cloud Print service to print to compatible printers on your network or save the email as a PDF file on the Google Drive cloud storage service. **Note:** Cloud Print is not the same as Apple's AirPrint service in iOS, and Cloud Print works with fewer printers than AirPrint. Cloud Print also requires setup, for which you can find instructions at www.google.com/landing/cloudprint.

- *Mark as Unread:* Does what it says.

See those check boxes to the left of each message in the message list? Tap them to select messages; then use one of the buttons at the upper right of the screen — Archive, Trash, or Menu — to act on all the selected messages at the same time.

Navigating Gmail's folders

✔ At the far left of the Gmail screen is a set of icons that represent common folders: Inbox (the tray icon); Starred (the Star icon); and Sent Mail (the icon of a paper airplane). Below them is the More button (shown here in the margin). Tap it to see all your folders, as shown in Figure 12-23, as well as all the labels you've created in Gmail. Tap a folder or label to see messages in it. Tap the Less button (the ^ icon) to hide the folder details.

If you can't find an email in the Inbox or other folder, go to the All Mail folder and look there. I suggest that you use the Search option at the top of the mail list when in the All Mail folder to more quickly find what you're looking for.

A label is not a folder but rather a tag on messages. Displaying a label "folder" simply shows all messages tagged with that label, no matter what folders they are actually stored in. Other such virtual folders automatically created by Google include Starred, Important, Personal, Receipts, Travel, and Work. Real folders are any you create in Gmail at its web page via your browser, plus Inbox, Sent Mail, Drafts, Archived, Trash, and Spam.

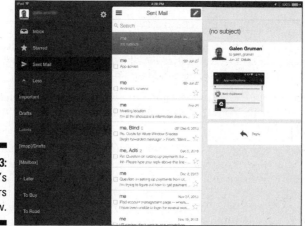

Figure 12-23:
Gmail's folders view.

Adjusting Gmail settings

If you show the Gmail folders, you see the Settings button (the gear icon) at the upper right of the folder list. Tap the Settings button to open a sheet of options:

- ✔ **Change Photo:** Lets you choose a different photo for your account.

- ✔ **Notifications:** Here, you enable or disable Gmail's notification of new messages. These settings override the On or Off setting you may have made for Gmail in the Settings app's Notifications pane.

- ✔ **Mobile Signature:** Lets you set up a different signature for emails sent from the iPad. By default, the signature you set up at the Gmail website is used.

- ✔ **Vacation Responder:** Lets you set up an automated reply to messages received during the period you specify. For example, you might say that you are on vacation and won't be reading emails for a while.

When you're done adjusting your settings, tap Save to save them and Cancel to cancel them; then return to the Gmail screen.

Going Wide with Mail+ and Boxer

If you need to use a different mail client for work than you use for personal email (or if for some reason you don't like the iPad's own Mail app), two good options are the $5.99 Mail+ for Outlook and the $9.99 Boxer. Both support all the popular email services, similar to the iPad's Mail app: Exchange, IMAP, Gmail, Yahoo!, Outlook.com, and AOL.

Mail+ and Boxer do support locally hosted Exchange servers, which is what most companies use, but they *don't* support Office 365 accounts, or at least they didn't when this book went to press. You need the iPad's Mail app or Microsoft's OWA app for that. And neither Mail+ nor Boxer functions as a contacts manager or calendar app; you likely have to stick with the iPad's own Contacts and Calendar for those needs.

Getting to know Mail+

Mail+, shown in Figure 12-24, has all the options you'd expect in an email app, along with a couple extras. Mail+ supports message conversations, flags, folders, email signatures, support for calendar invitations, message priorities, and so on. And its user interface is similar to Mail and Outlook, so getting up to speed with Mail+ is easy.

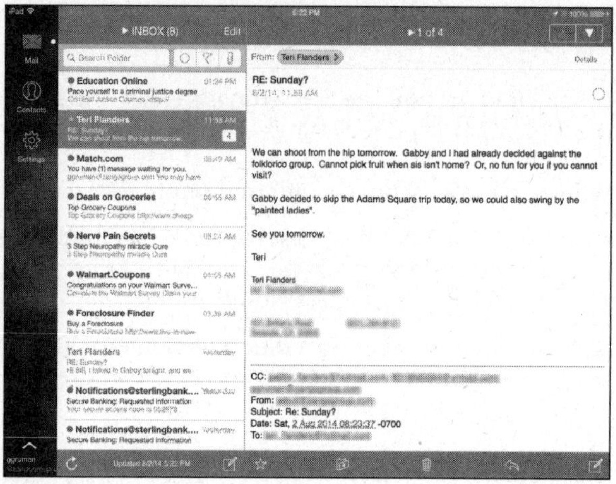

Figure 12-24:
The Inbox
for Mail+ for
Outlook.

But its remarkable capability is to attach files from your Box or Dropbox cloud storage accounts to your email — something that makes it a good fit for work usage, because don't we all send each other files via email?

Via its Settings pane, Mail+ also lets you set a passcode lock on the app, so if a child or spouse is using your iPad, he or she can't get to your email.

Where Mail+ is not so great is in its Contacts feature, which is nothing more than an alphabetical list of all people you've received emails from. You can search that list, but why bother? The app looks up that same data when you enter a person's name in an email's To, Cc, or Bcc field.

Getting to know Boxer

Boxer, shown in Figure 12-25, also covers the email capabilities you'd expect and works with the same set of accounts that Mail+ does, so it can cover every email service but Office 365. As with Mail+, Boxer supports file attachments from Box and Dropbox, plus it can send emails and their attachments to Evernote (see Chapter 9) for retention in your notes there.

You can also link Boxer to your Facebook, LinkedIn, and/or Twitter accounts to pull in people's photos and bios for display with their emails. A salesperson could find that feature handy for getting context about clients when reviewing emails.

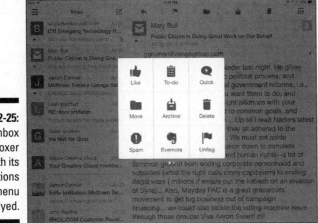

Boxer's creators like to trumpet its capability to use swipe gestures to easily delete, archive, and otherwise work with emails, but it's really no different in that regard than the iPad's own Mail app. I find Boxer's Actions button (the icon of a nine-square grid) at the upper right of the screen a faster, easier way to access its many functions.

Boxer does stand out in that it lets you treat emails as to-do items and assign them priorities and due dates. This is a cool idea because so many emails contain implicit and even explicit task information. To make an email into a to-do item, tap the Task button (the clipboard icon) at the upper right of the screen; then set the due date, priority, and/or assignee in the sheet that appears. That to-do email now displays in the Inbox's To-Do subfolder, and any deadlines show up with the email's subject line in the message list.

Where Boxer falls a bit short is in its approach to moving among accounts and folders. When you tap the Folders button (the icon of three lines) at the upper left of the screen, Boxer slides over your message list and your message, and you can no longer read the full message. You also lose access to the gestures you can use in the message list, as well as to the buttons in the upper right of the screen. In short, Boxer works best when you don't engage with your folders often.

But I do like Boxer's simpler arrangement of buttons and other controls; it's more straightforward than these controls in Mail+.

Chapter 13

Messaging and Conferencing

Although we tend to think of the iPhone as Apple's communications device, the iPad makes a great communications device, especially when typing or video is involved, because the iPad's larger screen makes both work better.

In this chapter, you learn how to use the iPad's immediacy-oriented communications capabilities (messaging and conferencing) to have those direct, collaborative dialogs from your iPad, where the work you're discussing is also likely to be.

Going Native with FaceTime and Messages

You iPad comes with two apps for real-time communication: FaceTime, for video and audio conferencing, and Messages, for text messaging (a.k.a. SMS on a cellphone).

The limitation of both FaceTime and Messages is that they are limited to interactions with people who have Macs, iPads, iPhones, and iPod touches — they're Apple-only services.

Well, not quite: On the iPhone only, Messages can also participate in text chats with any cellphone user, using the SMS technology that all modern cellphones now support. And the iPad, too, can participate in SMS texting, but only if you have an iPhone to receive and send those texts; iPads running iOS 8.1 and Macs running OS X Yosemite can access texts on an iPhone, and receive them from an iPhone, via iCloud syncing. Here's how: Sign in to the same iCloud account on your iPad as you have for your iPhone. That's all you have to do!

Figuring Out FaceTime

FaceTime started as a video-calling app for one-to-one sessions, but Apple has expanded it to also do audio-only conferences, which take much less bandwidth. As of iOS 8, you can add multiple people via FaceTime audio, so you can use it for a conference call as you would a phone.

To make a FaceTime call, follow these steps:

1. **Open the FaceTime app on your iPad.**

2. **In the pane at the left, tap Video to make a video call or Audio to make an audio call.**

   You can also tap the Video or Audio icon next to a person's name in apps like Contacts — and as of iOS 8, in the Recents list in the App Switcher — to initiate a FaceTime video or audio call, respectively.

3. **In the Enter Name, Email, or Number field, type in a name, email address, or phone number in the field in the pane at left, or tap the name of someone you've recently FaceTimed in the list below.**

   This places the FaceTime call request.

4. **Wait for the other party to accept the FaceTime request on his or her iPad, Mac, iPhone, or iPod touch.**

   Of course, the other party has to be connected to the Internet. When someone calls, the person receiving the call gets an alert on the iPad's screen with the option to accept or reject the call.

5. **Talk away!**

   When connected, you see and hear each other if doing a video call (shown in Figure 13-1), or just hear each other if doing an audio call.

6. **(Optional) While on the FaceTime call, you can do the following:**

   • *For video:* You can switch between the front and rear cameras using the Camera button. You can mute the audio by tapping the Mute button. You can also switch to another app; the iPad turns the status bar green so that you know an active call is going on, and the other person can no longer see you but you can still hear each other.

- *For Audio:* In addition to the options available for a video call, you can also turn the speaker on or off (you need a headset or earbuds if it's off). You can switch to a FaceTime video call by tapping the FaceTime button. And, new in iOS 8, you can tap Contacts or Add Call to add another person to the audio call. Tapping Contacts lets you find a person in your Contacts app, whereas Add a Call lets you enter the person's email address or phone number to make the connection. Figure 13-2 shows the FaceTime audio screen when connected.

7. **When done with the call, tap the End button (the phone icon) to end the call.**

Figure 13-1: A FaceTime video call in progress.

Figure 13-2: A FaceTime audio call in progress.

If a person is connected via a cellular network, FaceTime must be enabled to use the cellular network. You enable FaceTime in the Settings app's FaceTime pane by turning the FaceTime switch to On in the Use Cellular Data For list. Even then, a FaceTime connection might not work (especially for video) if the cellular connection isn't strong enough. Finally, keep in mind that videoconferencing uses a lot of data, so frequent cellular use could eat up your plan's data allotment quickly.

Your iPad can take and initiate phone calls with anyone via FaceTime Audio as well. That is, it can if you have an iPhone and both it and the iPad are running iOS 8.1, have Bluetooth turned on, and are within about 30 feet of each other. You enable this capability by going to the Settings app, tapping FaceTime to open the FaceTime pane, and setting the iPhone Cellular Calls switch to On. A Mac running OS X Yosemite can do the same: Open the FaceTime app, choose FaceTime➪Preferences, select the iPhone Cellular Calls check box, and close the Preferences dialog. (You can quit FaceTime on the Mac if you want; it will still detect an incoming call and launch itself automatically.)

Maneuvering through Messages

The Messages app lets you use Apple's iMessage service to text other people who also have iCloud-connected Apple devices. If your colleagues all use iPads and iPhones, it's a great way to message each other without incurring SMS charges — and your iCloud account stores the conversations indefinitely, so you can easily go back through a conversation to recall a detail or verify what someone wrote. And, as noted in the earlier section "Going Native with FaceTime and Messages," in iOS 8.1, you can enable SMS text syncing with your iPhone, so your iPad can send text to and receive texts from non-Apple users.

Messages works like any texting app. Here are the steps to create and send a message:

1. **Tap the New Message button (the paper-and-pen icon) to start a new message.**

2. **In the To field, enter the name, email, or phone number of the person you want to message, based on what the person has enabled in the Messages pane in the Settings app on his or her device.**

   Or tap the Add (+) button to choose people from your Contacts app's cards. ***Note:*** You can enter multiple people in the To field or via the + button to have a group texting session.

How do you know what to enter to reach that other person via iMessage? You don't, but if Messages can't send the text, it will display "Not Delivered" onscreen. Also, if the message is sent but the Sent button and message background are green, the message was sent via SMS, not iMessage. (iMessage messages have a blue Send button and blue message background.)

3. **Tap Send.**

4. **Type your messages in the iMessage field (called Text Message if you are sending via SMS) at the bottom of the right pane.**

   Your conversation appears on that right pane.

   A list of previous conversations appears in the left pane of the Messages app. Tap one to see it and to continue that conversation.

Attaching media files to your messages

In addition to sending text messages to each other, iMessage participants can also include photos, videos, and audio files in the messages.

Tap the camera icon to the left of the text field to insert a photo or video from your Photos app's Photo Library or to use the iPad's camera to take a picture or record a video.

In iOS 8, tap and hold the microphone icon to the right of the text field to record audio; release your finger to end the recording. When you release your finger, you see the controls shown in Figure 13-3. Tap Send (the ↑ icon) to send the recording, Cancel (the X icon) to delete it, or Play (the right-facing triangle icon) to listen to it (to see if you really do want to send it).

Figure 13-3: Messages' audio-attachment controls.

Managing the conversation and its contents

If you tap and hold the text in a conversation (that is, the text in one of the message "bubbles"), a contextual menu appears with two options:

- ✔ **Copy:** Copies the text for pasting into a new message or any iPad app that accepts text.

- ✔ **More:** Makes each "bubble" selectable, so you can delete specific parts of the text conversation by tapping the Delete button (the trash can icon) at the bottom of the screen. (Tap the Delete All button at the top of the screen to delete the entire conversation's contents.) You can also tap the Forward button (the curved arrow icon) at the bottom right of the screen to forward the selected "bubbles" to someone else via a new text conversation.

New in iOS 8 is the Details button, which opens the Details pane shown in Figure 13-4. Here, you get a raft of options:

Figure 13-4: Messages' Details pane offers a bevy of conver-sation-management controls.

- ✔ **Map:** A map shows the participants' locations if they've enabled Location Sharing in their iOS device's Settings app's Privacy pane or their Mac's System Preferences application's Security & Privacy pane.

- ✔ **List of participants:** Each participant is listed, with FaceTime audio and video buttons so that you can quickly initiate a FaceTime call with a participant. The Information (the *i* icon) shows what information the Contacts app has stored for that person.

- ✔ **Send My Current Location and Share My Location:** The Send My Current button lets you send just your current location to the participants, and the Share My Location button lets them see your location live as you move about. (If you tap it, the Share My Location button becomes Stop Sharing My Location.)

- ✔ **Do Not Disturb:** Turning this switch to On mutes the conversation so that you no longer get notifications of new messages. This is particularly handy for group conversations in which people are chatting away while you're busy. Set the switch back to Off to resume getting the notifications.

- ✔ **Leave This Conversation:** Available only for group conversations that you initiated, the Leave This Conversation removes you from the conversation while letting others continue to participate in it.

- ✔ **Attachment:** Available only if the conversation includes photos, videos, and audio attachments, the Attachment section shows thumbnails for every attachment in the conversation. Tap and hold an attachment to get a contextual menu with three options: Copy, Delete, and More. The More option displays a bar at the bottom of the pane with two options: Save Image and Delete (the trash can icon). Yes, that bar's Delete icon is redundant with the contextual menu's Delete button.

- ✔ **Cancel:** The Cancel button at the upper right closes the Details pane and returns you to the conversation pane.

Exploring collaboration services

A lot of services have come and gone in the last few years, promising to end "email hell" by replacing massive email group threads with collaboration tools that combine archived text chat, shared file repositories, onscreen presentations, and group to-do lists. The idea is to keep group communications on a product or project in a single communications space so that everyone has access to the whole picture and doesn't get lost in a sea of unrelated (email) communications.

Few have succeeded broadly, because email is universal, acts as a database for all the discussions and file attachments, and has tools like message rules that can help manage the communications well enough. But such tools do get raves from some work groups that are the right fit for whatever reason. So they're worth exploring.

Do note that besides the need to get everyone to use the same collaboration system for it to function as intended, your IT department may need to get involved to make sure that your chosen service doesn't violate legal requirements around restricting information access to just authorized users; that the data stored at the service is adequately protected and secured; and that interactions with other systems such as corporate servers or email don't cause unexpected problems.

Two examples of services to consider are Fleep and Slack. Both provide group and individual chat, the capability to search past discussions, and the capability to attach and review files. Fleep has Mac, Windows, Android, iOS, and web clients, and costs $60 per year per user. Slack has Mac, iOS, and Android clients — but not for Windows PCs or web browsers — and costs $80 per year per user for the basic business version and $150 per user per year for the advanced business version, which adds more detailed usage statistics and tighter integration with other services such as Twitter and Dropbox.

Using Commercial Services: GoToMeeting and WebEx

Most business use Citrix Systems' GoToMeeting or Cisco Systems' WebEx subscription-based online conferencing services to bring together people for virtual meetings. Both support audio conferencing via both phones and apps on computers, tablets, and phones. They also support video via their apps, as well as screen sharing so a presenter can show slides, web pages, or other digital content to the group.

Both GoToMeeting and WebEx have a free iPad app that lets you join in from your tablet if you have an Internet connection; you use the iPad's camera to participate via video if you'd like. And if you host the meeting, both apps let you share content to other participants.

If you switch to a different app while participating in GoToMeeting or WebEx, your audio is still live unless you muted the microphone in the app — so be careful what you say! The iPad reminds you that you're muted by making the status bar red until you return to the conferencing app.

You probably received the URL for the GoToMeeting or WebEx as well as the access code, via email — the conference host should do that so people know how to join. The best way, of course, is to send a calendar invitation (see Chapter 12) so that this information can be in your calendar.

Whether that URL is in your email or calendar, tap it to open the meeting. Your iPad first opens Safari and then switches to the appropriate conferencing app on your iPad. If all goes well, you'll be signed in, though you'll likely need to enter your name so that others in the conference know that you have joined.

However, this bounce from Safari to the app doesn't always work, so you may need to enter the conference ID into the GoToMeeting app (using the Join by Number button at the lower right of the screen) or WebEx app (via the Join Meeting button in the left pane).

In both apps, you're also asked whether you want to use Internet audio. I recommend that you say yes.

Participating in a GoToMeeting meeting

After you've joined a meeting in the GoToMeeting app, you see whatever the presenter is sharing, such as a web page (as shown in Figure 13-5), document, or video, as well as hear the audio from the presenter and any participants who speak.

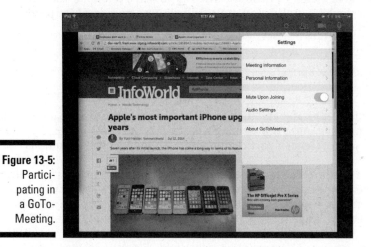

Participants get a row of buttons along the top of the screen, from left to right:

- ✔ **Exit (the icon in the top-left corner):** Disconnects you from the meeting.

- ✔ **Settings (the gear icon):** Lets you set personal information such as your name, have your audio muted by default when you join a conference, and set GoToMeeting to connect the voice portion of the conference via the cellular provider's phone channel rather than over the same data channel that the screen information uses.

- ✔ **Attendees (the people icon):** Shows who's joined the conference and lets you send text messages to any or all of them.

- ✔ **Video (the video camera icon):** Turns on your iPad's camera so that you can be seen by the others.

- ✔ **Audio (the microphone icon):** Turns your iPad's microphone on or off.

Hosts who initiate the conference from an iPad have most of the same options, as well as some new ones, as Figure 13-6 shows. But first they have to set up the meeting, which they can do from a computer or iPad.

To set up a conference on the iPad as the host, follow these steps:

1. **Tap My Meetings in the GoToMeeting app's left pane.**

2. **Tap the + button at the upper right of the right pane.**

3. **In the form that appears, fill in a title and the schedule for the meeting.**

4. **In that same form, set both the Audio Phone and VoIP switches to On so that participants can choose whether to use a phone or their computer or device's audio, and optionally enter a password for participants to use.**

5. **Click Done.**

   In the alert that appears, I suggest you tap Send Invitation to let people know about the meeting.

Tap the meeting in the app and then the Start button in the alert that appears, to begin the meeting. After the meeting has started, the controls you get as a host are the same as what a participant gets, with the following additions.

The Presenter button (the monitor icon) in the toolbar at the top lets you turn content presentation on or off; turn it on if you want to share files or web pages. It also lets you turn Audience View on or off. Audience View displays a small window of what the audience sees (visible in the upper right of Figure 13-6).

When you're presenting content, the toolbar adds a row of options. You can enter a web page's URL in the first text field to display that web page to your audience. You can tap the Cloud button to open files for display from either Dropbox or Citrix's own ShareFile service — PDF, Microsoft Office, and common image formats are all supported. Another way to share files is to open them in an iPad app and use the Share sheet to send them to GoToMeeting (if the file is compatible, of course).

Use the Back (<) and Forward (>) buttons on the toolbar to navigate among the websites and files you've shown during this presentation.

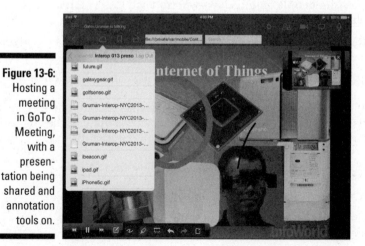

Figure 13-6: Hosting a meeting in GoTo-Meeting, with a presentation being shared and annotation tools on.

Tap the Play icon (the right-facing triangle) to share that content ("play" it) to your audience. You use the Rewind and Fast-Forward buttons in the contextual menu at the lower left to move among the slides of a PowerPoint presentation.

GoToMeeting also lets you draw on whatever is on your screen, as Figure 13-6 shows. In the contextual menu that appears on the bottom of the screen when you are presenting a document or web page, the drawing controls are as follows:

✔ **Drawing Tools (the icon of a pen in paper):** Turns the drawing tools on or off.

✔ **Freeform Line (the squiggle icon):** Enables the freeform tool, which draws a line that follows the movement of your finger on the screen. A pop-over also opens, in which you can set the color and highlight thickness.

✔ **Highlight (the marker icon):** Enables the highlighting tool, which places a color background along whatever you drag your finger across. A pop-over also opens, in which you can set the color and highlight thickness.

✔ **Whiteboard (the whiteboard icon):** Creates a blank screen on which you can draw, such as for sketches.

✔ **Undo and Redo (the curved-arrow icons):** Undoes or redoes previous actions.

✔ **Erase All Drawings (the icon of paper with an *X*):** Removes your annotations, such as when you want to go to a new page or slide and draw something new there.

Participating in a WebEx meeting

The WebEx Meetings app works similarly to GoToMeeting. WebEx is more capable than GoToMeeting with respect to file support, but it has no annotation capabilities.

If you're participating in someone else's WebEx, you see a screen like that in Figure 13-7 after you join. The controls at the top, from left to right, are the following:

✔ **Audio (the microphone icon):** Mutes or unmutes your iPad's microphone.

✔ **Video (the video camera icon):** Opens the preview pop-over showing what your iPad's camera sees, has a button to switch between the front and rear camera on the iPad, and has the Start My Video button to send your video to the other participants.

✔ **Participants (the person icon):** Shows who's on the conference and who's muted, as well as chat with anyone (tap their name first) or everyone.

✔ **Meeting Info (the *i* icon):** Shows the meeting ID and dial-in number.

✔ **Exit (the door icon):** Exits the conference.

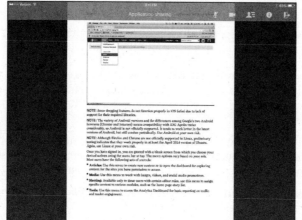

Figure 13-7:
Partici-
pating in
a WebEx
meeting.

If you are the host, you can schedule the meeting on your computer or the iPad. On the iPad, tap the + button in the upper right of WebEx Meetings' left pane and choose Meet Now or Schedule from the pop-over. If you choose Meet Now, the screen will show your meeting ID and dial-in number so that you can share it with others (such as via email). If you choose Schedule, you set the start and end dates and times for the meeting, add invites, and option- ally set a password for attendees in the pop-over that appears. Be sure to have WebEx open on your iPad when the meeting starts, and tap the meeting name that will be listed in the right pane to start it.

WebEx Meetings lets hosts share content with the audience by tapping the big Share Content button on the screen when you start or the Share Content button (the icon of a tray with ↑) later on. The Share Content button opens a pop-over, shown in Figure 13-8, in which you can select files from Box, Dropbox, GoogleDrive, or the iPad's Photos app. Use the Recently Shared option to choose files you've shown already. Another way to share files is to open them in an iPad app and use the standard iOS Share sheet (see Chapter 17) to send them to WebEx Meetings (if the file is compatible, of course).

Figure 13-8:
Sharing a
document
as a host
with WebEx
Meetings.

You scroll through Office files; for PDFs, thumbnails of each page appear at the left, as Figure 13-8 shows, so you can jump to any page. You can't navigate among the documents you've shared (you have to open them again in the Share Content pop-over), nor can you share web pages, as you can in GoToMeeting.

You also can't annotate your content in WebEx, but you do have a virtual laser pointer that you can use: Tap the Pointer button (the lightburst icon) in the toolbar and then tap and hold on the screen where you want the virtual laser pointer to appear.

To stop sharing a document, tap Stop Sharing.

Joining the Conversation with Google Hangouts

Google offers a lot of free services that work across Windows, OS X, Android, Chrome OS, and iOS — if you have signed up for a Google account. Google Hangouts is the conferencing component of those free services.

For business use, Google Hangouts may not be a workable option because you have to know a person's Google account's address — usually a Gmail address — to send invitations. That's rarely the same as a work address. But if the Google addresses are known, you can invite people to a conference that includes video, audio, and screen sharing, as Figure 13-9 shows.

Figure 13-9:
Partici-
pating in
a Google
Hangouts
meeting.

Participating in conferences

If you're invited to a Google Hangout conference, you need to have the free Google Hangouts app open to see the invitation and accept it. So just in case you don't have the app open, be sure to add the meeting to your calendar or, if you're the organizer, send an email or text when the meeting is about to start.

If you want to share documents or web pages, you must host the Google Hangout from a computer — the iPad app can't share content. Participants also have no controls while attending the Hangout conference.

Making video calls

You can initiate FaceTime-like video and audio calls from the Hangouts app. To do so, follow these steps:

1. **Tap Hangouts at the bottom of the left pane to switch to the Hangouts (conferencing) tab.**

2. **At the top of the left pane, tap the New Hangout button (the icon of a pen in paper).**

3. **Enter the person's Gmail account in the field at the top of the right pane.**

4. **Enter a message at the bottom of the right pane and tap Send (the airplane icon) when you're done.**

   After a few moments, the other person will get a text message within the Google Hangouts app.

   As the initiator, you'll see a video-camera icon to the right of the right pane. Slide it all the way to the left to initiate a video call. The other person should get a request to join. If he or she accepted it, you'll be video-chatting.

Making phone calls

The Hangouts app also lets you call regular phone numbers, which you do using the Calls tab. (You used to have to use a separate app called Google Voice, but it's now part of Hangout.) *Note:* To use this feature, be sure you have already set up Google Voice for your Google account via your browser.

To call a phone number, follow these steps:

1. **Tap the Calls button at the bottom of the left pane to switch to the Call tab.**

2. **Tap the Dial button (the keypad icon) at the top of the screen.**

   A form appears with a keypad.

3. **In the form's Keypad pane, enter the number and tap Call, or choose a contact from the People pane.**

   If you're calling a Google Voice phone number, that person gets a notification in the Google Hangouts app.

   You see a timer onscreen as you talk so that you know the call is still connected.

4. **(Optional) Add a person to the call to make it into a conference call by tapping the Contacts button (the people icon) and searching for someone in your contacts.**

   You cannot enter a phone number for additional participants; the people must be in your Contacts app so that you can select them from a list of contacts.

The Google Hangouts app often fails to receive video-call requests, and it sometimes can't hang up on audio calls (such as when voicemail kicks in).

Attending the Conference with Microsoft Lync

Lync is Microsoft's own conferencing service, and it requires that your company either run a Lync server or subscribe to a business version of Office Office 365.

To set up a Lync meeting, you need to use the Lync client application or the Outlook application's Online Meeting feature on a Windows PC or Mac — you can't do so from the iPad.

To join a Lync meeting as a participant from your iPad, you can tap a meeting in the Lync 2013 app (shown in Figure 13-10), a meeting event in the OWA for iPad app's calendars view, the Lync URL in Calendar, or the Lync URL in Mail. *Note:* All four options work for meetings sent by someone else in your organization, but people who aren't in your organization must use the Lync URL options and either connect from a computer browser or sign in as a guest via the Lync app.

Lync works fine for video and audio conferences, but the iPad app isn't compatible with all document and desktop presentations, so iPad participants aren't guaranteed to see such items.

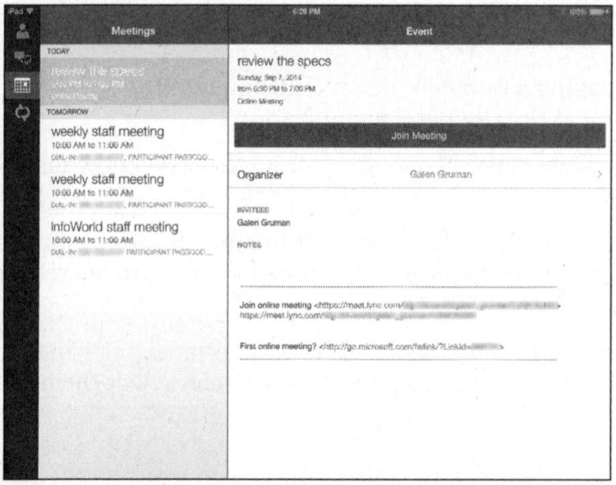

Figure 13-10:
Lync shows
you which
meetings
are in your
Exchange
calendar
and let you
join any that
have online
meetings.

When you do join a Lync meeting from the iPad, you see six buttons along the toolbar at the top:

- ✓ **Reveal Chats (the table icon):** Displays the left pane of scheduled Lync meetings.

- ✓ **Chat (the speech-bubble icon):** Lets you send text messages to other participants.

- ✓ **Audio (the phone icon):** Lets you switch to video, put yourself on hold (which mutes the microphone), and hang up the audio portion of the call.

- ✓ **Presenter View (the monitor icon):** Lets you see whatever document or web page the presenter is sharing. *Note:* You may well see the error message "The presenter is using a feature that isn't supported by this version of Lync" when trying to see such content. So you'll just have to listen at that point, until the presenter finishes sharing and the video returns.

- ✓ **Participants (the people icon):** Shows who's participating and lets you see their contact information, if available.

- ✓ **More (the . . . icon):** Lets you end the conversation or invite someone else.

Speaking via Skype

Chances are that you use Skype already on your computer, such as to keep in touch with friends and family. The Microsoft-owned service is very popular because it allows audio and video calls between Skype members for free and allows for audio calls to landlines and cellphones at inexpensive rates internationally, which is great for overseas vacationers and workers. And it works on all sorts of computers and mobile devices.

If you don't already use Skype, you need to get the free app for your iPad. Skyping someone is easy: Search for his or her username in the People pane of the free Skype app. The main Search field looks in your Skype contacts (not your iPad contacts); to search other Skype users, tap the Add button (the + icon) and choose Search Skype Directory.

If you sign in to Skype with your Microsoft account, searching contacts in Skype will look at both your Skype contacts and your Microsoft Messenger contacts.

Or tap the Dial button (the dial-pad icon) and enter a phone number. ***Note:*** You need to have purchased Skype call credits to dial a number. You can purchase such credits by tapping your name at the upper left of the screen and then tapping Skype Credit in the Profile pop-over that appears.

To initiate a Skype call, tap the person's name in your existing contacts list (a green check mark means that the person is online), enter a number via the Dial popover, or tap the desired name after conducting a search.

After you enter the number, you see as many as three options — Video Call, Voice Call, and IM (instant message) — depending on the recipient's capabilities. Figure 13-11 shows a video call in progress.

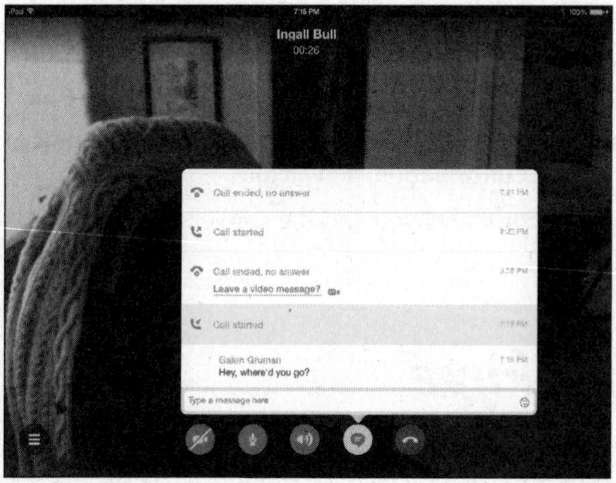

Figure 13-11: A Skype video call with text message.

To receive a call, the Skype app must be running. Tap Accept (the green phone icon) to take the call, and Reject to (the red phone icon) to dismiss the request.

Tap the screen to get these buttons at the bottom of the screen:

- **People (the icon of three lines):** Opens a list of active connections, the call history, and the People button that lets you see your contacts.

- **Video (the video-camera icon):** Lets you switch between the front and rear iPad cameras as well as disable the video from your iPad (the No Camera Option). If your iPad's camera is active, you see a preview screen in the lower-right corner of what it is showing the other person.

- **Audio (the speaker icon):** If you have a wired or Bluetooth headset connected to your iPad, tapping Audio switches the audio between that headset and the iPad's built-in microphone and speaker.

✔ **Chat (the speech-bubble icon):** Lets you chat with the person, as shown in Figure 13-11.

✔ **Hang Up (the phone icon):** Ends the call.

Texting with AIM

For years, AOL Instant Messenger, best known as AIM, was the popular texting service for computer users. So much so that Apple built AIM support into its own iChat application on the Mac (which became Messages a few years ago). These days, people use all sorts of chat services, and AIM is sort of old school, especially because it's limited to text.

But the free, ad-supported AIM app is still a good option if you want a texting system that works on Windows, OS X, Android, and iOS. Figure 13-12 shows an AIM chat session.

To use AIM, tap a buddy from the list at right. Add new buddies by tapping the Add button (the + icon) at the top of that pane and then select whether the person has an AIM or Google account. Enter his or her username.

You enter your text and see the chat in the middle pane, and you see a list of previous chats in the left pane, which you can tap to pick up where you left off.

When composing a text, tap the Attachments button (the paper clip icon) to the left of the text field. A pop-over provides buttons to attach a photo from the Photos app's Photo Library or from the iPad's camera, to share your current location, and to record and attach as much as 60 seconds of audio.

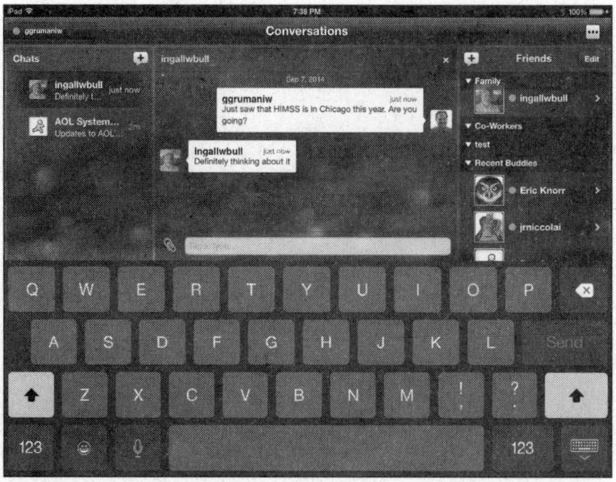

Figure 13-12:
An AIM text chat.

Part IV
Accessing Online Resources

Want to make your iPad act like a phone? If your iPhone is close by, you can! See how at www.dummies.com/extras/ipadatwork.

In this part . . .

- ✔ "Dagnabit! I left that file at work!" That's okay — just connect your iPad to your computer over the Internet. Yes, you can do that!

- ✔ Find out how your iPad can be your computer's second screen.

- ✔ Go surf the iPad way: Make the most of Safari, and get to know Chrome.

Chapter 14

Remotely Accessing Your Computer

. . . .

In This Chapter

▶ Making sense of VNC and RDP

▶ Remote-controlling your computer the basic way with VNC Viewer

▶ Accessing your computer remotely and in style with Jump Desktop

▶ Turning your iPad into a second screen for your PC or Mac

. . . .

*A*lthough an iPad can be your computer, sometimes you actually need your computer, or at least access to it. You can do that, too, from an iPad. Maybe you need a file that's on your computer that you didn't store in iCloud or other cloud storage service. Or, more likely these days, you have an app on your computer that has no iPad equivalent, and you need to run it but you're at home or at a conference or meeting with just your iPad handy.

There are several ways to access your PC or Mac remotely, but they all use a technology called *virtual network connection* (VNC). In a nutshell, VNC transmits your computer's screen to another computer (or iPad) and transfers back input such as clicks (or taps translated to clicks), mouse movements (or touchscreen movements translated to mouse movements), and keyboard entry so that you can control the computer and see the results of what you do.

You can also use VNC apps to remotely monitor activities on a computer, such as to follow along with a user who's in training or needs technical support. In this chapter, I show you how to use several VNC apps, so that you can select the best one for your needs.

There's another way to remotely access your computer that doesn't involve controlling it, and that way uses your iPad as a second monitor for your computer — a great use for your iPad when you are working at your desk. I explore two such apps, Air Display and Duet Display, at the end of this chapter.

Understanding VNC Technology

Because VNC is a standard technology, you'll find no shortage of apps that support it. Which app you pick comes down to a few factors: user interface, price, and any extra bells and whistles.

Some VNC apps are really services that require a subscription, such as LogMeIn and Citrix GoToMyPC. Those services limit your flexibility greatly, so I suggest that you avoid them unless your company's compliance requirements justify such a closed approach to remote access. This chapter showcases a few well-liked VCN apps that don't require a subscription, but feel free to try out others.

For remote access to work, your Mac or PC must be running and connected to the Internet, or at least on the network (if you're remotely accessing the computer from the iPad on the same network, such as if you are in a company conference room and want to access your PC at your work desk).

You should *never* enable a computer for remote access if that computer is not password-protected, whether through a sign-in to use the computer or a sign-in required of any remote user to connect. Be sure to use a password that is not easily guessed.

Making your computer remotely accessible

Before you can remotely access your computer via VNC or RDP (Remote Desktop Protocol, which is Microsoft's more capable variation of VNC), you need to tell your computer to let itself be remotely managed. Without that safeguard in place, anyone could take over your computer at any time.

To enable remote management, you usually need two ingredients: your computer's IP (Internet Protocol) address on your network and an app for your computer that works with your iPad's remote-access app to make the connection work.

Such apps aren't always needed: You can sometimes instead use the Mac's built-in VNC

feature or Windows' built-in RDP feature, at least for limited access. Here's how to find these features:

✔ **On a Mac:** Launch the System Preferences application, click the Sharing pane, and then enable Screen Sharing in the pane that appears. Click Computer Settings to set up a password for VNC users to gain access to your Mac.

✔ **In Windows:** Search your computer for Remote Desktop Connection, the included app that lets you enable RDP on your PC; then run that app to both enable RDP and set any parameters such as password requirements.

You get the computer's IP address as follows:

✔ **On a Mac (any version of OS X):** Launch the System Preferences application and go to the Network pane. If you're using a wired Ethernet connection, click Ethernet (or click Display Ethernet if you are using a Thunderbolt Display's Ethernet port) in the connections list at the left; you'll see the IP address listed in the pane at the right. If you're connected to the network via Wi-Fi, click Wi-Fi instead; you'll see the IP address listed in small text below the Status line at the right.

✔ **On a Windows 8 PC:** Open the Settings charm and click or tap the Network icon there. If the current network properties don't display, in the Network pane, click View Network Connections, click or tap Connections at the left in the pane that appears, and then double-click the network name at the right. The properties for that network should open, including the IP address (named IPv4 here).

✔ **On a Windows Vista or 7 PC:** Open the Control Panel and go to the Network and Internet Connections pane. Click View Network Status and Tasks in the Network and Sharing Center section. In the pane that appears, click Ethernet or Wi-Fi, depending on your current network connection, at the right side. In the dialog that opens, click Details to open yet another pane, where you'll see the IP address listed. Close the panes when done.

✔ **On a Windows XP PC:** Open the Control Panel and go to the Network and Internet pane; then click Network Connections from the icon list at the bottom. Click the active network connection in the pane at the right, then, at the bottom of the pane at the left, go to the Details section to see the IP address. (Click the Details label if this information does not display.)

As for the app you need to install on your computer, you get that from the company whose iPad app you're using. Note that these VNC server apps usually aren't free, even if the iPad app is; you either pay a one-time fee or a monthly subscription fee, and prices vary dramatically, so shop around. If the app's Help page or iTunes description page doesn't say where to download that app for your computer, go to the company's Home page and look around for it, such as in its Downloads section.

Make sure that the app is running on your computer — if not, you won't be able to remote in to it.

Testing the Waters with VNC Viewer

RealVNC's VNC Viewer app for the iPad and its companion VNC Server app for your computer are free. The viewer app is definitely free, but the server app's price ranges from free for a basic, one-user license (for five devices) with no security features to various "premium" offerings that can cost from $30 to $99 per computer. Updates and support after the first year require a paid subscription.

I like VNC Viewer as a basic tool and recommend that you start with this app to see how much you actually need and use VNC. If you find that you use it a lot and want something that encrypts your communications and performs other security validation, you can then step up to a different version of VNC Server or to a different product.

Setting up VNC Server and VNC Viewer

The first thing to do is set up VNC Server on your computer. After you install it and launch it, follow these steps on your computer's VNC Server app to set up the password requirement:

1. **Click the More button at bottom left to open a menu of options.**

2. **Click Options and enter your computer's admin password if requested.**

   The Options dialog appears.

3. **Go to the Users & Permissions pane, click the Password button, and in the sheet that appears, fill in the password required for access.**

VNC Viewer on the iPad is very easy to use: When you launch it, you see two buttons at the bottom: Address Book and Bonjour. Address Book lets you connect over the Internet to computers running VNC Server, and Bonjour lets you connect to computers on the current network that support the Bonjour protocol (Macs, Windows PCs running iCloud, and iOS devices).

If you tap Bonjour, all compatible detected devices display. Tap one to make a connection. Enter a username and the password that's been set in VNC Server; next, tap Done. Wait a few minutes, and you should see your computer's screen appear. Now you can work with it as if you were there, launching apps, navigating folders, and so on.

If you tap Address Book, any connections you previously created display. Tap them to sign in as you would for a Bonjour connection. To add a new connection:

1. **Tap the Add button (the + icon) at the upper right.**

2. **Enter the computer's IP address in the Address field and a name for that computer (so you'll know which one it is later).**

3. **Tap Save.**

   The computer now displays in the Address Book, and you see a window with three important buttons, as Figure 14-1 shows:

   - *Edit:* Tap this to change the settings.

   - *Done:* Tap this to close the window and see the Address Book list.

   - *Connect:* Connect to the computer you just set up.

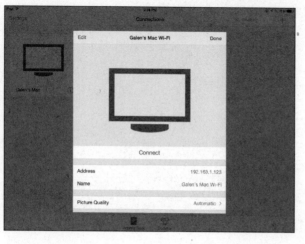

Figure 14-1:
Adding a new connection to VNC Viewer's Address Book. (An existing connection is visible in the background.)

When connecting, you may be asked to okay the use of an unencrypted connection if you're using the free version of VNC Server. (In the free version, you have no choice but to say yes if you want to make a remote connection, even though unencrypted connections are less secure.)

You will also be asked for your remote-access password unless you set the Remember Password switch to On when you connect. It's less secure to let VNC Viewer remember your password, because anyone who has your iPad could then connect to your computer. If your iPad is secured with a password and not shared with others, it's fine to let VNC Viewer remember the remote-access password.

Using VNC Viewer

When you're connected, you see your computer's screen, as Figure 14-2 shows.

The tricky part of using a VNC app is using the computer you're now remotely accessing. In the case, of VNC Viewer, you need to tell it what type of input you are using. You do this by using the toolbar at the top of the screen, shown in Figure 14-2. Tap the Keyboard button to open the onscreen keyboard, and tap the Mouse button to be able to control the pointer.

If you don't see the toolbar, swipe three fingers down to display it. To keep the toolbar onscreen, tap the Pin button; if the Pin button is blue, the toolbar will stay onscreen.

Figure 14-2:
The VNC
Viewer app
controlling
a Mac
desktop.

The trick to navigating the computer screen in VNC Viewer is that although you would expect your finger's position on the iPad screen to correspond to the pointer's position on the computer, it rarely does. As you move your finger on the touchscreen, pay attention to where the pointer is — because that's where the computer thinks your finger is. Make sure that the pointer (as opposed to your finger) is over whatever object you want to manipulate before you tap (to remotely click on the computer) and type.

VNC Viewer maps a variety of iOS gestures to computer mouse operations. Tap the question mark (?) icon in the toolbar to get an explanation of them all — many, such as how to drag an object, aren't ones you're likely to guess on your own.

Also, don't forget that you can use the standard iOS pinch and expand gestures to zoom in and out of the computer's screen, which almost certainly will be too small to easily work with if the whole screen is displayed on your iPad's smaller screen.

To end a connection, tap the X icon in the toolbar.

Getting a Better VNC Experience with Jump Desktop

A more sophisticated VNC/RDP client app is PhaseFive Systems' $14.99 Jump Desktop. It has more configuration features than VNC Viewer, and it's much easier to set up than VNC Server (described earlier in this chapter).

Jump's cost is higher than the free, basic edition of VNC Server, but cheaper than VNC Server's other versions. If you find yourself using the free VNC Viewer app a lot and are considering getting the premium version, I recommend moving up to Jump Desktop instead for its better user experience.

If you download the Jump Desktop app for your Mac from the www. jumpdesktop.com site, it's free. If you get it from the Mac App Store, it costs $30. That's because the one at the Mac App Store is both a server and a client. Because the Mac can act as a VNC server, the only reason to buy the Mac App Store version is to get the easier sign-in process from other devices to your Mac.

Setting Up Jump Desktop

The easy way to use Jump Desktop is to go to the company's website at www.jumpdesktop.com to download the free server app for your Mac or PC. The app does all the work for you in a wizard if you click the Automatic Setup button — but note that you must have a Google account to use the Automatic Setup option. For manual setup, click Set Up Your Computer instead.

On your iPad, open the Jump Desktop app and enter your Google account email and password when requested. As soon as your computer is set up, and Jump Desktop is running on both your computer and iPad (and both are connected to the same network or to the Internet), you see your computer listed as available in the Jump Desktop app on your iPad.

You can use Jump Desktop on your iPad to remotely access your computer without installing the Jump Desktop server app on your computer. If you've set up another VNC or RDP server on your computer, you can use its IP address and password from the Jump Desktop app instead. For example, if your company has set up VNC or RDF on its computers, you can choose to use Jump Desktop to access your work computer instead of whatever client IT gave you — or if it provided no iPad client.

Jump Desktop on the iPad also supports iCloud, so you can keep your connections synced across your iOS devices and Macs. The Jump Desktop Settings window also gives you control over many aspects of the app's operation, such as how gestures map to mouse operations; whether Num Lock is automatically turned on for RDP servers (meaning Windows); the capability to prevent the iPad from going to sleep while you're using Jump Desktop; and the capability to reconnect automatically should your connection get lost. You can also enter your Google account credentials if you didn't do that the first time you ran Jump Desktop.

To get to the Jump Desk Settings window, tap the Settings button (the gear icon) at the upper right of the screen.

Using Jump Desktop

Whether you use the automatic setup or manual setup, any available Internet connections display in the Jump Desktop screen when you open it. (On a PC, the app runs after you install it. On a Mac, you need to sign in the first time you use it from the Jump Desktop menu that appears in the menu bar after the app is running.)

Tap a connection to remotely access that computer. When requested, enter your password. "Which password is that?" you ask. "I didn't set up a password for Jump." No, you didn't: The password is the password used by your computer when you sign into it, if one is set up there. On a Mac, you must also enter the username set up for your Mac.

Jump Desktop for Mac relies on the Mac's built-in Screen Sharing application, which Jump offers to enable for you during setup. If Screen Sharing is not running when you use Jump Desktop, you can launch it by searching for it in Spotlight and then opening it there. Or, choose Diagnostics from the Jump Desktop menu in the menu bar to open the Diagnostics dialog. Click Fix It if it appears next to Screen Sharing in the dialog.

Figure 14-3 shows the Jump Desktop remotely accessing a Windows 8 PC. At the top is the toolbar, with buttons (from left to right) to open the onscreen keyboard, close the connection, hide the toolbar (pull the handle down that appears at the top of the screen to get it back), fit the computer's screen to the iPad's screen, set gesture and mouse options, and (again) open the onscreen keyboard.

As you move your finger on the screen, you see a larger circle follow you, to help you more easily find the pointer above it. Although Jump Desktop doesn't match the pointer's location to your finger's location on the iPad's screen, that circle is always the same distance from the actual pointer, so you can quickly select items and navigate them.

To get a sense of how gestures translate to mouse operations, tap the Options button (the wrench icon) and then tap the *i* icon to the right of the gesture profile in use. (Standard is the default.) You learn, for example, that to move a window, you tap twice quickly, holding your finger down on the second tap to start dragging the object.

Figure 14-3:
Jump
Desktop
controlling a
Windows 8
desktop.

Jump Desktop struggles, as do many PC owners, with getting Windows 8's Charms bar to appear. It's hard to position the pointer in that lower-right corner far enough and then hold the position to have the Charms icons appear so that you can open them. But it is possible: Just keep trying until it works. Jump modifies the iPad's onscreen keyboard to add special keys for Windows or Mac, depending on which computer you are remotely accessing. Figure 14-4 shows the two keyboards. As you can see, they add computer-specific keys in an added upper row that you'll need to use shortcut commands.

Figure 14-4:
Jump
Desktop
modifies
the iPad's
onscreen
keyboard to
add special
Windows
keys (top) or
Mac keys
(bottom) at
the top, as
appropriate.

Viewing More with Air Display and Duet Display

VNC apps are great for remotely controlling your computer from your iPad. But there's another type of remote access that is very handy: using the iPad as a second screen for your computer, both to view your computer screen and to interact with it (using touchscreen taps in place of mouse clicks).

Both Avatron Software's $9.99 Air Display and Rahul Dewan's $14.99 Duet Display do just that. If you put your iPad on a stand next to your computer screen so that both are in the same plane of view, this setup can work well to let you put secondary application windows on the iPad.

The Mac's OS X has long allowed such an extensible Desktop screen across multiple monitors if physically connected to your Mac, and Windows added a similar capability in recent years. But neither does so natively with tablets like the iPad.

Air Display works over a network connection, so there can be some delay in what appears on your iPad's screen. Duet Display works through a direct connection between your iPad's Lightning or Dock port and your Mac's USB port, so there's no lag — but it does not work with Windows PCs, just Macs.

 In both Air Display and Duet Display, you move the pointer between the iPad's screen and your computer's screen. That can take some getting used to. Use the Mac's Displays system preference or the PC's Display control panel to manage how the screens are related to each other, which determines which side of each screen flows into the other.

From your computer, drag windows from one screen to another to position them where you want them on the extended Desktop. *Note:* Some applications, such as Adobe's Creative Suite, use a docked set of panels that will not move to a different screen if the application's windows are moved.

Orchestrating two screens via Air Display

On the iPad, Air Display adds a row of Mac or Windows buttons to the onscreen keyboard so that you can use keyboard shortcuts on your iPad to work with your computer. There's a keyboard icon at the bottom of the Air Display screen to open that keyboard, as Figure 14-5 shows.

Air Display has to be on the same local network as your computer — it doesn't work via a remote Internet connection.

To use Air Display, you need the app on your iPad, of course. But you also need to install a host app and drivers on your Mac or PC. To get those files, go to www.getairdisplay.com, register yourself, and then click the download links sent to your email address. (If you use both a Mac and a PC, you can download both installers. Note that Air Display requires Windows 7 or later, or OS X 10.5 Leopard or later.)

At the website, you can find downloads for OS X and Windows to install the Air Display clients. These are *not* the files needed to extend your computer's screen to your iPad. Instead, they let a Mac or a PC act as a second screen to another computer, and they cost $19.99 per computer.

After you install the Air Display host app and drivers, you see the Air Display icon in your Mac's menu bar or PC's taskbar. Click the Air Display icon to open the host app, in which you can connect to a detected iPad. (That iPad must be running the client Air Display software and be on the same network.) You can also connect to another tablet or computer by entering its IP address. You also use this host app to end the Air Display session and gather all your open windows back on your computer's screen.

Figure 14-5:
Air Display is showing a second Mac screen on the iPad to extend the Mac's desktop.

Figure 14-6 shows the main Mac screen extended to the iPad in Figure 14-5. You can see the Air Display host app at the top of the screen.

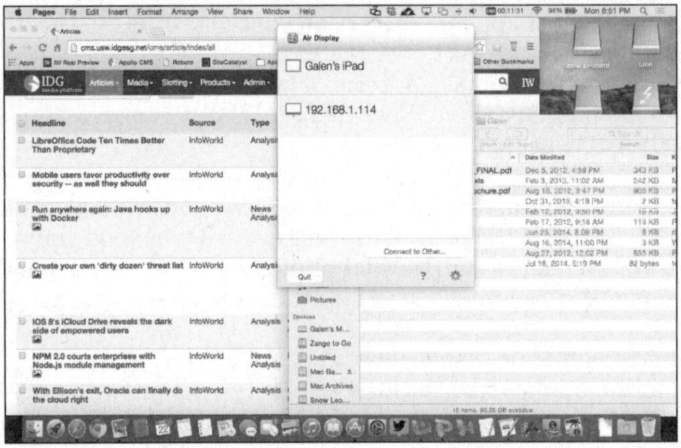

Figure 14-6: Air Display uses a host app on the computer to connect to or disconnect from an iPad used as a second screen.

Extending your Mac screen via Duet Display

The Duet Display app does a little less than Air Display does: It simply makes your iPad an additional Desktop screen for your Mac, as Figure 14-7 shows. Drag app windows from your main Mac screen to the iPad screen, as you would drag windows from one Mac screen to another, to arrange your extended Desktop as desired.

Figure 14-7: Using Duet Display to make an iPad the second screen for a Mac.

You can use the iPad's touchscreen to select items on the screen, but Duet Display assumes that you're controlling everything from your Mac's keyboard and mouse. Thus, selecting text from the iPad screen does not open the iPad's onscreen keyboard as it does in Air Display — you have to use your Mac's keyboard. But you can tap and double-tap items from the iPad screen as if it were a mouse.

To use Duet Display, you must install a Mac app, available for free at `www. duetdisplay.com`, as well as the App Store's Duet Display app on your iPad. (A reboot may be required.) Then, plug your iPad into your Mac via its Dock or Lightning connector, open the Duet app on your iPad, and wait a moment for the iPad to function as a second screen for your Mac. *Note:* If the iPad does not display your Mac's screen, unplug the connector, wait a few seconds, and then plug it back in — Duet Display may not work if you plug the iPad into the Mac before the Duet Display app is running on your iPad.

Chapter 15

Exploring Web Browsers

The web browser is your gateway to the Internet, and the iPad has a darned good browser included, called Safari. It has several features that make it easy to organize web pages for later reading, as well as to keep up on web content recommended in your social networks.

But Safari is not the only browser game in town. Several other browsers offer useful capabilities, and the beauty of the iPad is that you can use any or all of them.

In this chapter, I introduce you to several of the best browsers to consider using in addition to Safari.

Syncing with Safari

Safari for iOS is a great browser. It does everything you'd expect and then some. Among the capabilities it has that you'd expect are the following: open multiple web pages, create and manage bookmarks, save website forms' passwords, and enable private browsing (so that your visits aren't recorded in the browser history and cookies aren't saved).

Some other capabilities of Safari that you may not expect:

✔ Safari automatically syncs your bookmarks across Safari on your Mac, Windows PC, and other iOS devices, plus you can tell it to sync web forms' passwords and even credit card info.

✔ Safari automatically notes what web pages you've visited on each copy of Safari you use with the same iCloud account, and makes those pages available to all copies of Safari, as Figure 15-1 shows, in what is called iCloud Tabs. (Tap the Show All Tabs button, the icon of two overlapping squares, in the upper-right corner of the Safari screen to get to that view.)

✔ Safari lets you add websites to your Home screen as if they were app icons. Do so by tapping the Share button and then tapping Add to Home Screen in the Share sheet, as shown in Figure 15-2.

✔ Safari lets you save web pages for later reading, using what's called the Reading List (the tab with the eyeglasses icon in the Bookmarks sidebar), as Figure 15-2 shows. *Note:* Tap the Bookmarks button (the icon of an open book) to display the Bookmarks sidebar.

✔ Safari automatically gleans the web links in your social media streams and presents them to you in its Shared Links list (the @ tab in the Bookmarks sidebar).

✔ Safari lets you share URLs with other iOS devices and recent-model Macs via AirDrop, as Figure 15-2 shows. The Share sheet (which you open by tapping the Share button) also lets you share the URL via social media, email, copy and paste (to other apps), and print. On 2012-model and newer Macs running OS X Yosemite, it even automates that handoff using the, um, Handoff feature in iOS 8 and OS X Yosemite — no Share sheet required!

Figure 15-1:
Safari showing two open tabs and, below, the iCloud Tabs from my other devices.

Figure 15-2:
Safari
showing the
Reading List
pane at the
left and the
Share sheet
at the upper
right.

To see and manage your saved passwords and credit card info in Safari, go to the Settings app's Safari pane and tap the Passwords & AutoFill option; then tap Saved Passwords or Saved Credit Cards to see those items. You can turn off password sharing via the Saved Passwords switch, and you can turn off saved credit card info via the Credit Cards switch.

iCloud must be enabled and you must sign in using the same Apple ID on each computer or iOS device with which you want to sync bookmarks and other data. To synchronize passwords and credit card data across devices, iCloud Keychain must be enabled on each device, through the Settings app in iOS, iCloud system preference in OS X, and iCloud control panel in Windows.

Safari's sync features make it very easy to have all your devices keeping the same bookmarks, as well as pick up where you left off as you move from device to device. As someone who works on a variety of devices throughout the day, I can tell you how handy that is!

Cruising with Google Chrome

In the Windows PC world, Safari isn't that popular, but Google Chrome is. And even on Macs, lots of people prefer Chrome. On most Android devices, Chrome is what you get by default, and it's available for the iPad, as well.

Even if you don't prefer Chrome over Safari, you may want to use the free Chrome browser on your iPad. Why? Because you might want to use Safari for personal purposes and Chrome for work ones — or vice versa — so that your work and personal activities are kept more separated on your iPad (and computer).

As with Safari, you can set Chrome to sync bookmarks across all your devices that are signed into the same Google account. Do so in the Settings window, which you access by tapping the Settings button (the icon of a rotated ellipsis) at the upper right of the screen, and then tapping Settings from the menu that appears. You also set up and manage saved passwords through the Settings window. Figure 15-3 shows Chrome with the Settings menu, and Figure 15-4 shows the Settings window.

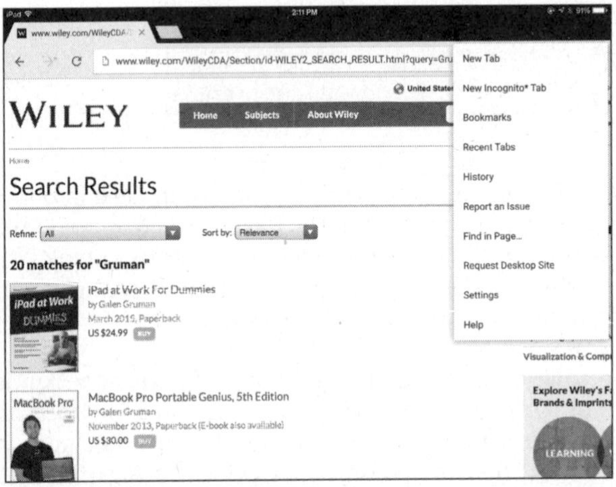

Figure 15-3: Chrome showing its Settings menu at the right.

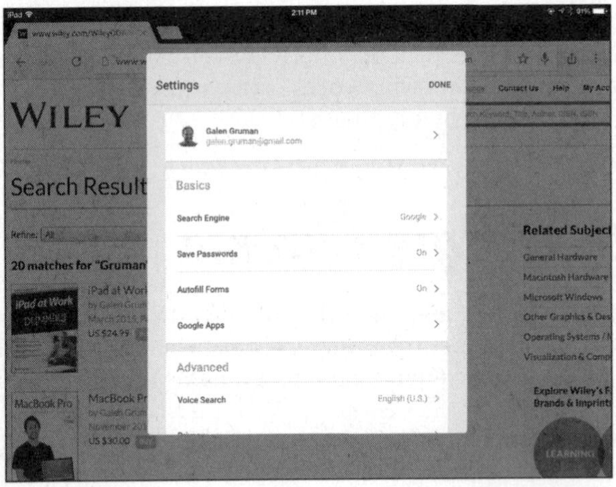

Figure 15-4: Chrome's Settings window.

Chrome also has its equivalent to iCloud Tabs. In the Settings menu, tap Other Devices to see recent web pages from other devices that sync Chrome bookmarks. In the same menu, the New Incognito tab does the same thing as the Private button in Safari's All Tabs view: It stops recording your browser history and disables tracking cookies so that no one else using your iPad can see where you've been — like looking at job openings elsewhere!

Chrome doesn't support Reading List, Shared Links, or AirDrop, but it does support Handoff (with your default browser on a Mac and with Safari on another iOS device). Chrome supports printing both through Apple's AirPrint technology and Google's CloudPrint service, which is supported by fewer printers than AirPrint.

But Chrome does do something that Safari can't: request the desktop version of a web page. Some websites are too smart for their own good, and when they see that you're using a mobile device, they provide a dumbed-down version of the page. On an iPad, that's rarely necessary because the screen is large enough for most regular web pages. The Request Desktop Site option in the Settings menu tells a site to send that normal version to your iPad. Just understand that not all websites will honor that request.

Investigating Mercury Pro and Atomic Web

For most people, Safari and/or Chrome are all the browser they need. But some people may need more. If you're one of them, I can suggest two browsers: the 99¢ Mercury Web Browser Pro and the $1.99 Atomic Web Browser.

Exploring Mercury Web Browser Pro

In addition to having the standard browser capabilities that you'd expect, Mercury Web Browser Pro, shown in Figure 15-5, has several capabilities that can be quite handy.

One of these capabilities is to pretend to be another browser, such as Chrome, Firefox, or Internet Explorer, so that you can see how a website would appear in another browser. That's useful for marketers, web designers, and testers. Tap the Menu button (the icon of three lines) at the upper left, tap User Agent, and then tap the desired browser in the list that appears.

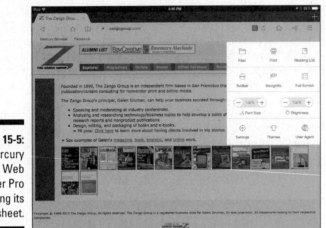

Figure 15-5:
Mercury
Web
Browser Pro
showing its
Menu sheet.

Another is that it can download links in the background: Just tap and hold a link to begin the download; then continue browsing. Tap the Menu button and then tap the File button to see the downloaded files, which you can organize into folders, copy, and share with other apps, email, or send to the Dropbox or Google Drive cloud storage services, as Figure 15-6 shows. (Tap Edit to get those capabilities.)

Tap and hold a file to open the standard iPad Share sheet, from which you can share the file via AirDrop, Mail, and Messages, open in a compatible app, print, or copy.

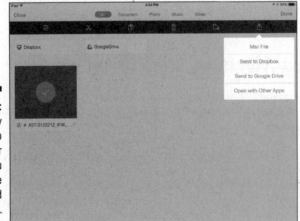

Figure 15-6:
Mercury
Web
Browser
Pro lets you
manage
downloaded
files.

You can even copy files from Dropbox or Google Drive into the Mercury file window so that you can then share from your iPad to other apps and via email. Of course, if you use Dropbox or Google Drive on your iPad, you can share files from those locations directly. The reason to copy them to Mercury is to keep files related to your web activities in one location.

A third nice addition is Mercury's capability to search a wider range of search engines than Safari or Chrome. When you enter a search term in the URL field, tap the icon of the current search engine (Google, by default) to change to a different search engine, including Bing, DuckDuckGo, Reddit, Wikipedia, and shopping sites like Amazon.com, eBay, and Walmart, as well as video sites like Flickr, Vimeo, and YouTube.

But, as they say on TV, "Wait, there's more!" — all of which is in the Menu sheet, where you can

- ✔ Increase or decrease the font size on the web pages you're viewing to improve readability.
- ✔ Change the display brightness for the browser without changing the screen brightness for the iPad's Home screen or other apps.
- ✔ Switch to full-screen mode.

You can also save web pages to your choice of either PDF (the default) or OS X Safari's WebArchive format (you need to set that in Mercury's settings). To save a web page, tap the Menu button (the triangle icon) to the left of the URL and tap Save Web Page in the menu that appears.

Exploring Atomic Web Browser

Shown in Figure 15-7, Atomic Web Browser is similar to Mercury, though its interface isn't as elegant. As does Mercury, Atomic lets you identify itself as a different browser (so that you can see how a website would appear in another browser), use a wide variety of search engines, change the font size, and manage file downloads from the web.

Atomic Web Browser can download files to Dropbox, though not to Google Drive. Although Atomic can't save web pages as PDF, it can save them as WebArchive or pure HTML files (via its Share button).

Figure 15-7:
Atomic Web
Browser,
with the text
enlarged.

But what can Atomic do that Mercury can't? Not much, though it has a couple
additional capabilities, all accessed via the Settings menu (the gear icon):

- ✔ Import and export bookmarks
- ✔ Control how web pages open, such as in a new tab

Part V

Structuring and Sharing Documents

In this part . . .

✔ Get your head in the cloud! You can find out all about using iCloud and other cloud storage services.

✔ The file shuffle: How to move documents from app to app as well as share them with other people.

✔ Make it and mark it: Use the iPad to create and annotate PDF files.

✔ Giving presentations is a snap with the iPad. The hard part is choosing the tool you like best!

✔ Words aren't always enough, but that's no problem thanks to the iPad's graphics, drawing, and diagramming tools.

Chapter 16

Exploiting Cloud Storage

*Y*ou don't have to bring your documents with you to have access to them. You can store them in the cloud (meaning on servers on the Internet) and have them available anywhere you have an Internet connection — and from any device, not just your iPad. It's like having an external hard drive that you can use anywhere you have an Internet connection — and that you don't have to carry with you. Apple's iOS 8 expands its support for cloud storage, but other options often play better outside of Apple's world.

This chapter tells you what the most popular cloud storage services offer and how to use them with your iPad and other iPad apps.

What's Out There? Knowing Your Cloud Storage Options

There are lots of those cloud storage options — more than anyone needs. But five services have the greatest popularity, and these are the most likely to be supported by the apps you use on your iPad: Apple's iCloud Drive, Box, Dropbox, Google Drive, and Microsoft OneDrive. All but iCloud Drive run on recent versions of Windows, OS X, iOS, and Android; iCloud Drive runs only on iOS 8, OS X Yosemite, and Windows 7 or later. All have free client apps and a base level of free storage, with tiered subscription pricing for additional storage amounts.

Chances are, you'll use one or more of these cloud storage apps. (You may use different ones to keep personal and private information separate, for example, or because different clients use different ones.) Others are available, such as SugarSync and Citrix ShareFile, but support for them in apps is quite limited. Unless your IT department forces you to use one of these, I suggest you ignore them.

Box, Dropbox, and OneDrive are available in enterprise versions that let IT impose rules on what you can access and who you can share with, to ensure that confidential company information stays that way. If you use one of those versions, note that the functionality may differ from what is described here based on whatever restrictions your IT staff imposes.

Some apps let you access cloud-stored files directly within them, but many don't. iOS 8 made it easier for developers to add cloud-storage access within their apps, so more and more apps will have this capability over time. For those that don't support direct cloud-storage access, you can use the iOS Share sheet to send files between a cloud storage app and an editing app on your iPad, as Chapter 17 explains. This round-tripping can make version control difficult if you're not meticulous about keeping the changed files consistent on both your iPad and the cloud storage service, but it's better than having to email the file to yourself for later synchronization.

Using Apple's iCloud Drive

iCloud Drive is not an app, so don't go looking on your iPad for its icon. Instead, iCloud Drive is part of the iCloud service that comes with all iPads, iPhones, iPod touches, and Macs — if you sign up for an iCloud account. You can also install iCloud Drive on a PC running Windows 7 or later; download the iCloud software from `http://support.apple.com/kb/DL1455`.

If an app is compatible with iCloud Drive, you may be able to navigate folders and files in iCloud from that app. iCloud Drive can appear in various ways, depending on your app: as a drive that you open; as a folder; as the default view; and accessible only as an import, share, or export option.

In some apps, all you see are the documents from specific folders in iCloud Drive. More commonly, you see those documents in the app's standard documents folder but have an option to see documents stored in iCloud Drive folders. For example, Apple's iWork apps use the Add button (+ icon) in the Documents window to let you work with files stored in other iCloud Drive folders (see Chapter 5).

In some apps, you may be able to access iCloud Drive only through the apps' import and export features. In those apps, you import a copy of the document to your iPad, working with it locally, and then you have to remember to export the changed version back to iCloud Drive to keep the versions in sync.

In other apps, you may have a direct connection to those apps' iCloud Drive folder *and* be able to import and export to other folders in iCloud Drive — not work directly on files in other iCloud Drive folders, as you can in iWork. GoodReader, shown in Figure 16-1, is an example of such an app that uses import/export to work with other iCloud Drive folders.

To quickly move among cloud storage services, tap the Locations button in the form in which you navigate iCloud Drive folders; a menu of other available cloud services displays, as you can see in Figure 16-1.

On your Mac or PC, you'll see and can work with the contents of each app's folders within iCloud Drive, as well as files not in those folders, as Figure 16-2 shows — as far as OS X and Windows are concerned, they're just folders and files on a network drive.

Whether an app shows the whole iCloud Drive folder hierarchy or just documents in the folder for that particular app, the files are synced to all computers and devices using the same iCloud account and signed in to iCloud Drive. So, unlike most cloud storage services, documents stored in iCloud Drive are available even when you are offline, after the files have had a chance to sync.

Even if your apps support iCloud Drive, they won't provide you access to it until you enable iCloud Drive on your iPad. You do so in the Settings app's iCloud pane: Set the iCloud Drive to switch to On. You may also need to enable iCloud Drive in your individual apps; most will ask you when you first launch them, as well as provide the option in their own settings either in the app itself or in its pane in the Settings app.

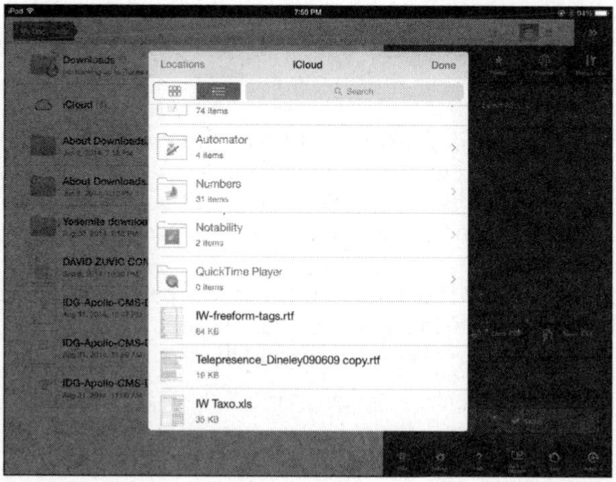

Figure 16-1:
Center:
Importing
a file from
iCloud
Drive in
GoodReader.
At left:
GoodReader
has direct
access to
its own
iCloud folder
as well.

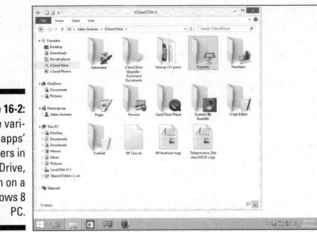

Figure 16-2:
The various apps' folders in iCloud Drive, seen on a Windows 8 PC.

Some apps may let you save to and read from other cloud services, such as Box and Dropbox. iPad apps can use as few or as many as such services — or none at all — as their developers choose.

To put a file into iCloud Drive from an app that doesn't support it, use the Share sheet (see Chapter 17) to send the document to a compatible app that does support iCloud Drive; then save it into iCloud Drive from there.

Moving Files to and from Your iPad with Box

The first time you use the Box app, you need to sign in (or "log in," according to Box) using the email address and password for your Box account. You can also create a new account from within the app.

When you open the app, you get the Files view, shown in Figure 16-3. It shows any folders and files already stored in your Box account, which you may have added there from your computer. *Note:* If you don't see the contents, tap the Files button (the folder icon) at the upper left of the screen.

Tap a folder to open it, and tap a file to download a preview of its contents to your iPad for viewing or sharing. (The file has to be in a format that Box can preview, such as PDF or one of the Microsoft Office formats.)

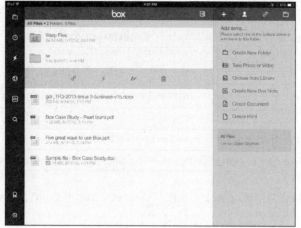

Figure 16-3:
Box's file
view, with
the options
available
for an
individual
file.

But note that this preview download is temporary: If you want to actually
download the file to the iPad so that it's available even when you don't have
an Internet connection, you need to make it available for offline access.

To make a file or folder offline-accessible, swipe to the left over it in the file
list. You see a gray bar with icons representing options on that bar, as shown
in Figure 16-3. Tap the bar's Offline button (the lightning-bolt icon) to make
a local copy that Box will keep synced with the master version on the cloud
service. You can see those offline files and folders by tapping the Offline
button (the lightning-bolt icon) in the left column.

That options bar has other options as well:

- ✔ **Share (the chain icon):** Tap this icon to open a pop-over that lets you
  send a link (not the file or folder itself) to other people via Mail or
  Messages, or copy that link so that you can paste it into another app.
  Note: This shares the link to the file, not the file itself, so the recipient
  will have to download the file from a browser or, if using an iOS device,
  from the link into his own copy of Box.

- ✔ **Rename (the pencil icon):** Tap this icon to give the file or folder a new
  name.

- ✔ **Delete (the trash can icon):** Tap this icon to remove the file from the
  Box storage service (making it no longer available to any computer
  linked to the same account).

To make a file no longer available offline, do not delete it — doing so removes
it everywhere. Instead, open the options bar and tap the Offline button again.

The selection method in Box is to tap and hold any file, and then tap the bubbles to the left of each name to select items. Doing so also displays the Copy, Move, and Delete buttons at the top of the screen, which you tap to do the desired action. Both Move and Copy place the selected files in the Box folders you select.

The Box app has several other controls to note. First, along the left pane is a column of buttons, as follows:

- **Files (the folder icon):** Shows you the file list.

- **Recent (the clock icon):** Shows you the files and folders you've recently previewed.

- **Offline (the lightning-bolt icon):** Shows you the files and folders available for offline use.

- **Preview (the globe icon):** Shows you a snippet of the last file you previewed. No, I don't get why it's there, either — you can get a complete preview simply by tapping the desired file in the file list.

- **Apps (the cloud-in-a-box icon):** Shows you featured apps that work with Box. This option is basically a promo for those apps.

- **Search (the magnifying-glass icon):** Lets you find files and folders by entering text in the Search field that appears. *Note:* You can't search for text in documents, just for text used in the file or folder names.

- **Upgrade (the ribbon icon):** Lets you buy more storage.

- **Settings (the gear icon):** Lets you set a warning when you're transferring files via your cellular connection, require a password to use the app, and control how you navigate document previews.

Along the top of the app in Files view are these buttons:

- **Close Pane (the icon with a → in a box):** Closes the right pane, which shows available options. If the right pane is closed, the icon becomes the Open Pane (the icon with a ← in a box).

- **Add Items (the + icon):** Lets you create new folders, take videos or photos using the iPad's camera, get a file from the Photos app, add a note (see Chapter 9), or create a document or HTML file by opening a compatible app.

- **Manage People (the person icon):** Lets you invite other Box users to get access to your files and folders, as well as see whom you've given such access to. *Note:* Whatever folder you are currently in is the one that is shared.

✔ **Share (the chain icon):** Works like the Share button in the options bar described previously. Except that it doesn't work — there's no way to select the files to share them. Yes, this is sadly true (at least at press time).

✔ **Folder Details (the folder icon):** Lets you sort the current folder's contents by name, kind, or size, as well as select files to be moved, copied,· or deleted, as previously described.

Box is not a complicated app to use. After all, its point is to make files accessible — and that's all it does. If you want to do more with your files, such as share them with other apps, skip Box and use one of the other services in this chapter.

Dealing with Files with Dropbox

The Dropbox app requires you to sign in the first time you use it, and you can also sign up for a Dropbox account then. After you've signed in, you see the files list shown in Figure 16-4. (Tap the Files button at the bottom of the left pane if you don't see the files list.)

Scroll to the desired file or folder. Tap a folder to open it and a file to preview it (as shown in Figure 16-4) if the file is in a supported file type such as PDF or Microsoft Office.

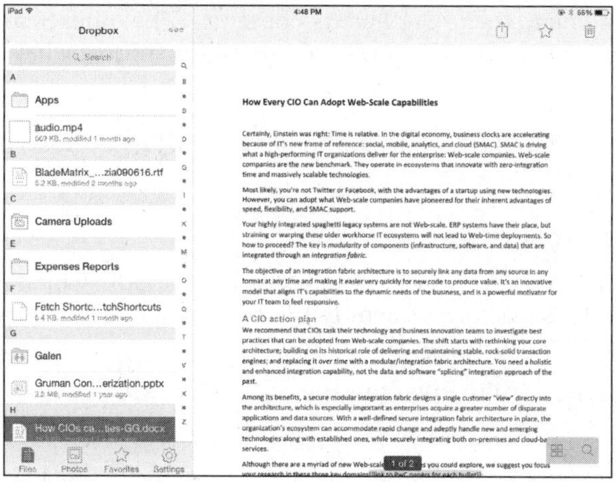

Figure 16-4:
Dropbox's file view, with a file being previewed.

By default, Dropbox shows you your files and folders organized alphabetically. But you can sort them by date by tapping the More button (the . . . icon) above the file list and choosing Sort by Date. That same menu lets you create a new folder, upload photos from the Photos app, or select files and folders so that you can delete or move them.

When you select a file (whether Dropbox can preview it or not), three icons appear at the upper right of the screen:

- **Share (the icon showing a ↑ emerging from a box):** Opens the standard iOS Share sheet, from which you can send a link to the file via Messages or Mail, or to a compatible app. You can also copy that link to paste it into an app. *Note:* Tapping this button shares the link to the file, not the file itself, so the recipient will have to download the file from a browser or, if using an iOS device, from the link into her own copy of Dropbox. But you can send the actual file to another app using the Open In button, or to another iOS device or Mac using the AirDrop feature in the Share sheet; both are described in Chapter 17. You can also use this feature to print any file that Dropbox can preview.

- **Favorite (the star icon):** Copies the file to your iPad's local storage, so it's available when you're not connected to the Internet. Dropbox still keeps the local copy in sync with the master copy stored in Dropbox's cloud servers. To see which files and folders are available for offline use, tap the Favorites button at the bottom of the left pane.

- **Delete (the trash can icon):** Deletes the file.

If you select a folder instead of a file, a Share button appears over the file list; tap it to share a link to the folder and its contents. (The other Share button remains visible over the preview area; you use it for sharing whatever you last previewed.)

The Settings pane (tap the Settings button to open it) lets you do the following:

- Purchase more storage

- Automatically upload your iPad's photos to Dropbox (which eats up your Dropbox storage allotment but does provide a secondary backup to iOS's own Photo Stream feature)

- Require a password to open the app

Getting to Files with Google Drive

Google Drive access is one of the things you get when you sign up for a Google account, such as when you sign up for a Gmail account or set up an Android device. On a computer, you use your browser to work with Google Drive, but in iOS, you use the Google Drive app because Google's services often work poorly on the browsers found on mobile devices like the iPad.

Figure 16-5 shows Google Drive with the Details pane open for a document. But before I get to the Details pane, I want to explain how to get your files in the first place.

Google Drive has two views: list and thumbnails (the list view is shown in Figure 16-5). A button at the upper right of the screen toggles between the two views. When you're in the list view, the button looks like four squares in a grid; tap it to see a grid of thumbnails. When you're in the thumbnails view, the icon looks like a bulleted list; tap it to see a list of files.

Tap a file to open it — and I mean open, not preview. If you have a compatible Google Apps app on your iPad, the file opens in that app — or asks you to download Google Apps from the App Store. (I cover Google Apps in Chapter 7.) In the Google Apps app, tap the ← button in the upper right of the screen to close the document; then tap the Menu button (the icon of three lines) to get the Google Drive option that takes you back to Google Drive.

In the list view, you see the *i* icon to the right of the file or folder name; it's in the bottom right of the file's preview or folder icon in the thumbnails view. Tap it to open the Details pane shown in Figure 16-5. The Details pane is where you manage the file or folder.

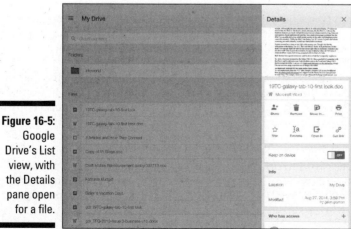

Figure 16-5: Google Drive's List view, with the Details pane open for a file.

The Details pane contains the following options for both folders and files:

- ✔ **Share:** Lets you invite other Google users to see and optionally edit the file or folder contents from Google Drive on their browsers or mobile devices.

- ✔ **Remove:** Deletes the file or folder from Google Drive.

- ✔ **Move To:** Lets you move the file or folder to a different folder.

- ✔ **Star:** Marks a file as a favorite. The button then becomes Unstar so that you can remove the favorites status from a file or folder later. *Note:* Tap the Menu button (the icon showing three lines) at the upper left of the Google Drive screen to get the option to see just favorite files and folders.

- ✔ **Rename:** Lets you give the file or folder a different name.

- ✔ **Get Link:** Creates a link that you can copy into an email or other message, which you can then send to someone so that he can access the file or folder from Google Drive.

The Details pane has the following additional options just for files:

- ✔ **Print:** Lets you print the file either via iOS's native AirPrint feature or Google's own CloudPrint service.

- ✔ **Open In:** Lets you open the file in another compatible app on your iPad.

- ✔ **Keep on Device:** Set this switch to On to keep the file available on your iPad even when you're not connected to the Internet. Google Drive keeps the contents synced with the master file on Google's servers when you regain Internet access.

To close the Details pane, click the Close button (the X icon) in its upper-right corner.

The Menu button (the icon of three lines) at the upper left of the Google Drive screen lets you narrow your view. The options in the Menu pane that appears are mostly self-explanatory: My Drive, Recent, Starred, and On Device.

The one that may not be so obvious is Incoming; it lists files recently shared by others to you so that you can add them to your own list of files in Google Drive. Tap the Pin icon (the pushpin icon) to the right of a filename to copy it to your Google Drive file list.

The Menu pane also has the Settings button (the gear icon), where you can require a password to open Google Drive and view how much of your account's storage is used up. You can also add more accounts here, which comes in handy if you have both work and personal Google accounts whose files you want to access from Google Drive on your iPad.

Managing Files with Microsoft OneDrive

If you've read the descriptions of the other cloud storage services in this chapter, this one will sound familiar. It should be obvious by now that although their user interfaces differ, the core functionality of cloud storage services is the same. This commonality makes sense because they all do basically the same things.

What distinguishes OneDrive from the rest of these services is that it is the native cloud storage service for Windows 8 and Windows Phone, much as iCloud Drive is for OS X Yosemite and iOS 8. But Microsoft has made the OneDrive app work on more devices than Apple has done with iCloud Drive: OneDrive supports Android and Windows Phone devices; iCloud Drive does not support either.

When you open OneDrive for the first time, you're asked to sign in using your Microsoft account (which you may have set up for OneDrive on your computer or as part of your Windows 8 PC's setup), or to set up an account. After you're signed in, you see the Documents window, shown in Figure 16-6, which by default shows the details for your files and folders.

For a more compact view, tap the More button (the . . . icon) at the upper right and choose Thumbnails View, which shows just the file type icons and the filenames. To get the Details view back, tap the More button and then choose Details View.

Figure 16-6:
OneDrive's
file view.

You open a file or folder by tapping it. If you open a Microsoft Office document, OneDrive will open the corresponding Office app on your iPad (or ask you to get the app from the App Store).

As Chapter 6 explains, Microsoft Office on the iPad lets you work with files stored in OneDrive for Business and Dropbox only if you have an Office 365 subscription. But you can use most Office editing capabilities on files stored on your iPad or in the standard OneDrive service without needing an Office 365 subscription.

If you tap another type of file, OneDrive shows a preview of the file if that file format is supported; Office files, PDF files, and most image files are supported. And if you tap the file, a row of buttons appears at the bottom; these buttons, from left to right, are the following:

- ✔ **Share (the icon with a ↑ coming out of a box):** Lets you invite other OneDrive users to see and work with your files, send a link to the file for others to view in their browser, and send the actual file as an attachment (as well as print it) using an abbreviated version of the standard iOS Share sheet, as explained in Chapter 17.

- ✔ **Delete (the trash can icon):** Removes the file from your OneDrive storage, including from any devices connected to it.

- ✔ **Files (the folder icon):** Lets you move the file to a different folder.

- ✔ **More (the . . . icon):** Lets you rename the file or open the file in another app using an abbreviated version of the iOS Share sheet.

Tap Documents at the upper left of the screen to return to the file list.

The More button in the upper right of the screen is where you primarily manage your files and folders. In the main files list, it has two options in addition to the Thumbnails View option described previously:

- ✔ **Add Items:** Lets you create a new folder, copy photos and videos from the iPad's Photos app (the Choose Existing option), or use the iPad's camera to take a photo or video.

- ✔ **Select Items:** Displays bubble selectors next to each file and folder. Select the items you want to manage; then tap the Share, Delete, or Files buttons at the bottom of the screen. (I describe what they do in the preceding list.) If you select just one folder, the More button at the bottom of the screen has the Rename Folder option. If you select just one file, the More button has the Rename File option and — for Microsoft Office files only — the Edit option to open them in the corresponding Office app on your iPad.

If you're in a folder, the More button at the upper right of the screen has two additional options in the main files list: Rename This Folder and Sharing and Permissions. The latter does for the folder's contents what the Share button does for an individual file. (See the bullet item describing the Share button earlier in this section.)

When you're viewing file lists, whether in the main window or within a folder, at the bottom of the screen are four buttons that let you filter what you see:

- **Files:** Shows all files.

- **Photos:** Shows photos stored in OneDrive.

- **Recent:** Shows recently added files.

- **Shared:** Shows files you've shared with others, as well as files that others have shared with you, each in their own folders.

Finally, there's the Settings button (the gear icon) at the lower right of the main window or within a folder. Its options include:

- **Camera Backup:** Enables camera backup, which can eat up your storage allowance but does give you a secondary backup to iOS's own Photo Stream.

- **Use Office Apps:** If you set this switch to Off, OneDrive does not open Office files in the Office apps on your iPad, and the Edit option disappears from the More menu for such files.

- **Sign Out:** Tap this option to sign out of the app, which means that you'll need to sign in again to use it. As with the password options in other cloud storage services, this feature is meant to keep people you let use your iPad from getting access to those files.

In contrast to Box, Dropbox, and Google Drive, OneDrive has no option to keep files on the iPad for offline access. (iCloud Drive keeps a local copy automatically within each app, so all the app's files are available for offline access.) So you must have an Internet connection to use OneDrive.

Chapter 17

Syncing and Sharing Files

. . . .

In This Chapter

▶ Transferring files between your computer with iTunes

▶ Exchanging files among iOS devices and Macs with AirDrop

▶ Sending files to other people via the iOS Share sheet — and receiving files from others the same way

▶ Moving files from Windows PCs and older Macs to your iPad via AirTransfer+

▶ Using GoodReader to exchange files from almost any server to your iPad (and back)

▶ Accessing your iPad's files from your computer via a direct connection in iExplorer

▶ Connecting to FTP servers via FTP on the Go Pro

. . . .

*T*he cloud storage methods covered in Chapter 16 are great, but they don't cover all the bases. Many apps don't work with cloud storage services, and even when they do, there are times when you want to share individual items outside the cloud.

Well, you can! The iPad provides multiple ways to share documents and other files with other devices and other people. In this chapter, I describe how to transfer files between your computer and your iPad via iTunes, AirDrop, and several other apps, as well as how to share files with others via the iOS Share sheet.

Syncing Files via iTunes

The iPad's original method for sharing files with a PC or Mac still works: iTunes file syncing. With the iPad connected to your Mac or PC via its USB cable or over Wi-Fi, open iTunes on the computer and follow these steps *on your computer:*

1. **Select your iPad in the Devices list (click the Devices icon at the upper left of the iTunes 12 screen to see the list).**

2. **Click Apps in the list of content in the left pane.**

3. **Scroll down the right pane until you see the Apps section.**

4. **Click the app you want to retrieve files from or send them to.**

   A list of files and folders, if any, displays at right, as Figure 17-1 shows.

5. **Select the folder and files you want to copy from the iPad to your computer; then click the Save To button at the bottom right of the currently selected app's file list.**

6. **In the dialog that opens, select the folder on your computer to save the files to; then click Save To.**

   Note that you cannot open folders on the iPad to select individual files within them; you just copy their entire contents to your computer.

7. **Click the Add button at the bottom right of the currently selected app's file list.**

8. **In the dialog that appears, choose the files and folders to copy to the iPad and then click Add.**

   After a few moments, the files are copied.

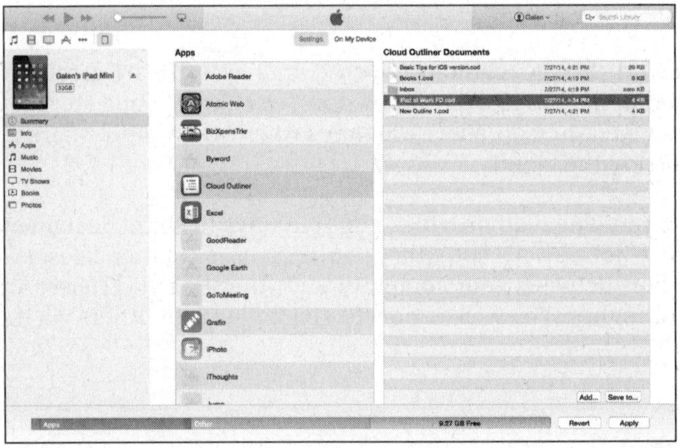

Figure 17-1:
iTunes can
copy files
between
your
computer
and your
iPad.

Sharing Content via AirDrop

Using iTunes to transfer files is, frankly, a bit clunky. And you're restricted to transferring files and other content (such as URLs in Safari) just between your computer and iPad — which is a limitation of iCloud Drive as well. But you can use Apple's AirDrop technology to move files among your iPad and other iOS devices and Macs, whether they are yours or not.

Sorry, AirDrop does not work with Windows PCs, Linux PCs, Android devices, or other non-Apple devices.

To work with AirDrop, the devices need to have both Bluetooth and Wi-Fi turned on, and they need to be in radio range of each other, which is usually no more than 30 feet, and often closer.

You can use AirDrop if your iOS devices and Macs are compatible, meaning that they support both Bluetooth Low Energy and Wi-Fi Direct, two technologies that require the use of specific internal hardware that only more recent devices have. Here are the devices that support AirDrop between your iPad and Mac or between your iPad and other iOS devices:

✔ Any 2012-or-later Mac model running OS X Yosemite. (To see whether your Mac is compatible, choose 🍎⇨About This Mac, click System Report, click Bluetooth in the left pane, and look for the Bluetooth Low Energy Supported row. If its value is Yes, you can use AirDrop with iOS devices; if not, you can use AirDrop only with other Macs.

✔ Any iPhone, iPad, or iPod touch that has a Lightning connector and is running iOS 8.

By default, AirDrop in iOS and OS X is configured to allow AirDrop sharing only with people in your Contacts list. You can change that behavior as follows:

✔ **iOS:** Swipe up from the bottom of the screen to display the Control Center, tap AirDrop, and choose Off to disable AirDrop or choose Everyone to share with any compatible iOS device or Mac that is in range of your iPad. Choose Contacts Only to restrict sharing with people in the device's Contacts app.

✔ **OS X:** Open a Finder window or tab and click AirDrop in the Sidebar. Click Allow Others to Find Me at the bottom of the window, and choose No One to disable AirDrop or choose Everyone to share with any compatible iOS device or Mac that is in range of your iPad. Choose Contacts Only to restrict sharing with people in the Mac's Contacts application.

The two faces of AirDrop on a Mac

A Mac that supports AirDrop with iOS devices can either share with both iOS devices and newer Macs or just with older Macs (those that don't support Bluetooth Low Energy and Wi-Fi Direct); it can't share with older Macs, newer Macs, and iOS devices all at the same time.

If you see Don't See Who You're Looking For? at the bottom of the Finder's AirDrop window, your Mac can share with compatible iOS devices and newer Macs, but not with older Macs.

Click the Don't See Who You're Looking For? text to open a pop-over and select the AirDrop with Older Macs check box. Now your Mac can't use AirDrop with iOS devices but it can use it with both older and newer Macs.

The Don't See Who You're Looking For? text changes to AirDrop with Older Macs: On.

Want to use AirDrop with an iOS device instead? Click the AirDrop with Older Macs: On text to get that pop-over where you deselect the AirDrop with Older Macs. The text changes back to Don't See Who You're Looking For?.

You can switch between Don't See Who You're Looking For? and AirDrop with Older Macs: On based on whom you want to share with at the moment.

Note: If clicking AirDrop with Older Macs: On doesn't open the pop-over, that means that your Mac doesn't support AirDrop with iOS devices, only with Macs.

AirDropping a file from an iPad to another iOS device

The process for using AirDrop to exchange files depends on what you're sharing from and to. Here are the steps for sharing from your iPad to another iOS device:

1. **Have the document or item you want to share open or selected in the app that contains it.**

2. **Tap the Share button in the app you want to share from.**

   In the Share sheet that appears, any available AirDrop devices show up at the top, as in Figure 17-2.

3. **Tap the person you want to share the file or content with.**

   You see "waiting" flash beneath that person's icon in the Share sheet.

   The Share sheet is actually a pop-over, but Apple calls it *Share sheet,* so I do, too.

The other person gets an alert on his or her device, with the option to Accept or Decline the content being sent by you. If the other person taps Accept, a list of apps compatible with the shared content appears, as Figure 17-3 shows. The person taps the desired app to open the content in.

Figure 17-2: The Share sheet shows who's available to have the current or selected content AirDropped.

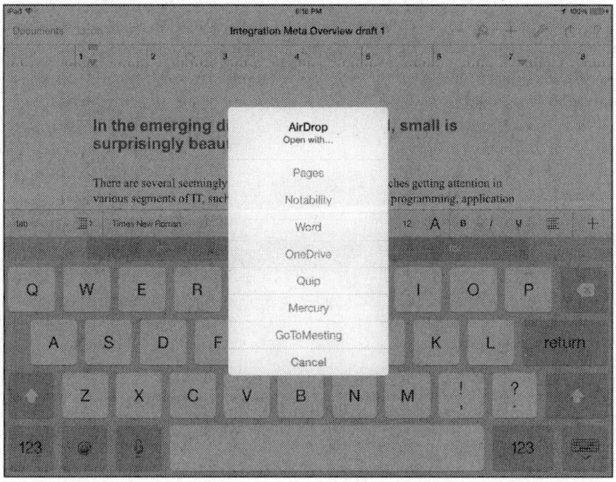

Figure 17-3: After another device's user accepts an AirDrop, he or she chooses the app to open it in.

AirDropping a file from an iPad to a Mac

The steps for sharing files from an iPad to a Mac are not quite the same as sharing from an iPad to an iOS devices; the differences are on the Mac's end. Here are the steps:

1. **Have the document or item you want to share open or selected in the app that contains it.**

2. **Tap the Share button in the app you want to share from.**

   In the Share sheet that appears, any available AirDrop devices show up at the top (refer to Figure 17-2).

3. **Tap the person you want to share the file or content with.**

   You see "waiting" flash beneath the person's icon in the Share sheet.

   The Mac user must have AirDrop open in a Finder window or tab. If so, that person will see an alert in the Finder with three options: Save and Open, Save, and Decline, as Figure 17-4 shows.

   The Mac user clicks Save and Open to copy the file to the Mac's Documents folder and open it in a compatible application, or the Mac user clicks Save to save the file to the Documents folder.

If you think you'll use AirDrop a lot, I suggest that you leave an AirDrop Finder window or tab always open on your Mac. You can minimize an AirDrop Finder window to the Dock if you want to keep it out of the way.

Figure 17-4:
An open Finder window or tab set to AirDrop displays any AirDrop requests.

AirDropping a file from a Mac to an iPad

To share content from a Mac application via its Share sheet, follow the same steps as for AirDropping from an iPad to another iOS device, using a Mac application instead of an iOS app as the source. To share a file via the Mac's Finder:

1. **Open a Finder window or tab and navigate to the file you want to share.**

2. **Drag the file into an AirDrop Finder window or tab over the icon of the person you want to share it with.**

   The other person gets an alert on his or her iOS device, with the option to Accept or Decline the content being sent by you.

   If the other person taps Accept, a list of apps compatible with the shared content appears, as shown earlier in Figure 17-3. The person taps the desired app in which to open the content.

Sharing with the Share Sheet

The Share sheet is meant for sharing — as you could no doubt tell from its name. In addition to making AirDrops from it, as described in the previous section, you can also use the Share sheet to share content through other means by tapping the appropriate button in the Share sheet, as Figure 17-5 shows.

Figure 17-5:
A standard
Share sheet.

The easy way to open files shared by others

The Open In facility used by the Share sheet also works to receive files, not just send them out.

If you open a file from a web link or in an email, iOS's Open In tries to determine the file type and then presents a menu of compatible apps to open the file in. Thus, an easy way to share files with an iPad is to make them available on a website (acting as if the website were a file server, basically) or send the files via email. You can then transfer the files to the iPad via Safari or Mail, respectively.

In fact, the website approach is particularly handy for work groups that need access to the same set of files. (You might want to password-protect the website so that only authorized users can get its files.)

The Share sheet shows buttons for any apps that have told iOS they can work with the specific file type you're currently using. Tap the desired app's icon to open the content in it — using what Apple calls iOS's Open In facility. If you don't see the app you want to share the content to, scroll to the right to see more apps, if available. When you tap an app, it opens with a copy of the shared content.

Not all apps use the standard iOS Share sheet, but their versions should work the same way, even if they look different. And whether or not they do use the standard Share sheet, they may require you to convert their files into a more widely used format before letting you select an app to open the file in.

 The Share sheet has a third row of icons, below the row of compatible apps. This third row contains available iOS services such as printing, adding to contacts, copying, and so on.

Syncing the No-Fuss Way with AirTransfer+

If you like the idea of AirDrop's simplicity but use a Windows PC or a Mac that doesn't support AirDrop exchange with iOS devices, the $1.99 AirTransfer+ app is a decent substitute.

The app uses your computer's browser as the portal to your iPad. AirTransfer+ displays a URL for your iPad, as Figure 17-6 shows, that you then enter into any of your computer's browsers to open.

Figure 17-6:
AirTransfer+
creates a
URL for your
iPad that
you can
then sync
to from your
computer's
browser.

Drag files into that browser window, as Figure 17-6 shows, and they are sent via the network to the AirTransfer+ app on your iPad, arranged in categories based on file type. Tap a category to see its files, open a file, and use the Share sheet to send it to other apps.

AirTransfer+ works on Macs and PCs in the Chrome, Firefox, and Safari browsers.

Figure 17-7:
Dragging
files into
an iPad's
AirTrans-
fer+'s
browser
window on
a computer
(here, using
Firefox in
Windows
8.1).

You can't use AirTransfer+ at all in the Windows 8.1 Start screen version of Internet Explorer because AirTransfer+ expects you to drag in files to be transferred, and all Start screen applications take up the entire screen. That means that no Desktop file list exists from which to drag files into Internet Explorer. You can use Internet Explorer in the Windows Desktop, but some features don't work, such as seeing what's on the iPad, so AirTransfer+'s developer, Darrinsoft, says to stick with Chrome, Firefox, or Safari instead.

Moving Files with GoodReader

iOS doesn't have a file system that you can access, meaning there's no way to get lists of files on the device, as you can in Windows' File Explorer, OS X's Finder, and Android's various folders such as Downloads and Gallery. Instead, iOS locks files inside the same "container" that holds the app. This means that each app stores all the files it works on, keeping them securely separate from other apps — viruses can't infect apps through files because of this approach, for example. But because practically every device we use has a file system, many people want to replicate that aspect in iOS.

The $9.99 GoodReader can act as a central file manager for iOS — sort of. It can't access other apps' files directly, but you can use GoodReader as a way station between apps and the rest of the world. It's a complex app, but if you master it, you'll appreciate all it can do.

GoodReader does many things, but for file syncing and sharing, the key to remember is that it can connect to both cloud services (such as those described in Chapter 16) and servers on your network, meaning computers, file servers, and even storage devices attached to your router. You can then move files between those network-accessible resources and GoodReader on your iPad.

Working with folders in GoodReader

When you open GoodReader, you see a list of any files stored in GoodReader, organized by folders. Tap the Home button to go to the main GoodReader file list, and tap a folder to open its contents. You can open folders inside a folder the same way. As you navigate the folder hierarchy, you see the path appear at the upper left of the screen, as Figure 17-8 in the upcoming section shows; you can tap any folder in that path to move directly to it.

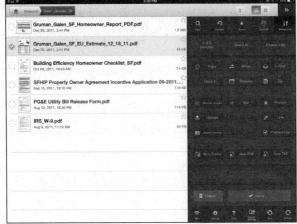

Figure 17-8:
GoodRead-
er's Manage
Files pane
is where
you upload,
download,
and share
selected
files.

You can make iCloud appear as one of those folders. Here's how:

1. **Tap the Reveal Controls button (the « icon at upper right) to reveal GoodReader's many controls.**

2. **Tap Settings at the bottom of the controls.**

3. **In the pop-over that appears, scroll down until you see the Use iCloud switch.**

4. **Set the Use iCloud Switch to On.**

5. **Tap Close to close the pop-over.**

Working with files in GoodReader

To work with files, tap Manage Files at the top of the controls to see the options shown in Figure 17-8. Then tap Manage Files at the bottom of the Manage Files pane; selection bubbles should appear to the left of the files and folders in the left pane.

Select files and folders in the left pane; then tap the button in the Manage Files pane at the right for whatever you want to do. For sharing, the three buttons that apply are Upload, Download, and Open In:

✔ **Upload:** Tap Upload to choose a server or cloud storage onto which to upload the selected items. (I explain how to set up those servers and cloud storage accounts in the next section.)

✔ **Download:** Tap Download to move a file from iCloud, other cloud storage, or server into the GoodReader app, in whatever folder is selected in the left pane. (If the selected file is not in a remote location, you won't see the Download button.)

✔ **Open In:** Tap Open In to open the Share sheet, from which you select which app to copy the selected file to (as well as open in that app).

When you're done with the selected files, tap the Done button in the Manage Files pane to be able to navigate GoodReader's folder hierarchy again.

Setting up servers in GoodReader

So how do you get GoodReader to access those cloud storage services and network servers in the first place? You do that in the Connect pane, which you open by tapping the Connect button at the top of the controls in the right pane. (Open that pane by tapping the « icon at the upper right.) Figure 17-9 shows the Connect pane, with a connected server's content open in the popover in the middle.

The Connect pane has four main sections related to getting content from outside your iPad: Web, Downloads, Remote Sync, and Connect to Servers.

The Web section has two buttons that let you find a website with files you want to download: Browse the Web and Enter URL. The first button lets you use a primitive browser to go to websites and navigate within them to the files you want; the second button lets you enter the URL directly.

Figure 17-9: Perusing files on a connected server in GoodReader.

The Downloads section lists all the files you've downloaded recently, and you can redownload any that were later deleted. Tap Show All to see the list, and tap the Refresh button (the curved-arrow icon) next to an item in that list to redownload it.

The Connect to Servers section is where you see all your servers. Tap Add to add a cloud service such as Dropbox or OneDrive, a WebDAV server, an FTP server, a Mac (called an AFP server), or a Windows PC (called an SMB server). You have to enter the appropriate credentials to sign in to the desired cloud service or remote server. After you do, it's available for downloading files from and uploading files to.

But wait, as they say on TV — there's more! Scroll to the bottom of the Connect pane and tap Reload List of Local Servers. All compatible servers on the current network display in the Servers Found via Wi-Fi list, and you can tap any to sign in; then you navigate its folder hierarchy to find files, as Figure 17-9 shows.

Tap the Pin button (the pushpin icon) to the right of a server to have GoodReader remember it, which places it in the Known Servers list for easy access later. Tap the Settings button (the gear icon) to the right of a server in the Known Servers list to enter your credentials for that server if you want GoodReader to sign in automatically the next time you open it.

You might have noticed that I skipped over the Remote Sync section. It lists the folder that you have set to sync to GoodReader (note that only one folder can be set to remotely sync). You use the Sync button below a folder to start the sync, which makes the contents of the remote folder and the GoodReader folder be the same. (Use the Delete button to end the automatic remote sync, and use the Settings button to change technical settings such as the server protocol, how deletions are synced across devices, and how filename conflicts are handled.)

But how do you set up remote sync in the first place? Here's how:

1. **Connect to the server via the Connect pane.**

2. **In the pop-over that opens, navigate to the folder that contains the folder you want to sync.**

3. **Tap that folder so that it's highlighted.**

4. **Tap the Sync button that appears at the bottom of the pop-over.**

5. **Tap Proceed in the alert that appears.**

6. **Select the folder within GoodReader that you want to synchronize that external folder to.**

   You can also create a new folder.

7. **Tap Download Here & Synchronize to make that local GoodReader folder be the one that syncs with the remote server's folder.**

8. **Tap Close to finish the setup, or Sync to both finish the setup and immediately sync the two folders.**

Exploring the iPad's Contents with iExplorer

Although the iPad's iOS doesn't have a file system that you can see and work with directly, it does of course have one that's working behind the scenes. Macroplant's $35 iExplorer application for OS X and Windows (download it from www.macroplant.com) lets you get into that hidden file system from your computer; you can do this for any iOS device connected via USB cable. You can use iExplorer to transfer files directly. It's similar to using the iTunes file syncing but with more access to files than iTunes provides.

Shown in Figure 17-10, iExplorer shows all iOS devices connected to your computer, and it shows all the folders in each device. Most folders are apps, because iOS stores files with their apps. Open a folder to see the contents.

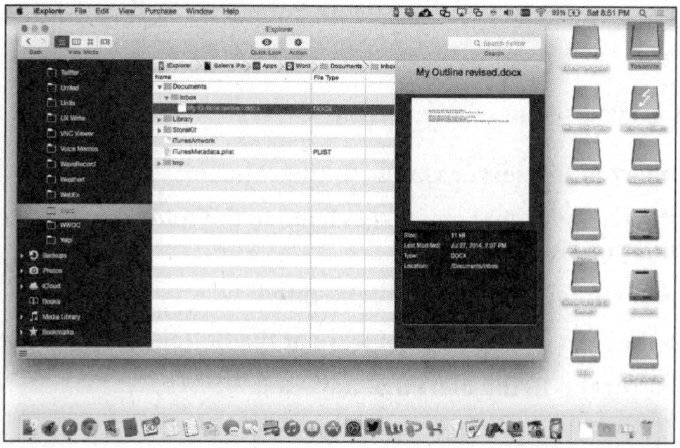

Figure 17-10: iExplorer for Mac and Windows lets you see the file-system guts of your iPad, and transfer files.

WARNING!

You're seeing the actual file system of iOS when you use iExplorer, so you're seeing not just document files but also the applications and their components as well. *Never move or delete these files!*

To upload files from your computer into an iOS folder, just drag them from the Mac Finder or Windows File Explorer into the folder shown in iExplorer's window. To download files from the iPad to your computer, drag them from the folder shown in iExplorer to the Mac Finder or Windows File Explorer. It's as simple as that.

Transferring Files the Old-School Way with FTP on the Go Pro

Long before there was an iPad, there was something called FTP, meaning File Transfer Protocol. It's an old standard, or protocol, for transferring files, as its name plainly says. (The SFTP variation means Secure FTP, by the way.) If you run a website, you very likely use FTP to upload your files to the server hosting the site. Well, you can use FTP to upload and download files between your iPad and such a server, too.

I mention earlier in this chapter that GoodReader can access FTP servers, and if all you need to do is transfer files to and from an FTP server, you should use GoodReader for that purpose, because you'll probably want GoodReader for its other capabilities anyhow.

But if you want an FTP app that acts more like a traditional FTP application that you use on a computer, I recommend the $9.99 FTP on the Go Pro app. It lets you access FTP and SFTP servers (of course), showing their contents and letting you upload files to them and download files from them.

You can connect FTP on the Go to your Dropbox account (via the Settings pane, which you open by tapping the Settings button in FTP on the Go Pro) so that you can transfer files between Dropbox and your FTP site. Also in the Settings pane, you can connect the app to the Photos app's Photo Library for easy image upload and download.

FTP on the Go Pro also lets you save your FTP bookmarks in iCloud so that you can then import them into your other iOS devices running FTP on the Go Pro. That saves a lot of data entry to set up your sign-ins.

As Figure 17-11 shows, FTP on the Go Pro also lets you edit text documents, including HTML files. That capability is really handy if you need to make a change to your website but don't have a computer with you to do that work.

Figure 17-11:
Editing a
downloaded
HTML file
via FTP on
the Go Pro.

Chapter 18

Working with PDFs and ePubs

The PDF (Portable Document Format) file is the one way to share richly formatted documents and know that everyone will see the same thing you do. The iPad can display PDF contents, but you can also get apps that let you create PDFs and annotate existing ones.

Sometimes you may also want to read or create an ePub (the most common e-book format) instead for a better tablet reading experience. You can do that, too!

In this chapter, I explain how to read PDF files, annotate them, and create them, as well as how to read and create ePub files on your iPad.

Reading PDFs through Quick Look

The iPad's iOS has a feature called Quick Look that lets apps preview files in popular file formats. For example, if you get an attachment in Mail, you can tap the attachment to have Quick Look display it in a screen as if it were open. You can also often use the Share sheet's Quick Look button as well.

You can't work on the previewed document, but you can see its contents, as Figure 18-1 shows. You can view files in Microsoft Office, Apple iWork, text, PDF, and a variety of graphics formats this way in Mail, for example, before deciding whether to use the Open In facility to open them in a compatible app.

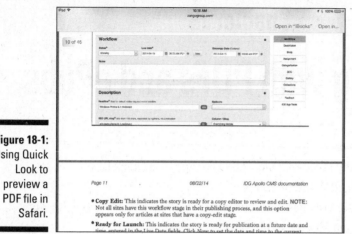

Figure 18-1:
Using Quick
Look to
preview a
PDF file in
Safari.

Quick Look can usually open Zip files as well and let you extract and preview their contents. When it can't, you need an app like the $9.99 GoodReader or the $4.99 WinZip that works with Zip files.

Tap in the previewed document to get two options to appear at the top of the screen: Done (the upper left) to close the preview, and Share (at the upper right) to open the Share sheet. Sometimes you may see the Open In option instead of the Share icon, as well as a third option: Open in iBooks.

Reading PDFs and ePubs in iBooks

Oddly enough, Quick Look can't preview ePub files as it can PDFs. But Apple's free iBooks app can display ePub files. (iBooks is preinstalled for you on new iPads purchased since October 2014. If you don't have it on your iPad, download it for free from the App Store.)

If you get an ePub file via email or a website link, use the Share sheet to open it in iBooks. Or tap the attachment or link to get an alert in which you can tap Open In iBooks; that alert will also have the Open In option to open the Share sheet, from which you can open the ePub in another compatible app.

When you open an ePub in iBooks, it appears like any other book, as Figure 18-2 shows. That's because it *is* like any other book — ePub is the standard format for iBooks' e-books.

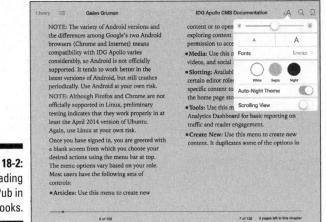

NOTE: The variety of Android versions and the differences among Google's two Android browsers (Chrome and Internet) means compatibility with IDG Apollo varies considerably, so Android is not officially supported. It tends to work better in the latest versions of Android, but still crashes periodically. Use Android at your own risk.

NOTE: Although Firefox and Chrome are not officially supported in Linux, preliminary testing indicates that they work properly in at least the April 2014 version of Ubuntu. Again, use Linux at your own risk.

Once you have signed in, you are greeted with a blank screen from which you choose your desired actions using the menu bar at top. The menu options vary based on your role. Most users have the following sets of controls:

• **Articles:** Use this menu to create new

content or to open
exploring content
permission to acce

• **Media:** Use this n
videos, and social

• **Slotting:** Availabl
certain editor role
specific content to
the home page sto

• **Tools:** Use this m
Analytics Dashboard for basic reporting on traffic and reader engagement.

• **Create New:** Use this menu to create new content. It duplicates some of the options in

Fonts   Iowan ›

White   Sepia   Night

Auto-Night Theme

Scrolling View

6 of 135   7 of 135   2 pages left in this chapter

Figure 18-2:
Reading
an ePub in
iBooks.

The ePub is copied into your main collection, the one called Books. A collection is essentially a folder for e-books; iBooks lets you create your own folders to organize your books the way you like. The default Books collection contains any new books you buy or add to iBooks, though you can move books to other collections if desired.

To move e-books into any other collection, follow these steps:

1. **Tap the Select button at the upper right corner of the iBooks app.**

2. **Tap the books you want to move to select them.**

3. **Tap the Move button at the upper-left corner.**

4. **Tap the destination collection in the pop-over that appears.**

5. **Tap Done.**

You navigate among collections using the menu button at the very top of the screen, which shows the name of the current collection.

If the ePub was created with a TOC and cover, you see those in the ePub, as Figure 18-3 shows, if you tap the Contents button (the bulleted-list icon).

iBooks can also open PDF files. You bring them into iBooks the same way you do an ePub: via the Share sheet, Open In menu, or one of the file-transfer methods described in Chapter 17.

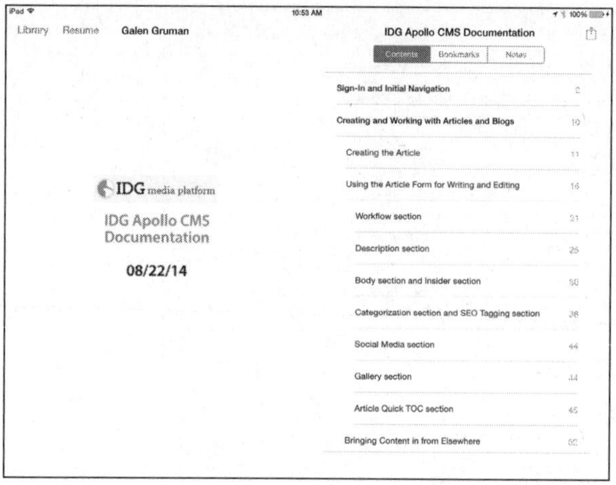

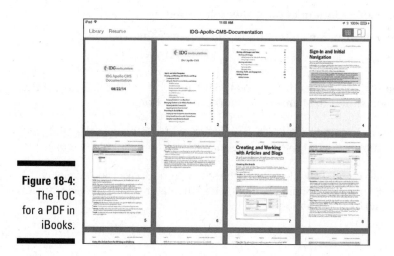

Figure 18-3:
The TOC for
an ePub in
iBooks.

PDFs are kept in the PDFs collection in iBooks — you can't move them to other collections. Also, PDFs appear a little differently than ePubs in iBooks. For example, if you tap the Contents button (the bulleted-list icon), you get thumbnail previews of all the PDF's pages, as Figure 18-4 shows.

You don't get the options to change text size, background, and scrolling options as you do with an ePub, as Figure 18-5 shows. But you can zoom the PDF's contents using the standard iOS expand and pinch gestures. And you do get the Share button for PDFs, so you can email them to others or print them — which you cannot do with ePubs.

Figure 18-4:
The TOC
for a PDF in
iBooks.

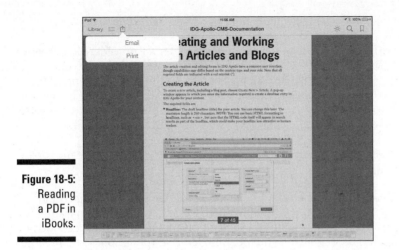

Figure 18-5:
Reading
a PDF in
iBooks.

Marking It Up with GoodReader

The $9.99 GoodReader app is really useful as a file manager and way station, as Chapter 17 describes. But it also is a full-fledged PDF annotation tool, letting you mark up PDF files — not just read them — and then share them with others.

Prepping for PDF markup

If you use GoodReader for PDF markup, the first thing you need to do is tell GoodReader your name so that it knows whom to ascribe your comments and annotations to. PDF files allow markup from multiple people, which is why markup tools need to know your name. To tell GoodReader your name, follow these steps:

1. **Open GoodReader and be sure to be in the documents view (tap My Documents if you're viewing a PDF file); then open the controls (by tapping the « button).**

2. **Tap the Settings button at the bottom of the controls pane.**

3. **In the Settings pop-over that appears, tap Viewing PDF Files.**

4. **In the PDF Files pop-over that appears, tap Author and enter your name.**

5. **Tap Close at the upper right of the pop-over.**

The author name you enter will be identified in all markup you perform.

To open a PDF file, just tap its name in whatever server or folder GoodReader holds it in. The PDF file displays onscreen. (If multiple PDF files are open, tabs appear at the top of the screen for each.) Tap the page or swipe to the right to advance forward in the file, or swipe to the left to advance backward. Double-tap to zoom in, or use the standard iOS pinch and expand gestures to zoom in and out.

Tap the center of the screen to expose the markup toolbar and the file toolbar, shown in Figure 18-6.

These toolbars disappear after a few seconds, so you may tap the screen frequently to bring them back when needed. But you can pin the markup toolbar (at right) to the screen so that it doesn't disappear after a few seconds of nonuse. Just tap its Pin button (the pushpin icon) at top; a solid blue pushpin icon indicates the toolbar is pinned and won't disappear on its own.

The toolbar at the right side of the screen handles PDF markup. The one at the bottom of the screen handles the PDF file itself.

Using the PDF markup tools

If you've used Adobe Acrobat or Adobe Reader, the markup controls will look familiar. They work pretty much the same way, too.

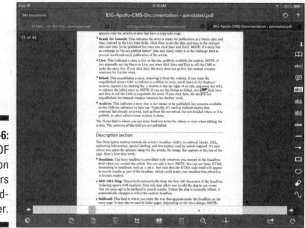

Figure 18-6:
The PDF annotation toolbars in Good-Reader.

The first time you annotate a PDF, GoodReader asks whether you want to annotate the original file or a copy of it. If you choose to annotate a copy, it makes a copy of the file and applies your annotations to it.

A horizontal variant of the markup toolbar appears as a contextual menu if you tap and hold on the screen or select text in the PDF. One option that the markup toolbar has that's not in the standard toolbar is Select All, which selects all text.

Here's what the markup toolbar's options do, from top to bottom (refer to Figure 18-6):

- **Add Bookmark (the open-book icon):** Adds a bookmark to the current page, with the text you enter in the box that appears. Tap OK when done.

- **Highlight Options (the abc icon):** Lets you highlight text with a color. When you tap this icon, a toolbar appears at the top of the screen with five buttons. The leftmost button (the abc icon) lets you choose the highlight method — the same ones that appear on the markup toolbar — and the second button from the left (the color swatch) lets you choose the highlight color. In other words, this menu lets you switch among various markup options rather than use the markup toolbar. No, I don't get that, either.

  Note: The two rightmost buttons let you navigate among pages, and in between them and the highlight control buttons is Cancel.

- **Add Comment (the speech-bubble icon):** Lets you add a sticky-note-style comment anywhere you tap.

- **Highlight Text (the abc icon showing black text on a white background):** Lets you highlight text with your finger as if it were a felt-tip marker, putting the color selected in the menu that appears behind any text that you run your finger over. Figure 18-7 shows an example. This highlighter is usually used to indicate text you want to review. Be sure to save your highlight when you're done drawing it. *Note:* You can also switch the highlighting tool and color here, in the same way as with the Highlight Options toolbar, plus you get navigation, Cancel, Redo, Undo, and Save buttons.

- **Underline Text (the underlined abc icon):** This works like Highlight Text except that a straight line is drawn under the text you run your finger over. You usually use this tool to indicate text that you want to give extra emphasis to.

- **Squiggle Text (the squiggly-underlined abc icon):** Works like Highlight Text except that a squiggly line is drawn under the text you run your finger over. It is usually used to indicate text you want reviewed.

- **Strikethrough Text (the abc icon with a line through it):** Works like Highlight Text except that a straight line is drawn through the text you run your finger over. This tool is usually used to indicate text to be deleted.

- **Line (the line icon):** Draws a line on the page. Tap the page; a line appears. Drag either control handle to resize and rotate the line as desired. In the contextual menu that appears, tap Cancel to remove the added line or Done to keep it. You can edit a line later by tapping it. In addition to getting the control handles, you get a menu of formatting options shown in Figure 18-8; these options are available for all sorts of objects, such as rectangles and ellipses, not just for lines.

- **Arrow (the arrow icon):** Draws an arrow on the page. The Arrow tool works like the Line tool except that one end of the line has an arrowhead.

- **Rectangle (the rectangle icon):** Draws a rectangle on the page, usually to put a box around a section you want to call attention to. The Rectangle tool works like the Line tool except that control handles are on all four corners of the rectangle.

- **Ellipse (the ellipse icon):** Draws an ellipse on the page, usually to put a circle around a section to which you want to call attention. The Ellipse tool works like the Rectangle tool, except for its shape.

- **Erase (the eraser icon):** Erases the part of a freeform line you run your finger over with it.

- **Freeform Line (the curved-line icon):** Draws a freeform curved line that follows your finger's movement on the screen.

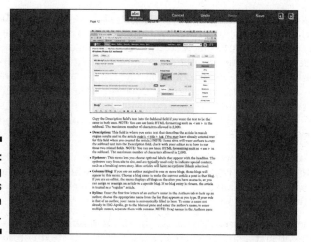

Figure 18-7:
Highlighting
a PDF file's
text in
GoodReader.

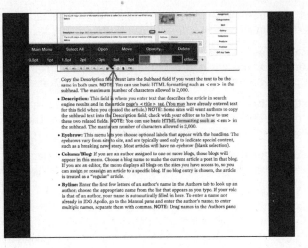

Figure 18-8:
The formatting controls in GoodReader for objects such as lines.

You can select any of the highlights, lines, and objects described in the previous list to edit them.

For text highlights (including underlines and squiggles), a contextual menu appears that provides tools to open a comment window to add a comment about the highlighted text (the Open button), delete the annotation, copy it, change its color, and show all toolbars (the Main Menu button).

For objects such as lines and rectangles, as Figure 18-8 shows, you can adjust the color, line weight, and opacity, plus select all text, open a comment window (the Open button), move it (which ensures the object's size is not changed when you drag it), delete it, and show all toolbars (the Main Menu button).

GoodReader's annotation tools take a little getting used to, both in how the controls work and how they react to your finger's movements, but after you get the hang of it, you'll be able to annotate pretty much as you can on a computer.

Using the PDF page tools

The file toolbar (refer to Figure 18-6) that appears at the bottom of the screen when you tap the center of the screen lets you manipulate the PDF file itself, rather than its annotations. Here are its controls, from left to right:

✔ **Page Navigation (the bar above the buttons):** This bar has Back and Forward buttons to move among pages, as well as thumbnails of every page that you can tap to go directly to a desired page.

✔ **Contrast (the half-circle icon):** Adjusts the contrasts of the entire PDF file. Tap it again to restore the original contrast.

✔ **Jump Back (the left-facing triangle icon):** If you navigate to a specific page using the Page Navigation controls, tap this button to jump back to the last page you were on (which could be anywhere in the document).

✔ **Text Reflow (the arrow-in-a-page icon):** Displays just the text of the PDF file in a new screen. Tap the My Documents button at the upper left of the screen to select the original PDF version to return to it.

✔ **Rotate All Pages (the page icon):** Lets you rotate all pages 90 degrees clockwise, 180 degrees, and 90 degrees counterclockwise, as well as restore the original orientation.

✔ **Pages Layout (the scrolled-pages icon):** Lets you control how PDF files' pages display in GoodReader: as single pages, as facing pages (double pages), and as facing pages with the first page alone (as a cover page).

✔ **Crop (the icon of a square with the diagonal line through it):** Lets you crop pages to be smaller, removing the cropped-out portions. You control whether the crop applies to all the pages by using the switch called The Same Crops for Odd and Even Pages, at the upper left. If the switch is set to On, all pages are cropped the same; if it is set to Off, the crop is applied to all odd-numbered pages if the current page is odd-numbered; if the current page is even-numbered, then the crop is applied to all even-numbered pages. Tap Done to accept the new crop, No Crops to reject them, and To Cur. View to crop to whatever is visible in the screen (such as after you enlarge the page using the expand gesture).

✔ **Annotations (the open-book icon):** Opens a sheet that lets you view the PDF file's bookmarks, outlines (TOC), and annotations. For annotations, you can use the Email Summary button to email the annotations to someone else (the PDF file itself is not attached).

✔ **Pages (the icon with four little rectangles):** Opens thumbnails of all pages in the document, as shown in Figure 18-9. At the bottom of the screen are buttons with which you can select to move, extract into a new PDF file, email, delete, rotate (individually), add a split marker such as to indicate a new section, or append (to add an external PDF file into the document). At the top of the page is the Add Pages button, which lets you insert blank pages to the document where desired. Tap Save to save your changes to the PDF file, or tap Cancel to reject them.

✔ **Search (the magnifying-glass icon):** Lets you search for text in the PDF file.

✔ **Navigate (the compass-like lock icon):** Lets you navigate through the document with access to the markup and file controls disabled. You see the Navigate icon at the upper right of the screen along with Back (←) and Forward (→) buttons. Tap the Navigate icon to return to the standard view.

✔ **Action (the icon of a curved arrow emerging from a rectangle):** Provides options to open the PDF in other apps; create a flattened copy (all annotations are made into part of the PDF images and are no longer editable or searchable); email the file, its summary, or both; and print the file or its summary.

✔ **Rotation Lock (the curved-arrow icon):** Tap this button to prevent pages from rotating even when you rotate the iPad. (When GoodReader's rotation lock is enabled, you see a lock icon inside a curved arrow icon.) Normally, when you rotate the iPad, GoodReader rotates the PDF file's pages at the same time, so your page is always facing "up" on the screen. That often makes sense for textual pages, but it comes at the cost of the page being shrunk to fit the screen when rotated — which you may not want to occur for some documents, such as those with intricate diagrams.

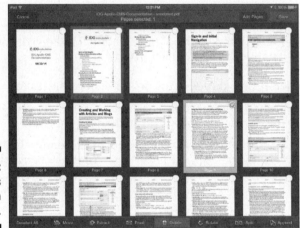

Figure 18-9: The Pages controls in GoodReader.

Putting Your Own Stamp on PDFs with PDF Expert

GoodReader does take some getting used to do when it comes to working with PDF files, though I've found no other app that can do as much as it can do. But if you prefer a simpler application that does most of what you'll likely need to do with PDFs — and a few things GoodReader can't, such as add stamps to PDF files — consider the $9.99 PDF Expert, shown in Figure 18-10.

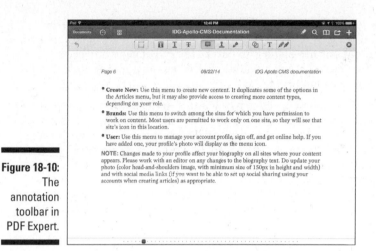

Figure 18-10:
The
annotation
toolbar in
PDF Expert.

To work with a document in the PDF Expert app, tap the document to reveal the annotation toolbar at top, and tap the Annotation button (the pencil icon) to keep it there. Its options are, from left to right:

- ✔ **Undo (the left-facing curved-arrow icon):** Undoes the last operation.

- ✔ **Select (the dashed-square icon):** This is supposed to let you select graphics in the PDF, but it doesn't do anything.

- ✔ **Highlight (the icon of a black T on a white background):** Highlights in yellow any text you drag your finger over. You can change the color, add a note, or clear the highlight by tapping the highlighted text and choosing the appropriate option from the contextual menu that appears.

- ✔ **Underline (the underlined-T icon):** Adds a red underline to the text you drag your finger across. Its contextual menu lets you change the color, add a note, or clear the underline.

- ✔ **Strikethrough (the T with a line through it):** Draws a red line through the text that you drag your finger across. Its contextual menu lets you change the color, add a note, or clear the strikethrough.

- ✔ **Add a Comment (the speech-bubble icon):** Adds a sticky-note-like note to wherever you tap. To delete a note, tap it to open it; then tap the trash can icon at its lower left). To reposition a note, drag it to its new location; then tap Done in the contextual menu that appears (or tap Cancel if you decide not to move it after all).

✔ **Stamp (the stamp icon):** Adds a stamp graphic to the location you tap. You get a menu of choices, as shown in Figure 18-11, or you can use the Custom tab to create your own stamp using your own text and images. After you insert a stamp, you can move it by dragging it and resize it by using its control handles. Tap the Done button when you've placed the stamp and sized it as desired. Tap a stamp to get a contextual menu in which you can delete, move, or copy it.

✔ **Signature (the pen icon):** Lets you create and add a signature to use as a stamp. Tap the Signature button and then draw your signature in the My Signature screen that appears; tap Save to save it as a graphic. Now tap and hold where you want to insert the signature graphic, tap Signature in the contextual menu that appears, reposition and resize the signature as desired, and tap Done. *Note:* If a signature already exists, it'll appear when you tap the Signature button. Tap Save to use it, or tap the Signature button (the pen icon) in the My Signature Screen to open a menu where you select the desired other signature; or tap New Signature to add a new one.

✔ **Shapes (the icon of a circle and square):** Tap this to get a menu of four shapes — rectangle, oval, line, and arrow — and buttons for the color, pen size, and opacity. Select the shape and its desired formats; then tap the screen to insert the shape, which you can reposition and resize as desired. Tap Done for that shape and then draw more shapes if desired. Tap the ✔ icon to close the Shapes menu.

✔ **Text (the T icon):** Lets you add text into the PDF file as independent objects. In the menu that appears, you can choose the font, size, and color and then tap the document to insert text at that point. Tap the ✔ icon to close the text menu. *Note:* You can't edit text in the PDF this way, just add your own text notes.

✔ **Freeform (the icon of two pens):** Opens a menu of pen styles. Select the desired pen, color, pen size, and opacity; then draw the desired freeform shape with your finger. If you want to erase part of what you've drawn, tap the Eraser icon and trace over what you want to delete. Tap the Eraser icon again to continue drawing. Tap the ✔ icon when done drawing. *Note:* If you tend to rest your wrist on the screen while drawing, tap the Wrist button (the hand icon) to tell PDF Expert to ignore your wrist so that it continues to draw lines normally.

✔ **Close (the X icon):** Hides the annotation toolbar.

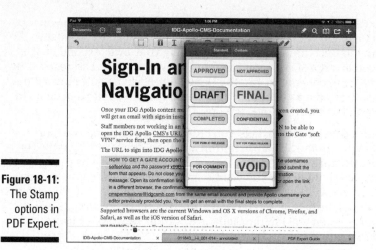

Figure 18-11:
The Stamp
options in
PDF Expert.

PDF Expert also has the following buttons at the top of the screen, from left to right:

- **Documents:** Shows the available documents in PDF Expert, as well as those in iCloud and on network file servers and cloud storage services that you make available by tapping Network in the left pane and then the Add button in the right pane.

- **Recents (the clock icon):** Shows recently opened documents for easy access to them.

- **Pages (the icon of four rectangles):** Shows thumbnails of all the pages in the current PDF file. Tap a page to jump to it. Tap Add (the icon of a page with a + symbol) to add a blank page. Or tap Edit to get the following controls for the pages you select (or tap Select All to select, um, all pages): Copy, Paste, Delete, Mail, Rotate, and Extract (into its own PDF file). Tap Done to apply your changes to the PDF file or tap Close to reject them.

- **Annotation (the pencil icon):** Enables the annotations described previously in this section.

- **Search:** Searches for text in the document.

- **Bookmark (the open-book icon):** Opens a pop-over with tabs to show bookmarks, outlines, and annotations in the current document. Tap Clear to remove all the items in the current tab.

- **Tools (the icon showing an arrow emerging from a rectangle):** Opens a menu with controls for going to a specific page, changing the brightness, cropping pages, emailing the PDF file, saving a copy of the PDF file, printing the PDF file, and opening the PDF file in another app.

✔ **New Bookmark (the + icon):** Adds a bookmark with the text of your choice on the current page. Tap Done to save it and Cancel to reject it.

Getting to the Basics with Adobe Reader

A very simple PDF markup tool is the free Adobe Reader. It lets you mark up your PDF with only basic annotations, shown in Figure 18-12. To get the annotation tools shown, tap the center of the screen to reveal the toolbars; then tap the Annotation tool (the icon of a speech bubble and pen) at the top right of the screen.

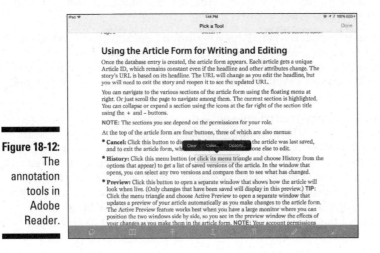

Figure 18-12: The annotation tools in Adobe Reader.

Now tap the desired annotation from the row of buttons at the bottom. From left to right, they are:

✔ **Note (the speech-bubble icon):** Adds a sticky note to wherever you tap. Enter the text in the blank note that appears, and tap Save to save it or Cancel to reject it. Drag a note's icon to move it. Tap a note's icon to open, edit, or delete it (you find the Delete button in the upper left of the note).

✔ **Highlight (the T-in-a-box icon):** Highlights with a yellow background any text you drag your finger over. Tap a highlight to open a contextual menu, in which you can delete the highlight (using the Clear button), change its color, and change its opacity.

✔ **Strikethrough (the T with a line through it):** Draws a red line through the text you drag your finger over. Tap a character that has strikethrough to open a contextual menu through which you can delete the strikethrough (using the Clear button), change its color, and change its opacity.

✔ **Underline (the underlined-T icon):** Draws a red line under the text that you drag your finger over. Tap an underline to open a contextual menu through which you can delete the underline (the Clear button), change its color, and change its opacity.

✔ **Text (the T| icon):** Lets you add text as an independent object to wherever you tap the page. You can drag the text to a different location. Tapping the text displays control handles at each corner; these handles let you resize the text. Tapping the text also opens a contextual menu with options for deleting the text, editing it, changing the text size, and changing the text color.

✔ **Freeform (the pencil icon):** Lets you draw a freeform shape based on your finger's movements on the screen. Tap Save when done or tap Cancel to reject the shape. You can tap a shape to open a contextual menu with options to delete it and change the line thickness, color, and opacity.

✔ **Signature (the pen icon):** Lets you add a graphic of your signature to wherever you tap. The first time you use this option, a screen appears in which you draw your signature with your finger and tap Save to use it. After that, when you use the Signature button, a contextual menu appears with two options: Add Signature, which adds the existing signature to that location, and Edit Saved Signature, which lets you modify that saved signature. You can tap a signature in the PDF file to open a contextual menu in which you can delete it or change its thickness, color, or opacity.

When you're done annotating in Adobe Reader, tap the Done button at the upper right of the screen. The standard controls are now available by tapping the center of the screen.

So what are those standard controls? Just these:

✔ **Documents:** Returns to your list of documents in Adobe Reader.

✔ **View Modes (the eye icon):** Lets you show the pages as a continuous scroll or as a series of individual pages that you swipe through. It also has the Night Mode switch, which reverses the PDF file's colors so that you get white text on a black background, making your iPad's screen less likely to annoy someone else in your bed at night when you're working late.

- ✔ **Tools (the icon of a wrench and page):** Opens a menu with an option to save the file to Adobe's Acrobat.com service (you must have an Adobe ID to use this) and with an option to export the PDF file as a Word, Excel, or RTF, with any scanned text converted to real text. This latter service requires a $24-per-year subscription.

- ✔ **Share (the standard iOS Share icon showing a rectangle with a ↑):** Lets you email the PDF file, print it, or open it in another compatible app.

- ✔ **Search (the magnifying-glass icon):** Searches the PDF for the text you enter.

That's it. Adobe Reader has no controls to rearrange pages, extract them, delete them, or rotate them, or to add stamps. Get PDF Expert or GoodReader if you need that level of PDF editing.

Exporting PDF and ePub Files

Some apps can create PDF files as part of their export capabilities, including the major office productivity apps covered in Chapters 5 through 7.

For example, Apple's Pages can convert documents to PDF and ePub formats when you use the Share button to email them or open them in another app, as Figure 18-13 shows. Apple's Numbers and Keynote can likewise convert their documents to PDF format.

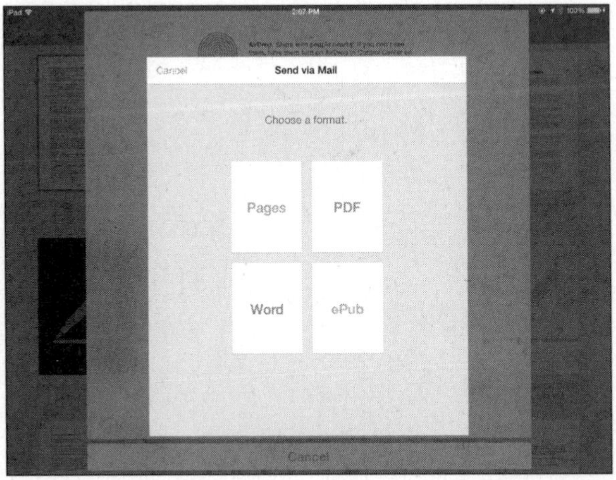

Figure 18-13: Exporting a document as a PDF or ePub in Apple's Pages app.

The ePub file that Pages generates is pretty messy on the inside. It'll display fine in iBooks or another e-reader app, but don't expect its TOC to be accurate. If you publish books through the iBooks Store, Amazon Kindle Store, Smashwords, or other such service, I don't recommend using the Pages-generated ePub files. You'll need to do the heavy lifting by using a tool such as Sigil on your computer instead.

Microsoft Word, Excel, and PowerPoint can also export documents as PDF files. The trick is to open the document and then tap the Share button (the person icon) from within the document. In the menu that appears, choose the Send PDF option. *Note:* If you use the Share sheet in the documents list, you *won't* get the option to send a PDF copy.

Google's Docs, Sheets, and Slides can also export PDF files. You can export either from the document list or from within the open document. Either way, tap the More button (the . . . icon), choose Share & Export, choose Send a Copy, and finally select PDF before tapping OK. (When you're in the document list, each document has its own More button, which is rotated 90 degrees; tap the More button for the document you want to export.)

There is no standard location for the export options in iOS apps, as you can see from the preceding examples. So, you may have to hunt around the apps you use to see whether they support PDF or (much less likely) ePub export. Chances are, the PDF and ePub export options, if they exist, will be somewhere you can send a file, print a file, share a file, or export a file.

Chapter 19

Giving Presentations

• •

In This Chapter

▶ Sending your iPad's screen to a TV or projector via AirPlay

▶ Presenting — and remote-controlling — your slideshow from Apple's Keynote

▶ Showing your slides from Microsoft PowerPoint

▶ Avoiding the potential display-compatibility problem via the SlideShark web service

▶ Displaying specialty presentations with Roambi and StoryDesk

• •

*T*he iPad is a great presentation tool. Sure, you can just hand someone your Pad so that the person can see whatever you want to show, such as a web page or presentation. But with Apple's AirPlay technology, you can share what's on your iPad screen to a whole group of people at one time via a TV or projector (using an Apple TV or through a cable).

In this chapter, I explain how to use AirPlay to display your iPad's screen on a TV or other screen. I then explain how to give presentations from your iPad using Apple's Keynote, Microsoft's PowerPoint, and Google's Slides apps — you may never run your presentation from a laptop again!

Using AirPlay

AirPlay is built into the iPad's iOS, so you always have it. But AirPlay doesn't work in a vacuum — it needs something to play *to*. That means that you need either an AirPlay device, such as an Apple TV or AirPlay-compatible speakers, or a cable connecting your iPad to a video playback device such as a TV or projector.

I firmly believe that every conference room and conference stage should have an Apple TV device in place, connected to the TV or projector. An Apple TV costs just $99 and can be remotely managed by IT, and it lets any iOS device or computer running iTunes send its display over the network to it.

For example, all the presenters in a meeting could simply beam their slides or videos to the TV in the room from their individual iPads, laptops, and even iPhones — no juggling of cable connections between presentations or collecting all the presentations before the meeting to put on a single PC.

If you have a TV or projector connected to the Apple TV's HDMI jack, and your iPad is on the same network as the Apple TV, you're ready to stream almost anything you want to the TV or projector.

If you don't have an Apple TV, you can directly connect your iPad to a TV via one of Apple's iPad video adapters, available at the Apple Store and other retailers for $39 to $49, depending on the model.

You plug the adapter into the iPad's Lightning or Dock port, and you plug one end of the VGA or HDMI cable (depending on the adapter you have and what your display device supports) into the iPad adapter and the other into the display device. That device is now an option in the Control Center's AirPlay menu. (Any AirPlay-compatible wireless speakers detected will also show up in that menu.)

Next, open the Control Center on your iPad by swiping up from the bottom of the screen. Tap the AirPlay button in the Control Center to reveal the controls shown in Figure 19-1. (No AirPlay controls? That means no Apple TV is in range; maybe your Wi-Fi is turned off. Nor do you have a physical connection to a playback device.)

Tap Apple TV to send your iPad's content to the Apple TV. If you're using a cable connection, tap the name of that device. If you're playing a video on your iPad, whether on a website, as shown in Figure 19-1, or in an app such as YouTube, the video on your iPad's screen gets replaced with a black box, and the device connected to the Apple TV shows the video full-screen instead. That's right: Even if the video is in a window on your iPad as in Figure 19-1, it's a full-screen display on the Apple TV-connected TV or projector.

If you're not showing video, set the Mirroring switch to On, as it is in Figure 19-1. Now, whatever is on your screen displays on the TV.

But don't worry if you're giving a presentation with Apple's Keynote or Microsoft's PowerPoint. Even though they require that Mirroring be set to On, they're smart enough to show only the presentation full-screen on that Apple TV-connected device. Your audience won't see the controls in either app, as long as you remain in the app's playback mode (which I describe in the "Presenting with Keynote" and "Presenting with PowerPoint" sections, later in this chapter).

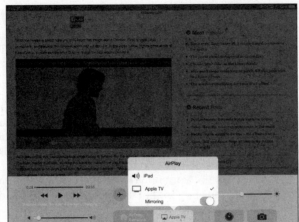

Figure 19-1:
The AirPlay controls on an iPad.

I recommend that when you're showing the whole screen, you turn on Do Not Disturb so that your viewers don't see your notifications on the TV or projector. Tap the Do Not Disturb button (the crescent-moon icon) in the Control Center to enable it; then tap it again when you're done to disable it.

AirPlay honors copy protection, so some apps and web videos may not play via an Apple TV or cabled connection to a TV or projector. That's because their creators have embedded a code in the video telling AirPlay not to retransmit it.

When you're done presenting, reopen the Control Center, tap AirPlay, and choose iPad as the source. Close the Control Center.

Presenting with Keynote

I believe that Keynote, covered in Chapter 5, is the best presentation app out there. I particularly love its iCloud support and its capability to remotely control a presentation.

That iCloud support means that your presentations are automatically synced to your other devices that are signed in to the same iCloud account. So if your iPad gets lost, forgotten, or damaged during a trip, that presentation is also on your iPhone, and you can present it from there just as you can from your iPad. I know: It has happened to me.

Using Keynote's tools while presenting

When you present with Keynote, tap the Play button (the icon of the triangular Play button in a box) to enter presentation mode. The iPad then sends out just the slides if you use AirPlay to display them.

When presenting, just tap your iPad's screen or swipe to the right to advance the slide or build the next transition. Or swipe back to go back a slide. While you present, Keynote shows the current time, so you can keep track of how you're doing in terms of schedule. (I promise it won't evaluate your performance!)

To simulate a laser pointer's hot spot on your slide, just tap and hold on the screen. When you release your finger, that "laser hot spot" disappears.

If you want to annotate a slide you're presenting, you can! Just tap the Annotation tool (the icon of a pen in a circle) to get the pen options shown in Figure 19-2. Draw away! The audience sees only your annotations as you make them, not the tools. Tap Done when you're done.

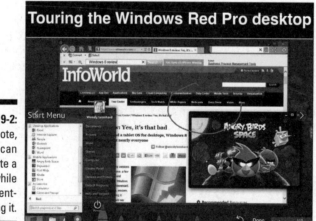

Figure 19-2: In Keynote, you can annotate a slide while presenting it.

If you want to read your presenter notes while presenting, tap the Layout Options button (the icon of a screen) and choose Current and Notes. You see the screen in Figure 19-3, but your audience sees just the slide you're presenting. (You can scroll through the notes vertically without affecting what the audience sees.)

To end your presentation, tap the Close button (the X icon) or use your choice of the pinch or expand gesture (they both work) on the current slide. (Be sure to turn AirPlay off as well in the Control Center.)

Figure 19-3:
The pre-
senter can
see the pre-
senter notes
while pre-
senting in
Keynote —
but the
audience
can't.

Remote-controlling a presentation

But we haven't gotten to my favorite feature in Keynote presentations:
remote control. Oh, but here we are. Keynote on an iPad, iPhone, or iPod
touch can remote-control another Keynote presentation on any of these
devices as well as on a Mac. An iPhone can remote-control an iPad, for example, and an iPad can control another iPad. But a Mac can't control anything.

To work, the devices need to have Bluetooth turned on, and this feature
works better if they're both on the same Wi-Fi network. Be sure that none of
the devices is locked.

The first thing to do is to pair the devices. You start with the device you want
to be the controller. In this section, I assume that's an iPhone. To pair your
devices, follow these steps:

1. **In Keynote on the iPhone, tap the Devices button (the icon of a remote
   control) in the Documents window, shown in Figure 19-4.**

2. **Tap the Devices button in the upper left to open the Manage Devices
   screen.**

3. **Tap Add a Device.**

   The screen shows that the iPhone is broadcasting its availability.

4. **On the iPad, open Keynote and tap the Tools icon (the wrench icon).**

5. **In the menu, tap Presentation Tools and then tap Allow Remote
   Control.**

6a. **If you want to control an existing device: In the Manage Devices screen that opens, tap the existing device to control it and tap Done to begin the remote control — you're done; skip Steps 7 and 8.**

6b. **If you're adding a device to be controlled, tap Add a Device and continue to Step 7.**

7. **In the pop-over that appears, set the Enable Remotes switch to On; then tap Link for the devices you want to control it, as shown in Figure 19-5.**

8. **After the devices connect, both show a confirmation passcode; if the passcodes match, tap Confirm on the iPad.**

Figure 19-4:
Keynote's
Documents
window
(here, on an
iPhone) has
the Remote
Control
button (at
upper left),
which you
tap to begin
the pairing
process
for remote-
controlled
presenta-
tions.

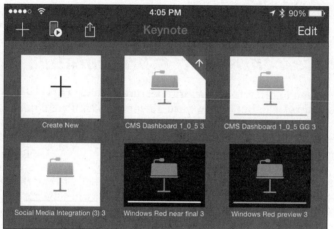

Now that the devices are linked, to remote-control the iPad from the iPhone, open Keynote in both devices. On the iPad, open the presentation you want to give. On the iPhone, tap the Remote Control button and then tap Play on the screen that appears. Keynote on the iPad switches to presentation mode, so be sure it's connected to the Apple TV or other presentation device.

Your iPhone screen now shows the slide and presentation notes as if you were presenting from it, as Figure 19-6 shows. You move among slides on the iPhone just as you would on the iPad, and you have the same annotation and view options as you do on the iPad. As long as the network connection between the two devices stays active, whatever you do on the iPhone is transmitted to the iPad, and from there to your audience.

Figure 19-5:
On the
iPad being
controlled,
link to the
device you
want to
control it
for Keynote
presen-
tations
(here, Test
iPhone 4S).

Figure 19-6:
An iPhone
controlling
a Keynote
presentation
on an iPad.

On the iPad, Keynote's Documents window has the same Devices button as it does on the iPhone, so you follow the same process to set up a link from the iPad to an iPhone, or from one iPad to another. But if you want to remote-control a Mac, on that Mac you choose Keynote⇨Preferences to open the Preferences dialog in Keynote and set up the link to the controlling device in the Remotes pane there.

I like using the iPad Mini as the remote control because the bigger screen makes the presenter notes more readable, but I can still hold the iPad Mini in one hand as I walk the stage.

Presenting with PowerPoint

Microsoft's PowerPoint (see Chapter 6) also has a few presentation tricks you should know. (Google's Slides has none — you can't even see your presenter notes while presenting, which defeats their purpose!)

After you open a presentation in PowerPoint, be sure to go to the Slide Show tab — this is critical if you want to be able to see your presenter notes while presenting via the Presenter View feature.

In the Slideshow tab, tap Presenter View to get the screen shown in Figure 19-7. *Note:* Presenter View is available only if you have an Office 365 subscription.

Figure 19-7:
Power-
Point's
Presenter
View of a
presenta-
tion, with
the pen
options
visible.

The current slide is the big one, and your other slides are shown below. To the right of the current slide are its presenter notes (which you can edit right there). Tap the Notes button at the top (the page icon) to hide or show the presenter notes.

To simulate a laser pointer's hot spot, just tap and hold on the slide where you want that "laser hot spot" to appear; then release your finger to make it go away.

To make live annotations while you present, tap the Annotation button (the pen icon) and draw away. You can change the pen settings by tapping the Pen Settings button (the icon showing a pen and a gear) to open the pop-over shown in Figure 19-7. Note the Clear Pen Markings button: It erases anything you've drawn on the current slide — a nice touch when you want the annotations there for only a little bit.

There's not much more to presenting with PowerPoint. You can black out the screen by tapping the Blank button (the shadowed black rectangle icon) and then resume your slide by tapping it again. You might use this feature when a video from another source is shown in the middle of your presentation, for example.

Also, you can enter full-screen mode on your iPad by tapping the Full Screen button at the upper right. The full-screen mode hides the controls on your iPad but doesn't affect what the audience sees — though if you're using Presenter View, the audience sees only your slides anyhow.

Tap End Slide Show when done to close Presenter View and return to the standard PowerPoint editing controls.

If you don't have an Office 365 subscription, you can still use many of the Presenter View capabilities. After you tap Play to begin presenting your slides, swipe down on the screen to reveal a limited version of the Presenter View toolbar. It provides the annotation, blackout, and full-screen capabilities, and the laser-pointer feature works, too. But you don't the presenter notes or thumbnails of the other slides in your presentation to navigate with.

Staying True to PowerPoint with SlideShark Presenter

A popular presentation app is SlideShark Presenter. A Pro subscription (an in-app purchase) costs $95 per year, letting you store up to 1GB's worth of your favorite PowerPoint presentations on an Internet-connected server so that they're available for presentation on the iPad via the SlideShark Presenter app.

SlideShark is popular because it does what it does very well: Present PowerPoint presentations exactly as designed. Yes, you can import PowerPoint presentations from your PC into Keynote or PowerPoint for iPad, but the fonts and other items will look different on the iPad — especially the fonts, because the iPad doesn't have most of the fonts available that a Mac or Windows PC does. Videos and images can also "break" — not display or display with errors — when transferred to the iPad, especially if they are in a file format that the iPad doesn't not support.

Yes, you can design slideshows that are compatible across Macs, Windows PCs, and iPads, but doing so imposes some design limits. As a result, many presenters don't like to use Keynote or PowerPoint on the iPad. That's especially true in sales organizations that do most of their work on PCs and don't see the need to do custom iPad presentations for the subset of iPad users.

Pro subscribers can also send their presentations to people over the Internet via their browser, such as for conference calls. And they can share their presentations with other iPad users, such as in a conference room without a big monitor.

But you don't need a Pro account to use SlideShark Presenter. It can also connect to several cloud storage services — including Box, Dropbox, and Google Drive — to bring those original PowerPoint slideshows into the iPad unmolested. But be patient: It can take several minutes for each file to be imported by SlideShark Presenter.

After a file is ready, tap its Play button to begin. Well, first make sure that AirPlay is active, because if it's not, you see a black screen on your iPad. Tapping Play displays the screen shown in Figure 19-8.

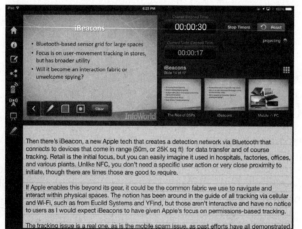

Figure 19-8:
Presenting
with
SlideShark.

The current slide is the big one. The other slides are to its right. You can tap the big slide or swipe to the right to advance it, or tap a specific slide to jump to it. Swipe left on the big slide to go back a slide. Tap and hold on the big slide to display a simulated laser pointer. (Yes, all these controls work like Keynote and PowerPoint.)

If you want to see all your slides, tap the grid icon above the slides scroll; a grid of slides appears over the presenter notes, which you can then navigate. To hide that grid, tap the down-pointing double-chevron button (shown here in the margin), which is at the upper left of the slide grid.

You can also turn on a timer with the Start Times button to track your total time and the time for the current slide, as Figure 19-8 shows.

Another feature of SlideShark is the capability to make live annotations on the slides while presenting. Tap the Annotations tool (the pen icon) at the left side of the screen; then select the desired color and pen size from the menu that appears at the bottom if the current slide, as Figure 19-8 also shows. Tap Clear to remove the annotations from the slide.

Some other controls to note are the following:

- ✔ **Presenter Mode (the easel icon):** Shows or hides presentation notes, as well as displays the screen in full-screen mode (as your audience sees it).

- ✔ **Remote Control (the remote-control icon):** Opens a pop-over in which you enable remote control from an iPhone and see the PIN that the iPhone needs. (The iPhone also needs to be running the SlideShark Presenter app, and Bluetooth has to be turned on for both devices.)

- ✔ **Save Annotations (the icon of a pencil in a frame):** Saves the annotations you made during the presentation into the PowerPoint file itself.

- ✔ **Play Options (the *i* icon):** Opens a grid of all the slides as well as three controls: Auto Play (for a self-advancing presentation); Slide Delay (which lets you change the default 3-second delay between auto-played slides); and Loop Presentation (which keeps playing the slideshow over and over).

- ✔ **Home (the house icon):** Shows all slideshows downloaded to the iPad.

Showing the Data with Roambi Analytics

Marketers and salespeople often fall in love with Roambi Analytics, an early iPad app that showed just how useful the iPad is. Roambi Analytics is more than an app — it's a whole service that your company has to subscribe to (at $39 per user per month) and connect to your various data sources to pull together the data that looks so beautiful on the iPad. In other words, this is the kind of app you can use only if you have a marketing support team at the office that does the real work and makes its reports available to you.

But assuming that you have such a team pulling your data into reports, you'll be able to download the kinds of reports you see in Figure 19-9. Swipe up or down to scroll through the pages (what Roambi Analytics calls "cards") in the reports.

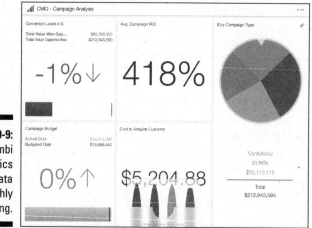

Figure 19-9:
Roambi
Analytics
makes data
look highly
compelling.

These can make great presentations on the road. And you can take a screen shot of a Roambi presentation to put in an actual presentation, such as through Keynote or PowerPoint. To do so, display the card you want to use and press the Home button and Sleep/Wake button at the same time. You hear a shutter sound, and a photo of your screen is now in the Photos app's Photo Library for use by other apps.

Roambi Analytics also lets you draw some basic annotations on your cards. To do so, tap the More button (the . . . icon), and in the pop-over that opens, tap the Share button at the bottom; then tap Annotations in the Collaboration pop-over that opens. You now get several pens at the bottom of your screen; tap one and begin drawing. That's it!

Going Nonlinear with StoryDesk

Another app that requires your company to have a subscription — with fees running between $15 and $39 per user per month — is StoryDesk. This app lets you create presentations on your iPad, as well download them from your corporate StoryDesk server. What sets StoryDesk apart is what it calls its nonlinear flow for presentations, as Figure 19-10 shows.

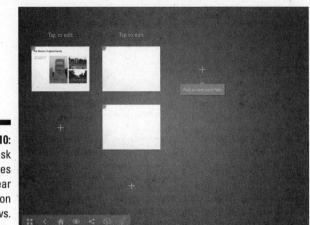

Figure 19-10:
StoryDesk
enables
nonlinear
presentation
flows.

A StoryDesk presentation can go in several directions, with the idea being that when a prospect is intrigued by a high-level slide, the salesperson can then go into the details for that slide, rather than be stuck in the one-way sequence of a traditional slideshow.

What you don't get in StoryDesk, unless you do custom work, are the fancy bells and whistles that you expect from Keynote or PowerPoint, such as transitions, embedded videos, and font formatting.

Chapter 20

Dealing with Graphics and Drawings

*T*he iPad is both a natural medium for drawing and an unnatural one. Natural because finger painting is something most of us know from childhood as one of our first artistic outlets, and the iPad's screen makes for a nice canvas. Unnatural because the finger is not really suited for fine lines or precise drawings, as a pen is, whether on paper or a computer.

Still, it's amazing what you can do on the iPad to create artwork or business diagrams — especially if you invest in a stylus whose smaller surface makes fine lines more possible and whose pencil-like form makes it easier to control in fine movements.

Never use a hard-surfaced item as a stylus, such as an actual pen or pencil or one of those hard-plastic styli you might remember from the days of the Palm Pilot. They damage the iPad's glass screen or at least its protective coating. You want a stylus with a soft, pliable tip that feels more like a finger than a stick.

Many companies make iPad-safe styli, so check out the description before buying. There are even pressure-sensitive styli from Adonit, Hex3, and Ten One Design that vary the thickness of a stroke based on how hard you press the stylus to the iPad's screen. (They communicate that pressure to an app via the iPad's Bluetooth radio.)

In this chapter, I explore several graphics apps that are useful in business — Photoshop Touch, Concepts, SketchBook Pro, and Grafio — and explain the basics of using them.

Compositing in Photoshop Touch

In the computing world, Adobe Photoshop is the tool that nearly everyone uses to create and manipulate digital drawings. Its wide variety of brushes, effects, and text formatting make it amazingly powerful. Adobe has a version of Photoshop for the iPad called — appropriately enough — Photoshop Touch ($9.99), which makes a subset of the Photoshop experience available to iPad users.

There's a catch, of course: You need an Adobe Creative Cloud account to work on your Photoshop Touch drawings using Photoshop CC on your computer. That'll cost you anywhere from $120 per year for just Photoshop CC to $600 per year for the whole Creative Cloud suite.

You also need to install the Touch App Plug-ins on your computer via Creative Cloud to be able to open the native Photoshop Touch (`.psdx`) files in Photoshop on your computer; if you use the standard Photoshop format (`.psd`) in Photoshop Touch, all your layers get merged into one. As any Photoshop expert knows, that's a bad thing. *Note:* Adobe says that a future version of Photoshop CC will support the layer-preserving `.psdx` files without requiring an add-in.

You can also export JPEG or PNG versions of your drawings — good enough for sketches but not for, say, marketing use.

So, what can you do in Photoshop Touch, exactly? It's definitely not a drawing program — there are no brushes for you to create lines, curves, shapes, and the like. No, Photoshop Touch is an image manipulator in which you can work with photographs and text, layering them and applying special effects to create the kind of artwork you see done in, well, Photoshop. It's what designers call *compositing*.

Figure 20-1 shows the Photoshop Touch screen for an image with layers.

Bringing images into Photoshop Touch

When you open Photoshop Touch, you get the projects screen that shows any existing folders (such as the Tutorials folder, which contains really useful interactive tutorials) and any existing images. At the top of the projects screen are six buttons:

✔ **Creative Cloud (a chain link icon):** Syncs files in Photoshop Touch with files in your Creative Cloud account's online storage.

✔ **Share (the standard iOS share icon):** Uploads selected files to Creative Cloud, saves them to the iPad's Camera Roll in the Photos app, copies them to iTunes on your connected computer, and opens the standard Share sheet so that you can share files via social media, messaging, and email, as well as print them, assign them to contacts, copy them for pasting into other apps, and open them in other apps. *Note:* When you share images, you have to decide what format to use (JPEG, PNG, .psdx, or .psd).

✔ **Folders (the folder icon):** Creates a new folder or moves selected files to a folder that you specify.

✔ **Duplicate (the overlapping-pages icon):** Copies the selected files within Photoshop Touch.

✔ **Delete (the trash can icon):** Deletes the selected files.

✔ **Settings (the gear icon):** Opens the Settings screen, where you can sign in to your Creative Cloud account, set import resolution, set up a stylus's touch sensitivity, and sign into your Facebook account (for photo access).

Figure 20-1:
Photoshop
Touch with
the layer
controls
visible.

To create a new file, you use one of the two buttons at the bottom of the initial screen:

✔ **New Blank Project (the + icon):** Creates a new, blank project, the Photoshop Touch term for a file.

✔ **New Project From (the icon of a picture with a + symbol):** Creates a new project from an image you select from the iPad Photo app's image library, your Creative Cloud account, the iPad's camera, or your Google or Facebook social accounts. The selected image becomes the base layer for your new project.

Using Photoshop Touch's image-editing tools

When you have a project file open, you can do your compositing work. As you can see in Figure 20-1, shown earlier, a stack of layers appears at the right side of the screen.

Throughout Photoshop Touch, you see two icons that let you undo (the left-pointing rotated arrow) and redo (the right-pointing rotated arrow) an action.

As Photoshop users know, layers are the key to compositing: You add images, text, and special effects to layers; then you manipulate attributes such as transparency and blend modes and they combine (or composite) to create your final image.

Tap a layer to move to it. Drag a layer to change its order in the compositing stack. Tap the + icon to add a new layer, and tap the Layers button (the stacked-diamonds icon) to show the layer controls, also shown earlier in Figure 20-1: Opacity; Blend Mode; Match Color (the palette icon); Merge Layers (the layers icon with a ↓); and Delete Layer (the trash can icon).

A blend mode controls how a layer interacts with the layers beneath it, in terms of overlapping items. It's hard to describe, but easy to see for yourself: Add a text layer above a photo (using the Text option). Then experiment with different blend modes for that text layer. The Match Color lets you apply the colors from the layer below to the current layer's objects.

After you create a text layer, you cannot edit its text, even though you can apply other transformations and effects to it. The text is converted into a graphic image automatically. (Strange, I know, but it does eliminate the issue of missing fonts as you move the file from your iPad to a computer.)

To select part of an image, you can draw a marquee with your finger just as you can on a computer by using a mouse or trackpad: Tap and hold on the screen and then drag to create a rectangle (called a *marquee*). When you take your finger off the screen, the marquee appears as a dashed rectangle, and your actions in the Edit menu affect that selection area.

You can use the two selection mode icons — Add to Selection (the icon of a marquee with a +) and Remove from Selection (the icon of a marquee with a –) to refine your selection. If you draw a new marquee after tapping Add to Selection, that new area is added to the previous selection. If you draw a new marquee after tapping Remove from Selection, that new area is removed from the previous selection.

At the top of the screen are nine buttons that contain most of the special effects you can apply (the rest are in the layer controls):

- **Back (the ← icon):** Brings you back to the main Photoshop Touch projects screen. You're prompted as to whether to save the changes to the existing project file.

- **Add Image (the picture icon with a +):** Lets you add an image to the existing project as a new layer. Figure 20-2 shows the Add New Image screen, which is identical to the New Project From screen mentioned earlier.

- **Edit (the pencil icon):** Provides the Cut, Copy (as a new layer), Copy Merged (into the current layer when pasted), Paste, Clear, and Extract (keep only the selected area in the current layer) options to work on selections for the current layer, as well as the Show Pointer icon to show a pointer similar to what you'd see if you were using a mouse on a computer.

- **Select (the marquee-with-gear icon):** Provides controls for working with selections: Select All, Deselect, Select Pixels, Inverse (select everything but the current object), Feather (create a soft border for the selected area), Transform (shown in Figure 20-3), and Refine Edge (lets you modify or erase the existing edge of the selection using your finger as a pen).

- **Transform Layer (the + icon with arrowheads):** Provides the same controls as Select, but applies them to the entire layer.

- **Adjustments (the icon of two slider controls):** Provides color-enhancement controls such as Invert, Saturation, Black & White, Auto Fox, and Curves. These controls do what they do in any photo-enhancement tool.

- **Effects (the *fx* icon):** Provides the image filters you know from Photoshop if you're familiar with it, such as Gaussian Blur, Glow, Halftone Pattern, Chalk & Charcoal, and TV Monitor. These change the fundamental character of your image by simulating various artistic styles.

- **More (the & icon):** Provides a grab bag of additional capabilities: Crop, Image Size, Rotate, Fill & Stroke, Text (creates text layers using the font and size you specify), Warp, Gradient, Fade, Lens Flare (shown in Figure 20-4), and Camera Fill (which uses whatever the iPad camera sees as a fill for the current selection). These controls work like their counterparts in Photoshop.

- **Image Only (the icon of a rectangle within a dashed border):** Removes the various controls so that you can see the image with no distractions.

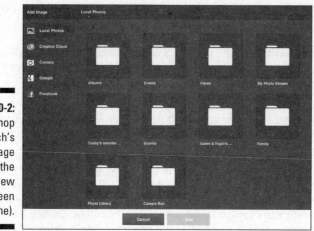

Figure 20-2:
Photoshop
Touch's
Add Image
screen (the
Create New
From screen
is the same).

Figure 20-3:
Transfor-
ming a
selection
(rotation,
here) in
Photoshop
Touch. The
panel at
the bottom
shows the
controls for
constraining
the transfor-
mation.

Although the visual appearance is a bit different, the Transform Layer panel's controls in Photoshop Touch work like their counterparts in Photoshop, but you use the Skew and Rotate handles near the marquee to implement either of those adjustments; you use the eight sizing handles to resize the selection; and you use the alignment, aspect-ratio lock, and snap-to controls to determine how your transformations are constrained. Tap ✔ to apply your changes, or X to cancel them.

Figure 20-4:
Applying a lens-flare effect — a favorite of movie director J.J. Abrams — to a layer in Photoshop Touch.

In the Transform Layers panel, tap the button that's shown here in the margin to expand the controls to show precise dimensions, rotation, angle, and so on (refer to Figure 20-3).

Likewise, Refine Edges works like its Photoshop counterpart. Tap the Pen or Erase button to add or remove edges using your finger movements; tap Size to change the "pencil" size of your finger.

The various filters and adjustments require less mental adjustment to use than Transform and Refine Edges because, well, their options are much closer to what you know from Photoshop.

Where the iPad's Photos app fits in

You may wonder why you would bother with a tool like Photoshop Touch, considering that the iPad comes with its own photo editor, called Photos. The answer is the degree of sophistication you need. Photos is great for basic image enhancements, such as cropping, rotating, red-eye removal, and color adjustments. If you simply want to make your photos look better, Photos may be all you need, especially because Apple plans a major overhaul of Photos to debut in early 2015 (after this book went to press) that incorporates much of the capabilities in its now-discontinued iPhoto app for the iPad and Mac.

Certainly, if your need is image enhancement, rather than image creation and compositing, start with Photos. And consider also using other powerful photo-enhancement apps, such as Google's free Snapseed or Adobe's free Photoshop Express.

Getting Precise with Concepts

Plenty of tools for the iPad let you draw in freeform mode with your finger or a stylus — which is great for rough sketches but not for the kinds of drawings you'd show a client. Fortunately, plenty of good precision-drawing tools are available for the iPad, too. A well-regarded one is the free Concepts, which with the $5.99 Pro Pack in-app purchase becomes business class.

Concepts is a great tool for freeform drawings, with a selection of pen types, weights, and colors, as Figure 20-5 shows. With the Pro Pack add-in, you can bring in images from your iPad's Camera Roll or camera to draw on, as well as work with your strokes in layers, so you have more control over which display, as well as the capability to modify them. Concepts also supports several popular pressure-sensitive styli.

Using Concepts' Share tool, you can share your drawings via email and social media, print the drawings, copy them for use in other apps, open them in other apps, and share a link to the drawing (uploaded to the public Concepts server on the Internet for anyone to see). Your drawings can be exported or shared as JPEG or PNG bitmap images and as SVG vector images.

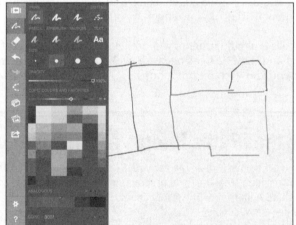

Figure 20-5: Concepts' Pen tool provides a nice selection of pen types, sizes, and colors.

Creating precise drawings

The Pro Pack add-in brings the precision tools that make Concepts shine. You can create precise lines and curves that, optionally, snap to the grid points on your virtual canvas. Concepts assumes that your next shape should be like the last one, so you can quickly create a series of similar shapes (clones, basically) when needed. And you can switch to a different one when you need to do that, too.

The tricky part is that you first have to create the outline and then apply the pen to it. That's not an obvious approach.

What I mean is that you first have to select the Precision Drawing tool, which by default looks like a dashed line but changes to a dashed shape based on the last shape selected. To create and work with a shape, follow these steps:

1. **Double-tap the Precision Drawing tool to get the set of options shown in Figure 20-6: straight line, curve, angled curve (like V shapes), ellipse, and rectangle. Select the desired shape and snap-to options.**

2. **Place two fingers on the iPad's screen, and draw them apart to create your shape. Take your fingers off the screen when the shape is roughly at the size and location you want.**

3. **With one finger, drag the selection handles to resize any side of the object, to adjust the curve, or to rotate the object. With two fingers, drag the object to a new location.**

4. **To actually draw the shape (that is, give it a visible edge), trace along it with one finger; whatever settings you made in the Pen tool (the squiggly-line icon) is applied to the portion of the shape you trace over.**

   Figure 20-6 shows an example of several shapes that have some of the edges traced to display edges.

5. **To add another shape of the *same type,* repeat Steps 2 through 4. To add a *different* shape, repeat Steps 1 through 4.**

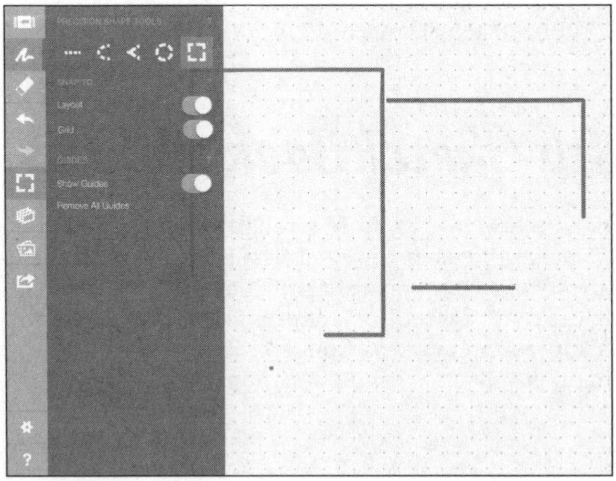

Figure 20-6:
Concepts'
Precision
Drawing
tool ensures
shapes that
look like
they were
drawn with
a mouse
in an illus-
tration
program.

The Concepts method is a bit awkward at first, but if you're trying to create a series of similar shapes, it can't be beat. Each new shape of the same type you create in Step 5 mirrors the dimensions or curve of the one you just created, essentially cloning that previous shape as the default for your new one.

Modifying your drawings

To edit a drawn object, you can select its layer by tapping the Layers tool (the icon of three stacked rectangles), tapping the Adjust button, and then selecting the desired layer. If you swipe across the layer, you can change the object's opacity, lock or unlock the layer, copy the layer, or delete the layer using the contextual menu that appears.

You can also modify a drawn object by first making sure that the Precision Drawing tool is not active (tap its tool so that it's no longer highlighted) and then tapping and holding on any part of its stroke. Just be careful: It's easy to end up drawing a new freeform object instead of selecting the existing object.

You use the standard iOS rotate, expand, pinch, and drag gestures to adjust the selected object or the selected layer's contents. (If no object or layer is selected, the gestures are applied to the entire drawing.) You can also change the pen settings by selecting the object or layer and then switching to the Pen tool to adjust its settings, such as stroke type, size, and color.

Use the Eraser tool (the eraser icon) to erase strokes, the Undo tool (the left-facing curved arrow) to undo the most recent action, and the Redo tool (the right-facing curved arrow) to reinstate the most recent undo.

What you can't do in Concepts is edit an object after you've moved on to something else — the adjustment handles are no longer available for the existing objects, only for new shapes.

Sketching with SketchBook Express

The SketchBook Express app is a more straightforward drawing tool than Concepts, which makes it easier to use at first but also lacks the benefit of being able to quickly create precise shapes in a series, which is Concepts' big draw. (Sorry for the pun!) SketchBook Express also can't enforce the creation of straight lines and exact curves as Concepts can — it's only as precise as your finger or hand is.

SketchBook Express is free, but to really take advantage of it, you need to buy one or more of the three brush packs, which are 99¢ each. These are in-app purchases that you make by tapping the Info button (the *i* icon) at the top of the screen and then choosing the Store menu option.

As with Concepts, you can't edit an object after you've created it, such as to move its line segments or change its curves. You *can* transform an object, sort of — what you can do is move, resize, and/or rotate a layer, so to be able to work on individual objects means that each must be on its own layer.

Creating and opening drawings

When you open SketchBook Express for the first time, you're asked whether to save your drawing on iCloud or on your iPad. The choice you make becomes your default storage for future drawings.

After you've created and saved a drawing, SketchBook Express opens with its My Gallery view, which shows thumbnail images of your drawings, whether on iCloud or on your iPad. Double-tap a drawing's thumbnail to see it at full size. Tap a drawing and then tap Edit to open it for further work.

Or create a new one using the buttons at the bottom left of the screen:

- ✔ **Create (the + icon):** Creates a new, blank drawing at the dimensions you specify (768 x 1024, 1536 x 20148, 1800 x 2400, or 1000 x 1000). You can change that square size's default by tapping the > icon to its right.

- ✔ **Duplicate (the icon of two + symbols):** Copies the selected drawing, which you can then open.

- ✔ **Create From (the flower icon with a +):** Creates a drawing at the size specified using an image at the location specified: Photo Library (meaning the iPad's Photos app), iTunes, Dropbox, or the iPad's camera.

Additionally, the row of icons at the bottom left has three more buttons on the right side to note; select a drawing to use them:

- ✔ **Share (the icon showing a flower with a →):** Copies the drawing as an image to Photos, iTunes, Flickr, Facebook, or Twitter; saves it to Dropbox; emails the file; or prints the drawing.

- ✔ **Upload to iCloud (the iCloud icon showing a ↑):** Moves the file to iCloud; an iCloud logo appears on the upper left of the drawing's thumbnail.

- ✔ **Delete (the trash can icon).**

Creating and editing drawings

The top of the screen contains the buttons you use when editing or creating a drawing:

- **My Gallery (the icon of four rectangles):** Returns to the My Gallery view and lets you save or discard the changes made to your drawing, as well as save the changes to a new copy.

- **New (the + icon):** Lets you create a new blank drawing, with the option to save the current drawing or discard your changes.

- **Settings (the *i* icon).**

- **Undo (the left-facing curved arrow icon) and Redo (the right-facing curved arrow icon).**

- **Pen (the brush icon):** Tap this to get a pop-over of brush controls, as shown in Figure 20-7, such as pen tip, opacity, stroke color, fill color, and "ink flow" (the button that looks like a set of slider controls). Ink flow simulates a real pen tip by adjusting the appearance of the stroke based on the pressure and angle of your pressure-sensitive stylus, if you're using one. Think of how a felt-tip marker stroke changes based on how you hold it and how hard you press on it when drawing on paper. (Set the stylus you're using in the Settings pop-over, accessed via the *i* button.)

- **Shape (by default, the freeform-stroke icon):** Use its pop-over to select four types of shapes to draw: freeform, line, rectangle, and ellipse. Whichever you select displays as the button's icon.

- **Symmetry (the icon of a squiggle next to a dashed line):** When you see one squiggle on the icon, SketchBook Pro draws objects normally. Tap the object to enter Symmetry mode (the icon now has the squiggle on both sides of its dashed line). In Symmetry mode, anything you draw is drawn twice, with a mirror image created automatically for you. For example, if you were drawing a violin, you'd enable Symmetry mode and draw just one side of the violin, letting SketchBook Pro create the other side as a mirror image.

- **More (the . . . icon):** Here, you can choose:

  - *Text:* For entering text labels.

  - *Transform:* To display controls for moving, rotating, resizing, and flipping the current layer.

  - *Time-Lapse Record:* To create a movie of your drawing as you draw it.

  - *Duo Sketch:* To enable shared editing with another iPad user of SketchBook Pro or with an iPhone, or an iPod touch user of SketchBook Mobile. Both people must tap this option; then one of them must invite the other to share the drawing by tapping that other user's device name. Both users can draw on the shared canvas as well as send notes to each other. When they end the connection, both users have a copy of their shared drawing (as separate files).

✔ **Layer (the icon of two stacked diamonds):** In addition to hiding the layer (by using the eye icon) and adjusting its opacity, this pop-over lets you create new layers. You see each layer, and you can delete a layer by tapping its – icon or move it by dragging its Reorder handle (the icon of three lines) within the layers stack. Along the bottom of the pop-over are four icons:

- *Add Layer* (the + icon).

- *Duplicate Layer* (the icon of two + symbols).

- *Import Layer* (the icon of a flower and a +): Imports an image as a new layer.

- *Merge Down* (the ↓ icon): Merges the current layer into the one beneath it.

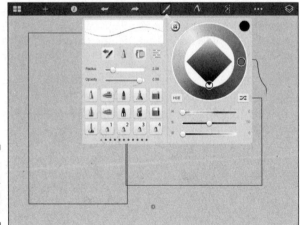

Figure 20-7:
SketchBook
Pro's Pen
pop-over.

You don't need to keep opening the Pen pop-over to change your brush settings. Instead, tap the little ring icon at the bottom of the screen to display the brush controls along the left and right sides of your screen, for continuous access, as Figure 20-8 shows. You also see the Brush Editor wheel in the center of the screen: Drag down within it to reduce the opacity and up to increase it; drag left within it to decrease the pen size and right to increase it.

To zoom in or out of the canvas, use the standard OS pinch and expand gestures. To move within the canvas, use the standard two-finger scroll gestures.

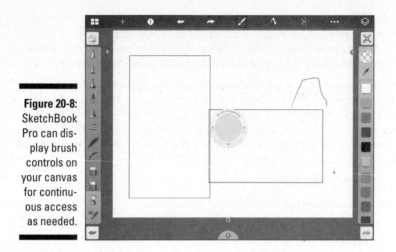

Figure 20-8:
SketchBook
Pro can dis-
play brush
controls on
your canvas
for continu-
ous access
as needed.

Diagramming with Grafio

Working with graphics at work doesn't always entail illustrations or compos-
ited marketing images. Sometimes it means diagrams, such as for flow charts
or org charts. Chapter 11 covers tools that include diagramming as part of
brainstorming activities, but if you just want to draw diagrams, consider the
$8.99 Grafio instead. It's simple but powerful.

As do many graphical tools for the iPad, it displays its drawings as thumbnails on its main screen. Tap a drawing to open and work with it, or tap the
Add button (the + icon) to create a new one.

When you're creating or editing a diagram in Grafio, you see a bevy of controls at the top of the screen. But you'll work with just a few of those most
of the time.

Drawing and formatting diagrams

The two key tools are Draw (the pencil icon) and Select (the icon of an index
finger). You tap Draw when you want to draw something, and you tap Select
when you want to adjust or format something.

By default, when you draw on the screen with your finger or stylus, Grafio
tries to recognize the shape and clean it up for you. So your uneven circle
becomes a nice ellipse, and your slightly wiggly line becomes a straight line.

You can modify a shape by tapping it once to get the controls shown in Figure 20-9 and then, after a brief pause, tapping it again to get the resizing handles that practically every graphics program uses. Drag a handle to resize or reshape the object as desired.

If you want to draw truly freeform shapes, tap the Preferences button (the icon of a page with a gear) and set the Shape Recognition switch to Off in the Preferences pop-over that appears. You also have options for snapping objects to each nearby one, for easy object alignment, and to display a grid for easier visual alignment.

You set the stroke and fill for both new and selected objects using the buttons in the center of the button row: Stroke, Fill, Text, and Connectors. (The Connectors button appears only if a line is selected or if the Draw tool is active.) Tap a button to get its formatting pop-over.

Connectors are lines that connect objects to each other, optionally with arrowheads or corners. Grafio knows that you want a connector when you draw a line from one shape to another. The trick is to start that line inside an object and end it inside the other object that you want to connect. Figure 20-9 shows a simple drawing with connectors.

If you want a special shape, you can get it from the Library (refer to Figure 20-9). Tap the Library button (the icon of a collection of shapes) and then choose the desired category of shape to see what's available. Drag the desired shape onto your canvas to add it to your drawing.

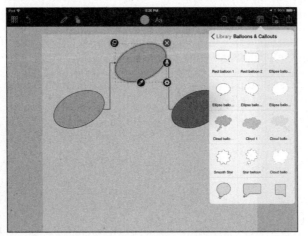

Figure 20-9: Grafio lets you create flow and other diagrams with consistent shapes.

Refer to Figure 20-9 to see the buttons that appear when you select an object, as follows:

- ✔ **Copy (the icon of overlapping squares):** Copies the shape you select.

- ✔ **Delete (the X icon):** Deletes the selected object.

- ✔ **Voice memo (the microphone icon):** Lets you record notes for an object via the iPad's microphone. If an object already has a voice memo, the icon changes to a Play button.

- ✔ **Formatting (the gear icon):** Displays the Fill pop-over. But you could just as easily tap the Fill button instead, as well as the Stroke, Text, or (for connectors) the Connectors buttons to change those attributes for a selected object.

- ✔ **Sample (the eyedropper icon):** Applies the colors of an object you tap to the current object.

The other buttons to note when drawing are the Undo button (the left-facing curved arrow icon) and the Redo button (the right-facing curved arrow icon).

Sharing your diagrams

Grafio saves your changes as you make them, so it has no Save option anywhere. But it does have the Share button that, as it does in any app, lets you email, print, and share a drawing via social media. The Share button also lets you copy the drawing to iTunes, Box, or Dropbox, or open the drawing in any compatible app on your iPad.

But the Share pop-over has one feature that you won't find elsewhere: the capability to create a video from your drawing, via the Video Presentation option. This feature creates a video saved in the Photos app that re-creates the drawing step by step in the same sequence as you built it in Grafio. It's a great tool for showing a flow in action.

Part VI

The Part of Tens

Go to www.dummies.com/extras/ipadatwork for tips on printing from your iPad. And for ten Settings app preferences every business user should know, check out the additional Part of Tens chapter at www.dummies.com/extras/ipadatwork.

In this part . . .

- ✔ It's the little things: Find out about utilities that make the iPad even more useful.

- ✔ There's a lot more than you might realize in the App Store, if you know where to look. (And I show you!)

- ✔ Apps as special as your work: I take you on a tour of industry-specific apps.

Chapter 21

Ten Useful Utilities

Some apps just don't fit in the major categories of apps that a business user may need. The PC industry calls those odds and ends "utilities" — and so do I! Here, I've gathered utility apps that I suspect you'll find really useful in your daily use of the iPad, some for when you travel and others no matter where you are.

Doing the Math with Calculator HD and Calc

Even though computers have probably replaced a lot of what used to be on your desk (paper, especially), and a smartphone has probably replaced your wristwatch, I bet you have a pocket calculator on your desk.

Crunching the numbers with Calculator HD

One of the nicest freebies on the iPhone is its Calculator app, which gives you a pocket calculator on a device that's already in your pocket. The iPhone Calculator does both the standard calculator we all (used to) use and, if you rotate it, the scientific calculator that you might remember from calculus class in high school or college.

But the iPad has no Calculator app! Sure, you can use your iPhone or an actual calculator, but if you're already working on your iPad, why switch devices?

You don't have to, because plenty of calculator apps are available for the iPad. My favorite is CrowdCafé's 99¢ Calculator HD, shown in Figure 21-1. It's got basic, scientific, and paper-tape modes, and you can mail or print that paper tape. It works like the kind of calculator that you already know how to use, and it's got a clean, simple interface.

Doing advanced math with Calc

If you're an engineer or scientist, I recommend the 99¢ Calc as a full-featured scientific calculator, shown in Figure 21-2. But you probably don't need its $1.99 Converter in-app purchase, which converts various measurements.

Calc takes a little getting used to. It builds your calculations as you enter them, though you can tap into the calculation shown at the top to edit it — such as to add parentheses when you realize that your calculation is getting more complicated than originally planned. Also, a difference to note from many standard physical scientific calculators is that in Calc you enter a function like sin before the value you're applying it to, not afterwards as with many physical devices.

Figure 21-1:
Crowd-Café's Calculator HD offers a paper tape display.

Figure 21-2:
QApps' Calc
is a real
scientific
calculator.

Managing Measurements with Units

Another tool that is handy on both your iPhone and iPad is Units, a free (ad-supported) app that converts measurements across several dozen categories, from ladies' shoe sizes to electrical voltage. Figure 21-3 shows the screen for currency conversions. You enter a value in any field, and the others display the equivalent values. It's really simple, almost in a "d'oh!" way, but it does the job quickly. The hardest part about using Units is finding the category for which you want to convert values, because the list is so long.

Figure 21-3:
The Units
conversion
utility.

Keeping Time with Clock

The iPad comes with the Clock app, an app you might not think much about. But it is actually quite handy. The World Clock view shown in Figure 21-4 lets you easily figure out what the time is somewhere else, whether you're traveling or simply want to know what time it is for someone you want to call or text. As the figure shows, you can add whatever cities you want, as well as manage the order of cities (using the three-line Reorder handles) and delete them.

Clock has several other useful features as well, available from the buttons at the bottom of the screen:

✔ **Alarm:** Lets you set alarms, such as when at a hotel or simply during a meeting to give you a signal that it's time to wrap up.

✔ **Stopwatch:** Acts as, well, a stopwatch, recording elapsed time. Giving a speech? Use it to track your timing as you rehearse — or someone else's. It also supports laps, which probably won't matter to your work needs unless you're a sports coach.

✔ **Timer:** A countdown timer. On my iPhone, I use it to make sure that I know when the parking meter is about to need a refill. On my iPad, I use it to track how much time is left for a meeting or a presentation — the countdown shows up not just in the app but also on the Lock screen, so I can glance quickly at my iPad to see the remaining time available.

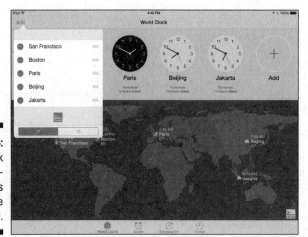

Figure 21-4:
The Clock app showing times across the world.

Going Paperless with Scanner Pro

A vast amount of information is available digitally these days, as web pages, Word documents, PDF files, and so on. But there are times you still have paper to deal with. The $6.99 Scanner Pro is available for those times when you have to deal with paper but would prefer not to.

Scanner Pro uses the iPad's camera to take pictures of paper documents, converting them into crisp electronic images, with shadows, colors, and the like removed — and the text's readability enhanced.

Scanner Pro does not use OCR technology to convert the photo to actual text; you need to do that using an OCR app on your computer. There are some OCR apps for the iPad, but none that I can recommend.

Figure 21-5 shows a scanned jury notice as an example that I wanted to make sure I had in case I lost or forgot the original paper version on my desk. You can take multiple "scans" to build a multipage document. Tap the < button to navigate back to the list of your saved documents, and tap a document to open it.

You can share a document using the Share button via email, send it to your Evernote account, send it to a cloud storage service (Dropbox, Google Drive, or a WedDAV-compatible server), or even print it (such as if you lost the original or want to make a copy but have only a printer available to you).

You can also require a password to open a specific scanned document; in the Share pop-over, tap More and then Lock to set the password.

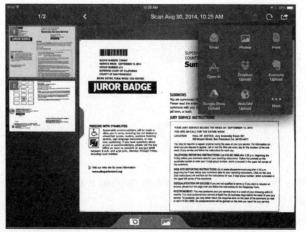

Figure 21-5: Scanner Pro converts photos of paper documents into digital ones.

Finally, you can fax your scans if you have a live Internet connection (Wi-Fi or cellular). In the Share pop-over, tap More and then Fax to get the form in which you enter the addressee's fax number and optionally create a cover sheet. Faxing costs 99¢ per unit (in Scanner Pro, "unit" is a fuzzy concept based on the number of pages, country being faxed to, and number of recipients), which you pay for through in-app purchase when you send a fax. That's pricey, but usually cheaper than using a FedEx Office/Kinko's or UPS Store/Mailboxes Etc.

Automating It with IFTTT

The free IFTTT app — the acronym comes from its full name, If This Then That — lets you automate activities between apps, sort of like scripting or, if you use a Mac, creating Automator actions. You basically create "recipes" that tell IFTTT to do Y if X occurs. For example, in Figure 9-8, I'm telling IFTTT to send a notification when I leave a specific location.

You need to create or have an existing IFTTT account to use the app. The iPad's iOS doesn't let apps control each other (a security feature), so apps need to send notifications instead to IFTTT's servers, which then send a notification to the other app. That also means that you need an Internet connection for many recipes to work. (Some iOS services can communicate directly on the iPad, such as accessing location or contacts if you give permission, so those recipes don't need an Internet connection to work.)

The process is simple, as shown in Figure 21-6, though not immediately obvious.

Figure 21-6: Creating a rule in IFTTT.

1. **Slide the Browse switch to the left so that it becomes Manage.**

2. **Tap the + button to the Manage switch's left.**

3. **Tap the blue + button to create the "if" rule.**

4. **Tap the app you want to trigger the "if" rule; then tap the + button to the right of the trigger action in the list that appears below.**

   You may be asked to sign in to the app or give permission to use the specific service.

5. **Tap the red + button to create the "then" rule.**

6. **Tap the app you want to perform the "then" rule; then tap the + button to the right of the desired action in the list that appears below.**

   You may be asked to sign in to the app or give permission to use the specific service.

7. **Tap Finish when done.**

   The new action shows up in the list of actions at right. ***Note:*** You can turn individual actions on or off using the switch to its right.

Keeping Warm and Dry: Yahoo Weather and Weather Channel

You don't need to be a road warrior to worry about weather conditions during your workday. If you make local sales calls, are a consultant, deliver products, make estimates, or do other service work in the field, knowing the weather outlook is important.

Chances are, you use your iPhone or other smartphone to check immediate weather conditions, but the iPad is a better tool to use to get a sense of the details for the day as a whole, or to track an incoming storm so that you can adjust the rest of the day's plans.

The free Yahoo Weather app by Yahoo! is a visually slick app, displaying the details when you scroll down from the simple forecast view that appears when you go to a city, as shown in Figure 21-7. You use the Menu button (the icon of three lines at the upper left) to edit the saved locations you want to track, and then swipe among them on the main screen. (Your current location is always the first screen.)

The Weather Channel app is free though ad-supported, and like any weather app will show you the current conditions and forecast for the current location or any location you choose. What makes it stand out is its Travel Weather feature, accessed by using the Travel button (the airplane icon) at the bottom right. Enter the city you're going to and the dates, and you see the forecast weather if your trip is occurring soon, or the usual conditions if the trip is further out, as shown in Figure 21-8. The app saves your travel plan so that you can quickly get updates to the weather as your trip nears.

Figure 21-7: Yahoo Weather presents detailed weather conditions for your bookmarked cities.

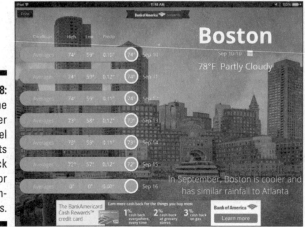

Figure 21-8: The Weather Channel app lets you track weather for your upcoming trips.

Tracking Your iPad with Find My iPhone

Apple's free Find My iPhone app's name is misleading — it'll find your iPhone, iPad, iPod touch, and Mac based on the device's last connection to the Internet. (Location services has to have been turned on, of course, which is the default for iOS devices.)

In fact, it can find other people's devices, too. Enter a person's Apple ID and password in the app (after you sign off from your account, if you're already signed in), and that person's devices will display on a map. Tap a device to get the controls shown in Figure 21-9 to sound an alarm, lock the device, or even wipe it clean.

If you don't have an iOS device handy, you can still use the Find My iPhone functionality by going to www.icloud.com from a Windows, OS X, Linux, Android, or other browser, signing in with the appropriate Apple ID and password, and tapping Find My iPhone button to get a screen similar to that in Figure 21-9.

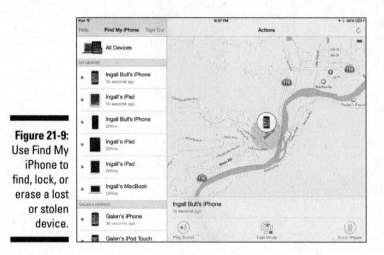

Figure 21-9:
Use Find My iPhone to find, lock, or erase a lost or stolen device.

Tracking People with Find My Friends

Like Find My iPhone, Apple's Find My Friends is a free app that uses the location services in an iOS device or Mac plus a person's iCloud account to find out where that person is if he or she has an active Internet connection.

In addition to tracking people's location on a map, the app can notify you when a person leaves or enters a location you specify — or notify him or her when you do. After selecting a person in the app by tapping the List button (the bulleted-list icon) at the upper left and then tapping that person's name in the list that appears, tap Notify Me to receive such notifications. Or, to notify that person, tap More and then Notify *person's name.*

Although the app is designed to let family friends keep track of each other's location, the app is useful for business users, too.

For example, if a group of co-workers is at a conference, they could invite each other for location tracking, as shown in Figure 21-10, so that they can more easily meet up for dinner or a conference check-in. Likewise, a sales or field-support team manager could track colleagues' locations to see who's closest to a client in need.

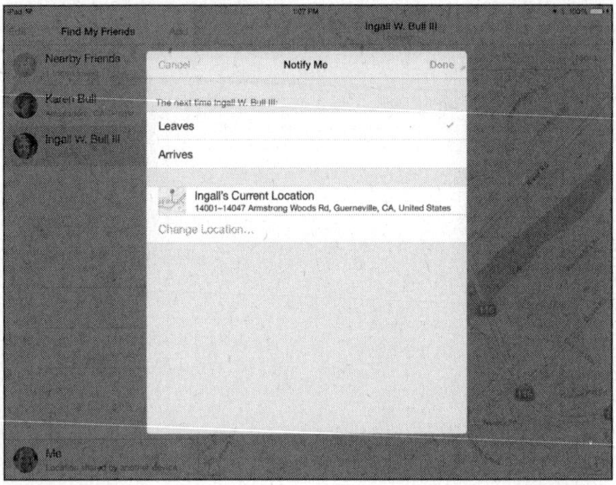

Figure 21-10:
Find My
Friends in
action.

A person must accept an invitation to be tracked; Find My Friends won't let you track people without their consent.

You can manage how you are tracked by tapping Me in the list of tracked people. Tap the Info button at the upper right to open the Info pane at left. There, you see the Share My Location switch that you use to hide your location when desired. You also control which device, if you have several, is shown as your current location — that's typically your iPhone because you usually always have that with you.

If you scroll down, you see a list of people to whom you gave permission to track you. Tap a person and then tap Remove from Followers to revoke her capability to track you. If you want to stop tracking someone, tap her name in the list of people, tap More, and then tap Remove in the pop-over that appears.

Finally, as you scroll down the Info pane, you also see the Allow Friend Requests switch; if it's set to Off, no one can even ask to track you.

Checking on Your Print Jobs

Yes, this is the eleventh item in this list of ten. But I hate to think of it as an app because it's really a feature in iOS — just one that hardly anybody knows is there. "It" is Print Center, an app that lets you monitor what you're currently printing from your iPad, and even cancel a print job.

To get to Print Center, double-tap the Home button to open the app switcher and then scroll to the left (*not* to the right as you usually would) to see Print Center. (There is no icon for Print Center in any of your Home screens.) Tap the preview to open the app, shown in Figure 21-11.

In Print Center, you see the status of whatever is currently printing as well as the Cancel Printing button, which you can use to stop the printing.

Don't see Print Center? That's because the print job is already done. Print Center appears only while the iPad is actively sending a print job to an AirPrint-compatible printer. So you have to move fast to see it.

Figure 21-11:
The Print
Center
lives only
in the app
switcher.

Chapter 22

Specialty Apps for Ten Industries

. . . .

In This Chapter

▶ Knowing how to get the most out of the App Store

▶ Locating apps for accountants, Realtors, lawyers, doctors, and more

. . . .

*T*here are productivity apps most people can use, and then there are productivity apps designed for specific tasks and industries. You'll find both types of apps for the iPad, but finding the ones designed for specific needs in specific industries is, admittedly, harder.

But with some work, you can.

Finding Specialty Apps

The place to start in your search for apps that are specific to your professional needs is the App Store. Sure, you see the broadly applicable tools featured — including some of those recommended in this book. But if you drill down a bit, you start to find specialty apps.

At the bottom of the App Store is the Explore button; tap it to do that drill-down in the Explore tab. On that tab, you find categories in the left pane and descriptions of apps in the right pane. Tap a category to see its subcategories, and tap a subcategory to see its apps. Figure 22-1 shows an example of what might come up when you tap the Productivity category and then its Engineering category.

Depending on your industry, I recommend that you start exploring the Business, Finance, Medical, Music, Productivity, and Reference categories, because these are most likely to contain apps you can use in your work.

Notice the hierarchy at the top of the left pane: You tap entries there to move back to those higher levels.

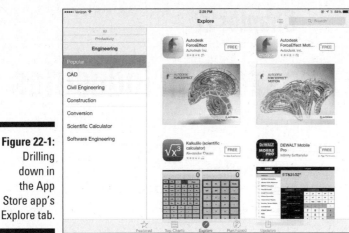

Figure 22-1:
Drilling
down in
the App
Store app's
Explore tab.

Searching the App Store using keywords in your industry is also a good way to look for useful apps.

Some companies create their own apps or get through them through the Business App Store, a private venue that Apple has set up to let companies provide apps to employees and contractors directly. In that case, your IT department should have a web page or app portal that lists the available apps for you to download to your iPad.

These apps can include apps developed by your company or apps developed by other companies that are licensed for your company to distribute to its employees and contractors. Your business can also distribute books, such as manuals, this way. (And if your company doesn't do this, ask why not! It can get the details at www.apple.com/business/vpp/.)

What follows are examples of the kinds of apps you can find for your iPad work, to whet your appetite.

Surveying Apps for Accounting and Estimating

2ndSite has the free Freshbooks app for its $19.99-per-month service that provides time tracking, invoice management, and expense capture. It's designed for small businesses as a cloud-based suite.

Intuit, the big name in small-business accounting, also has its free QuickBooks Online app, which requires its $124.99-per-year service to use.

If you're a contractor, consider Joist's free Contractor Invoicing and Estimating Tool, which requires that you sign up for it but currently has no subscription cost. (The company says that it plans to introduce paid premium features in the future but that it doesn't make money from your data in the meantime.)

Landing Apps for Architecture and Real Estate

The MagicPlan app converts photos of buildings into interactive maps of floor plans, which is useful for architects, designers, building inspectors, insurance agents, and contractors. The app is free but a subscription for unlimited floor plans costs $99.99 per year; other plans are available for those who work with just a few floor plans.

AutoCAD is the mainstay tool for architectural and engineering drawings, and AutoCAD 360 is its iPad companion version. The app is free, but to be able to work on drawings stored on a website, you need a Pro subscription, which starts at $49.99 per year.

If you're a real estate agent, your brokerage or Multiple Listing Service may have its own apps to manage listings and contracts. But you should also consider Open Home Pro, which lets you manage your prospects. The app is free but there's also the $9.99-per-month Pro subscription that lets you send emails and other marketing materials to your prospective clients.

Learning with Apps for Education

Showbie is a free app for teachers that lets them gather homework assignments from their students, comment on it, and then provide feedback to the students with it. A limited version of the service is free, so you can try it before deciding to get a paid license for your school.

Keeping track of students and seating charts is something every teacher has to do and often would love some help with. The TeacherKit apps provide that help. The basic version is free, but the $6.99 in-app upgrade is what you need to print what you track in it. If you want online access to your tracked activities, you need the $39.99-per-year Online Edition in-app purchase as well.

Feedback is important for students, but remembering the details you want to convey is often hard. The ClassDojo app lets you collect those details during the course of your teaching day, and send feedback to students and parents. (Of course, you can overdo it and get caught up in overanalyzing and over-reporting.) ClassDojo currently has no cost, but ITWorx, the company behind TeacherKit, hopes to find a way to charge teachers, parents, or schools for it after it has a lot of users.

Evaluating and Planning with Apps for Enterprise Systems

If your company uses the Oracle Business Intelligence suite, you may want to use the free companion Oracle Business Intelligence Mobile app to be able to see and analyze your analytics on the go. Oracle has apps for many of its other enterprise software modules as well.

Likewise, SAP offers the free SAP Business One app to give customers of its enterprise resource planning suite access to ERP data when they're away from their desk. SAP also has iPad apps for some of its other enterprise software modules.

In the same vein, Workday for iPad provides Workday customers access to the suite of financial, human resources, along with analytics applications from their tablet.

Getting Creative with Apps for Entertainment and Sports

Apple provides the iMovie video-editing app and GarageBand music-editing app for free, but those just scratch the surface of apps for those in the entertainment business.

The Musicnotes Sheet Music Viewer app turns your iPad into a music stand so that you can see, move through, and annotate your sheet music while playing. It works with scanned PDF files as well as the Musicnotes subscription service for sheet music. You get to work with all that sheet music while having nothing extra to carry around — or worry about losing.

Memorizing lines, tracking script changes, and keeping the context of the scene are all critical activities for actors. The $9.99 My Lines app helps both stage and film actors do all that.

Coaching sports is similar to directing a movie, concert, or play, with the same need to put on the best performance for the audience. The TeamSnap app helps you manage the team logistics so that you can spend more time on coaching players on the art of the game. The annual subscription starts at $59.99 per year.

Programming and Networking Apps for IT Management and Development

The $9.99 Kodiak for JavaScript is an offline HTML5, CSS3, and JavaScript web development environment with a WebKit-based internal browser that can play back your code as if it were live. It includes the jQuery library and 50 other JavaScript libraries and frameworks. There's also the similar $9.99 Kodiak PHP app that helps you create PHP programs for web browsers.

If you work in IT and manage remote Windows clients, you may want the free Microsoft Remote Desktop app, which lets you manage Windows computers — including the latest version, 8.1 — with a tool that does it all. And it comes from the same company, of course, as the operating system you're managing.

The $4.99 Cathode is another must-have tool for IT admins. The multisession secure-shell (SSH) tool is essential for working with routers, switches, and other networking equipment.

Organizing and Tracking Apps for Lawyers

The $89.99 TrialPad app lets litigators organize, manage, and present the evidence used in their trials.

Most law firms and independent lawyers subscribe to the Lexis service to keep track of court activities, case law, legislation, and other legal news. The free Lexis Advance HD app brings that online database to the iPad if you have a Lexis subscription.

You have a lot to manage as a lawyer, which is what the MyCase service helps you do, from calendars to documents and from client data to invoices. The online service costs $39 per month per lawyer and $29 per month per legal assistant. The free MyCase app lets you access and handle all that case management from your iPad.

Tracking Projects and Employees with Apps for Managers

The Basecamp service is widely used to manage and communicate around project tickets. The free Basecamp app ensures that you can manage those activities and stay updated from your iPad. The service cost ranges from $20 to $150 per month for an unlimited number of users, based on the number of projects and data storage used.

Whiteboarding is a powerful way to work through projects and ideas. The Trello app combines the whiteboarding approach with project management, letting you visually manage your team's work. The Trello app is free, and the Trello Business Class service costs $45 per user per year.

A big part of a manager's job is tracking employee performance for use in evaluations and assignment decisions. The $9.99 Employee Tracker Pro app helps managers keep track of both the problems and accomplishments of each employee. It's essentially a tool to centralize your employee documentation.

Reporting and Management Apps for Marketing and Sales

Salesforce1 is the iPad app that collects all your Salesforce customer activities into one place. It's free, but of course your company needs to have Salesforce.com's cloud apps deployed.

Managing social media posts can be a lot of work, given the number of services you might post to. The free HootSuite app and the HootSuite service can help for Twitter, LinkedIn, Facebook, Google+, and more than 30 other social services. The basic free service is meant for individuals to manage their posts; the Business and Enterprise service tiers add campaign management and analytics capabilities, with prices based on the number of users and volume of posts.

Like it or not, businesses run on paperwork, and that means forms. For those forms that need to remain paper forms, such as work orders and inspection reports, the ProntoForms app lets you bring them to the iPad so that you can fill them out on the device and then print the forms as needed. The app is free, but the service for creating forms and capturing their data costs $299.99 per year.

Tracking and Research Apps for Medical Practice

WebMD has become a major source of medical news and data for doctors, nurses, and other health are professionals, and the free Medscape app brings all that information to the iPad. The service is also free, but you do have to register for an account at WebMD.

The PatientKeeper service is used by many hospitals to provide physicians access to patients' clinical notes and data, from lab orders to dispensed medications. The horribly named but free PK53284R app provides them with access to that data when away from their desks (if the hospital has PatientKeeper's service, of course), though historical data is not available.

One of the oldest iPad apps — it was in fact one of the first Phone apps, before there was an iPad — is the free Epocrates app, which lets you research drug interactions and side effects before prescribing. The $159.99-a-year in-app Essentials subscription adds disease information, alternative medications, and a variety of clinical tools.

Index

About the Author

Galen Gruman is author or coauthor of 40 books covering the iPad, the Mac, OS X, Windows 8, iBooks Author, and desktop publishing. He is an executive editor and the columnist covering mobile technology at InfoWorld, a website focused on business technology. He has also been executive editor of *Macworld*, *Upside*, and *M-Business* magazines, as well as West Coast bureau chief at *Computerworld* and a contributor to *CIO* magazine. Gruman has also presented on mobile business technology trends and best practices at conferences such as Interop, the CIO Global Forum, the Southland Technology Conference, ITxpo, and CIO Perspectives.

Acknowledgments

It takes a team to create a good product, and I've been fortunate to have had a strong team in making *iPad at Work For Dummies* a reality. Thanks are due to Aaron Black, who asked me to take on this project and has been a driving force behind many Wiley book projects I've had the pleasure of writing. I also appreciate the excellent editing by Susan Christophersen, who made the book better through her questions, edits, and comments — although invisible to the reader, editors make authors look good, and we can't do it without them.

Thanks are also due to tech reviewer Russ Mullen and Ryan Faas, who had several excellent suggestions to improve the book's content, and to Katie Mohr, who managed the whole affair so that you could have this book in your hands. And let me not forget David Sparks, the author of *iPad at Work*; I had the pleasure of editing and producing that book and now of carrying his vision to a new level of depth.

I'm also grateful to my readers at InfoWorld and the many industry insiders who have kept me current on key mobile trends, issues, and solutions. They provided the groundwork for the advice and explanations in this book.

Dedication

To John Gallant, the man who ensures that InfoWorld and all IDG publications remain the shining examples of excellence that they are.

Publisher's Acknowledgments

Senior Acquisitions Editor: Katie Mohr

Project and Copy Editor: Susan Christophersen

Technical Editors: Russ Mullen, Ryan Faas

Editorial Assistant: Claire Johnson

Sr. Editorial Assistant: Cherie Case

Project Coordinator: Patrick Redmond

Cover Image: © iStock.com / SelectStock